ANTIQUE

Golf Collectibles

A Price and Reference Guide

2nd Edition

Chuck Furjanic

Published by

krause
publications

700 E. State Street • Iola, WI 54990-0001
Telephone: 715/445-2214

Please, call or write us for our free catalog of antiques and collectibles publications. To place an
order or receive our free catalog, call 800-258-0929. For editorial comment and further information,
use our regular business telephone at (715) 445-2214

Library of Congress Catalog Number: 99-66998
ISBN: 0-87341-790-9

Printed in the United States of America

DEDICATION

To Julia, for her patience and love

TABLE OF CONTENTS

Acknowledgments 7

Preface 8

Foreword: Rives McBee 9-10

Foreword: Peter Georgiady 11

About the Author 12

Chapter 1: Collecting Antique Golf 13
    The Heritage of Golf by Archie Baird
    Collecting Golf Memorabilia by Johnny Henry
    Collecting Pre-1875 Golf Artifacts by Will Roberto
    A Brief Introduction to Patent Clubs by Gordon Page
    Musselburgh, Prestwick and St. Andrews by Keith Foster

Chapter 2: Collecting Societies 47
    Welcome to the Golf Collector's Society by Tom Kuhl

Chapter 3: A Guide to Values 51

Chapter 4: Antique Golf Clubs 55
    Introduction to Collecting Wood Shaft Clubs
    Prices: Golf Clubs: The Most Collectible Makers

Chapter 5: Antique Golf Balls 177
    Introduction
    My Passion for Old Golf Balls by Jim Espinola
    Prices: Golf Balls
    Ball Boxes and Containers

Chapter 6: Signature Balls 241
    Collecting Signature Golf Balls by Paul Biocini
    Collecting Signature Ball Boxes by Gary Hilgers
    Prices: Signature Balls

Chapter 7: Collecting Autographs 255
    Golfing Autographs: A Brief History by Mark Emerson
    Prices: Autographed Items

Chapter 8: Golf Tees 269
    An Introduction to Golf Tees by Lee Crist
    Prices: Golf Tees

Chapter 9: Collecting Books on Golf 281
    Collecting Golf Books by Joseph Murdoch
    Determining Condition and Value of Books by George Lewis
    Prices: Golf Books

Chapter 10: Collecting Golf Art 297
    The Pictorial History of Golf: A Suggestion for Collectors by Martin Hardie
    Prices: Golf Art

Chapter 11: Collecting Golf Ceramics and Glass 309
    Golf Ceramics by Wayne Aaron
    Collectible Glass by Jerry Sprung
    Prices: Golf Ceramics
    Prices: Glass Collectibles

Chapter 12: Golf Medals and Trophies 331
    Collecting Medals by Art DiProspero
    Golf Trophies by Dr. Hank Alperin
    Medals and Trophies by Bob Burkett
    Prices: Golf Medals
    Prices: Golf Trophies

Chapter 13: Golf Trading Cards 343
    The History of Golf Cards by Mike Daniels
    Prices: Golf Cards

Chapter 14: Silver and Gold Golf Collectibles 353
    Introduction
    Prices: Silver and Gold Collectibles

Chapter 15: Miscellaneous Golf Collectibles 363
    Introduction
    Prices: Miscellaneous Golf Collectibles

Chapter 16: A Short History of Golf Bags 381

Chapter 17: How and Where to Purchase Golf Collectibles 391

Bibliography 398

Contributors 400

Index 403

ACKNOWLEDGMENTS

I would like to express my sincere gratitude to the many people who helped put this book together, without them this presentation would have never become a reality: Wayne Aaron, Hank Alperin, Archie Baird, Paul Biocini, Bob Burkett, Jim Cooper, Lee Christ, Mike Daniels, Art DiProspero, Mark Emerson, Jim Espinola, Keith Foster, Pete Georgiady, Roger Gilchrist, Bob Gowland, David Griffiths, Gary Hilgers, Roger Hill, Johnny Henry, Tom and Karen Kuhl, Bob Kuntz, George Lewis, Ralph Livingston, Dick Moore, Norm Moreau, Joseph Murdoch, Gordon Page, Don Paris, Will Roberto, Tim Smartt, and Jerry Sprung. Dan Alexander provided the impetus and a multitude of photographs for this reference.

A special thank you to Teresa Ferrieri-Bisigato for her enthusiasm and research assistance.

PREFACE

For the past twelve years, I have heard thousands of collectors, club professionals, antique dealers, and curious people with collectibles, ask the same questions: "What is this worth?" and "Is there a reference book giving current pricing for all golf collectibles?"

This book is designed to answer both these questions, and more.

Collecting old golf memorabilia, clubs, books and balls is not a new fad. Classified advertisements for "Feather Balls," old "Gutta Percha Balls" and wooden head clubs made by "Hugh Philp" were published in the British publication, "Golf Illustrated" circa 1900. Harry B. Woods assembled a very fine collection and, in 1911, published *Golfing Curios and the Like*.

In 1987, my thirst for information concerning collectible golf equipment was at its peak. The references available were Stirk and Henderson's *Golf in the Making*, *The Encyclopedia of Golf Collectibles* by the Olman's, the Golf Collectors Society's *Bulletin*, a few dealers publishing catalogues, and auction catalogues from several British auction houses.

Determined to acquire and share up-to-date information, I began publishing a retail catalogue in 1989. In 1991, interesting articles by expert collectors and dealers were also included helping the catalogues become both informative and a retail sales vehicle. The catalogues include a wide variety of golf collectibles, such as wood shaft clubs, balls, books, tees, memorabilia and ephemera, all offered for sale. There is also a listing of events, gatherings and meetings involving golf collectors and collectibles, articles that will bring you back to the nostalgic times, and offerings of hard to find grips, tacks and whipping for care and repair of old hickories. I am presently the only dealer publishing a monthly catalogue for the golf collectibles hobby, and have published nearly 120 as of this writing.

In 1993, I began conducting mail auctions that provided two essential services to the collector: A way to sell duplicates from their collection and a way to add collectibles at "their price." Chuck Furjanic, Inc. now holds four auctions each year: Spring and Fall live sales and Winter and Summer absentee sales. If a collector cannot attend the auction "in person," where lots may be viewed prior to sale, a profusely illustrated catalogue allows them to bid confidently by mail.

When Dan Alexander, former president of Books Americana, suggested I write a price and reference guide on golf collectibles, the intent was clearly set in producing a truly comprehensive work encompassing the entire spectrum of golf collectibles. To accomplish this, I called for input from a number of knowledgeable, well respected dealers and collectors who are experts in their field. Throughout the years, I have been privileged of knowing the finest of these experts, and several of them assisted in presenting accurate, up-to-date information and pricing of collectibles. Their perspective and knowledge are a refreshing and valued addition to this price and reference guide.

It was also the goal of my publisher, the contributors, and mine, to provide as many photographs as possible to make these listings and prices come alive for the collector. Anyone using this guide will find the photographs incredibly helpful in bringing you back to the times and the history of the game, as well as providing visual references to the collectibles.

Thus, this guide is the result of such an effort; I am very confident it will be of great help to the numerous collectors asking that familiar question, "How much is this item worth?"

Golfingly,
Chuck Furjanic
Irving, Texas, 2000

FOREWORD

by Rives McBee

People often ask me, what do you collect and why do you collect? My answer to them is, "I collect almost anything that is related to the game of golf," and that includes classic clubs; hickory shafted clubs; clubs with unique shafts, fancy faces and clubheads; golf balls; logo golf balls; golf bags; golf books; golf art; golf autographs; and golf bronzes. I have done exactly what most expert collectors say don't do—that is, get into many areas of different collectibles. Most collectors choose one particular area such as scorecards, pencils or tees and stay with just these items. I have chosen to spread out into several areas because I have yet to find the one area that intrigues me the most. I usually can't resist buying something if it is different from what I am looking for originally. An old leather bag may contain a putter or a wood that I want and I buy the whole bag full of clubs.

Why do I collect? It all started in 1966 after my first major tournament appearance, the 1966 United States Open Championship at the Olympic Club in San Francisco. In the second round of the tournament I shot a score of 64, which set the course record and tied the all-time low round for an Open. I went on to finish, tied for thirteenth in the championship, and returned to Midland, Texas, and my job as an assistant golf professional. When I got home I put the clubs (I had used in the Open) in the closet along with a place mat autographed by all of the contestants at the Open. I still have the clubs and the place mat. This started me in the wonderful world of golf collectibles. Adding to my collection has given me many hours of pleasure, and meeting fellow collectors around the country has been a fabulous experience.

Collecting can be fun and it can be expensive. Sometimes the pleasure of finding a unique club or ball far outweighs the cost of the item. When a fellow collector asks if he paid too much for a particular find I usually respond with, "You bought it because you wanted it, so you didn't pay too much." An item is worth what you are willing to pay for it. Most people who sell memorabilia are willing to negotiate and this too can be fun if you know what you are doing.

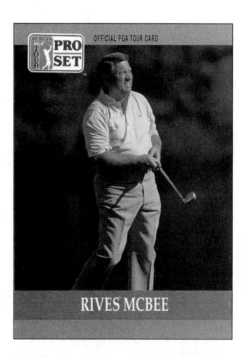

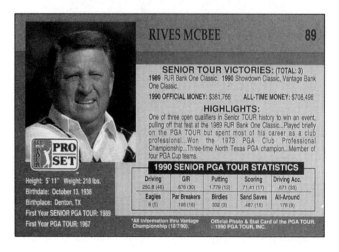

Now my good friend, Chuck Furjanic, has found a way to help the collector, old and new, by providing this reference and pricing guide. It is filled with illustrations of clubs, golf balls, pottery and ceramics, autographs, golf cards, and many more antique golf collectibles. This book should help all of the new collectors in their search for those "precious finds" at the garage sale or auction, and give them an approximate price for these items. I wish that I would have had this book to help me in my early years of collecting, but I still probably would have done what so many of my fellow collectors do. If I like it and can afford it, I buy it!

Golfingly,
Rives McBee
Irving, Texas

FOREWORD

by Pete Georgiady

Twenty years ago there was nothing.

By that I mean there were no ready resource materials for the collectors of old golf clubs and other golf memorabilia. It didn't much matter because there were almost no collectors. The prospect changed abruptly in 1978 when Englishmen David Stirk and Ian Henderson wrote Golf in the Making. This eclectic volume combines colorful bits of golf history with profiles of important club makers, and short but tantalizing notes on old clubs and other golf items that were rapidly becoming collectible. It is a book that many consider to be the "Bible" for golf collectors and deserves a great deal of credit for launching the activities of many of today's collectors.

Without going into great detail, I can say that the shortcomings of one or two of the club-related sections of the Stirk and Henderson book gave me cause to begin my own explorations into the whos, whys and wherefores of old clubs and club makers. The result of my research is a small group of books devoted to clubs and club makers, the two topics, which I have found most self-enlightening. Thus, the pioneering contribution of Stirk and Henderson spawned other collector-writers like myself who will leave teachings for the next generation of golf enthusiasts. After all this time, there is a crying need for even more information about many aspects of the golf collectibles field. Frequently I am asked if a guide book has been written on this topic or another, and sadly, the answer is usually "No, not yet." Perhaps golf collectors, most of whom are also golfers, take their game so seriously that it leaves no time for scholarship. Who can blame them?

Voids still remain in the information web but sooner or later they will be filled. One addition to the collector's library is undoubtedly the volume you are now holding. It has emerged from one among us who has espoused the spirit of old golf with an evangelical fervor. Chuck Furjanic possesses a unique story within the golf collectibles field. A lifelong golfer, coach and friend of the game, he has made the world of golf collectibles his business. His ability to amass considerable familiarity with clubs, balls, art and other areas of golf collectibles, as well as a knowledge of the persons who were specialists in those areas, has made him a beacon in the field of golf collectibles. This book is a marriage of those two worlds: his daily handling of the game's antiques and his regular contact with novice and expert collectors.

There is no single person who knows everything about all the disciplines of the collectibles we seek, so the natural ideal is a book with an aggregation of information from those highly knowledgeable in the different fields. Chuck has delivered just that. In the years ahead, more books to assist and instruct golf collectors will materialize. Maybe the authors of those future volumes will have been inspired by this price and reference guide just as we were inspired by another book of twenty years ago.

Pete Georgiady
Greensboro, N.C.

The seeds of Pete's interest in old golf clubs germinated while he was a graduate student at Scotland's Dundee University in the early 1970s. After many years of research and gathering information on old club makers and the clubs they produced, his knowledge has been disseminated in a series of books which include the Compendium of British Club Makers, Collecting Antique Golf Clubs, Views and Reviews: Golf Clubs in the Trade Press, Wood Shafted Golf Club Value Guide and North American Club Makers.

A collector of over 20 years, Pete is a regular contributor on golf topics to golf magazines, the GCS Bulletin and Chuck Furjanic's monthly catalog.

ABOUT THE AUTHOR

Charles Michael Furjanic Jr. began playing golf at age 10 during the summer of 1953. Thanks to the parish priest, Father Charles Georgavich, Chuck was gifted his first set of clubs...two woods, four irons and a putter...all with hickory shafts. In his sophomore year at Swissvale High School in Pittsburgh, Pennsylvania, Chuck persuaded a faculty member to sponsor the school's first golf team. Chuck attended Slippery Rock University of Pennsylvania, where he played without compensation. Chuck would, in 1979, establish the "Doc-Chuck" Golf Scholarship Fund in co-sponsorship with coach Dr. Albert "Doc" Schmittlein, providing financial assistance to more than thirty golf students through 1996.

Chuck's life-long love of golf and collecting led him to turn professional in two areas. Golf came first. He taught lessons at a driving range and played in tournaments, good enough to avoid embarrassment, but not well enough to win much more than gasoline money. After nearly four years, he was convinced professional golf was not going to be his lifelong vocation.

Turning to his other love, numismatics, Chuck became one of the nation's leading coin experts and enjoyed working with collectors, building meaningful collections. Chuck was a contributing editor for *A Guide Book of United States Coins (Red Book) for nearly fifteen years, and for the Handbook of United States Coins (Blue Book). He authored articles for CoinWorld, Numismatic News and CoinAge, gave talks and presentations at local and national organizations and taught numismatic courses at Allegheny College in Pittsburgh.*

In 1986, when packing to move from Pittsburgh to Irving, Texas, Chuck found some old friends in a corner of the garage. The original seven wooden shafted clubs rekindled his interest in golf collectibles and he began in earnest to develop a business around golf, focusing on the collector.

He published his first retail golf collectibles catalogue for the hobby in February 1989 and launched a new career, not as a professional golfer, but as a golf professional, dealing with collectors and collectibles.

Conducting several successful Mail Bid Sales gave him the expertise to sell the late Linda Craft's golf estate in May 1995 (Linda was an LPGA pro and long-time golf collector). Because of that auction's success, Chuck now conducts spring and fall public sales geared to the collector from both the consignment and sales aspect.

Nearly a hundred catalogues and this book later, Chuck has found his comfort zone—golf, collectors and collectibles.

"My philosophy has always been the collector should come first. Customer satisfaction is my most important product, and if the collector is not happy, I'm not happy.

"Yes, we all would like to make mega-thousand dollar sales each time the phone rings, but the collector, who spends his grocery money to buy that $50 ball or $65 hickory shafted club, is the real foundation of the hobby. I take as much time and care filling a $50 order and helping the collector get what he wants, just as I do for the $1,000 buyer. I personally try to answer every incoming call because listening to collectors, and helping them find the collectibles or information they seek, is very important to me and essential to the hobby.

"If you are in the Dallas area, bring your hickories—not your collectibles, but your playables—there's always a 'game' available! On second thought, bring your collectibles and your stories too, and we will sit down for a friendly chat—after the 'game.'"

TO CONTACT THE AUTHOR
Chuck Furjanic
P.O. Box 165892
Irving, TX 75016
Phone: (972) 594-7802
Fax: (972) 257-1785
furjanic@directlink.net
web site: http://www.golfforallages.com

Chapter 1

COLLECTING ANTIQUE GOLF

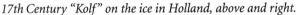

17th Century "Kolf" on the ice in Holland, above and right.

The Heritage of Golf

by Archie Baird, Aberlady, Scotland

Archie Baird is an avid golf collector and historian as well as a good golfer and past Captain of Gullane. He is a member and a Director of both the British and American Golf Collectors' Societies and founder and curator of the Golf Museum next to the pro-shop at Gullane Links, Gullane, Scotland. He is one of the most knowledgeable and respected authorities on clubs, balls, books, and golf memorabilia in the hobby.

EARLY GOLF 1300-1700 AD

We begin with the Dutch derivation, and by means of paintings, prints and photographs, show the variety of conditions and costumes in which the game was played. It was played in church yards, on the streets and roads, on the fields and harvest, and on the ice in winter.

Who brought golf to Scotland? It may have been soldiers or sailors. There were many Scottish mercenary soldiers in Holland, and dozens of marriages between these soldiers and Dutch girls are recorded. If the wind was unfavorable, Scottish sailors would be forced to stay in Holland for days or weeks, giving them plenty of time for golf. The Van der Velde painting of 1668 shows two kilted players with clubs.

This painting is of early 19ᵗʰ Century golf in Scotland. Pre-1900 art is a popular collectible.

The flowerings of Dutch landscape paintings coincided with the popularity of the game. In most outdoor scenes in these paintings, at least one figure carries a club. The game disappeared about 1700 and was succeeded by an indoor variation.

The spread to Scotland from Holland looks likely after studying the maps marked with the early Scottish links. They are all near east coast ports e.g. Dunbar, North Berwick, Aberlady, Musselburgh, Leith, Elie, St. Andrews, and so on up the coast to Dornoch. The earliest inland golf was at Bruntsfield Links, just South of Edinburgh Castle.

Golf on the Scottish links, circa 1900.

All of these new links were rolling hills and land where rabbits and grass vied for existence. Smooth areas nibbled short and marked by rabbit "scrapes" (the 1st hole?) alternated with rough grass. The "greens" were connected by sheep paths of varying widths. Rabbits and sheep were therefore the first golf course architects!

THE FEATHERY BALL ERA

Up until 1850 the feather ball was used. It was a leather stitched case stuffed with a top-hat full of boiled feathers. It was a skilled and arduous job to make a feather ball and a man could only complete two or three in a day. This made them as expensive as a club, and controlled, to some extent, the popularity of golf.

Because the "feathery" was easily damaged by iron clubs, irons were only used in sand or in a rut. The player carried nearly all wooden clubs and there was a great variation in loft and length. The first club makers were bow makers who fashioned beautiful delicate woods, and carpenters who made heavier, clumsier clubs. There were no "sets" of clubs. Players chose or ordered each club to their preference, and no two clubs made before 1890 were the exactly the same. The heads were long, narrow and shallow with a concave or "hooked" face. They were made of beech, apple, pear or thorn. The shafts were ash or hazel until about 1830 when hickory was found to make much better shafts.

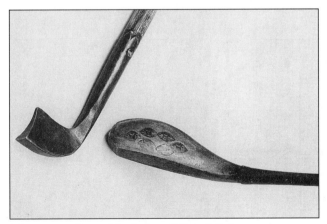

These are replicas of the famous "Troon" clubs.

The wood heads were attached to the shaft by a long diagonal splice or "scare." These are known as "scared head" clubs. They had lead poured into the back and a strip or horn was fitted into the leading edge of the sole. Very early clubs had no grips and the shafts were thick enough to grip. Sheepskin was used as a grip from about 1800. Leather became popular much later, about 1880. Early irons were made by blacksmiths and were heavy and cumbersome. They were only used "in extremis" for fear of damaging the leather cover of the feather ball. The hosel was thick and the shaft was fitted into the socket, which was "knurled" to help grip the wood shaft. The cruder the "nicks", the older the iron. During the "feather" era there were two main irons: the sand iron, with a large concave face, and the rut iron with a very small head to play out of the tracks formed by carts bringing back sand from the beach.

The courses at this time were as nature made them. There was very little green keeping and the golfers played the ball as it lay. Rules were simple and about 14 in number. Stroke play was very rare, match play was almost always the game. Societies were few, only 17 being formed by 1850. Dress was a personal choice except that most societies made the wearing of red jackets compulsory so that golfers could be seen easily on the busy links. Colored facings and lapels were often described, and silver or brass buttons with a club insignia and motto were increasingly popular.

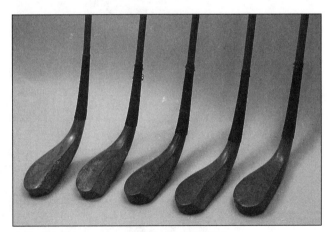

A "set" of long-nose woods circa 1800-1820.

COSTUME

The story of golf clothing is more varied than the clubs and the balls.

In the "feathery" era, red coats with swallow tails and even the occasional top hat were seen. A man's everyday suit was considered correct and the ladies wore the long-skirted gowns that were fashionable at the time. An unbuttoned jacket was rare before 1920.

Waterproof clothing and spike shoes are fairly recent innovations. There is surely a wonderful book to be written on golfing costume.

MRS. CHARLES S. BROWN.
CHAMPION WOMAN GOLFER, 1896.

MISS BEATRIX HOYT,
WOMAN CHAMPION GOLFER '97-'98.

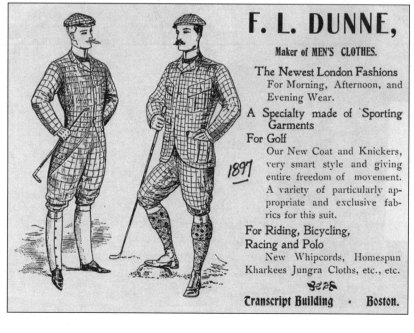

F. L. DUNNE,

Maker of MEN'S CLOTHES.

The Newest London Fashions
For Morning, Afternoon, and Evening Wear.

A Specialty made of Sporting Garments

For Golf
Our New Coat and Knickers, very smart style and giving entire freedom of movement. A variety of particularly appropriate and exclusive fabrics for this suit.

For Riding, Bicycling, Racing and Polo
New Whipcords, Homespun Kharkees Jungra Cloths, etc., etc.

Transcript Building • Boston.

A print by F. T. Richards depicting an Elizabethan women's golf costume.

A print by F. T. Richards depicting an Elizabethan men's golf costume.

PERSONALITIES

Being essentially a solo game, golf has had its share of personalities. The Parks and the Morrises; the Triumvirate; Braid, Taylor and Vardon; Harold Hilton and John Ball, Hoylake's tremendous pair; the prince of them all Bobby Jones; Joyce Weathered and Babe Zaharias; Hagen and Hogan; Player and Palmer; Nicklaus and Watson are only a few.

Any golfer could add a hundred names because no two people ever played the game the same way.

WHAT GUTTA-PERCHA DID FOR GOLF

Just before 1850, probably in Musselburgh, the first gutta-percha balls were produced by immersing the gum-like substance in hot water and hand rolling until round. They were cheap and tough

Antique Dutch Kolf Balls. Made out of Boxwood (hardwood root), two decorated with nails and screw heads.

Examples of smooth, hand hammered and line cut gutta-percha balls. Left—1850s, middle—1870s, and right—1890s.

and a man could make dozens in a day. But they would not fly properly, originally having been made smooth. At first they were hand hammered to produce a rough surface. Then they were made in molds with a wide variety of patterns. Bramble, dimple squares and circles are only a few. They were never painted successfully and survivors are all dark brown. Like the featheries, they were made in varying weights and sizes. Their moderate price and resilience allowed golf to grow quickly. The Scots had kept the game alive for 400 years, and now it began to expand rapidly.

GOLF CLUBS AND SOCIETIES

Year	1850	1870	1890	1910
No. of Clubs and Societies	17	34	387	4135

This expansion was aided by the spread of the railways, but the "gutta" and its composition successor, the "guttie," made it possible.

They also changed the shape and the choice of clubs. The long-nose woods that swept the "feathery" along could not stand up to the "gutta-percha." Leather faces and vulcanite insets, brass soles and broader heads all appeared. Irons became more popular and blacksmiths who made clubs became "cleek-makers," refining the sand iron and the rutiron into niblicks, mashies, and cleeks. They even made iron putters!

Greenskeeping became a necessary and canny craft. The skills became more specialized and numerous, and the local club maker or professional had seldom the time or the inclination to "keep the green."

RUBBER CORE

At the turn of the century came the "Haskell" ball from the U.S.A. This was made by winding hundreds of feet of elastic onto a central core, then coating it with gutta-percha. These balls flew farther—a bad shot could go a long way! The rubber core ball traveled so far, golf courses had to be changed to contain it.

On the negative side, the cover was easily cut on these new balls. Many improvements have been tried over the last 75 years. Recently, some solid one-piece balls have gained in popularity with manufacturers, who are always trying to improve them further.

During the gutta and rubber core domination, club face design became important. Lines or dots on the face enabled backspin to be applied to the ball. When the grooves became too deep, the R & A ruled them illegal. Hickory shafts finally gave way to steel in the 1920s, partly to steel's superiority, but mostly because the hickory forests were depleted.

Collecting Golf Memorabilia, A Collector's Personal View

by Johnny Henry

I've known Johnny Henry for nearly 12 years. He can still shoot his age with steel or hickory clubs (72), has a fine collection of golf artifacts, and just about the finest collection of golf related memories and friends of anyone I know. A book on collecting golf would not be complete without including his impressions.

People frequently ask me when I started collecting old golf items, and I always reply, "I don't know, but I was collecting for a long time before I knew it." Golf has been a large part of my life since I started playing at age six (in 1933) with a set of Spalding juvenile, hickory-shafted clubs. Since then, I have been involved with golf-oriented occupations: Toro turf equipment salesman, golf course irrigation designer, PGA professional, golf architect and greenskeeper. Over the years, the opportunity had arisen to probe for clubs at the various golf courses and I had amassed some 18-20 hickory clubs. Then, in 1975, my wife gave me a golf trip to Scotland for an anniversary gift, and that was a serious mistake! While on the trip, I met Ken Smith (GCS #0076); he suggested I join the Golf Collectors Society, then, just a small group of people who had the same interests as us.

Before Phillips, Christie's and Sotheby's auction houses began to have golf sales. About 1980, it was possible to ferret out collectible clubs from individuals—retired professionals, widows, caddies, "boot sales"—as well as thrift shops and pros at old courses in Great Britain. This was the "fun era" of collecting.

While touring the various courses in Scotland and England, I would find pros who would have a few hickories on the wall or back in the club storage area that were for sale. In many cases, they would also give me leads as to where I might find clubs in the area.

Sadly, those days are gone forever. With headlines in the London Times reading "GOLF CLUB MAKES RECORD PRICE AT SOTHEBY'S SALE" the public became reluctant to sell for fear the old clubs in their possession were worth more than this "Colonist" was offering to pay. Other than flea markets, estate sales, thrift shops and other collectors, probably the best source is purchasing items from dealers. They attend auctions here in the USA and in the UK to maintain inventories of items we all look for.

Display cabinet filled with porcelain, glass and silver golf collectibles.

An assortment of wood head clubs circa 1880-1900.

My collection, while modest in quantity (240 clubs), is adequate in quality. It consists of 25 long-nose clubs, including a Philp and an 18th century play club made by a bow and spear maker. I also have most of the patent clubs such as the Cran, Seely, spring face, Lard whistler, anti-shank irons, Mills aluminum clubs, along with a giant niblick, transitional woods, bulger scares and deep-grooved irons. There are about 50 putters including: a Calamity Jane, Gassiat, Schenectady, a Kismet with rollers on sole, Ivora Perfection, and various blade and Mills putters.

My collection of balls include two featheries, 20 gutties, and about 100 wound balls with different markings.

Scattered about in my golf room are various miscellaneous items relating to golf, including pottery by Doulton, O'Hare, Carlton, Wedgewood, Weller, and others. There are also silver and gold medals, silver hat pins, spoons and glass items by Cambridge and Steuben. My library has about 150 books, none of which are "classic" volumes, but those that I like to read.

This room is an excellent place to relax after a hard day on the links. While sipping a beverage, I can scan the walls, and each club has a story behind it. I can remember where I was, from whom it was acquired, and the circumstances and haggling that transpired. Collecting memories, friends and reminiscing is as important to me as the collection itself. It's amazing how close a bond exists among people with a common interest.

Collecting Pre-1875 Golf Artifacts

by Will Roberto

Will Roberto, Attorney at Law, is a long-time collector who specializes in pre-1875 golf collectibles and artifacts. Mr. Roberto has kindly outlined this era.

Pre-1875 golf artifacts are very scarce and seldom offered at auction or private sale. The few examples known are in museums, clubhouse displays and in several advanced collectors' hands. The USGA at Far Hills, New Jersey, has an outstanding display of long-nose and early hammer-forged iron head clubs. In St. Andrews, Scotland, there is a museum, and in the Royal & Ancient Club House, the Members Room is adorned by many golfing artifacts. Historical courses such as Royal Liverpool, Prestwick, and The Royal Company of Edinburgh Golfers at Muirfield, have extensive displays of clubs and balls. The clubhouse at Gullane has an outstanding display of balls, one of which is the "Map of the Globe" ball. Archie Baird also has a small museum next to the pro shop at Gullane where, by appointment, Dr. Baird will conduct a personal tour.

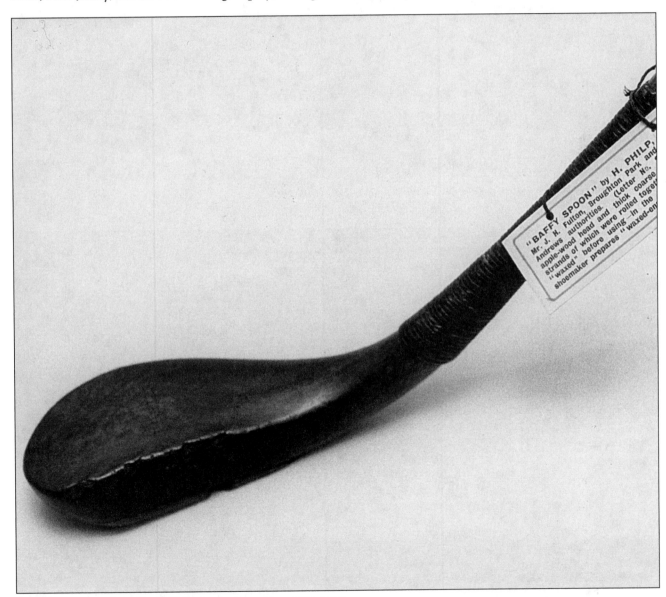

A Baffy Spoon made by Hugh Philp, St. Andrews Circa 1840-1855

A wonderful den display with a St. Andrews Captain's jacket as the centerpiece.

Hand painted ceramics and china are some of the most sought after golf collectibles.

Pre-1875 Artifacts

This period of collecting covers the era starting in 1457—a span of nearly 420 years of golf history—but is really a short blip on the collecting scene. Golf during these times was limited to royalty, clergy and the wealthy businessman, as only the affluent had the time and money to pursue the sport. Most of the highest quality artifacts are impounded in museums and clubhouse displays, and of those available to collectors, many are below average or damaged pieces not worth having in a serious collection. As a result, very few quality collectibles are available and collectors diligently seek them when offered privately or at public auction.

The recent auction of the Thistle Club memorabilia pushed ephemera prices to an all time high. Some of the earliest scorecards, notebooks and letters have since been sold at more than twice the auction prices. Collectors have realized these one-of-a-kind historical items are just as collectible as early clubs, balls, and medals. These are "history" in the hand of those unknown players who kept the game alive when it almost died out in the early 1800s in Scotland.

GOLF CLUBS

During this era, very few iron-head clubs were marked with manufacturers' identification and are difficult to date and authenticate. Wooden-head clubs were usually marked with the maker's name, but use, abuse, refinishing and repair render many unidentifiable, some not worthy of an advanced collection. With these items, accurate provenience, or opinions from experts would be the only way a collector could feel comfortable before and after acquisition. There are about fifty major collectors worldwide and a few dealers who concentrate on pre-1875 memorabilia. They could be good sources for identification, dating and authentication. Elsewhere in this book is mention of the Golf Collectors Society and other worldwide organizations who can supply names of experts.

Since the previous edition of this book, current scholarship has advanced the push that the earliest known golf clubs currently in major collections are the spur toe irons which are light and heavy irons. These clubs date to the 17th century. There are also several wooden clubs which may be late 17th century but most certainly of early 18th century vintage. As these clubs have no makers names or marks, and only limited provenance to assist in dating, the collector golf historian must rely on the crudeness of manufacture, larger size, as compared to clubs of a more certain vintage, and written references describing these earliest bludgeons as they are indeed massive tools of the game. Among the few known examples, they appear to have several generations of design advancement, which only the most expert eye can notice.

Several new theories about wooden club head sizes and shapes have been advanced. Foremost

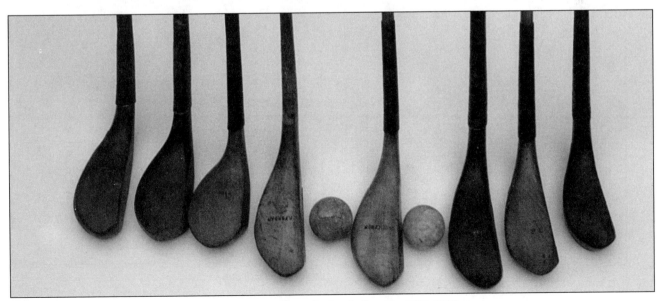

An assortment of long-nose clubs, circa 1840-1890, and two feather balls, circa 1840-1860.

among these is that due to the difficulty of travel in the earliest days of the game (50 miles was considered a long trip) many seaside makers of woods and irons never saw what their inland counterparts were producing unless a traveling player was in town for a game or needed a repair. Sometimes the differences were no doubt adopted by the repairer or maker seeing the idea for the first time. The theory as propounded is that inland makers, due to the firmer soils of inland "greens", made wood clubs that had larger, heavier heads characterized by thicker necks and deeper faces; whereas, the early coastal club makers such as Philp & McEwan made smaller more delicate heads for use on the softer links land such as St. Andrews, Leith links & Musselburgh. Early irons being "trouble clubs" have not shown such a difference whether made by early inland or seaside makers. They tended to be stout and heavy clubs used to extricate featheries and early gutties from the worst of lies.

The most difficult to obtain are pre-1800 clubs. There are very few authenticated and properly dated pre-1800 clubs in collector hands. Most of these are wooden-headed clubs, as the early players only carried a few irons for use from trouble lies. There are also some pre-1800 iron putters to be found, but not many.

The period from 1800 to 1850 provides the collector more clubs than the pre-1800 period—most likely based on age and preservation rather than numbers originally manufactured. The numbers of golfers did not vary substantially from 1750 to 1845; in fact, during the period from 1820 to 1845 golf nearly died out in Edinburgh. Robert Forgan wrote in a letter to T. H. Bairnsfather, Feb. 3, 1899, "...there was not work for three men making golf clubs in 1856 when I first went to it..." The attrition rate of pre-1800 artifacts was far greater than clubs from the first half of the 19th century. Again, most of the clubs from the 1800-1850 period in collectors' hands are woods with a few bunker, rut and putting irons.

Clubs from the period 1850 to 1875 are somewhat more plentiful but cannot be considered common. Some pre-1875 clubs have a maker's name or mark on them that can help date them.

How can a collector date woods and smooth-face irons with or without identifying markings? Many wood clubs were marked with the maker's name and sometimes with his mark. Reference books listing known makers can help place a "McEwan," "Philp" or "Jackson" stamped club in a probable time period by size and shape of the stamping and general overall construction of the head and neck.

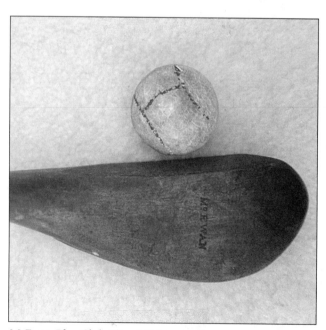

McEwan Play Club Circa 1800.

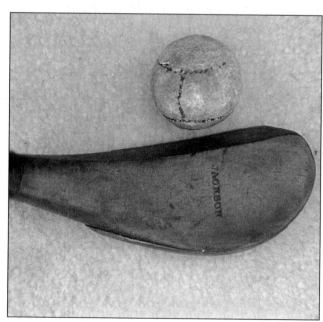

Jackson Short Spoon Circa 1825.

Many uninformed collectors assume unmarked irons are rare. Most clubs forged in the 1880s and early 1890s were made to look like the old style but were imprinted with the maker's name or mark. Caddies used "Emory" paper to clean rust from the iron heads and while sanding away the rust, the caddies also sanded away the markings. Rare unmarked irons were usually made by a blacksmith and have a crude hammered appearance, longer hosels, heavier hosel nickings and usually exhibit forging lines or seams. The hole at the top of the hosel where the shaft is inserted is usually wider in diameter than clubs forged by the post-1885 club maker. Many pre-1875 irons had shafts made of ash, not hickory.

Collectibility of these pre-1875 clubs is determined by quality, provenience, the maker's place relating to the history of the game as a player, maker, or both, and the scarcity of a particular club. A club from 1870 would be far more valuable if the owner could produce a provenience verifying

Examples of Blacksmith made iron-head clubs in use prior to 1875.

young Tom Morris used this particular club while winning three British Opens, versus one without provenience probably belonging to a businessman or clergyman.

BALLS

As with clubs, pre-1800 balls are scarce. Pre-1860 gutty balls are scarcer than featheries. Named maker balls of both types are even scarcer. Balls with markings on them from this period are among the rarest. There are also a few balls painted for winter play that are highly sought after. While most are red or orange, there have been blue, yellow and black balls noted.

Early balls continue to be found, with the unusual marked gutties pushing the envelope on auction prices. Marked feather balls by the earliest makers continue to command premium prices and those few of the rarer named featheries rival the gutties.

Early gutty balls were hand rolled and smooth. The early players realized they flew poorly and marked them by hand using a hammer or knife. (Some gave the smooth spheres to caddies to

Smooth gutta-percha balls, circa 1950s.

Line cut gutta-percha balls, circa 1885-1900.

knock them around before play, rendering them with cuts and marks, thus making their flight more consistent.) Later patterns, such as those made by Forgan, became more common and other makers developed different styles as a form of advertising. Just as club making became more sophisticated, so did ball making.

As golf grew, and with it the demand for balls, heavy iron molds (rare and very collectible) were used to mold and mark the gutta-percha spheres. Various devices to cut patterns in the balls were developed in an attempt to improve the flight of the ball.

BOOKS

Pre-1875 books are very scarce as few were written. Major titles are Robert Clark, *Golf—A Royal and Ancient Game,* 1875; H. B. Farnie, *A Golfer's Manual,* 1857; Robert Chambers, *A Few Rambling Remarks on Golf,* 1862.

Pre-1875 books have achieved record auction prices in some cases regardless of condition, primarily based on rarity. Easier to come by and equally important are some books published 1875 to 1910.

ART

Very little pre-1800 art, not already in museums, is available to private collectors and these pieces rarely appear at auctions. There are, however, many fine prints, pieces of sculpture, and paintings being offered from time to time. Also many later generation reproductions of fine quality are available to decorate a collection room.

Several fine pieces of pre-1900 art have sold in the last couple of years. Paintings by J. Michael Brown, Thomas Hodge, Major Hopkins (Short-spoon) and several others have seen record prices achieved.

GENERAL

Many important items associated with the game are available. Original letters between players challenging one another are very rare and expensive. Written documents of the game such as rules, scorecards, receipts, club secretary records, and notebooks, occasionally become available.

Clothing, such as the red coats worn by the captains at St. Andrews, leather caps, top hats, tweed waistcoats and wool plus fours are prized pre-1875 collectibles.

Smoking-pipes with carved golfing scenes, pottery, mugs and beer bottles as well as jewelry, watch fobs, and whiskey flasks are also highly sought after by the historically bound collector.

Club maker's tools and maker's die stamps are another avenue as well as feather ball maker's tools. At an auction in 1989, a complete set of feather ball tools in a wooden case was offered for sale.

These are two of the cornerstone books of a collector's library.

Hand painted Daulton ceramics are quite scarce.

MEDALS

The early clubs and golf societies gave prizes of balls or clubs, a claret of wine, but most often medals. There are numerous medals won by competitors on display at old links like Muirfield, St. Andrews, Prestwick and in museums. On occasion, medals are sold through auction and their value is determined by the club that gave the medal, names of winners thereon, and whether the medal is gold or another metal. Most British-made medals were of 9kt. gold, sterling or bronze.

There have been several good, but very few, early medals at recent auctions. As expected, those from the earliest clubs have done well.

It is suggested that new collectors contact the many dealers and advanced collectors who can advise and assist in assembling a collection or refining an existing one.

Knowledge in any antique hobby takes years of research, and in this hobby it requires many nights of reading old, scarce books (when they can be accessed) and/or trips to visit private museum collections in the U.S. and abroad.

With thousands of dollars often changing hands for sought after items, subtle variations that shave only a few years off an item's age often mean the difference between a good buy and overpaying.

SUGGESTIONS FOR A PRE-1875 STARTER COLLECTION

• *Long Nose Woods -*	T. Morris, Forgan, McEwan and Park.
• *Blacksmith Irons -*	No maker's name - early cleeks, lofters, general irons c. 1860 or earlier in any condition are scarce if not rare.
• *Named Irons -*	c. 1850-1860 by Carrick, Gray c. 1870s R. Wilson, W. Wilson, Park, Forgan, Morris, Anderson
	Some of the named clubs were made for the seller, often a player or a manufacturer of wooden clubs, but are still attractive period pieces.
• *Books -*	R. Clark *"Golf A Royal & Ancient Game"*
	John Kirr *"Golf Book of East Lothian"*
	Alastair Johnston, *"Chronicle of Golf"*, 1990
	These are cornerstone books for all collectors.
• *Art -*	Watercolors by Hodge or Hopkins.
• *Medals -*	Any pre-1890 medals from the early Clubs.
• *Balls -*	Feather balls, named or unnamed. Smooth gutty, hand hammered gutty, line cut gutty.
• *Ceramics -*	Pieces that can be dated to pre-1900.

Sometimes these differences are so subtle, some of the more sophisticated dealers and collectors miss them due to specialization within the hobby. There are, however, several well-known collectors and dealers with in-depth knowledge willing to help newcomers avoid the heartbreaks. The old doctrine "Caveat Emptor" applies for at least two reasons. The well intentioned advisor could not have been negligent due to the limited information in the public domain and because of security concerns, it was difficult to see or handle pieces in museums and private collections.

The sand tee box dates this painting near 1900.

An early depiction of St. Andrews, from the Road Hole (#17) by Thomas Hodge, 1881.

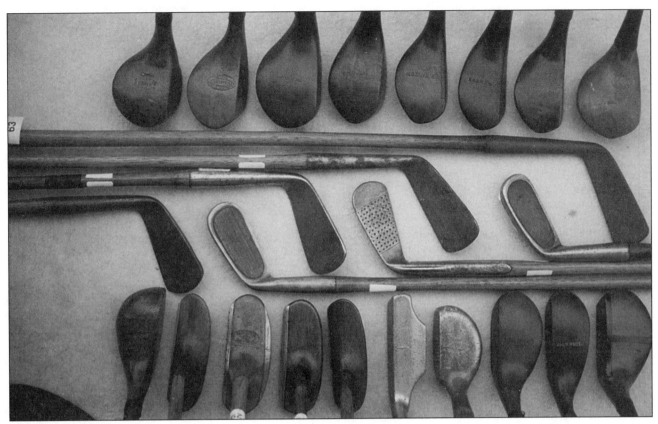

An assortment of patent clubs, woods and putters circa 1900-1920.

A Brief Introduction to Patent Clubs

by Gordon Page

Most clubs in the patent category tend to visually stand out and say "I am different, interesting and have a story to tell." In addition to dramatic visual appeal, many of them represent a particular period in golf history and reflect some of today's designs. They also can be found in price ranges from moderate to high. Thus, they can be purchased and admired by the beginning collector on a budget to the veteran collector eyeing the highly treasured ones. Variety is definitely the spice of patent life, and one can probably never run out of items to look for.

Let's reflect a moment on history and its relationship to many of the patent clubs. From the 1890s through the early part of the 1900s, several events brought forward the proliferation of unusual clubs:

- The industrial revolution brought manufacturing techniques to the golf industry not available prior to that time. Hand forging, with its limited volume, started to be replaced by mass production and the ability to work with various metals in new and sometimes very unique designs. Instead of hundreds or thousands of clubs being produced, the industry was producing millions, yes, millions of clubs.

- The interest in golf was exploding. Where the game was previously played by a few on few courses, golf courses were being built at a rapid pace for the multitude of eager novices.

- As companies looked for an advantage to help sell their clubs and profit from this groundswell of interest, designers conceived hundreds of patentable club shapes, sizes and forms.

- The golfer picked up the game with a fervour and many looked for the magic club to assist them in getting from tee to green in as few strokes as possible.

Information on patent clubs could cover several large books; it is my intent, however, to only show some examples of woods, putters, and irons, why they were invented and, also, to categorize them by availability. I have concentrated on the period of 1890s to the 1930s, when patent clubs proliferated the golfing field. An overly simplistic statement about availability suggests that, the less the patent appealed to the golfer at the time, and the less it improved his game, the fewer they made. Thus, the least desirable clubs of that era are the most desirable to today's collector and the price follows availability.

The first list gives some examples of moderately priced, more available clubs (generally under $500), followed by the higher priced, rarer clubs.

MODERATELY PRICED WOODS

Face Inserts were used to protect the impact area, and frequently utilized brass, steel or ivory type materials to enhance the appearance of the insert (fancy faces). Suggested makers are MacGregor with its Chieftan series, Spalding's Kro-Flite series, and Wilson's Walker Cup.

Club head materials

Fancy faces

Head Materials were developed with the intent to make the head impervious to the elements and included aluminum, molded and compressed synthetics and combinations of these. Suggested makers include Standard Golf of Sunderland, England with its many aluminum "woods," Forgan's Forganite and Kroydon's Kroydonite compressed wood models.

Structural Designs were fairly standard in that one club shape pretty much looked like another after the turn of the century. The Streamliner by MacGregor broke this trend. Its unique bullet head shape was an attempt at aerodynamics for club head speed. It has an early chromed steel shaft, but is one steel shaft club worth collecting.

Streamliner

Neck Designs to look for include the Scott patent fork splice and the Spalding triple splice, both developed for stronger head/shaft construction.

Forked splice

MODERATELY PRICED IRONS

Sweet Spot weighting was in favor throughout the industry and included a wide diversity of patented designs. Suggested makers are T. Stewart for mussel back and diamond back styles and William Gibson for flange backs and heel/toe weighting.

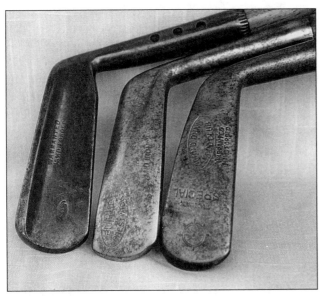

Sweet spot weighting

Hosel Designs were also developed to add weight to the club head by removing it from the hosel. Two popular designs are the Maxwell designed holes in the hosel, as seen on some Gibson clubs, and the slotted holes in the hosel as seen on some MacGregor clubs. These two patents were also designed to improve the snug fit of the shaft. A third design was the Carruthers short hosel with bore through shaft as seen on some Spalding clubs. It is interesting to note modern club designs went 180 degrees away from sweet spot weighting and developed the cavity back to enlarge the sweet spot.

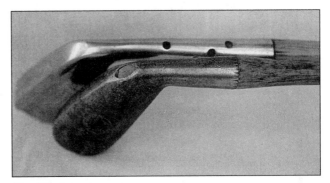

Hosel designs

Deep Grooved clubs were developed to allow the golfer to put spin on the ball in order to "bite" and stop on the green. Suggested makers are MacGregor for the deep slot and corrugated styles; Spalding for their waterfall, and Burke for their "stars and stripes." Other designs to look for are the brick, waffle and deep dimple styles. Many of these designs were declared illegal by the R&A and the USGA in the 1920s.

Deep grooves

Waffle face

Concave face

Anti-shank Designs were developed in two styles, both with the same purpose of preventing the dreaded shank! The two designs lifted the hosel connection to the top of the club. A Smith patent and a Fairlee patent were produced and seen almost exclusively on Scottish clubs. Most anti-shank clubs were made by Gibson.

Materials used to protect from rust, other than forged iron, included a bronze like substance, AMPCO and Radite, MacGregor.

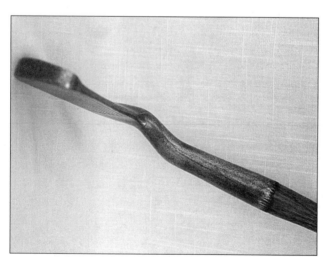

Antishank

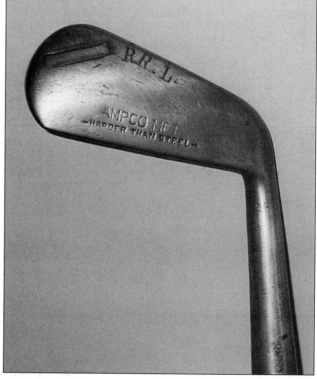

AMPCO material

Flanged Niblics were designed as players recognized their lack of a good wedge to negotiate out of soft sand. The most popular of these from a collecting standpoint is the Walter Hagen sand wedge with its very large flange and concave face.

MODERATELY PRICED PUTTERS

Putter designers must have been tuned into the golfer's feeling of inadequacy on the putting green. There was a prodigious number of patents on putters.

Hosel/Neck Designs were developed to give the golfer a better view of the blade striking area by bending the hosel "out of the way." The William Park bent neck putter was one of the first.

Mallet heads

Unusual designs included the Sayers' Benny putter with a ribbed sole, Spalding hollow back, MacGregor's aluminum mallet with a lead face insert, and a steel blade lead face by Noirit.

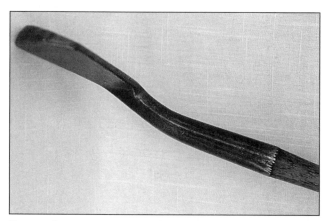

Bent neck

Weighting of the head for feel and balance included heavy flange back; Burke; GEM style (like a 1/4 round molding), Gibson; hollowback, Spalding; mallets of aluminum, Standard Golf and Schenectady; brass mallets, Anderson; or wood mallets, MacGregor, Burke, and Spalding.

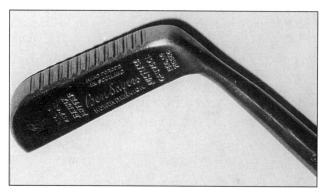

Ribbed sole

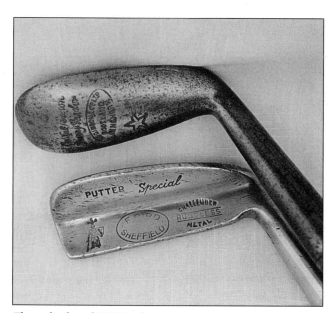

Flange back and GEM style

Hollow back

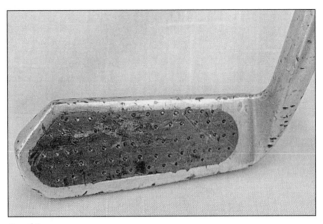

Lead insert

The following list is for those collectors wanting to expand their collection to include the rare patent clubs.

WOODS

Neck designs to strengthen the head and shaft included a screw-in shaft by Slagenzer, one piece woods by B.G.I., Spalding, and MacGregor.

Duplex and one piece

Structural designs would include clubs like the Brewster Simplex, which is shaped like an elongated triangle, the streamliner clubs (previously mentioned), and the aluminum Duplex clubs by Standard Golf.

IRONS

Deep groove clubs such as the Spalding Double Waterfall, the Spalding "Cran Cleek" with a wood face insert, and the Spalding Spring face.

Double waterfall

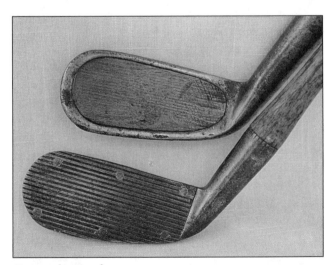

Cran and spring face

Club head size was exaggerated. Giant niblic examples by Winton and Hendry & Bishop are the most popular.

Giant niblick

Clubs were designed with a hosel that could be adjusted to vary the loft of the face—one club that can do the job of all the clubs in the bag. The most popular of the available patent clubs is the Urquhart.

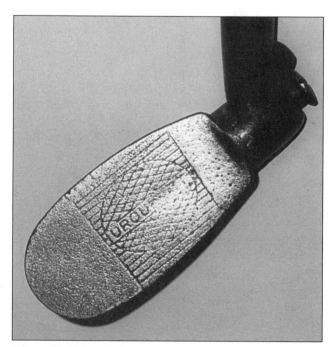

Adjustable iron

Unique and unusual designs such as the Brown's Rake Iron and Perforated face water irons were designed to make trouble shots easier.

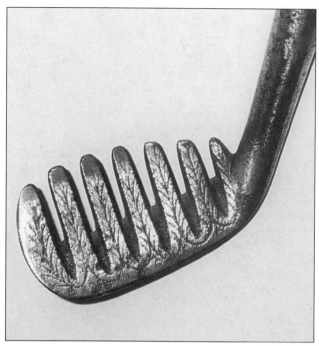

Rake iron

PUTTERS

A wood mallet head putter by Jean Gassiat had the large wooden head shaped like a grand piano.

A unique center shafted putter with a bifurcated hossel and aluminum head was patented by Otto Hackbarth.

A combination of steel head and brass hossel by Bussey is another unusual patent collectible.

Gassiat

Forked hosel

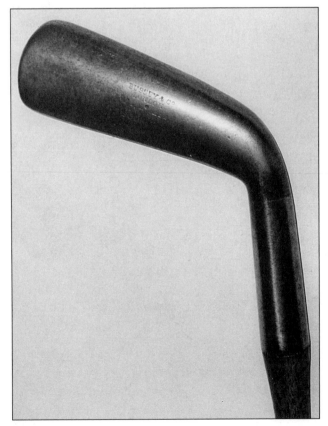

Bussey

Adjustables allowed for left or right handed putting, changing the lie and loft for approaching. These highly collectible putters included the Sprague and the Baltimore.

Adjustable putter

Gordon Page is a long-time friend, dealer in antique golf collectibles, and an avid collector of patent clubs. We thank Gordon for his expertise and photographs. Mr. Page can be contacted by e-mail at: gpage@innet.com

Prestwick, St. Andrews and Musselburgh

THE THREE COURSE "ROTA" FOR THE BRITISH OPEN FROM 1872 TO 1889, THEIR SIGNIFICANCE TO THE GAME, AND THEIR INFLUENCE ON COURSE DESIGN TODAY.

by Keith Foster

Keith Foster is a golf course designer who has two great Texas courses to his credit; The Quarry and Texas Star. He is currently reconstructing the bunkers and greens at Colonial CC, home of the prestegious PGA Tour Colonial Invitational Tournament, Ft. Worth, TX. He is an avid collector and has a particular fascination for pre-1890 left handed longnose clubs.

All who embrace the wonderful game of golf know that nothing contributes more greatly than the endless variety of courses, shots or conditions. This variety is a very distinct feature of the game. Such variety can be found at golf's hallowed grounds at St. Andrews, Prestwick, and Musselburgh. Most of us are already familiar with St. Andrews, less knowledgeable of Prestwick and have heard little or nothing of Musselburgh. Yet, the three courses were the gold centers of the game within Scotland back in the early, mid and late 1800s.

St. Andrews, Prestwick and Musselburgh were golf's big three courses and they formed the Open Rota from 1872 through 1889, while also hosting most of the big matches of the day.

In today's game, it is easy to look at the three courses for what they are not. But rather, to truly appreciate the game and its history, it is far better to look at St. Andrews, Prestwick and Musselburgh for what they were and still are to the game.

Consider that St. Andrews was once 22 holes, Prestwick was originally 12 holes, while Musselburgh started out as five holes and then pushed out to total nine holes.

The charm of all three courses is the simple truth. There are the holes, play them as you like. That is how the game was intended to be played. Today we expect courses to fit our games, our talents. This was not the case with early golf courses where golfers were to discover and improvise golf shots for a given situation.

GROWTH WITHIN THE GAME

While this chapter will look at the three courses more closely, it is helpful to understand how golf courses were maintained then and what helped spread the game within Scotland itself.

Early in the game, the "Featherie" was the ball used. Its cost was so high that this alone kept few from enjoying the game, except the well-to-do. But in 1848, the introduction of the Gutta-Percha ball opened the game to the common man.

The Gutta-Percha ball also created a rift between Tom Morris and Allan Robertson in St. Andrews. A couple of years later, Tom Morris moved to Prestwick.

As for early golf course maintenance, it should be noted that until the 1860s early golf courses had no real water source. During droughts, the links simply had to weather as best they could. In the 1870s, some courses sunk wells to keep greens moist during extended periods of drought. Around the turn of the century, courses began to introduce primitive watering systems for greens.

The equipment of the day was one's back, a wheelbarrow, shovel and a spade. Holes were hand cut by a knife to a diamater of 4-1/2", still the standard today. It wasn't until Old Tom put in a lead liner at the soft 7th green at St. Andrews around 1880 that anyone had ever even thought of a cup for the hole in the ground.

The introduction of mechanized equipment to mow turf followed shortly. Thereby beginning the quest for improved turf conditions and further grooming of the links.

MUSSELBURGH

Golf in Edinburgh was originally played on Bruntsfield Links or Leith Links. In 1836, overcrowding at Leith Links moved the Honorable Company of Edinburgh Golfers to Musselburgh. Two years later in 1838, the Royal Burgess Society left Bruntfield for the same reason. By 1840, there were four major golfing clubs playing at Musselburgh, making it the golf center of Edinburgh.

With the top four Edinburgh golf clubs now at Musselburgh, Edinburgh, club maker "McEwan" and William Gourlay, the "best ball maker," both set up shops adjacent to the links. Add to this, Musselburgh was the home of Willie Park, the first

Musselburgh Original
7 Hole Layout

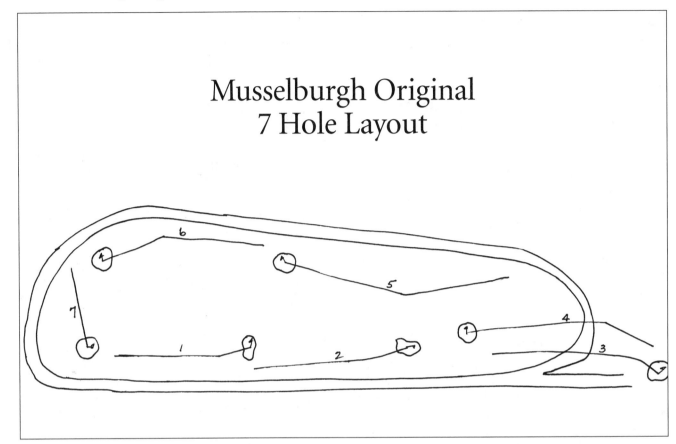

MUSSELBURGH LINKS GOLF COURSE *(Not to scale)*.

Modern Layout

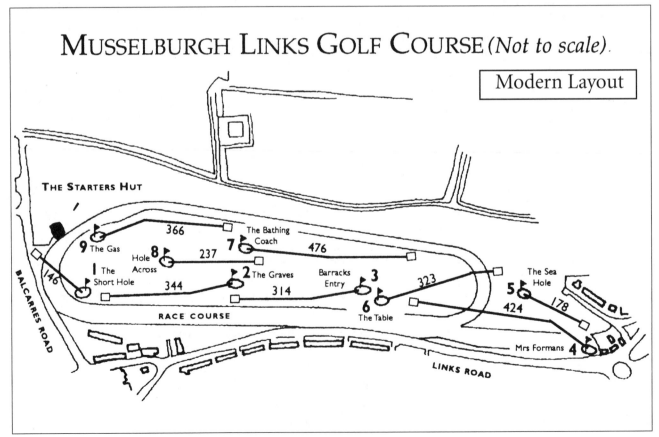

Main Street Musselburgh at dawn. A hotbed of golf in the 19th Century. Willie Park Jr. and Sr., Douglas McEwan, J. & D. Clark, R. Neilson, Mungo Park and Waggott all had club making businesses here. The Musselburgh links hosted six British Opens from 1874 to 1889.

Open Champion in 1860. In its day, Musselburgh had the largest concentration of men skilled in playing, clubmaking and ballmaking. This is quite a fact when you consider that Musselburgh was a very tight and compact nine hole course.

As for the Musselburgh course, it was originally a five hole course. Supposedly, Mary Queen of Scots was said to have whacked a ball around the links. Musselburgh was the nearest test of golf to a true links course for Edinburgh. Its compact site is rather flat and devoid of cavernous features, yet within each hole, there were sound design principles; namely, that there is a right line and a wrong line to each hole. This design principle still is the hallmark of sound design today.

One interesting feature of the course was the Bankers' holes which were adjacent to the 5th green. The Bankers' holes consisted of four holes, each 30 yards long. Willie Park, with his incredible short game, once scored a five on the four hole course.

Musselburgh's demise came from changes within the game and at the hand of Muirfield. In the late 1880s, Musselburgh became so heavily played that the Honorable Company of Edinburgh Golfers had acquired their own property, and in 1892 wanted the Open Championship to be held on their new course, Muirfield.

Musselburgh remains today as a reminder of how simple the game once was and how big the game has become.

PRESTWICK

With the railway now going through Prestwick around 1840, a primitive links was being started. Tom Morris was persuaded to leave St. Andrews in 1851 and routed a 12 hole course within the linksland.

The original 12-hole loop was framed by the railway tracks on its eastern boundary; to the west, the sea. The town was its south boundary and a short stone wall its northern edge. Such great history was made on this rugged ground.

Consider that on such bold terrain there was no machinery, hence nothing could be knocked down or cut into. As such, construction, as we

Early play at Prestwick. The caddies played an important part of pre 1900 golf. Note the clubs were carried under the arm, not in a bag. (Allan Robertson 3rd from the left, Old Tom Morris 5th from the left.)

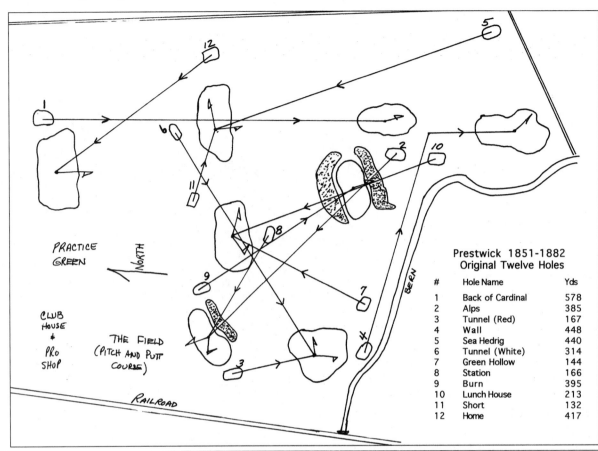

Prestwick 1851-1882
Original Twelve Holes

#	Hole Name	Yds
1	Back of Cardinal	578
2	Alps	385
3	Tunnel (Red)	167
4	Wall	448
5	Sea Hedrig	440
6	Tunnel (White)	314
7	Green Hollow	144
8	Station	166
9	Burn	395
10	Lunch House	213
11	Short	132
12	Home	417

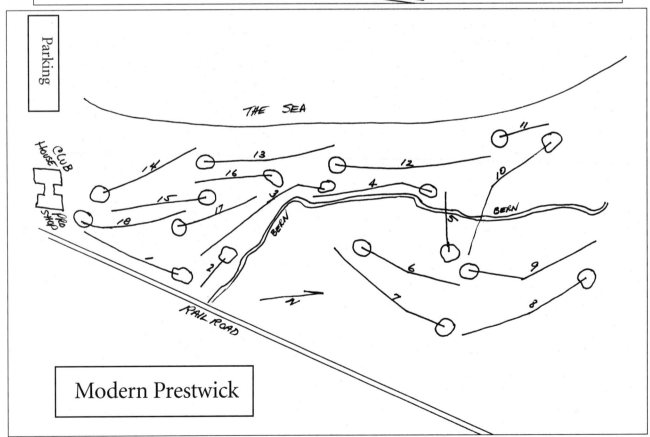

Modern Prestwick

know it, was impossible. The routing of the course at Prestwick worked carefully through and on top of the massive dunes, as in the case of the Alps. Back then, blind shots were regarded as a test of manhood.

Prestwick's early claim to fame was their promotion of the Open Championship, and from 1860 through 1871, hosted the first 12 British Open Tournaments. The 12 hole course, although charming, must have been chaotic, due to the number of times holes played across others.

Between 1851 and 1882, Prestwick was and remained a 12 hole course; however, after Tom Morris had returned to St. Andrews, Prestwick followed St. Andrews' lead and became 18 holes. Many of the original greens still remain today, but only the Cardinal (now the 3rd) and Sea Hedrig (now the 13th) play as they did originally.

The conversion from 12 to 18 holes was not a smooth one. Prestwick was no stranger to controversy, as some prominent golfers truly loved the rugged and blind shots while others felt the course could be improved by the new routing. Prestwick members still play a tournament on the original 12-hole loop.

Prestwick remains a wonderful golf course where history has been written. Of particular note is when the re-routing occurred in 1883, many fine holes were created.

The present 1st hole was never part of the original layout, yet I cannot imagine Prestwick without it. "The Cardinal," which was originally the 4th hole and now the 3rd, remains a testament of the boldness of Prestwick. The 5th hole, "The Himalayas," is of great fame, and was one of the new holes, while the final loop of four holes, which contain holes 15, 16, and 17, are as exciting as any holes in the world. But Prestwick's biggest contribution to golf course architecture might be the 4th. It was the first use of the dogleg, having established the principle of changing direction after the drive.

In 1925, Prestwick's association with the Open was severed, not because of the course, but rather its unsuitability of handling the crowds and its lack of lodging.

Score cards for the 1872 BR. Open Chapionship.

A view of the clubhouse at St. Andrews from the Swilken Bridge.

ST. ANDREWS

There is never enough that can be said concerning the links at St. Andrews. St. Andrews is after all, the home of the game. Nothing can compare with the town, the shops, the people and its history. To be at St. Andrews is to be at golf's heavenly gates.

The course at St. Andrews is an acquired taste. At first view, there doesn't seem to be much there. The course is all but fair, yet therein lies its charm. Bobby Jones once commented that the more he studied the Old Course, the more he loved it. Time has not changed this fundamental truth.

Long before there was golf, St. Andrews was the pre-reformation capital of Scotland. It is interesting that the routing itself forms a shepherd's crook. The Old Course owes more to the hand of God than that of man and is acknowledged as a masterpiece.

SIR HUGH LYON PLAYFAIR

The concept of the double greens was probably the idea or implementation of Sir Hugh Lyon Playfair, the Provost of St. Andrews from 1842 to 1861. He was also the Captain of the R & A in 1856. Sir Playfair was also credited with carrying out the land reclamation of what is now the 1st and 18th holes.

THE RETURN OF TOM MORRIS

In 1865, Tom Morris returned shortly after the death of Allen Robertson, and was paid £50 a year as "Keeper of the Green," taking entire charge of the course.

Prior to Tom Morris' return, the course at St. Andrews was a narrow and penal golf course. But under his watchful eye and careful study of the course, Old Tom began to enlarge the greens. The purpose being to provide a more confortable area in which outbound and inbound players could co-exist in safety.

Tom began to learn that the key to links golf was sand. David Honeyman was Old Tom's foreman and Old Tom's words to him would be: "Saund, Honeyman, saund and then mair saund."

Early after Tom Morris' return, he re-grassed several of the greens and claimed ground on the west side of the Swilican Burn, which golfers today play as the 1st green. By the early 1870s, Tom was re-turfing the 1st and 18th fairways which then led to the re-positioning and enlargement of the 18th green.

With the introduction of the new green west of the Swilican Burn, golfers realized the course could

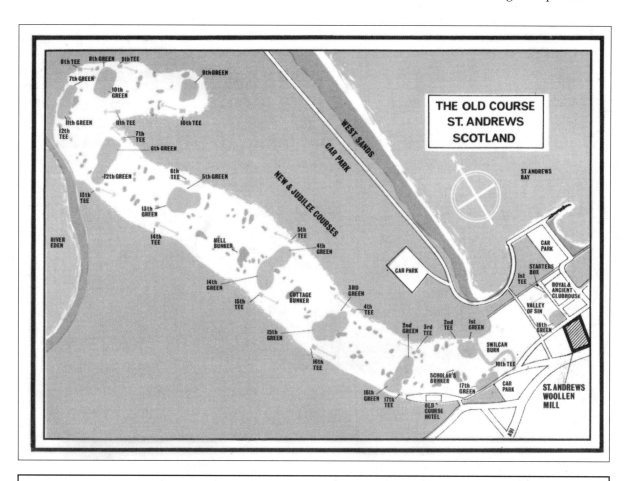

OLD COURSE, ST. ANDREWS

Hole	Name	Distance yds.	Par	Str.	Score
1	Burn	370	4	15	
2	Dyke	411	4	3	
3	Cartgate	352	4	13	
4	Ginger Beer	419	4	9	
5	Hole o' Cross	514	5	1	
6	Heathery	374	4	11	
7	High	359	4	7	
8	Short	166	3	18	
9	End	307	4	5	
	Outward	3272	36		

TOTAL DISTANCE 6566 yds.   Par and S.S.S. 72

Hole	Name	Distance yds.	Par	Str.	Score
10	Bobby Jones	318	4	10	
11	High	172	3	17	
12	Heathery	316	4	6	
13	Hole o' Cross	398	4	12	
14	Long	523	5	2	
15	Cartgate	401	4	8	
16	Corner of the Dyke	351	4	14	
17	Road	461	4	4	
18	Tom Morris	354	4	16	
	Inward	3294	36		

Marked by		Total	
		Handicap	
Date		Nett Score	

LOCAL RULES

1. **OUT OF BOUNDS (Rule 27-1)**
   (a) Beyond any wall or fence bounding the Course
   (b) Beyond the Swilken Burn on the right of the 1st hole and in or beyond the trench marked by stakes on the right at the 2nd hole.
   (c) Beyond the fence behind the 18th green and 1st tee and on or over the white line between sections of this fence
   Note: The trench on the right of the 12th and 13th holes is not out of bounds

2. **WATER HAZARDS (Rule 26)**
   (a) Those parts of the Swilken Burn which are unmarked or are marked with yellow stakes are ordinary water hazards (Rule 26 1a and 1b)
   (b) Those parts of the Swilken Burn to be treated as lateral water hazards are marked with red stakes (Rule 26 1c).

3. **GROUND UNDER REPAIR (Rule 25)**
   Play is prohibited within a GUR demarcated area (Rule 25 1a and 1b applies)

4. **ROADS AND PATHS**
   All roads and paths are integral parts of the Course. The ball must be played as it lies or declared unplayable (Rule 28)

5. **OBSTRUCTIONS (Rule 24)**
   March stones are immovable obstructions (Rule 24-2).

6. **FIXED SPRINKLER HEADS**
   All fixed sprinkler heads are immovable obstructions and relief from interference by them may be obtained under rule 24-2. In addition if such an obstruction on or within the two club-lengths of the putting green of the hole being played intervenes on the line of play between the ball and the hole the player may obtain relief without penalty as follows
   If the ball lies off the putting green but not in a hazard and is within two club lengths of the intervening obstruction it may be lifted, cleaned and dropped at the nearest point to where the ball lay which (a) is not nearer the hole (b) avoids such intervention and (c) is not in a hazard or on a putting green.

7. **STONES IN BUNKERS**
   Stones in bunkers are movable obstructions (Rule 24-1 applies).

A match at St. Andrews.

be played clockwise and counter clockwise. For several years, the Old Course routing varied during alternate weeks. The original, preferred routing was and is the way in which we play St. Andrews today.

OF WHINS AND BUNKERS

Within the Old Course, it should be noted that the natural, deep bunkers (those with colorful names) are on the left side of the course. Most of the bunkers on the right of the outward holes are man-made; strategically sited to replace the vast thickets of whin which once covered the links. Much of the widening of the links was overseen by Old Tom Morris and was completed by the turn fo the century.

Old Tom did remove a few bunkers, but one made a triumphant return, that bunker was Sutherland at hole number four. The tale of Sutherland begins with the man.

Sutherland was a flamboyant character, completely and utterly obsessed by golf. Golf was his whole life; anyone who had no knowledge of or no interest in the game was "an ignorant lout." A. G. Sutherland spent his winters on the links at Musselburgh and his summers in St. Andrews.

Old Tom Morris

In August 1869, he walked over the course one day and discovered the bunker had been filled in. He wrote to Major Broothby of the R & A's Green Committee asking if the bunker had been filled in on the authority of the Committee, and at the same time, reminded him that the Committee had no power to remove any bunker from the course. He suggested that the Committee should restore the bunker to its former state or answer for their action in a court of law.

Major Boothby replied he was not aware of any special orders having been given by the Committee for filling up the bunker, but Tom Morris, as Custodian of the Links, had taken the opinion of many golfers who considered that the bunker was unneccessary.

Sutherland was furious. He denied that Tom had the right "to destroy or remodel the links as it pleases him and his clique," and he repeated his conviction that neither the R & A, the Green Committee, nor even the proprietor of the links had the right to change the face of the ground "as nature has placed it."

The lost bunker became the talking point of the day. It was certainly the talking point at a private dinner on August 10, 1869 given by publisher John Blackwood. Sir Alexander Kinlock and Mr. Robert Dalzell (both of whom were to become captains of the R & A) were guests at the dinner; and they agreed that the vandalism of the Green Committee was not to be allowed. They made their way to the links where they labored all night, and by morning the bunker was restored. Before they left, they wrote the name "Sutherland" on a piece of paper. Everyone thought it was Sutherland's work, and the bunker is known by the name Sutherland to this day.

THE GAME'S FOUNDATION

Unlike all other golf courses in the world, there is the air of permanence at St. Andrews, and it will forever be linked with the game's origins.

COLLECTIBLES

There are many collectibles available relating to the British Open and the three courses. Actually the list is endless. Here are a few broad suggestions:

Scorecards
Ball Markers
Logo Balls
Programs
Golf clubs made and sold at the courses
Medals & Trophies
Golf Cards (Wills Tobacco)
Post Cards
Photographs
Art
Books

Even Presidents
Enjoy Golf Collectibles

Former President George Bush visited Montgomery, Alabama, November 8, 1996, and played golf at the Montgomery Country Club. While at the club, President Bush expressed an interest in the golf collectibles on display there. Forrest McConnell, the club's historian, gave the president the grand tour of the collectibles on display in the club house. The president seemed knowledgeable about antique golf artifacts, wooden-shafted golf clubs and the makers.

On display were several clubs made by Willie Park Sr. and Willie Park Jr. and President Bush was keenly aware of the Parks, including when and where they made their clubs. He was also keenly aware of their collectible popularity, value and historical signifi-

cance in the development of modern-day golf equipment. He was entranced by the long-nose putter and rut iron made by Willie Jr. and inspected them closely with the help of Mr. McConnell.

The president expressed that he was a student of golf history and has visited many of the old courses in Scotland and England. He is especially fond of the club room at the Royal & Ancient, and the Museum at St. Andrews.

Forrest McConnell is a long-time collector specializing in the history and club making of the Park family. As the historian at Montgomery C. C., Forrest has developed interesting and informative golf displays centering around the Parks. We thank Mr. McConnell for sharing the president's visit with our readers.

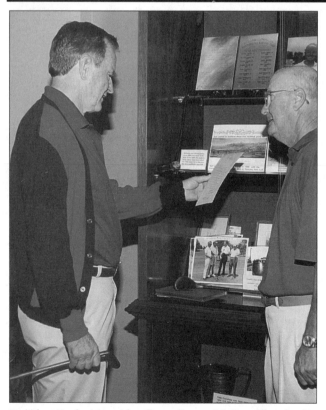

President Bush visits with collector Forrest McConnell at the display in the clubhouse at Montgomery (AL) Country Club.

President Bush inspects a long-nose wood with collector Forrest McConnell.

Chapter 2
GOLF COLLECTOR SOCIETIES AND ORGANIZATIONS

Bob Kuntz, co-founder of the Golf Collectors Society and Paul Wood inspect clubs.

No one likes to collect alone. Collectors want to hear from others with their same interests, meet, talk and show off their prized possessions. One way to meet others is to join an organization or society. Here we will list five which provide a printed bulletin or newsletter for their members.

Welcome to the Golf Collectors Society!

Any new collector of golf memorabilia (or antiques in general) will eventually come to the point where he or she will seek broader horizons, branch out, and want to meet other people who share the same enthusiasm for the game and its various artifacts. Golf collectors have been around for many years—long before the game arrived in America—but they were always scattered hither and yon and never organized. A famous early collector was Harry

Wood, an Englishman from Manchester who wrote the masterpiece on collecting, *Golf Curios and the Like* in 1911, now a valuable item in any golf book collector's library. Other early prominent golf collectors of the 20th century include Alex Findlay, O. M. Leland, Jack Level, and Otto Probst. They, and others like them, shared an intense passion for the memorabilia of the game. Not until 1970 was an official body of golf collectors organized under the title of the Golf Collectors Society.

It began with a small band of 27 collectors in September 1970. In 1995, on the 25th anniversary of the Golf Collectors Society (GCS), there were more than 2,200 members from America, with nearly 200 others from all parts of the golfing globe. The largest foreign contingent is from the United Kingdom and Canada, with other members from Japan, Taiwan, Australia, South Africa, continental Europe, and a dozen or so other nations.

From the very start, and on into the present day, the purpose of the GCS is: *To serve as a means of getting golf collectors together... To establish friendships between those who share a love of the game... And to facilitate the exchange of information about collecting and the game.* Founded in 1970 by J. Robert Kuntz of Dayton, Ohio, and Joseph Murdoch of Philadelphia, the GCS remains a not-for-profit fraternal organization.

GCS members collect all golf memorabilia from A to Z. Some specialize in old hickory-shafted clubs, or even older valuable long-nose playclubs from the mid-19th century. Others might collect balls, books, ceramics and artwork, medals, old tees and ephemera, early magazines and tournament programs, or maybe just modern era putters only, or a varied combination of all the numerous collecting categories...and a whole lot more!

While some members might specialize in collecting items as small as ball markers or scorecards, there are others who own museum quality collections of the highest caliber. And speaking of museums—the curators of all the world's great golf museums are GCS members as well, including the USGA's Golf House; the R. & A. Museum at St. Andrews; the James River (Virginia) C. C. Museum, the oldest private golf museum in the United States; the Ralph Miller Library and Museum at City of Industry, California, named after one of the GCS founding members; and the

new World Golf Hall of Fame, now under construction near St. Augustine, Florida. All of these people have a mutual love for the game and its artifacts. They share the express purpose of the Society: to bring people together and to exchange memorabilia and information. The fact that several dozen books exist on golf collecting, authored by GCS members, indicates that information on collecting for new and veteran members alike is a highly sought after commodity.

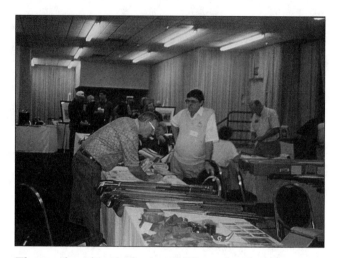

The author (center) at a GCS trade show.

One of the single most unifying events toward this stated purpose is the regional trade show and Hickory Hacker. Based on membership population density, the GCS has a Board of Directors covering ten geographical regions. Several times per year, within each region, a GCS gathering of varying size occurs. Generally speaking, it comprises a one or two day show where golf memorabilia is bought, sold, traded or just simply exhibited for educational or entertainment purposes. Members enjoy these events if for nothing more than to meet and share their knowledge, ideas, and experiences concerning the game, its artifacts and treasures.

But the accumulation of knowledge and golf memorabilia is not always the primary focus for many GCS members at these regional meetings. To get out on the golf course and play with the old "weapons of the game" is a fun occasion that members look forward to. In these Hickory Tournaments—or Hickory Hackers, as some like to affectionately refer to them—participants often outfit themselves in the old plus fours (or knickers as they are called here in the USA) and play with the old hickory-shafted clubs from the 1920s or earlier. Like Jones, Sarazen, Vardon, Hagen, and all of the early golfers before them, the GCS Hickory Tournament participants go back in time to the days of golf when wood—not steel or graphite—was the shaft that made the ball go "far and sure."

At these regional trade shows—and especially the GCS Annual Meeting in late September or early October at various locales across the country—expect to find any golf collectible your little heart desires. The Annual Meeting is by far the largest show, with more than 200 display tables and 500-600 collectors commonly in attendance. Among others, the following large and long-running regional golf collecting shows take place annually. All members and collectors from anywhere in the world are always invited.

- "Cabin Fever," January, Dayton, Ohio

- USGA, early Spring, Far Hills, New Jersey

- The Texas gathering, March or April, Irving

- A South Florida event, February, and another at Dunedin, usually in March

- The Midwest event in Chicago, May, Rolling Meadows

- Three or four events throughout the year in the Mid Atlantic region, near Washington, D. C.

- The Carolinas gathering, at least twice per year

- Western meeting, November or December, Southern California

- Heart of America, June, Kansas City, Omaha, or Iowa

- Two or three Canadian events, Toronto area

You won't find anyone pitching golf resorts or golf course real estate, or too much mention of overpriced and oversized "new stuff" at these shows. Instead, you will find tables full of the old hickory-shafted clubs, common and rare, or the more valuable and unusual implements of the game. Then there are collectible clubs of the more "modern era" of the game: Tommy Armour woods, Pings and highly collectible Wilson putters from the 1960s. Back to the good old days—you might discover mesh and gutty balls and usually some pre-1850 featherie balls. You'll see early and modern books offered by a number of collectors, as well as recognized golf book dealers; fine old golf pottery, ceramics, jewelry, and the like; long out-of-print golf magazines, hard-to-find autographs, medals, and much, much more. As our GCS co-founder, Joe Murdoch, has stated time and again when talking about the regional and annual meeting trade shows, "If you think you have seen everything there is in golf, you'll be pleasantly surprised to see something new and different at the trade show."

Each GCS member receives our newsletter, *The Bulletin*, on a quarterly basis. Articles include golf history, collections and collectors, golf book reviews, patent information, unusual clubs and artifacts, current golf auction news and results, and coverage of GCS regional events. It also has a small classified ad section, where members are offered buy/sell/trade opportunities.

Members also receive an annual Membership Directory issued in the first quarter of the year. Among the address, telephone and e-mail numbers, vital collecting interests of each individual member are identified.

The Director of the Golf Collectors Society is Bud Thompson. The mailing address is: P.O. Box 241042, Cleveland, Ohio 44124 (phone 216-861-1615; Fax 216-861-1630).

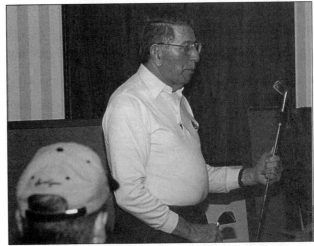

Bob Kuntz gives an interesting talk at a "Club Forum" during a GCS annual meeting.

The Golf Club Monthly

This newsletter is published monthly. For a membership fee of $40 per year, members are entitled to a 75-line free advertisement each month. An average of 50 dealers/collectors advertise on a regular basis. Most of the ads deal with steel-shafted "classic" clubs from the 1950s to the 1980s, modern clubs and accessories for play.

This is an excellent source for finding a replacement for a lost or broken club, finding out how much your "Ping" putter is worth, or buying a used set of clubs for play. This is a very worthwhile organization.

Contact: 4620 Deer Creek Trail, Bessemer, AL 35020. Phone 205-428-0078.

The Golf Club Collectors Association

The GCCA was founded in 1987 and was organized to include collectors of classic clubs as well as collectors of wooden-shafted clubs and related memorabilia. The purpose of the GCCA is to introduce golf collectors to each other, and to identify, trade, and share information.

A newsletter is published every three months and a membership directory is published annually that includes names, addresses, phone numbers and collecting interests of all active members. Annual dues are $30.

Members are informed through the newsletter, by both editorial content and advertisements, about the increasing desire to collect golf clubs and golf related items. They are encouraged to submit articles, classified ads, or news of trade shows and auctions.

Regional get-togethers are encouraged, and a mail-in/phone-in auction is held annually. For a nominal charge, a catalogue is available for the identification of classic golf clubs.

Contact: Dick Moore, Executive Director, 640 E. Liberty Street, Girard, OH 44420-2308, 330-545-2832, 330-545-2718 (FAX), Internet: gccagolf@aol.com

The Golf Club Historical Society of Canada

The Golf Historical Society of Canada was formed in 1988 when four founding members reasoned that there must be other souls who share a love of golf and the game's rich heritage. Today, this collective helps members indulge in their passion for golf history, its artifacts and treasures.

A quarterly bulletin is published covering a wide range of member interests. Trade shows are organized so that members can share their knowledge and build their collections of golf books, trophies, clubs and memorabilia. Special interest is placed on the preservation of Canadian golf history and traditions. A spring and fall "Hickory Hacker" golf tournament is held and many sets of restored wooden-shafted clubs once again help their owners enjoy the "Grand Ould Gayme."

Contact: 555 Eastern Avenue, Toronto, Ontario, Canada, M4M 1C8 , Tel. 416-465-8844.

The British Golf Collectors Society

The British Golf Collectors Society exists to promote an interest in the history of golf and the collecting of items connected with that history. The Society's journal, *Through The Green*, is published quarterly and distributed to some 460 members residing in the UK and seventeen overseas countries, including 80 members in the USA. It contains articles of historical interest and collecting related topics.

The Society has three major golfing meetings: President's Day at the Royal Liverpool G.C., Hoylake, in May; The Scottish Hickory Championship, in which wooden-shafted clubs must be used, at Gullane near Muirfield, in May; and The Open Championship meeting at a course (usually one of the Open qualifying courses) in the vicinity of the Open on the Wednesday before it starts. There are also a number of regional meetings and the Society regularly fields a team, in period dress and playing with wooden-shafted clubs, in matches associated with the Centenary celebrations of clubs.

Contact: The Hon. Secretary, BGCS, P. O. Box 13704, North Berwick, East Lothian, Scotland EH39 4ZB.

Chapter 3
A GUIDE TO VALUES

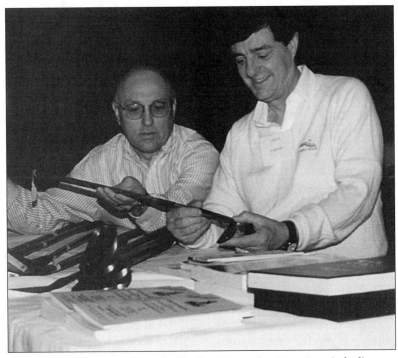

Chuck Furjanic, right, and noted golf collectibles author Peter Georgiady discuss a rare club at the Midwest Golf Collectors Show and Sale, Chicago.

"How much is this Calamity Jane putter worth?"

"What condition is this book, The Curious History of the Golf Ball?*"*

"How much is this sterling silver trophy worth in this condition?"

"How would you rate that Vardon Flyer ball on a 1 to 10 scale?"

Condition affects value, and experience is the collector's best ally in understanding how condition can determine the value of golf collectibles. Many collectors purchase only the best quality items; though their collection may be small, it is of high quality. Other collectors acquire items simply because they are available regardless of condition. The ultimate common thread is receiving value for dollar spent, no matter what golf collectible you buy. There is an old cliché worth mentioning here: "Quality remains long after the price has been forgotten." Quality and value go hand in hand.

How to Receive the Best Value For Dollar Spent

Set collecting goals. If your goal is to collect everything related to golf, or only long-nose putters made by Robert Forgan during September 1886, stick with your goal. Acquire what you like and achieve your collecting goals rather than purchasing golf collectibles touted as a good buy.

Acquire collectibles in the best condition you can afford, even if it means buying a G-2 condition scarcity or rarity that fills a void in your collection. Most of all, be happy with the items you acquire. Sort out the items that do not conform to your collecting goals and find collectors or dealers who will take them in trade towards items that will enhance your collection.

Learn as much as possible about the golf collectibles you have set out to acquire. Building a good reference library to go with your golf collectibles will be an invaluable asset.

Once you have set your goals and have armed yourself with knowledge, you can begin locating dealers and collectors who will respect your collecting aspirations and help you fulfill them. If purchasing from a dealer, buy only from those who offer return privileges, regardless of reason. If you buy at auction, inspect lots or have someone you trust inspect and bid on your behalf. You can bid confidently by mail if the auction company will allow you to return lots you are not happy with.

What Determines the Value of a Golf Collectible?

Value is based on condition, rarity, availability, competition and desirability.

Rarity is based on the availability of a golf collectible factored by its condition and desirability.

For example, a McEwan Play Club from 1880 is moderately scarce, but frequently available in the marketplace in grades ranging from G-5 to G-8. In near mint condition (G-9), it is decidedly rare and highly desirable.

Common mesh pattern golf balls—circa 1930 from Worthington, Dunlop or Spalding—in above average condition (G-7) sell for about $75. An identical ball, but with a cover cut, or teeth marks from the family pet, will bring only $10 or $15. "Faroid" or "Park Royal" are two types of balls that are so rare and seldom offered that even damaged examples are highly sought after and bring premium prices.

Availability of a golf collectible has a great effect on the price, especially at public auctions. Let's imagine a nice example of John Kerr's *The Golf Book of East Lothian*, limited edition, signed and numbered, is offered at auction. We know the book is not rare because there were 250 copies printed in 1896. But, this is the only example to be offered publicly for nearly a year and three book collectors attending the sale are interested in bidding on the book. In this case, availability and competition will determine the ultimate value.

In another example, two Royal Doulton punch bowls in similar condition were offered by two different companies at their July auctions held during British Open week. Only two serious pottery buyers were in attendance, and each is able to acquire one at a reasonable price. Availability, in this scenario, has had an adverse affect on value, even though the punch bowls are quite rare.

Let's use our imagination again. We are back in 1980 and a famous collection is being auctioned. A circa 1865 rut iron by Carrick is touted as the finest example available to collectors. At the time, only four or five collectors worldwide have enough sophistication and knowledge to believe the cataloguer; only one attends the auction and the club brings a modest $200.

Ten years from now, let's say the same club is offered when literally thousands of collectors are actively seeking clubs and several hundred have the knowledge, sophistication and resources to take the cataloguer seriously. Several hop a flight, inspect the club, and try to determine who in attendance will be competition for acquiring it. Dealers carefully inspect the club, try to "feel the mood" of those present, and contact anxious clients to determine if a high "four figure" or low "five figure" bid is appropriate.

If you think the last paragraph is pure folly, think again! Let's look at what actually took place at an auction during 1996. A Willie Dunn "Stars & Stripes" ball in mint condition was estimated at the $6,000 level. Three bidders were actively bidding at $18,000 and the final hammer price was $26,000 plus a ten percent buyer's fee for a total of $28,600! And to top that off, the collector who purchased the ball was offered a handsome profit (which he graciously refused) within a short time after the auction.

What does this mean to the antique golf collector? Since the mid-1980s, thousands of new collectors have entered the hobby. In addition, tens of thousands have expressed curiosity in golf antiques. The highly visible collectibles, such as long-nose woods, feather balls, art, pottery and any other memorabilia, will be the center of attention, and quality will become the determining factor of value.

A Grade Scale for Golf Collectibles

Any golf collectible that has deviated from its initial manufactured mint new condition must be evaluated by how much change it exhibits. A grade scale (G-) on a basis of 1 to 10 has been formulated to evaluate the golf collectibles in this reference.

G-10

Absolutely mint new as it left the factory. Showing no signs of wear, circulation, play or any deviation from "as made."

G-9

The ultimate collectible, but not mint new. Exhibits "as made" originality with virtually no imperfections.

G-8

An outstanding example with minor imperfections and minimal wear.

G-7

A desirable collectible in an above average state of preservation. A nice example exhibiting all the characteristics of originality, but with evident imperfections and visible wear.

G-6

A slightly better than average collectible. Should look original with evident imperfections and wear. Still very desirable to the collector who cannot locate a better example because of rarity or financial reasons.

G-5

An "average" example showing moderate to heavy wear. An affordable collectible with moderate desirability.

G-4

A below average collectible, with moderate to major problems. Unless the collectible is very scarce or rare, the advanced collector will not be interested in an item of this grade.

G-3

Collectibles with obvious major problems such as broken parts, and/or replacement parts that are not matching. Unless the collectible is very scarce or rare, the advanced collector will not be interested in an item of this grade.

G-2

A collectible that borders on being a non-collectible. Only the scarce or rare items will have any collectible interest.

G-1

A non-collectible item.

Chapter 4
INTRODUCTION TO COLLECTING WOODSHAFT CLUBS

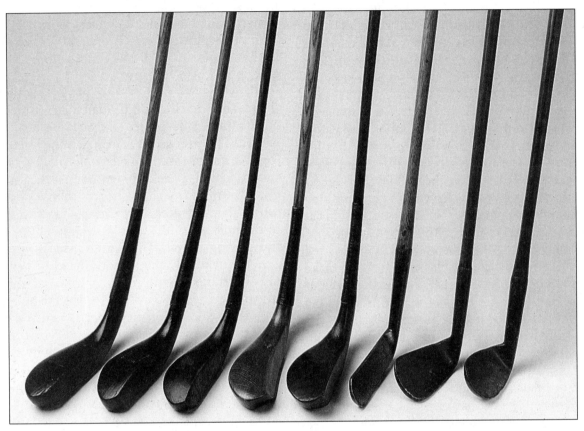

Classic 19th Century clubs - a typical play set prior to 1880.

THE EARLIEST CLUBS

Feather ball-era clubs were usually made by carpenters, bow makers, barrel makers, wheelwrights and other craftsmen with woodworking backgrounds. The irons were forged by the local armor maker or blacksmith.

The woods were very long and narrow, almost half-pear-shaped, with a head usually measuring between five and six inches in length. The face was shallow and slightly hooked to promote control of the feather ball. The neck was delicate and curved usually producing a flat lie. The shaft was long and whippy, about 44 to 47 inches, which permitted the ball to be "swept" from the turf. The head and shaft were joined together by a "scare" or "splice"

usually five to seven inches in length. The shaft and neck were glued together and a heavy linen twine was wrapped over the splice to help reinforce and strengthen. The linen twine was treated with "pitch" to act as adhesive and preservative for the splice. The grip was formed by an underlisting of wool wrappings tacked to the end of the shaft and covered by goat, lamb, sheep or deer skin.

A "play club" was used from the teeing ground, a "brassie" was used to strike long, low shots from the fairway. The "long spoon" and "mid-spoons" were used to hit moderately long-lofted shots and the "short spoon" (sometimes called a baffie) was used to hit short-lofted shots around the green or over trouble. Next time you play golf, look at the variety of woods in the bags: Ginties with runner soles, No. 5, 7, 9 and 11 woods—even some *I've* not heard of. The feather ball era was not much different, as many players had variations of clubs made of a long spoon or baffie to suit a particular playing style or even a specific type of terrain.

The iron-head clubs generally consisted in sets of three, although all golfers did not carry all three. The "rut" iron had a small, rounded head with the face concave or cupped. The hosel was generally five to six inches long and very thick as this club was a "trouble" club—it was used to extricate the ball from cart ruts, hoof prints or bad lies in the gorse and heather. The club was designed to propel the ball for only a few yards, from impending disaster to a more playable lie. According to the player's preference, there were tiny heads (2 to 2-1/4 inches wide) and larger heads (2-1/2 to 2-3/4 inches wide) with anything in between. The concavity of the face also varies from being nearly straight to "ice cream scoop" proportions, and some were made with twisted hosels. During this era the blacksmith didn't make clubs until he had an order. The clubs were, therefore, made to the golfer's specifications. In many cases the golfer brought the club back to the blacksmith having him re-heat and re-hammer the head to produce just the right loft or concavity to suit his game.

The "bunker" or "sand" iron was a large-head, concave-faced, heavy gauge metal iron with the similar use of our modern sand wedge. Most courses were laid out over links land between the sea and arable land, and most of the terrain was sandy, creating the need for this club. The head was rounded and generally three to four inches wide with a thick hosel usually about five inches long. The stoutness of shaft and hosel combined with the heavy weight of the head, afforded the golfer to take a forceful slash at the ball, propelling it, with moderate distance, back into play, or onto the green.

The "cleek" was an iron with very little loft and a long face that could measure four to five inches in length. Usually the heel and toe were nearly the same depth giving the head a "rectangular" appearance. The hosel was generally very long, as much as six inches, and the shaft was held in place with heavy nicking hammered down into the shaft. Many old re-shafted irons had the nicking sawed

off to remove the shaft. When I see an older style club without nicking, this indicates to me that the shaft is a replacement and the original heavy saw-toothed hosel nicking was sawed away when removing the original shaft. The hosel pin replaced nicking as a head and shaft fastener. The cleek was primarily used for hitting long, low shots from bad lies instead of using a long spoon or brassie which were more susceptible to damage when not swung with a sweeping motion. The cleek was also used to hit low shots into a strong wind or to hit running approach shots to the green.

Many players carried two putters, sometimes three. The "driving" putter had a large thick head with a rather deep face and a large heavy back weight. This was used to approach the hole from a long distance over a relatively flat area. The "approaching" cleek, or putter, was a slightly lofted iron with a shaft shorter than a cleek, but longer than a putter. This was used to run the ball to the hole when the terrain prohibited the use of the driving putter. The "holing out" putter was either a delicately made wood-head putter or an iron-head putter with minimal loft used for more control and accuracy when close to the hole.

A very heavy white linen thread or cord was used at both ends of the grip. It was coated with pitch and many weathered whippings appear more brown than black. This same thick thread or cord was used for covering the splice joint of shaft and head on the woods and putters. A thick coating of tar or pitch was used to cover the splice whipping for added protection from moisture and handling.

CLUBS FROM THE 1890S THROUGH THE EARLY TEENS

During the boom period beginning with the 1890s, many innovations in club making took place. There were many patents filed on clubs of all types: aluminum heads, adjustable heads, laminated heads, laminated shafts, one-piece woods, screw-socket woods, bifurcated hosels, steel sockets, one-piece grips, various back weightings, socket wood joint, cushioned iron face, wooden face irons, rake irons, waterfall irons, concave face irons—the list goes on and on.

Club makers went from hand forging to drop forging to conserve time and increase production. The cleek maker that could hand forge only hundreds of clubs a month was replaced by factories (or he built his own) producing thousands of clubs a week. With the advent of the rubber-cored "Haskell" ball, golf went into another gear, and companies such as Spalding, MacGregor, Stewart, Anderson, Nicoll, Forgan, and Gibson produced millions of clubs yearly.

CLUBS FROM THE TEENS THROUGH THE 1930S

During the roaring 1920s and early 1930s new American companies such as Burke, Hillerich & Bradsby, Wilson, Kroydon, Draper-Maynard, and Scottish companies like Cochrane's Lt'd, Hendry & Bishop as well as the aforementioned Forgan, Nicoll, etc. produced more than 100 million wood-shaft clubs of various quality. Millions upon millions of low quality clubs were made, by Burke, Wright & Ditson, and others, to be marketed at department, hardware and sporting good stores.

With the advent of legalization of steel-shaft clubs, for the 1926 season in America, and 1930 in Great Britain, Spalding, MacGregor, Walter Hagen, Hillerich & Bradsby, Forgan, Sayers, Nicoll, Gibson and other mainstream makers began to market sets of high quality hickory-shaft clubs. The Gibson "Stella" series was a great playable iron, as well as MacGregor's "Duralite," Burke's "Long Burke" and Spalding's "Kro-Flite" series just to name a few.

HOW MUCH ARE THESE COMMON CLUBS WORTH?

Every day, someone calls our offices saying "I can't find this club in your book."

It is our intention to list collectible clubs in this reference. Listing all the clubs that were made would require volumes. The following will help you understand why most clubs you encounter may not be in this book.

Chuck Furjanic, Peter Georgiady and Bub Duffner, *Golfiana Magazine (1987-1994)* have collaborated to bring you the following information:

Auction houses and club dealers usually sell the finest-grade museum quality scarcities or rarities. Reports of these prices realized cause the uninformed to overestimate the value of grandpa's clubs. Metal shafted clubs with coated or painted shafts made to look like "cane" or "wood" have no collectible value to the woodshaft collector.

Wooden-shafted clubs in this section will be valued on a scale of ten grades as outlined in Chapter 3. Current prices will be provided in conditions G-5, G-7 and G-9. The criteria for these conditions are as follows:

G-9

The ultimate collectible, but not *mint new*. Exhibits "as made" originality with virtually no imperfections. The head, shaft and grip must be original. Head, whether wood or metal, must be "as made." Shaft will be straight and have original finish. Grip must be an original or a replacement done "in-period" in order to appear as the original when inspected by the most fastidious experts. Whipping may be replacement, but must be the correct size and color for the club's period.

G-7

A desirable collectible in an above average state of preservation. A nice example exhibiting all the characteristics of originality, but with evident imperfections and visible wear. Imperfections may include an "in period" grip, signs of moderate play or a weak "maker's mark." A very desirable collectible. Clubs prior to 1890 will show more use and the woods may have slight grain separations or a leather face insert nicely done "in period." This club must be aesthetically appealing. For the collector who wants the best, but finds it difficult to locate a better example.

G-5

An "average" example showing moderate to heavy wear. An affordable collectible with moderate desirability. May exhibit a slight warping of the shaft or a tattered original looking grip. If there are any markings on pre-1900 clubs, they should be readable enough to properly identify the maker. An acceptable example for the person not seeking perfection, or on a limited budget. A well done in-period cracked shaft repair can actually add "character" and desirability.

Collectors and dealers feel fewer than five percent of all wood shafted clubs have interest or value beyond decorative or playable worth. In effect, this means about 24 out of every 25 clubs you have, or encounter at flea markets or garage sales, are common.

One must realize during the period 1920-1935, millions of low grade clubs were made and sold through department, hardware, and sporting goods stores. Spalding, MacGregor, Burke, Kroydon, Hillerich & Bradsby, Wilson, Wright & Ditson and scores of others made clubs with line, dot, hyphen and other face markings. 99% of these are common and have no value beyond decorative, conversational or playable items.

YOU CAN IDENTIFY COMMON CLUBS BY:

* No manufacturer's name, or names like: Biltmore, Hollywood, Thistle, Bonnie, Metropolitan, Columbia, Ace, Majestic, etc.
* Metal caps at the end of the grip.
* Yardage ranges stamped on the back (145-155 yds.).
* Chromed, chromium, or stainless steel heads.
* Numbered irons from sets, or "matched set" irons.
* Irons with dots, hyphens, lines or other face scoring.

Clubs that have not been "cleaned" or "refinished" that look all original and slightly used, are worth more than clubs that show use, have some rust, or are not of "high quality." Clubs that have been restored, cleaned, have warped or cracked shafts and/or hosels, heavy rusting, pitting, bad or missing grips, bring substantially less.

RETAIL PRICES FOR COMMON CLUBS IN OUTSTANDING MUSEUM OR PLAYABLE CONDITION:

IRONS	$45.00 to $75.00
PUTTERS	$50.00 to $90.00
WOODS	$85.00 to $135.00

HERE'S HOW TO IDENTIFY SCARCE OR RARE CLUBS:

* Irons with no face markings, or unusual face markings.
* Irons or putters with unusual head shapes, wood head putters.
* Woods with a thick, curved, oval neck covered with four or five inches of string whipping.
* Smooth-face irons with the following names: Anderson, Army & Navy, Ayres, Carrick, Forgan, Gray, Morris, Park, and White. Certain Spalding, MacGregor, Condie, Nicoll, Stewart, Gibson and Wright & Ditson with smooth-faces.

Clubs are valuable because collectors want them! Common clubs are not in demand by collectors.

PRICES
GOLF CLUBS: THE MOST COLLECTIBLE MAKERS

G-5 G-7 G-9

AITKEN, ALEX
GULLANE, SCOTLAND

Aitken was the professional at Royal Portrush from 1892-1895 and at Gullane Links from 1905-1917.

RUSTLESS PUTTER $60   85   150
Circa 1915. Offset blade. Stamped "Alex Aitken, Maker, Gullane."

ACCURATE PUTTER $60   85   140
Circa 1910. Offset blade. Stamped "Alex Aitken, Maker, Gullane." Photo below.

SOCKET WOODS $90   120   175
Circa 1910-1915. Driver, brassie or spoon marked "A. Aitken."

SPLICED-NECK WOODS $300   400   850
Circa 1890-1895. Transitional bulger beech-head play club marked "Aitken."

JOHN ALLAN
WESTWARD HO!

Allan was the professional at Royal North Devon (Westward Ho!) from 1867-1886 and at Prestwick, St. Nicholas from 1886-1895. He made long-nose and transitional putters and woods. He was a well respected clubmaker.

LONG-NOSE PUTTER $1500   2500   4800
Circa 1880-1890. Beech-head driving putter stamped "J. Allan."

LONG-NOSE WOODS $2000   3300   7000
Circa 1880-1890. Beech-head play club marked "J. Allan."

TRANSITIONAL WOODS $500   750   1850
Circa 1885-1895. Beech-head play club or brassie marked "J. Allan." Photo below.

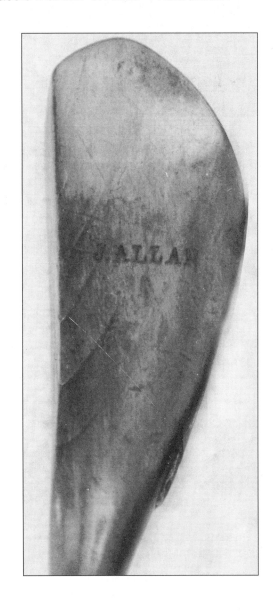

AMPCO MFG CO.
MILWAUKEE, WI

Ampco began forging clubs about 1926 and by the early 1930s were out of business. They made irons and putters from an alloy resembling bronze or brass. When cleaned or polished they have a golden appearance.

| AMPCO PUTTER | $65 | 90 | 125 |

Circa 1926-1930. Line-scored face.

| AMPCO IRONS | $60 | 85 | 125 |

Circa 1926-1930. Line-scored. All irons.

| AMPCO ALUMINUM WOODS | $300 | 400 | 600 |

Circa 1926-1930. Driver, brassie or spoon. "Ampco, Milwaukee, Wis." on crown with a brass face insert. Photo below.

ANDERSON, ANDERSON & ANDERSON

Anderson, Anderson & Anderson clubs were made by Anderson of Anstruther and bear the large "Lion and Globe" mark.

| LONG BLADE PUTTER | $200 | 350 | 600 |

Circa 1895-1905. "Lion and Globe" maker's mark. Smooth-face blade.

| PUTTING CLEEK | $200 | 300 | 500 |

Circa 1900. "Lion and Globe" mark.

| LION & GLOBE IRONS | $200 | 300 | 500 |

Circa 1895-1905. Smooth-face iron, mashie or mashie-niblick. Large "Lion and Globe" mark. Photo below.

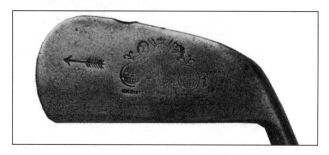

| BRASS-BLADE PUTTER | $250 | 400 | 650 |

Circa 1900. Steel face inlay. "Lion and Globe" mark.

ANDERSON & BLYTHE
ST. ANDREWS

The firm of Anderson & Blythe began operations shortly before 1910 and was dissolved prior to 1915. They made wooden-head putters, but iron-head clubs with their stampings were forged by other makers, principally Tom Stewart.

| WEYMESS PATENT IRON | $100 | 140 | 250 |

Circa 1910. Dot-faced iron. Two level back marked "R E Weymess Patent No 16070."

| LONG-NOSE PERSIMMON PUTTER | $250 | 375 | 650 |

Circa 1908-1914 stamped "Anderson & Blythe."

| SOCKET WOODS | $100 | 140 | 225 |

Circa 1910. Driver brassie or spoon marked "Anderson & Blythe Special."

| WOODEN-HEAD CLEEK | $125 | 175 | 250 |

Circa 1910. Small persimmon head. Lofted wooden cleek.

ANDERSON, D. & SONS
ST. ANDREWS, SCOTLAND

Club and golf ball production began in St. Andrews about 1893 with David and his five sons. They exported many clubs to the United States. They were instrumental in the revival of ash shafts during the mid 1890s.

| LONG-NOSE PUTTERS | $700 | 1150 | 2250 |

Circa 1893-1900. Spliced-neck, beech-head stamped "D Anderson."

| GLORY PUTTER | $85 | 115 | 175 |

Circa 1915. "Diamond" back design. Photo below.

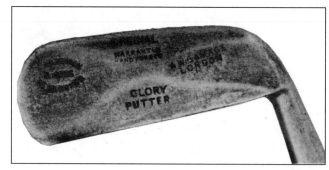

| BRASS-HEAD PUTTERS | $80 | 100 | 150 |

Circa 1910. Dot Ball-face.

| LINE-SCORED PUTTER | $60 | 75 | 100 |

Circa 1920s. "Double Circle and Ribbon" mark.

| EXCELSIOR PUTTER | $65 | 85 | 135 |

Circa 1910. "Diamond-Dot" face scoring.

SPECIAL ACCURATE PUTTER $50   65   100
Circa 1920s. "Calamity Jane" style offset blade.

MONARCH PUTTER $50   65   100
Circa 1920s. "D. Anderson & Sons" in a circle mark. Photo below.

MAXWELL HOSEL PUTTER $80   100   150
Circa Teens. Flanged back with Maxwell holes drilled into hosel. Photo below.

BENT NECK PUTTER $75   115   175
Circa 1900-1910. "Criss-cross" with "diamond-dot" face scoring.

D. ANDERSON IRONS $60   90   150
Circa 1900. Cleek, iron and lofting iron. Smooth-face.

MONARCH IRONS $45   60   90
Circa 1920s. All irons.

GLORY IRONS $55   80   135
Circa 1915. "Diamond" back design. Dot-punched face.

MAXWELL HOSEL IRONS $60   85   150
Circa 1910-1915. Flanged back with Maxwell drilled holes in hosel.

SAMMY IRON $70   110   175
Circa 1910-1915. Rounded sole. "Diamond" back.

GLORY JIGGER OR CLEEK $75   100   150
Circa 1915. "Diamond" back design. Dot-punched face.

ANTI-SHANK IRONS $150   235   325
Circa 1920s. Stainless steel "Smith's Mashie."

SPLICED-NECK WOODS $190   290   550
Circa 1900. Beech-head driver, brassie or spoon marked "D. Anderson, St. Andrews." May have a leather face insert. Photo below.

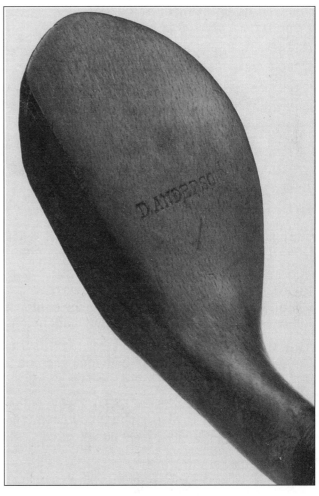

SPLICED-NECK WOODS $175   250   450
Circa 1910. Driver, brassie or spoon. "D. Anderson & Sons, St. Andrews, Special" in Gothic lettering.

SOCKET WOODS $80   120   175
Circa 1915. Driver, brassie or spoon with "D Anderson & Sons, St. Andrews" on the head.

ANDERSON OF ANSTRUTHER
ANSTRUTHER, SCOTLAND

BRASS-HEAD PUTTERS $125   150   250
Circa 1890. Straight blade putter with small "Circle" mark.

SMOOTH-FACE PUTTER $125   150   250
Circa 1895-1900. Rounded back with small "Circle" mark.

DEEP-FACE PUTTER $60   80   150
Circa 1905. Smooth-face with small "Circle" mark.

BRASS-BLADE PUTTER $90   125   225
Circa 1900. Smooth-face blade. Small circle mark. Large "P" stamped at the toe.

BRASS MALLET PUTTER $200   300   550
Circa 1915. Brass-head with a steel face plate. Double circle mark. Photo below.

DIAMOND BACK PUTTER $50   85   150
Circa 1910. Smooth-face. Bent neck hosel. Small circle mark.

RIDGE BACK PUTTER $190   275   475
Circa 1915-1920. "Ridge" runs along the center of the back. Dot-punched face. "Arrow" mark at toe.

TRIUMPH PUTTER $225   325   600
Circa 1920. Pyramid top line of blade. "Diamond-dot" face scoring.

JAMES ANDERSON IRONS $300   400   700
Circa 1880-1890. Lofted general purpose iron with small "Circle" mark. Photo below.

JAMES ANDERSON IRONS $450   700   1800
Circa 1870-1880. Cleek. Small "Circle" mark. Five inch hosel.

SHORT BLADE CLEEK $70   100   225
Circa 1900. Small "Circle" mark.

FOR ARMY & NAVY STORES $100   140   250
Circa 1900. Cleek, iron, or lofting iron marked "A N C S L" with small "Circle" mark.

SMALL HEAD NIBLICK $300   550   1150
Circa 1895-1900. Smooth-face rut niblick. Small "Circle" mark. Photo below.

VARDON SIGNATURE IRONS $65   100   160
Circa 1905-1910. All irons. "Arrow" mark at toe.

VARDON SMALL
HEAD NIBLICK $250   400   900
Circa 1905-1910. Small smooth-face niblick. "Arrow" mark at toe.

SMOOTH-FACE CLEEK $55   85   135
Circa 1910-1915. Large double circle mark.

DEEP-FACE MASHIE $60   90   140
Circa 1910. Smooth-face. Large double circle mark.

OVAL-HEAD NIBLICK $60   100   150
Circa 1915-1920. Line or dot-face. Arrow and large double circle marks.

MUSSEL BACK IRONS $60   95   145
Circa 1920s. Cleek, iron, mashie or mashie-niblick. Arrow and large double circle marks.

CRISS-CROSS FACE IRON $60   90   150
Circa 1905-1910. "Arrow" mark at toe.

CONCAVE FACE IRONS $100   145   225
Circa 1915. Mashie-niblick 30. Dot-punched face. "Arrow" at toe.

DIAMOND BACK IRONS $50   75   110
Circa 1920. Driving iron, mid-iron, mashie, jigger, mashie-niblick or niblick. Large double circle mark.

PYRAMID BACK IRONS $50   75   110
Circa 1920s. All irons. Arrow and large double circle mark.

BALL-FACE LOFTING IRON $70   100   160
Circa 1905-1910. Deep face. Small circle mark.

MAGIC MASHIE $100   125   200
Circa 1920-1925. A raised ridge bisects back from heel to toe. Lined face. Large double circle mark. Photo below.

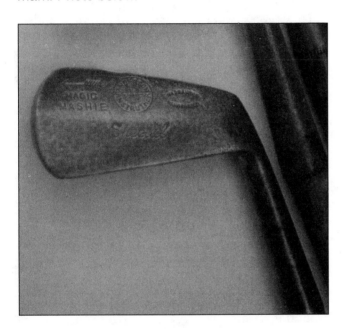

"A 5" SAMMY IRON $150   200   350
Circa 1920. Ridge bisects the back from heel to toe. Box-dot scoring.

RUSTLESS NIBLICK $50   65   90
Circa 1925-1930. Dot-face. Large single circle mark.

SMITH ANTI-SHANK IRONS $150   235   325
Circa 1920-1925. All irons.

JAMES ANDERSON RUT IRON $800 1150   2500
Circa 1885. Tiny rounded head. Small "Circle" mark.

ANDERSON, ROBERT
EDINBURGH, SCOTLAND, PRINCESS STREET

Began making clubs during the early 1890s. Patented the first through-hosel shafted woods.

BRASS-HEAD PUTTERS $90   150   275
Circa 1890-1900. Smooth-face blade marked "R. Anderson & Sons, Princess St. Edinburgh."

CONCENTRIC-BACK CLEEK $80   140   250
Circa 1900. Shallow smooth-face cleek.

SMOOTH-FACE IRONS $90   150   275
Circa 1895-1905. Cleek, iron, or lofter. Marked "R. Anderson & Sons, Edinburgh."

GENERAL PURPOSE IRON $125   225   475
Circa 1890-1895. Long, moderately lofted smooth-face. "Anderson & Sons, Princess St., Edinburgh" markings.

CRESCENT HEAD IRON $1200 1600   2400
Center shafted crescent shaped head. Photo below.

THROUGH HOSEL PATENT
WOODS $100   150   250
Circa 1900. Driver, brassie or spoon marked "Anderson & Sons, Edinburgh, Patent."

THROUGH HOSEL PATENT
WOODS $150   275   475
Semi-long-nose, circa 1891-1900. Play club, brassie or spoon marked "Anderson & Sons, Edinburgh, Patent."

ALUMINUM WOODS $275   425   750
Circa1900-1910. Various lofts. Head marked "Anderson, Edinburgh."

ANDERSON OF ANSTRUTHER, SCOTLAND

by Pete Georgiady

Most collectors have seen the circular mark containing the name "Anderson-Anstruther" at one time or another but few realize the history behind the firm. That mark was used by a father and son whose club production spanned 75 years. Their business was located in the Fife coastal town of Anstruther (pronounced "anster") located about 25 miles from St. Andrews.

The firm's founder, James Anderson, was born in 1845 and became a blacksmith and ferrier. He was undoubtedly approached to make a club head or two at some point and did such a fine job that more such work was sent his way. This is conjecture but it makes for a sound hypothesis since at that time, the early 1860s, Anstruther had no golf links and Anderson himself was never known to have played golf.

There is no acknowledged year when he made his first club heads but several sources suggest either 1862 or 1865, in a decade when John Gray and the Carricks would have been his chief competition. Anderson quickly prospered and by 1880 he had moved primarily into golf club heads and was probably not shoeing horses any longer.

He eventually became a master smith and among the alumni of those once apprenticed to him was Robert Condie who started his own golf club forge in St. Andrews and achieved considerable fame in later years.

In 1892 Anderson patented his first club, a roll face putting cleek that he named the Kurtos model—Kurtos meaning curved in ancient Greek. Since he ran the premier cleek-making business of his day, many other makers and patentees sought him out to produce their iron heads. He forged Carruthers' (drilled hosel), Forester's (concentric) and George Lowe's (anti-shank) patent club heads as well as many others for F. H. Ayers, Willie Park Jr., and Robert Anderson.

Some people credit James Anderson with the invention of the diamond-back shaped iron club head. Whether or not this is true, he produced some magnificent old irons with that design in the late 1880s and early 1890s.

James Anderson died early in life in 1895 and was succeeded in the business by his son Alexander. Alex did a fine job of transitioning the company from his father's moderately sized shop to a large volume production company making heads in the hundreds of thousands yearly.

Anderson used several cleek marks over the years. James' first mark appeared in about 1875 and was used up to his death in 1895. It is the classic Anderson-Anstruther name in a circle measuring only 1/2- inch in diameter, usually stamped in the center of the back of the club head. Alex then switched to a similar mark with a double circle that he used for about 15 years before reverting to the original design his father used, only in a slightly larger 5/8- inch circle.

It was Alex who began to use the "arrow" cleek mark for which the firm is now so famous. Also around this time, 1905, Anderson devised a numbering system for club heads to increase sales through catalogs. A two- or three-digit model number can be found stamped on most of their heads. Many Anderson heads were exported to North America and one of the largest sellers of Anderson headed clubs was The Golf Shop, Chicago, a MacGregor retail outlet. Alex Anderson produced a registered design bent neck putting cleek (#277771) similar to that of Willie Park Jr. around 1900. He also produced a wide variety of iron heads in many styles including concave faced irons, "Hold-em" model deep groove irons as well as a healthy variety of putter types.

ARMY & NAVY COOPERATIVE STORES, LTD:

Began selling clubs about 1885 and began manufacturing and assembling clubs during the early 1890s. The mark they used was "A & N C S L" and usually included "London" on the pre-1900 wood head putters and semi-long-nose woods.

STEEL BLADE PUTTER $60   85   120
Circa 1905-1910. Large double circle mark. Photo below.

LONG-NOSE PUTTER $650   1150   1900
Circa 1890-1900. Beech-head spliced-neck marked "Army & Navy C S L, London."

DEEP-FACE MASHIE $100   160   290
Circa 1900-1905. Stamped "Hold Fast" and "A & N C S."

SMOOTH-FACE IRONS $125   175   325
Circa 1890-1900. Iron or lofting iron. "A & N C S L" on head. Photo below.

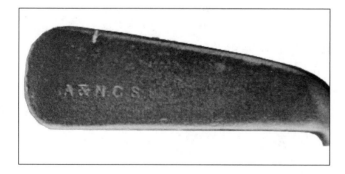

SPLICED-NECK WOODS $225   350   625
Circa1900-1910. Driver, brassie or spoon. "Army & Navy A N C S L, London."

LONG-NOSE WOODS $1150   1850   3750
Circa 1890. Play club or brassie. Beech-head marked "Army & Navy C S L, London." Photo below.

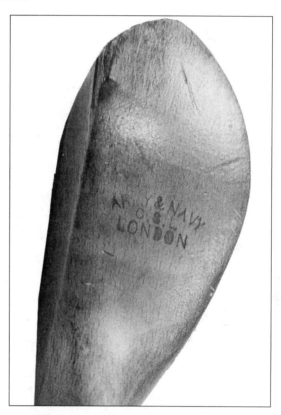

ASHFORD, W & G
BIRMINGHAM, ENGLAND

Made clubs during the mid-1890s. They used a "Fox" head as a maker's identification mark. Many clubs had the patented one-piece sewn grip.

SMOOTH-FACE IRONS $225   300   600
Circa 1893-1897. General purpose iron or lofting iron. Marked "W. & G. Ashford, Mild Steel" with "Cat" mark. Many have a one-piece leather grip.

SHORT-BLADE CLEEK $225   375   600
Circa 1893-1897. Stamped "W. & G. Ashford, Mild Steel" with "Cat" mark. Many have a one-piece leather grip. Photo below.

DRIVING IRON $250   400   650
Circa 1893-1897. Driving iron marked "W. & G. Ashford, Mild Steel" with "Cat" mark. Many have a one-piece leather grip.

SPLICED-NECK WOODS $450   850   1750
Circa 1893-1897. Pear-shaped heads with "Cat" and "W. G. Ashford" markings. Many have a one-piece leather grip. Photo below.

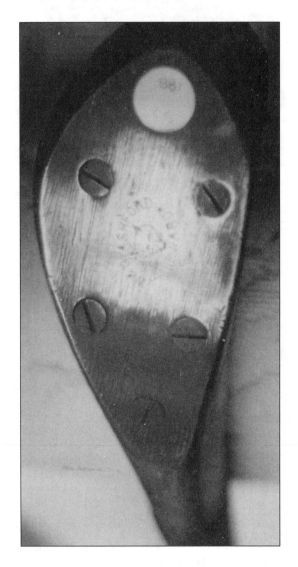

AUCHTERLONIE, D & W
ST. ANDREWS, SCOTLAND

David and Willie Auchterlonie formed their company during the late 1890s. Their mark was simply "D. & W. Auchterlonie, St. Andrews."

STAINLESS STEEL PUTTER $60   75   110
Circa 1930-1935. Offset flanged back blade putter. Marked "D. & W. Auchterlonie, St. Andrews."

D & W BRAND PUTTER $90   125   190
Circa 1910-1915. Patent No. 726896. Two-level back. Dot-face.

RIDGE-BACK PUTTER $200   275   400
Circa 1905-1910. Patent No. 405445. Fancy "Chain Link" face scoring.

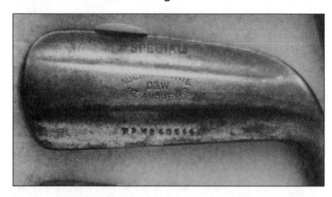

ALL SMOOTH-FACE IRONS $65   95   140
Circa 1905-1910. Stamped "D. & W. Auchterlonie, N B, St. Andrews." Photo below.

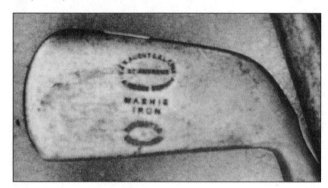

SOCKET WOODS $90   120   175
Circa 1915-20. Driver, brassie or spoon. Marked "Auchtie" in script below "D. & W. Auchterlonie, St. Andrews."

SPLICED-NECK PUTTERS $300   625   1150
Circa 1910-1915. Long-nose style persimmon head. Marked "Auchterlonie Special."

AUCHTERLONIE, TOM
ST. ANDREWS, SCOTLAND

He began his business in St. Andrews at the turn of the century and continued until the 1980s. His mark was "T. Auchterlonie" in block lettering.

ELLICE PUTTER $55   75   100
Circa 1925-1930. Bent-neck line-scored blade.

WOOD HEAD SOCKET
PUTTER $225   375   550
Circa 1910-15. Marked "T. Auchterlonie."

HOLING-OUT PUTTER $275 400 650
Circa 1920. Wide sole and beveled heel and toe.

SPLICED-NECK PUTTERS $300 525 900
Circa 1910. Long-nose style putter. Marked "T. Auchterlonie." Photo below.

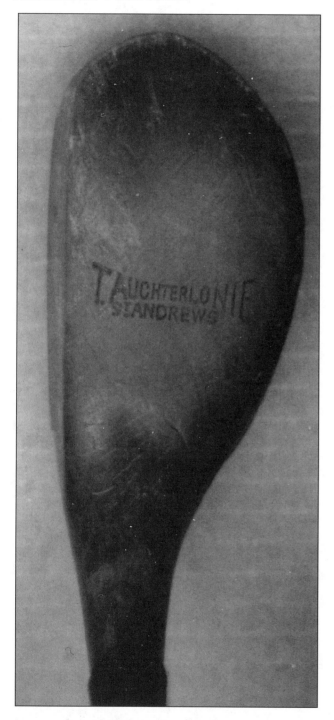

"AUCHTERLONIE" IRONS $45 65 90
Circa 1925. All irons. "Auchterlonie" in large script.

"IT-Z-IN" SERIES IRONS $75 110 160
Circa 1920s. All irons. Marked "Patented by Tom Auchterlonie." Photo below.

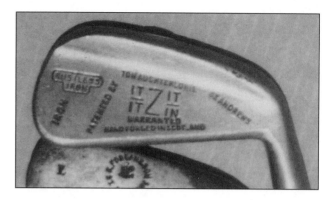

DELUXE SOCKET WOODS $90 120 175
Circa 1920s. Driver, brassie or spoon. Stamped "T. Auchterlonie, St. Andrews, Deluxe."

HAND MADE SOCKET WOODS $90 120 175
Circa 1920s. Driver, brassie or spoon. Stamped "Auchterlonie Special, Hand Made."

GOLD MEDAL SOCKET WOODS $90 120 175
Circa 1920s. Driver, brassie or spoon. Stamped "Auchterlonie Gold Medal."

AYRES, F. H.
LONDON, ENGLAND

F. H. Ayres began as a sporting goods house at the beginning of the 19th century. About 1885 it purchased clubs from different manufacturers, and stamped them with their "F. H. Ayres, London" block letters mark. It also began making its own clubs and used the same mark until about 1900 when it began to use the "Maltese Cross" mark. The business ended during the dark days of the Great Depression. Many of the original shafts were marked "F. H. Ayres & Co."

FLANGED BACK PUTTER $60 90 150
Circa 1915-1920. Offset blade stamped with the "Maltese Cross" mark.

GEM PUTTER $60 90 150
Circa 1915. "Maltese Cross" mark and "Putter" at toe.

STRAIGHT BLADE PUTTER $80 120 190
Circa 1890. Smooth-face with "P" at toe. Steel head.

FACET PUTTER $75 120 160
Circa 1915-1920. "The Facet" in a "Triangle Sweet Spot" on a dot-faced straight blade. "Maltese Cross" mark at toe.

STRAIGHT BRASS-BLADE
PUTTER $100   140   250
Circa 1890. Brass-head. Smooth-face with "P" at toe.

WINKWORTH SCOTT
PUTTER $250   350   575
Oval hosel and oval shaft putter similar to the "Winkworth Scott" Patent. "Rainbow" face.

LONG-NOSE PUTTERS $600   950   1800
Circa 1890-1900. Transitional shorter rounded-head putter. Beech-head.

LONG-NOSE PUTTERS $750   1500   2750
Circa 1885-1895. Long-nose putter. Beech-head. Photo below.

BOBBIE IRON $55   75   110
Circa 1915. Rounded sole. "Maltese Cross" mark.

VARDON SERIES IRONS $70   100   150
Circa 1920s. All irons. "Maltese Cross" mark at toe.

ROUND FACE NIBLICK $75   100   175
Circa 1910-1915. "Maltese Cross" mark. Dot-punched face.

DRIVING IRON $100   150   300
Circa 1890-1900. "D" marked at toe. "F. H. Ayres, London" mark.

SMOOTH-FACE IRONS $120   200   450
Circa 1885-1895. Large block letters. Photo below.

ANTI-SHANK IRONS $140   200   350
Circa 1915-1925. All Smith Patent irons.

THE CERT IRONS $175   225   350
Circa 1920s. "Maltese Cross." Sole extends below the heel and toe. Photo below.

ANTI-SHANK IRONS $175   250   400
Circa 1900-1910. All Fairlie Patent irons with smooth-face.

SMALL-HEAD NIBLICK $190   300   550
Circa 1900-1905. "Maltese Cross" mark.

RUT IRON $450   850   1900
Circa 1885-1895. "Maltese Cross" mark.

SOCKET WOODS $90   120   175
Circa 1915-1925. Driver, brassie or spoon. "F. H. Ayres" mark.

SOCKET WOODS $110   140   125
Circa 1915-1925. Wood cleek or Bull Dog trouble wood.

SPLICED-NECK WOODS $200   325   550
Circa 1895-1910. Traditional head shape. Driver, brassie or spoon. "F. H. Ayers" stamping.

LONG-NOSE WOODS $550   950   1750
Circa 1895-1900. Transitional semi-long-nose driver, brassie or spoon. "F. H. Ayers" stamping. Photo below.

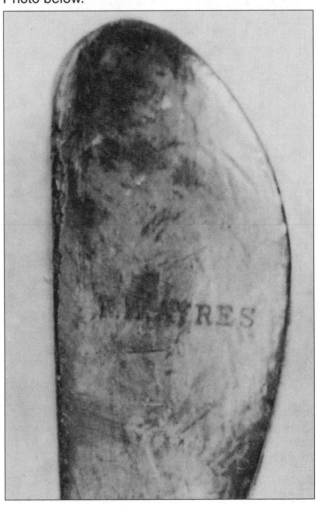

LONG-NOSE WOODS	$1150	1900	3250

Circa 1885-1895. Play club, brassie or spoon. "F. H. Ayres" on beech-head. Photo below.

SPLICED-NECK WOODS	$375	575	900

Circa 1890s with transitional pear shaped heads, many stamped Shinnecock Hills. Photo below.

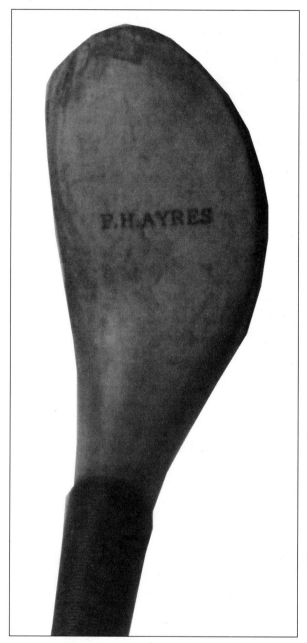

BEVERIDGE, JAMES
SHINNECOCK HILLS

Beveridge began making clubs in Scotland about 1880. He immigrated to America in the early 1890s and was the professional at Shinnecock Hills until his death in 1899. His clubs are highly collectible as he was an important early American clubmaker.

SMOOTH-FACE CLEEK	$175	250	425

Circa 1890s stamped Southhampton, NY.

BLACKSMITH MADE

Clubs made by makers of armor, wheelwrights, metal workers, etc. and blacksmiths. Usually made prior to the 1870s and have crudely forged heads and heavy hosel nickings.

SMOOTH-FACE CLEEK $1750   3250   7000
Circa 1840-1860. Five-inch-long hosel with crude heavy nicking. Photo below.

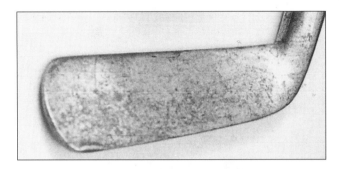

HOLING-OUT PUTTER $1900   3750   7500
Circa 1840-1860. Very thick long hosel with crude heavy nicking. Photo below.

RUT IRON $1800   3750   8500
Circa 1840-1860. Small cupped face. Long thick hosel with heavy nicking. Photo below.

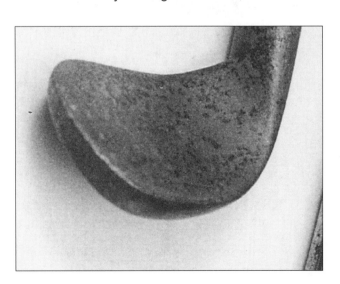

BUNKER OR SAND IRON $2500   6500   12500
Circa 1840-1860. Very thick long hosel with crude heavy nicking. Usually with a concave face. Photo below.

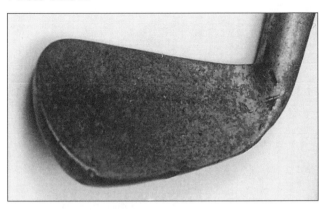

BRADDELL
BELFAST, IRELAND

BRASS-BLADE PUTTER $125   175   300
Circa 1895-1900. Stamped "Braddell, Belfast."

SMOOTH-FACE CLEEK $75   125   250
Circa 1900 Stamped "Braddell Patent."

ALUMINUM-HEAD WOODS $450   700   1350
Circa 1900-1910. Model C or G. Stamped "Braddell Patent." "Carruthers" shafting and a leather face insert.

ALUMINUM-HEAD WOODS $450   700   1350
Circa 1894-1900. "Braddell Patent 4624." Leather face insert. Photo below.

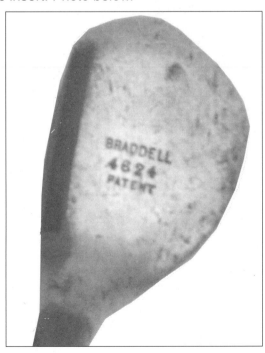

BRAND, CHARLES
CARNOUSTIE, SCOTLAND

Charles Brand was from Carnoustie and began making clubs about 1890. His mark was a "C. Brand, Carnoustie" in block letters, inside a double oval and he also used a "Lion" mark. He produced clubs until his death in 1922.

IRON-HEAD BLADE PUTTER $60   90   150
Circa 1910-1915. Stamped "C. Brand, Carnoustie." Hatched face scoring.

BRASS-HEAD PUTTERS $100   140   225
Circa 1900-1910. Stamped "C. Brand, Carnoustie." Smooth-face.

WOOD-HEAD SOCKET
PUTTER $250   375   700
Circa 1900-1910. Stamped "C. Brand."

SPLICED-NECK PUTTER $600   1000   1800
Circa 1895. Stamped "C. Brand" on beech-head.

LINE-SCORED IRONS $50   70   100
Circa 1920s. All irons. Stamped "C. Brand, Carnoustie" in a double circle.

SMOOTH-FACE IRONS $90   140   250
Circa 1895-1905. Cleek, iron, and lofter. Stamped "C. Brand, Carnoustie."

BRIDGEPORT GUN & IMPLEMENT CO.
BRIDGEPORT, CONNECTICUT

Bridgeport Gun Implement Co. produced clubs, balls and bags from 1896 to 1904 in their Bridgeport, Connecticut plant. Most pre-1899 clubs sold by B. G. I. were imported or made by Spalding before J. H. Williams Co., Brooklyn, New York, became its major supplier. Many aluminum-head putters and fairway woods were imported from Standard Golf Company, Sunderland, England, and were stamped "B G I, CO" on the sole. Some Anderson of Anstruther clubs can also be found with the block letter "B G I CO." stamp. About the turn of the century, B. G. I. began numbering their clubs and placed those numbers on the shaft, just below the grip, and on the heel of the wood head clubs.

Their clubs were of high quality and very popular, competing favorably with MacGregor and Spalding. Today many collectors focus on B. G. I clubs as they represent a good portion of early American golf history.

Other brand names B. G. I. used were Fairfield, Edinboro, Aberdeen and Dunn Selected. The Fairfield and Aberdeen marked clubs are priced slightly less than the other B. G. I. marked clubs.

In 1904 the company was sold to the Bridgeport Athletic Mfg. Co. and the "BAM" trademark, 1904-1907, replaced the familiar B. G. I. oval marks.

Don Paris, who is currently writing a book on B. G. I., has contributed photos, information and pricing to this price and reference guide.

Jim Cooper has written the definitive work on Spalding, which is profusely illustrated and contains sections on B. G. I. and Wright & Ditson as well. Every B. G. I. collector should have this reference in his library. It is available from the author, or Jim Cooper. There are also B. G. I. Retail Catalogue reprints from 1900, 1903 and 1904 available from the author of this book.

PUTTING CLEEK $65   115   200
Circa 1900. #110 on shaft. "Diamond W" mark on the hosel. Photo below.

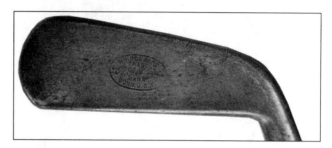

FAIRFIELD PUTTER $65   115   200
Circa 1900. "Fairfield" in script. "220" on the shaft .

DEEP FACE BLADE PUTTER $85   150   275
Circa 1900. Smooth-face. "B. G. I." oval mark. "Diamond W" mark on the hosel.

BRASS-HEAD PUTTERS $75   150   275
Circa 1900. Two-way blade. "BGI" oval mark.

PARK-STYLE PUTTERS $125   190   375
Circa 1900. Goose Neck, severely offset blade. "BGI Arrow" mark.

SCHENECTADY-TYPE PUTTER $200   375   550
Circa 1903-1904. "BGI Co" on the sole.

SPLICED-NECK PUTTER $500   900   1500
Circa 1899-1901. "Arrow-BGI-Arrow" mark. Dogwood head. #96 on heel. Photo below.

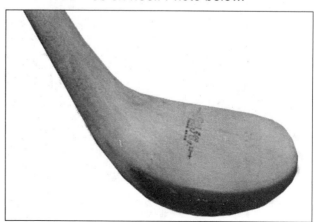

SMOOTH-FACE IRONS $50 100 175
Circa 1900. All irons. "BGI" oval mark.

CENTRA-JECT MASHEY $65 125 225
Circa 1899-1904. Weight concentrated in center of back. #105 on shaft. Photo below.

FAIRFIELD IRONS $50 90 150
Circa 1900. All irons.

CARRUTHER'S MODEL CLEEK $80 140 275
Circa 1900. #103 on shaft. Carruther's through hosel shafting.

SPLICED-NECK WOODS $190 375 550
Circa 1900. "Arrow-B G I-Arrow." All woods. Photo below.

SOCKET WOODS $110 190 325
Circa 1900-1905. "Arrow-B G I-Arrow" mark. All woods.

FAIRFIELD WOODS $100 170 290
Circa 1900. "Fairfield" in script. All woods. Socket heads.

FORKED SPLICE WOODS $450 750 1150
Circa 1900. All woods.

ONE-PIECE WOOD $1400 1800 3000
Circa 1898-1902. Driver or brassie one-piece hickory head and shaft. Has a leather face insert. Photo below.

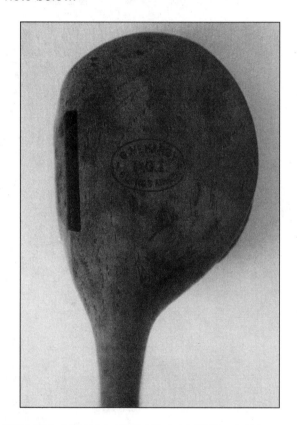

BUHRKE CO., R. H.
CHICAGO, IL

Began making clubs in the early 1920s. R. H. Buhrke made many different clubs, mostly department or sporting goods stores quality clubs. The most sought after series is the "Classic" with a brass "plug" in the face. They used a "Key" mark and used trade names of "Medalist," "Burr-Key-Bilt," "Classic," "Finalist" and others.

ANDY ROBERTSON IRONS $35 48 80
Circa late 1920s. All irons. Line-scored face. Chromed head.

ANDY ROBERTSON PUTTER $40 55 90
Circa late 1920s. Line-scored face. Chromed head.

CLASSIC SERIES PUTTER $70 100 150
Circa 1920s. Brass plug face insert in sweet spot.

STYLIST SERIES IRONS $35 48 80
Circa 1925-1930. All irons. Line-scored blade, "Flower" at the sweet spot. Chromed head. Photo below.

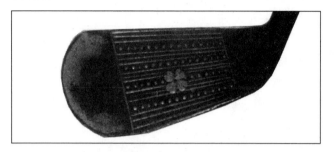

MAJESTIC SERIES IRONS $35 48 80
Circa 1920s. All irons. Line-scored face.

CLASSIC SERIES IRONS $65 85 115
Circa 1920s. All irons. Brass plug face insert in sweet spot. Photo below.

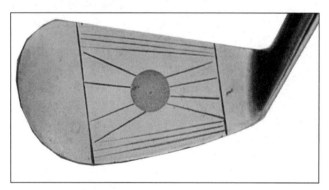

KILROY IRONS $35 50 80
Circa 1920s. All irons. "Burr-Key-Bilt" mark with "Key." Photo below.

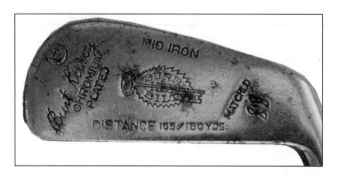

PRETTY FACE WOODS $95 125 190
Circa 1925. "Burr-Key-Bilt Regal." Driver, brassie or spoon.

PRETTY FACE WOODS $125 200 300
Circa 1925. Half-moon aluminum face insert. Driver, brassie or spoon.

MAJESTIC SERIES PUTTER $40 55 90
Circa 1920s. Line-scored face.

STYLIST SERIES PUTTER $40 55 90
Circa 1925-1930. Line-scored blade. Chromed head.

BURKE MFG. CO.
NEWARK, OH

Burke began forging irons about 1910. They made millions upon millions of low and medium quality clubs that were sold in dry good and department stores throughout the Midwest. They used many marks including a "Hand with Scales," "Bee," "Daisy," "Thistle," "Crown" and others. Their top-of-the-line clubs were the "Grand Prize" series.

MONARCH PUTTER $40 55 90
Circa 1920. Flanged back hyphen scored blade with a large "Crown" mark.

PICCADILLY PUTTER $90 150 225
Circa 1920s. Large flange with a "Swastika" type mark.

STERLING PUTTER $40 55 90
Circa 1920. Square punch marked face. Crown and Lion marks.

PRESTWICK PUTTER $40 55 90
Circa 1920. Line-scored blade putter.

ST. ANDREWS SPECIAL PUTTERS $40 55 90
Circa 1915-1920. Dot-punched face. "Crown" mark.

GRAND PRIZE PUTTERS $40 55 90
Circa 1920s. Hyphen scored face.

BEE AND FLOWER MARK PUTTERS $40 55 90
Circa 1920s. Various assemblers.

COLUMBIA SPECIAL PUTTERS $40 55 90
Circa 1915-1925. "Rampant Lion" and "Crown" markings.

GLENCOE PUTTERS $80 120 190
Circa 1920s. Flanged back putter with alternating "Line and Dot-punched" face scoring.

GRAND PRIZE PUTTERS $40 55 90
Circa 1920s. Offset hosel blade.

X 69 PUTTER $100 140 225
Circa 1920s. Flanged back, wide sole.

GIRAFFE-NECK PUTTER $120 175 250
Circa 1920s. Six-inch-long pencil-thin hosel.

ALUMINUM-HEAD PUTTER $100 125 175
Circa 1920s. Mills-type aluminum-head mallet.

Hagen's Own Clubs—for You!

WALTER HAGEN—the Incomparable Sir Walter—has granted Burke (and only Burke) the right to copy his bag of clubs.

So here are shown the leading Burke-Hagen models—*actual duplicates* of his record-breaking clubs, each autographed *Walter Hagen*.

If Walter uses them, they MUST be unrivalled in design, in material, in finish. Have you ever wondered how a set of these *proven* clubs will help your score?

Quit wondering—and find out!

In Monel metal or in steel at Pros and Sporting Goods Stores

Hagen Driver: Socket model. Deep face with metal insert. Easy to learn.

Hagen Brassie: Made exactly as the Driver but with a little more loft.

Hagen Driving Iron: A confidence-building club for the long one-shotters.

Hagen Mashie Iron: His pet club. You will use it more than any other in a round.

Hagen Mashie: Well lofted. Medium in size and weight. Practical in every way.

Hagen Mashie Niblick: Heavy head but a small blade. An excellent trouble-escape.

Hagen Putter: Slightly gooseneck. His selection from 100 models.

GRAND PRIZE

BURKE
CLUBS·BAGS·BALLS

A COPY of the new Burke Catalog, picturing and describing the full line, sent on request.

The Burke Golf Company
NEWARK, OHIO, U.S.A.

No. 2 Spoon

Burke Grand Prize Wood Clubs

No. 1 Spoon. Small Head. Deep Face.
No. 2 Spoon. Medium Size Head. Medium Deep Face.
No. 11 Splice Spoon. Large Head. Rounding Sole.
No. 14 Spoon. Bull Dog Type. Large Head. Round Sole. Made in Fiber Face Only.
No. 522 Spoon. Confidus Model used by J. H. Taylor Bulging Sole makes this model very effective in securing distance from cuppy lies. Made with Fiber Face Only.
No. 875 Spoon. Bull Dog Type. Round Sole. Extremely Deep Face. Made with Fiber Face Only.

Wood Cleeks

No. 44 Wood Cleek-Splice Model. Small Head. Shallow Face.
No. 45 Wood Cleek-Socket Model. Same as No. 44.

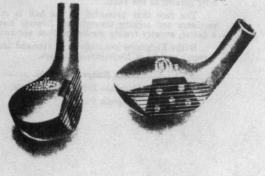

No. 45 Wood Cleek. Fiber Face

Page Thirteen

The Burke Golf Company
NEWARK, OHIO, U.S.A.

No. 872-874 Driver and Brassie

Burke Grand Prize Wood Clubs

Drivers and Brassies

No. 800-802 Driver and Brassie. Small Head. Narrow Face. Medium Lie.
No. 864-866 Driver and Brassie. Medium Size Head. Long Deep Face. Medium Lie.
No. 868-870 Driver and Brassie. Small Head. Deep Face. Medium Lie.
No. 872-874 Driver and Brassie. Made in Black Fiber Face only. Bulldog Model with Rounding Sole. Upright Lie. Deep Face.
No. 10-12 Splice Driver and Brassie. Pear Shaped Head. Bulger Face. Upright Lie.

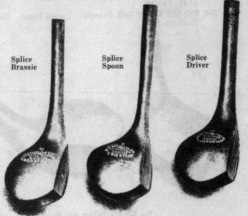

Splice Brassie   Splice Spoon   Splice Driver

Page Twelve

Burke 1922 Catalogue.

X 78 BENT-NECK PUTTER $100   125   175
Circa 1920s. Park-style, severely bent neck, smooth-face putter.

CRESCENT-HEAD PUTTER $125   150   250
Circa late Teens. Crescent head, broad sole and pointed toe.

END GRAIN PUTTER $350   450   750
Circa 1920. Rectangular wood head.

DIAMOND BACK IRONS $50   65   90
Circa 1910-1915. "Rampant Lion" mark at the toe.

PRESTWICK IRONS $35   45   75
Circa 1920. All irons.

ST. ANDREWS SPECIAL IRONS $35   45   75
Circa 1915-1920. Dot-punched face. "Crown" mark at the toe.

GLENCOE IRONS $35   45   75
Circa 1920s. All irons.

COLUMBIA SPECIAL IRONS $35   45   75
Circa 1915-1925. All irons. "Rampant Lion" and "Crown" markings. Photo below.

COMMANDER IRONS $35   45   75
Circa late 1920s. All irons. Grip has aluminum end cap.

BURKE STAINLESS IRONS $35   45   75
Circa 1925-1930. All irons.

GRAND PRIZE IRONS $35   45   75
Circa 1920s. All irons.

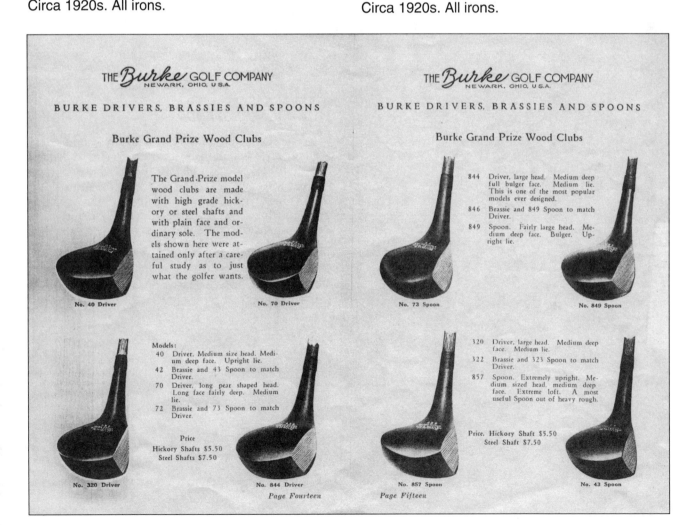

GRAND PRIZE IRONS $100   125   175
Circa 1915. Foulis-type concave head.

HARRY VARDON
SIGNATURE IRON $35   50   90
Circa 1925-1930. All irons.

TED RAY SIGNATURE IRONS $35   50   90
Circa 1925-1930. All irons.

MONEL METAL IRONS $40   55   95
Circa 1920-1930. All clubs.

DEEP GROOVE IRONS $100   140   200
Circa 1915-1922. Corrugated deep grooves. All irons.

DEEP GROOVE IRONS $110   150   225
Circa 1915-1922. All clubs. Monel metal heads.

DEEP GROOVE IRONS $120   150   225
Circa 1915-1922. Slot deep grooves. All irons.

ROTARY ILLEGAL IRONS $300   425   750
Circa 1920. All clubs. Half waffle pattern, half slot deep groove. Monel metal. Photo below.

LONG BURKE IRONS $35   45   75
Circa 1925-1930. All irons. "Shield" mark. Photo below.

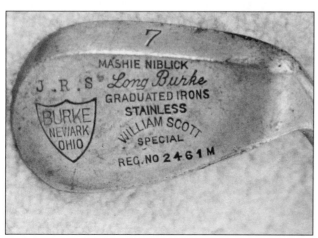

BRASS-HEAD NIBLICK $150   175   250
Circa 1925. Large hyphen scored brass-head.

CHAMPION WOODS $75   100   150
Circa 1920s. Driver, brassie or spoon.

GRAND PRIZE WOODS $75   100   150
Circa 1915-1925. Driver, brassie or spoon.

GLENCOE WOODS $75   100   150
Circa 1920s. Driver, brassie or spoon.

COLUMBIA SPECIAL WOODS $75   100   150
Circa 1915-1925. Driver, brassie or spoon.

VARIOUS WOODS $75   100   150
Circa 1925-1928. Driver, brassie or spoon. "Golfrite," De Luxe," "Plus-Four," Autograph series," "Sportsman" and "Skippers."

PRESTWICK WOODS $75   100   150
Circa 1920s. Driver, brassie or spoon.

JUVENILE CLUBS $30   40   70
Circa 1920s. All irons and putter. Smooth-faces.

JUVENILE CLUBS $60   80   140
Circa 1920s. All woods.

HAGEN SERIES IRONS $40   50   85
Circa 1925. All clubs.

BUSSEY & CO.
LONDON, ENGLAND

George Bussey began making clubs in London during the late 1880s and made a two-piece club called the "Patented Steel Socket." He also patented a one-piece grip that was sewn up the back. He used a monogram "GGB" mark with an arrow through it and "Thistle." On many clubs, the name of the club (mashie, iron, etc.) was stamped on the shaft.

STEEL SOCKET PATENT
PUTTER $175   250   450
Circa 1890-1900. "Bussey & Co, London" and "Thistle" marks. Photo below.

STEEL SOCKET BRASS
PUTTER $275   450   850
Circa 1890-1900. Brass-blade, steel socket. "Bussey & Co, London" and "Thistle" marks. Many have a one-piece leather grip. Photo below.

STEEL SOCKET PATENT IRONS $175   250   450
Circa 1890-1900. Smooth iron or mashie. "Thistle" below "Bussey & Co., London." Photo below.

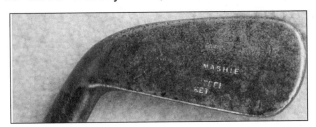

STEEL SOCKET PATENT CLEEK $225   275   500
Circa 1890-1900. Smooth-face cleek. "Thistle" below "Bussey & Co., London."

BUTCHART-NICHOLLS
GLENBROOK, CT

They were famous for shafts made of alternating strips of bamboo and hickory. They used a "Bird" mark and the letters "BTN."

BAMBOO-SHAFT PUTTER $55   65   100
Circa 1920s. Dot-punched face.

BAMBOO-SHAFT IRONS $45   55   90
Circa 1920s. All irons. Dot-punched face.

BUTCHART BILT WOODS $100   140   200
Circa 1920s. Driver, brassie or spoon. Many have steel face inserts. Laminated bamboo shaft.

CANN & TAYLOR
LONDON, ENGLAND

A London-area firm. They used "Cann & Taylor, Winchester" in block letters 1894-1897, "J. H. Taylor" signature and an odd looking "Flywheel" mark into the 1930s.

TWISTED HOSEL PUTTER $90   140   275
Circa 1905-1915. "Cann & Taylor" with "J H Taylor" signature marks.

DOT-FACE BLADE PUTTER $50   60   100
Circa 1910-1915. "Cann & Taylor" with "J H Taylor" signature marks.

ALUMINUM MALLET PUTTER $225   325   475
Circa 1915 with a raised sight line. Photo below.

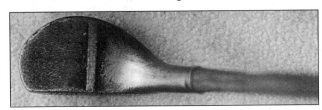

GEM PUTTER $80   100   150
Circa 1910-1920. Flywheel mark. Rounded back. Dot-punched face.

SMOOTH-FACE PUTTER $90   125   225
Circa 1900. "Cann & Taylor, Winchester and Richmond" stampings.

CYNOSURE SERIES IRONS $45   55   85
Circa 1925. All irons. "Flywheel" mark.

AUTOGRAPH MODEL IRONS $50   60   95
Circa 1915. All irons. Bordered hyphen face. Photo below.

CONVEX FACE NIBLICK $60 70 100
Circa 1920.

SMOOTH-FACE AUTOGRAPH
IRONS $75 95 150
Circa 1900-1910. Cleek, iron, mashie and lofting iron.

RADIAL SOLE DRIVING
MASHIE $80 110 150
Circa 1915. "Flywheel" mark.

DRIVING MASHIE $80 100 150
Circa 1920. "Flywheel" mark.

RUT NIBLICKS $140 200 350
Circa 1900-1905. Stamped "Cann & Taylor Niblick."

CYNOSURE SERIES WOODS $95 125 190
Circa 1920s. Driver, brassie or spoon.

SPLICED-NECK WOODS $150 225 350
Circa 1910-1915. Driver, brassie or spoon.

SPLICED-NECK WOODS $300 450 850
Circa 1891-1897. Transitional beech-head. Leather face insert. Bulger driver or brassie.

CARRICK, F. & A.
MUSSELBURGH

The Carrick brothers, who were initially blacksmiths, began forging iron heads about 1860 through the early 1900s. They used two marks: "F & A Carrick, Musselburgh" and simply "Carrick" in block letters. All their clubs carried a "Cross" cleek mark. They are quite scarce and highly collectible.

STEEL-BLADE PUTTER $350 550 1200
Circa 1890-1895. Smooth-face blade putter. "Cross" mark.

EARLY STEEL-BLADE PUTTER $475 650 1500
Circa 1870-1885. Smooth-face straight blade. "Cross" mark.

GENERAL PURPOSE IRON $450 650 1350
Circa 1870-1880. "F & A Carrick, Musselburgh" above the "Cross" mark.

CROSS MARKED CLEEK $500 700 1400
Circa 1870-1880. Stamped "F & A Carrick, Musselburgh."

CROSS MARKED CLEEK $525 750 1500
Circa 1870-1880. Stamped only "Carrick." "Cross" mark. Photo below.

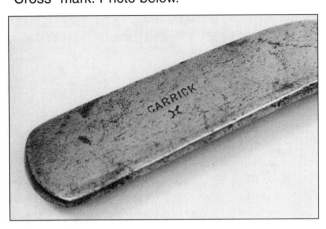

CASSIDY, J. L.
ALDBURGH, ENGLAND

Cassidy began making clubs shortly after the turn of the century. He is known for his patented "V" sight line aluminum putters.

PERSIMMON HEAD PUTTER $175 275 450
Circa 1910. "Cassiday, Aldburgh" on the socket, semi-long-nose head.

ALUMINUM HEAD MALLET $120 175 275
Circa 1910. "Cassidy 'V'" on the sole. Photo below.

CLARK, J. & D.
MUSSELBURGH, SCOTLAND

The Clark brothers apprenticed under Willie Park and many of their clubs were made by Park or in his style. In the short period of time during the late 1890s and early 1900s, they used two marks: "J & D Clark, Musselburgh" in a circle similar to Park's mark, and the same in very tiny letters.

LONG-NOSE BEECH-HEAD
PUTTER $950 1650 3000
Circa 1890-1895 most likely made by Willie Park.

SMOOTH-FACE BLADE
PUTTER $100 135 225
Circa 1895-1905. Stamped "J & D Clark Musselburgh."

BRASS-BLADE PUTTER $125   175   325
Circa 1895-1905. Stamped "J & D Clark Mussel-burgh."

MARKED FACE IRONS $60   90   150
Circa 1910-1920. All irons. Stamped "J & D Clark Musselburgh."

SMOOTH-FACE IRONS $90   125   200
Circa 1895-1905. Cleek, iron and lofting iron. Stamped "J & D Clark Musselburgh." Photo below.

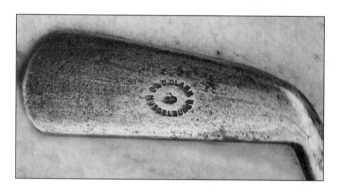

SPLICED-NECK BRASSIE $350   550   1000
Circa 1895. Transitional pear shaped head stamped "J & D Clark Musselburgh."

COCHRANE'S LTD.
EDINBURGH, SCOTLAND

This Edinburgh-based firm used several marks including the "Knight in Armor" holding a sword, and a "Bowline Knot." They also used "J P Cochrane's, Lt'd, Edinburgh" in script. The company made clubs well into the late 1930s.

OFFSET BLADE PUTTER $50   60   95
Circa 1915. Knight mark. Dot-punched face .

PUTTING CLEEK $50   70   110
Circa 1910-1915. "Knight" mark. Hyphen scored straight blade putter.

MUSSEL-BACK PUTTER $55   75   125
Circa 1920. "Knight" mark.

WALTER HAGEN PUTTER $55   75   120
Circa 1925-1930. Stainless steel putter. "Bowline" mark.

PUTTING CLEEK $55   75   120
Circa 1920. Dot-faced blade. "Bowline Knot" mark.

"NIGGER" PUTTER $150   250   425
Circa 1920. 7-inch long hosel. Dot-faced blade. "Bowline Knot" mark. Photo below.

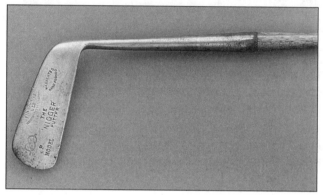

FLANGED BACK PUTTER $60   75   120
Circa 1920-1925. "Knight" mark.

BENT NECK PUTTER $60   75   120
Circa 1915. Stamped "Bent Neck Putter." "Knight" mark.

HOLEM PUTTER $80   110   175
Circa 1915. "Mussel" back. "Knight" mark.

CHALLENGER RUSTLESS PUTTER $95   150   250
Circa 1920s. "Knight" mark. Park-style severely bent neck hosel.

"X X X" FLANGED PUTTER $100   150   225
Circa 1920. Flat hosel and shaft.

U O T PUTTER $450   750   1150
Circa 1920. "Knight" mark. "Spur" at toe.

CRUICKSHANK SIGNATURE IRONS $45   60   90
Circa 1925-1930. "Bowline Knot" mark.

CARDINAL SERIES IRONS $45   55   80
Circa 1920s. 1 through 9 irons. Dot-punched face.

HAGEN SERIES IRONS $50   60   80
Circa 1930. All irons marked rustless. "Bowline Knot" mark.

STAINLESS IRONS $55   65   90
Circa 1925-1930. All stainless irons. "Bow-line" mark. Photo below.

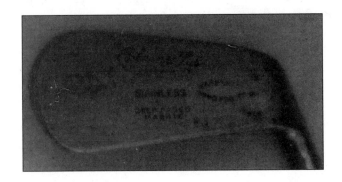

LIGHT MASHIE $60   80   120
Circa 1920-1925. "Knight" mark. Line-scored face.

MAXWELL HOSEL IRONS $60   80   140
Circa 1910-1920. All flanged back irons. Maxwell holes drilled in hosel.

CARDINAL SERIES IRONS $90   120   190
Circa 1920s. Dreadnought niblick.

DEEP GROOVE IRONS $120   175   275
Circa 1915-1922. "DEDLI" pitcher with five slot grooves.

GIANT NIBLICK $1250   1600   2400
Circa 1925-1930. "Mammouth Niblick." "Stainless" "Fort Mason, Picadilly, London" "Bowline Knot" mark.

CARDINAL GIANT NIBLICK $1250 1750 2600
Circa 1920s. Bowline knot mark.

PRETTY FACE WOODS $100   135   190
Circa 1910-1920. Driver, brassie or spoon. "Triangular" black face insert.

KIRKWOOD SERIES WOODS $100 135 190
Circa 1925-1930. Driver, brassie or spoon. "Genuine Joe Kirkwood Model."

HAGEN SERIES WOODS $100   135   190
Circa 1925-1930. Driver, brassie or spoon. "Genuine Walter Hagen Model."

SEMI-SOCKET PATENT $150   200   325
Circa 1910.

SPLICED-NECK WOODS $150   250   390
Circa 1900-1910. Driver, brassie or spoon. Persimmon head.

CONDIE, ROBERT
ST. ANDREWS, SCOTLAND

Robert Condie began as a cleek maker during the early 1880s in St. Andrews. His mark was "R. Condie, St. Andrews" surrounding a "Flower" mark. More than 10 different sizes and shapes of Condie's "Flower" have been catalogued. During the 1890s he briefly used single and double "Fern" marks. Clubs with the "Fern" marks are very scarce and are highly sought after by collectors.

EXCELSIOR PUTTER $60   70   120
Circa 1920. Dot-faced blade. "R. Condie, St. Andrews" surrounding his "Flower" mark.

CALAMITY JANE TYPE $60   75   125
Circa 1910. Offset blade. "Flower" mark.

PUTTING CLEEK $70   95   150
Circa 1900-1910. Smooth-face blade. "Flower" mark. Photo below.

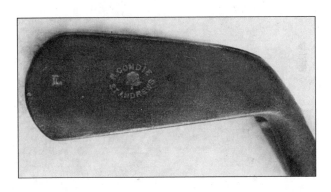

BRASS-HEAD PUTTERS $80   120   180
Circa 1900-1910. Smooth-face blade. "Flower" mark.

LINE-SCORED JIGGER $50   70   100
Circa 1920. "Flower" mark.

ROUND-HEAD NIBLICK $55   65   95
Circa 1915-1920. "Flower" mark. Dot-punched face.

OVAL-HEAD NIBLICK $55   65   95
Circa 1915-1920. "Flower" mark. Dot-punched face and offset hosel.

SMOOTH-FACE IRONS $60   75   120
Circa 1900-1910. Iron or lofter. "Flower" mark.

SMOOTH-FACE CLEEK $60   75   120
Circa 1900-1910. "Flower" mark.

EARLY CONDIE IRONS $100   150   250
Circa 1890-1900. Smooth-face iron or lofter. "Flower" mark. Shafted and stamped by D. McEwan, Ben Sayers, R. Simpson and others.

SWILCAN PITCHER $90 120 175
Circa 1920. "Flower" mark. Wide sole, beveled heel and toe. Dot-punched face.

SMOOTH-FACE NIBLICK $95 125 190
Circa 1900-1910. "Flower" mark.

EARLY CONDIE CLEEKS $100 150 250
Circa 1890-1900. "Flower" mark surrounded D. McEwan, Ben Sayers, R. Simpson and others.

CONCAVE FACE LOFTER $125 175 275
Circa 1895. "Flower" mark.

ANTI-SHANK IRONS $140 200 325
Circa 1900-1910. Fairlie Patent smooth-face iron, lofter or niblick. "Flower" mark.

SINGLE FERN IRONS $275 350 550
Circa 1890-1895. Iron or lofter. Photo below.

SINGLE FERN CLEEK $300 375 600
Circa 1890-1895.

DOUBLE FERN IRONS $325 425 650
Circa 1890-1895. Iron or lofter.

DOUBLE FERN CLEEK $350 450 650
Circa 1890-1895.

CRAIGIE, J. & W.
MONTROSE, SCOTLAND

The Craigie brothers began forging clubs during the mid-1890s and continued through the 1920s. Their mark was "J & W Craigie, Montrose" in block letters and they used a "Rifle" cleek mark.

OFFSET BLADE PUTTER $55 65 100
Circa 1915-1920. "Rifle" mark.

SPLICED-NECK PUTTER $550 950 1900
Circa 1895. Transitional shaped beech-head. "Craigie" in block letters.

DOT-PUNCHED FACE IRONS $55 65 90
Circa 1915-1920. All irons. "Rifle" mark. Photo below.

RUT NIBLICK $200 275 450
Circa 1900-1905. Smooth-face. "Rifle" mark.

DINT PATENT GOLF CO., LTD.

Made wood clubs with "Dint" in script on the sole plate. The one-piece face and sole plate were made of silver.

SILVER DINT WOODS $200 275 450
Circa 1915. Driver, brassie or spoon. Patented one-piece silver face and sole plate. "Pat No. 22777/13."

SILVER DINT WOODS $225 300 475
Circa 1915. Wooden baffie. Patented one-piece silver face and sole plate. "Pat. No. 22777/13." Photo below.

DONALDSON, J.
GLASGOW, SCOTLAND

James Donaldson made clubs from the early 1920s through the early 1930s. He used a "Rangefinder" circular mark.

RANGEFINDER IRONS $55 65 85
Circa 1925-1930. All rustless irons. Dot-punched face. Photo below.

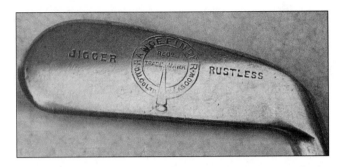

THE SKELPIE IRONS $60 75 110
Circa 1925-1930. All rustless irons. Dot-punched face.

RANGEFINDER WOODS $100 135 190
Circa 1925-1930. Driver, brassie or spoon. Two-tone heads.

DUNN, JOHN D.
BOURNEMOUTH, ENGLAND

Began making clubs in the early 1890s. He patented the "One-Piece" wood while in Bournemouth, England, circa 1894. He later moved to New York.

BRITISH MAKE IRONS $70 90 150
Circa 1900. All smooth-face irons.

ONE-PIECE WOOD $1200 1750 2700
Circa 1895. "John D Dunn, Bournemouth" on shaft.

PARK-STYLE PUTTER $125 150 250
Circa 1900-1910. "Dunn Selected" mark. Severe bent neck.

IONIC IRONS $60 75 100
Circa 1915-1920. All line-scored irons. Photo below.

CROWN MARKED WOODS $100 135 190
Circa 1905-1910. All socket woods.

DUNN, SEYMOUR
LAKE PLACID, NY

Made clubs in America circa 1910-1920. Used a large "Crown and Ribbon" mark.

DOT-FACE IRONS $75 90 140
Circa 1915. Large "Crown and Ribbon" mark.

SMOOTH-FACE IRONS $95 125 175
Circa 1905-1910. All irons. Large "Crown and Ribbon" mark. Photo below.

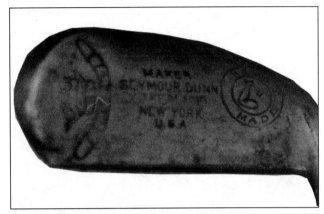

ANTI-SHANK IRONS $175 275 500
Circa 1910. Fairlie style. Smooth-face mashie-niblick or niblick. Large "Crown and Ribbon" mark.

SOCKET WOODS $100 145 210
Circa 1910. Driver, brassie or spoon. Large "Crown and Ribbon" mark.

DUNN, WILLIE
NEW YORK

Willie Dunn began forging clubs in the late 1880s at Westward Ho! In 1895 he began a club-making business in New York. His clubs were marked "Ardsley C. C., New York." During the period from 1897 to 1900 he worked as club designer for B.G.I., MacGregor, and Spalding. After 1900 his clubs were marked "Dunn Selected" or "Willie Dunn, New York" in block letters.

OFFSET BLADE PUTTER $75 100 150
Circa 1910. "Rampant Lion" mark.

BALL-FACE BLADE PUTTER $75 100 160
Circa 1910. "Rampant Lion" mark.

SMOOTH-FACE BLADE
PUTTER $80 110 200
Circa 1900-1905. Stamped "Willie Dunn, New York."

DUNN IRONS

ARDSLEY CASINO, NEW YORK $190   275   450
Circa 1895. All smooth-face irons with tiny "Eagle" mark. Photo below.

DUNN SELECTED IRONS $85   130   195
Circa 1900-1905. All smooth-face irons.

APPROACHING CLEEK $125   160   275
Circa 1897-1903. "Willie Dunn, New York" in block letters.

SMOOTH-FACE IRONS $125   160   275
Circa 1897-1903. All irons stamped "Willie Dunn, New York" in large block letters. Photo below.

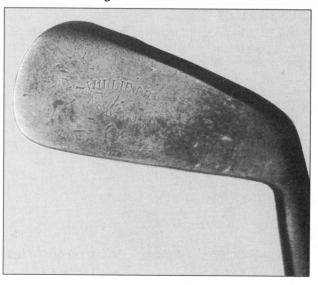

DUNN SELECTED WOODS $125   175   275
Circa 1900-1905. Socket-head driver, brassie or spoon.

SPLICED-NECK WOODS $200   350   550
Circa 1900-1905. Spliced-head driver, brassie or spoon.

DUNN SELECTED WOODS $200   350   550
Circa 1900-1905. Spliced-neck driver, brassie or spoon.

FORGAN, ANDREW
GLASGOW, SCOTLAND

Brother to Robert Forgan. He made clubs only during the mid-1890s. He used the marks "A. Forgan, Glasgow" in block letters and a "Pear" tree with "Regd" beneath.

STEEL BLADE PUTTER $125   150   250
Circa 1895-1900. Pear Tree mark. "Andrew Forgan, Glasgow" stampings.

BRASS-BLADE PUTTER $150   200   300
Circa 1900. Pear Tree mark. "Andrew Forgan, Glasgow" stamping. Photo below.

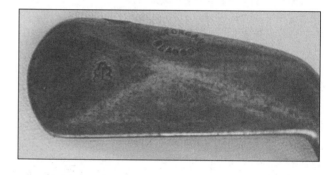

SPLICED-NECK WOODS $250   375   650
Circa 1895-1900. Driver, brassie or spoon. "Tree" mark. Photo below.

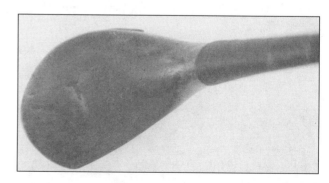

FORGAN, ROBERT
ST. ANDREWS, SCOTLAND

Robert Forgan was one of the foremost and prolific clubmakers of his time. His shop was adjacent to the

18th green of the Old Course in St. Andrews, Scotland.

Robert apprenticed under Hugh Philp (Philp died in 1856). During that time, his reputation had grown to capture the Prince of Wales' attention, who commissioned him to make his clubs. This explains why the firm used the Prince of Wales "Plume" mark as their trademark from the 1880s onward. When the Prince became King Edward in 1901, the firm adopted the "Crown" mark and used it until about 1910 and subsequently during the late 1920s.

When the firm of James Spence was acquired in 1926, its "Flag in the Hole" maker's mark was also used. Each club had "R. Forgan & Son, St. Andrews" stamped into the head as well as the "mark" (woods sometimes did not bear the "trade mark"). Pre-1910 clubs and post-1910 premium quality clubs usually had "R. Forgan & Sons, St. Andrews Selected" stamped into the shaft just below the grip.

Today the St. Andrews Woolen Mills occupies the building, which still has "R. Forgan & Son" spelled out on the sidewalk in front of the main entrance as a reminder of their glorious club making past.

EARLY STEEL PUTTERS $250   350   500
Circa 1880-1890. "R. Forgan and Sons, St. Andrews" marking. Face nearly two inches vertically.

PLUME MARK BRASS
PUTTERS $100   175   290
Circa 1895. Smooth-face brass-blade with a short, straight, thick hosel. "R. Forgan & Sons, St. Andrews" mark. Photo below.

CROWN MARKED PUTTERS $70   120   200
Circa 1901-1908. Smooth-face. Heavy gauge steel.

CROWN MARKED PUTTERS $70   110   150
Circa 1901-1908. #100 dot-faced, centra-ject back weighted.

CROWN MARKED BRASS
PUTTERS $75   100   175
Circa 1901-1908. Brass-blade with "R. Forgan & Sons, St. Andrews" mark.

SCOTIA SERIES PUTTER $45   60   110
Circa 1920. Line-scored blade.

GEM PUTTER $70   100   150
Circa 1926-1930. Wide rounded back broad sole. "Forgan" in large block letters on back.

GIRAFFE NECK PUTTER $150   200   300
Circa 1920. "Flag" mark. Slender five-inch-long hosel.

MAXMO PUTTER $175   275   450
Circa 1920. Persimmon head mallet. Metal sole plates at heel and toe. Wood portion of sole marked "R. Forgan, St. Andrews."

TOLLEY PUTTER $250   350   550
Circa 1925-1930. Heel shafted socket putter made of "Forganite," a plastic-type material. Photo below.

PUTTERS EXPORTED TO
INDIA $125   175   275
Circa 1901-1908. Brass-blade putter. "Crown" mark. "Wager & Co., Bombay" stamping.

LONG-NOSE PUTTERS $1700   2800   4800
Circa 1856-1870. Beech-head. "R. Forgan" large block letters mark. Long head. Large lead back weight.

LONG-NOSE PUTTERS $1250   1800   3250
Circa 1870-1890. "R. Forgan" and "Plume" mark. Medium-size head. Medium weight. Photo below.

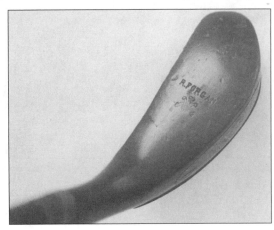

SPLICED-NECK PUTTERS $275   500   900
Circa 1910-1920. "R. Forgan" in block letters on long narrow head.

GOLD MEDAL SERIES IRONS $50   65   100
Circa 1920s. All irons with line-scored face.

DIAMOND BACK IRONS $55   70   110
Circa 1920s. Photo below.

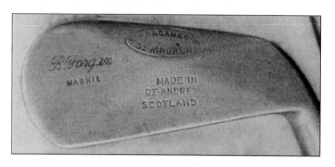

PLUME MARKED IRONS $100   150   300
Circa 1890-1900. Lofting iron marked "R. Forgan & Sons, St. Andrews."

PLUME MARKED IRONS $100   150   300
Circa 1890-1895. Long blade cleek marked "R. Forgan & Son, St. Andrews."

PLUME MARKED IRONS $225   350   700
Circa 1880-1890. Large head lofting iron marked "R. Forgan & Sons, St. Andrews."

PLUME MARKED IRONS $900   1500   3000
Circa 1880-1890. Rut iron with a small cupped head. "R. Forgan & Sons, St. Andrews" marks.

CROWN MARK IRONS $60   80   150
Circa 1901-1908. Cleek or driving iron with a smooth-face. Photo below.

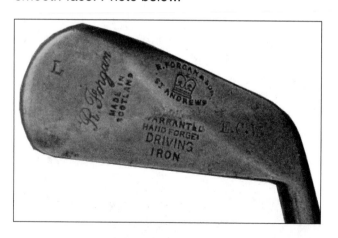

CROWN MARKED IRONS $75   100   150
Circa 1901-1908. Jigger marked "R. Forgan & Sons."

CROWN MARK IRONS $75   100   150
Circa 1901-1908. Diamond back and dot-punched "BALL" face.

CROWN MARKED IRONS $100   140   225
Circa 1901-1908. Driving mashie with a smooth-face marked "R. Forgan & Sons, St. Andrews."

CROWN MARKED IRONS $300   450   750
Circa 1901-1908. Niblick with a rounded head and smooth-face. "R. Forgan & Sons, St. Andrews" markings.

CELTIC SERIES IRONS $50   65   100
Circa 1920s. All irons with dot-punched face.

FLAG-IN-HOLE SERIES IRONS $50   65   100
Circa 1926-1930. All irons with dot or lined face. Photo below.

SELECTED SERIES IRONS $50   65   100
Circa 1920s. All irons with line-scored face.

BIG BALL SERIES IRONS $50   65   100
Circa 1930. All irons marked "Made especially for the big ball."

ROYAL SERIES IRONS $50   65   100
Circa 1930. All irons line-scored face.

SCOTIA SERIES IRONS $50   65   100
Circa 1920s. All irons with dot-punched face.

SMITH ANTI-SHANK IRONS $120   175   275
Circa 1915-1920. Dot-face. Cleek, mid-iron, mashie, mashie-niblick and niblick.

ANTI-SHANK IRONS $140   190   300
Circa 1900-1915. "Fairlie's Patent" cleek, mid-iron, mashie, mashie-niblick and niblick.

JUVENILE CLUBS $50   70   110
Circa 1926-30. Smooth-face. "Flag-in-Hole" mark.

LONG-NOSE WOODS $2000   4000   8000
Circa 1860-1880. Long-nose without "Plume" mark.

PLUME MARKED WOODS $500 1100 1900
Circa 1885-1895. Play club, brassie, spoon. Beech transitional pear-shaped head.

PLUME MARKED
LONG-NOSE WOODS $1500 2800 5250
Circa 1870-1890. Play club, brassie, spoon. Beech transitional pear-shaped head. Photo below.

PLUME MARKED WOODS $400 700 1450
Circa 1890-1900. Spliced-neck bulger face play club, brassie and spoon. Photo below.

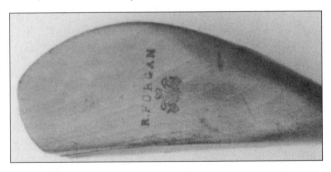

CROWN MARKED WOODS $100 140 250
Circa 1901-1908. Driver, brassie or spoon. "R. Forgan, St. Andrews" above "Crown" mark.

GOLD MEDAL SERIES WOODS $90 120 190
Circa 1920s. Driver, brassie or spoon marked "Forgan, St. Andrews Gold Medal" on persimmon head.

SCOTIA SERIES WOODS $90 120 190
Circa 1920. Driver, brassie or spoon. "R. Forgan & Son, St. Andrews" mark.

FORGANITE WOODS $100 175 290
Circa 1910-1915. Driver, brassie and spoon. "Forganite" in an elongated "Diamond." Forganite is a plastic-type material. No sole plate.

DREADNOUGHT WOODS $125 175 275
Circa 1920. Large head driver, brassie or spoon. "R. Forgan" in block letters. Black triangular face insert.

ANGLE-SHAFT WOOD $190 275 500
Circa 1905-1910. "Crown" mark, "Angle-Shaft Patent No. 10194" and "R. Forgan" markings. The shaft is oval shaped and "Angled" for strength.

FORRESTER, G.
EARLSFERRY, ELIE, SCOTLAND

George Forrester began making clubs in the late 1880s and continued through 1930. His mark was "Geo. Forrester, Elie, Earlsferry" in block letters.

BRASS-HEAD PUTTERS $80 120 175
Circa 1895-1900. Long face blade putter. "George Forrester, Earlsferry, Elie" circle mark.

CONCENTRIC BACK IRONS $100 135 225
Circa 1900. Smooth-face. Patent "No. 125240."

GENERAL PURPOSE IRON $150 200 350
Circa 1890. Smooth long face. "George Forrester, Earlsferry, Elie" circle mark.

ROUNDED FACE IRONS $175 250 400
Circa l895-1900. "Patent #53386" rounded back cleek or iron. The face is rounded from heel to toe, much like a "bulger" face wood.

SPLICED-NECK WOODS $175 250 375
Circa 1900-1910. Driver, brassie or spoon. Stamped "George Forrester, Elie, Earlsferry." Photo below.

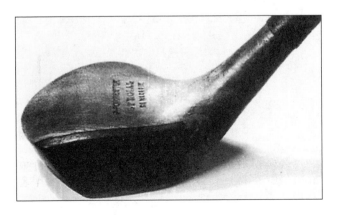

FOSTER BROTHERS
ASHBOURNE

The Foster Brothers produced clubs for only a short time after WWI. They used a human "Skeleton" swinging a club as their mark. They also made clubs bearing "The Bogee" stampings.

ALUMINUM BOGEE PUTTER $250   350   500
Circa 1920. "Registered No. 696416." Wide soled sloped back aluminum-head putter. Square hosel. Photo below.

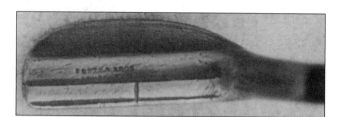

BOGEE IRONS $75   125   190
Circa 1915-1920. All irons. Dot-punched face. Their mark was a "Skeleton" swinging a club.

FOULIS, JAMES
WHEATON, IL

SMOOTH-FACE IRONS $150   220   300
Circa 1900. Iron or lofter. "J. & D. Foulis, Selected" mark.

SMOOTH-FACE CLEEK $175   250   350
Circa 1900. "J. & D. Foulis, Selected" mark.

FOULIS, JAMES, WHEATON, IL

By Pete Georgiady

On his first day attending St. Andrews University, Charles Blair MacDonald was taken to meet the Grand Old Man of Golf, Tom Morris. The Morris shop was one of Scotland's golfing headquarters. Situated close to the 18th green, it was a place where golfers gathered and stories were told by the game's early devotees. Spending time in the company of those golfers left its mark on the student. MacDonald and he knew exactly who to call when the club he formed, The Chicago Golf Club, required a pro—a real Scottish pro. Old Tom, himself, was entrusted to nominate a suitable candidate for the Chicago Golf position. Thus Tom went to his foreman James Foulis Sr., the father of five sons, each of whom played a highly respectable game, and encouraged him to send his best to America where golf missionaries were required.

But James Foulis Jr. was not the first choice for the position. Brother Robert was already a professional at the Ranfurly Golf Club, Bridge o' Weir, and the most experienced, but he turned down the opportunity. Instead of moving to Chicago, he chose to honor his one year contract and suggested that Jim take the job offer instead. Jim was, after all, the better golfer and he arrived in Wheaton, Illinois, in March 1895 ready to assume his responsibilities.

Strictly speaking, young Jim Foulis was not a golf professional in 1895. Foulis' occupation was a clubmaker in the Robert Forgan works, at the time, the world's largest clubmaking firm. The rules defining golf professionalism allowed him to compete as an amateur. A member of the famed St. Andrews Golf Club, he was a skilled competitor and at age 22 won the club's 1893 medal competition. Although not highly competitive, his family had been in the golfing world for many years. James' great-grandfather, a shepherd, had also mown the grass on the St. Andrews links during the time of George III. His father was employed in the Morris Club Works for more than thirty years.

With golf courses being created all across America, the need for more professionals and greenskeepers was quickly growing. Once in Chicago, Jim sent for younger brother David to be his assistant. Soon after that, Foulis wired home again and instructed Robert to join him immediately, "expenses paid!" Once Bob arrived, he was quickly put to work overseeing the final phases of construction at the Lake Forest Golf Club (the name would shortly be changed to Onwentsia) finishing the work Jim had begun that spring. He was appointed Lake Forest's first pro and stayed for another five years.

Jim played in the first U.S. Open at Newport in 1895, winning $50 for finishing third behind Horace Rawlins and Willie Dunn. The following year the Open was played at Shinnecock Hills and the train from Illinois carried two challengers from the American West, Jim Foulis and C. B. MacDonald.

PATENTED MASHIE-NIBLICK $175 250 375
Circa 1905. Concave smooth-face. Photo below.

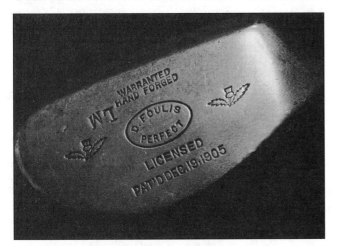

SOCKET WOODS $150 250 425
Circa 1905. Driver, brassie or spoon.

SPLICED-NECK WOODS $300 450 850
Circa 1905. Driver, brassie or spoon.

GASSIAT, JEAN

BIARRITZ, FRANCE

He made the famous "Grand Piano" style head putter, circa 1910, that today is called simply "The Gassiat." He used his name in script as his mark.

PIANO-SHAPED WOOD
PUTTER $500 750 1200
Circa 1910."Jean L Gassiat" and "Regd. No. 627732" on the broad wood head.

The '96 Open would be remembered for two important non-events outside the tournament. The threatened boycott of professional contestants opposed to the entry of two local Shinnecock caddies, John Shippen and Oscar Bunn fell apart two days before the championship. The other mix up occurred when Willie Park Jr., the odds-on favorite to clean the field, arrived a day after the tournament had ended, having missed his original steamship to New York.

In the early days of the U.S. Open only two 18-hole rounds were played, both on the same day. Jim Foulis shot a 78 in the morning round, leaving him in a six-way tie for the lead among the 33 contestants. In the afternoon, he deftly stroked a 74 to outdistance defending champ Horace Rawlins by three, setting an 18-hole record that was not broken until the advent of the rubber-wound ball. It is interesting to note that James Foulis Jr. stood only five feet five inches tall, but had a barrel chest, stout arms and legs, and enormous hands which gave him excellent club control.

One of the trademarks Jim Foulis applied to the game was the invention of the special Foulis patent mashie-niblick. The American game differed from Scottish golf in large part because of course design and native vegetation. Thick long grass around greens prohibited the traditional Scottish approach shot we now refer to as the "bump and run." A lofted shot, hopefully stopping dead, was required and to this end Foulis perfected a new club. It had a deeply concaved face with a blade rounded on top and very flat at the sole. It assumed the name of the "Foulis club" and every manufacturer on both sides of the Atlantic copied it after its introduction in 1904. Earlier, he had invented a club called the Octagon Niblick with its modified diamond-back design.

America was good to the Foulis family. In 1899, with three sons enjoying successes in American golf, James Sr. brought the remainder of the family—wife, daughter and two sons—to Chicago to live permanently. Robert subsequently moved to Minneapolis and, afterward, St. Louis, initially to Glen Echo and later became the first pro at Bellerive. David worked with Jim at Chicago Golf (clubs marked "J & D Foulis") and was made the club's professional after Jim moved to Calumet C. C. on Chicago's far south side in 1905. Later Jim received the appointment to the pro's post at Olympia Fields. The fourth brother John Foulis worked at Chicago Golf as a ball maker until his untimely death in 1907. The youngest brother, Simpson, remained an amateur throughout his career.

The life and career of James Foulis are interwoven with the very heart of early American golf history. He was the second national champion and had a close relationship with C. C. MacDonald, a founding father of the USGA, Chicago Golf and National Links clubs. He served as the first professional at America's first full 18 hole course and the first golf pro west of the Alleghenies. Foulis was an expert clubmaker and inventor, and with his brothers he had a hand in laying out more than 20 courses in the Chicago and St. Louis areas.

GIBSON, CHARLES

WESTWARD HO!

Charles Gibson began making clubs about 1890 and used the mark "Charles Gibson, Westward Ho!" in block lettering on his earliest clubs. About 1910 he adopted a "Rampant Stallion" mark and later the "Phoenix" bird mark.

RUSTLESS PUTTER $125 175 275
Circa 1925-1930. Long blade with "G-in-Star" mark. Corrugated sole.

RUT NIBLICK $200 300 550
Circa 1895-1900. Stamped "C. Gibson, Westward Ho!"

SOCKET WOODS $100 135 190
Circa 1910-1915. Driver, brassie or spoon. "C. Gibson, Westward Ho!" mark.

OFFSET BLADE PUTTER $75 100 150
Circa 1915-1920. Rampant Stallion mark. Photo below.

SOCKET-HEAD PUTTER $250 325 450
Circa 1915-1920. Persimmon mallet. Stamped "C. Gibson Special."

PHOENIX MARKED IRONS $50 70 100
Circa 1925. All irons. Line-scored face. "Phoenix" bird mark.

EXCELLAR IRONS $55 70 100
Circa 1920. All irons. "Phoenix" bird mark.

MAXWELL HOSEL IRONS $60 85 125
Circa 1915-1920. All irons. Flanged back. "Rampant Stallion" mark.

GENERAL PURPOSE IRON $125 190 325
Circa 1890. "C. Gibson" mark.

TRANSITIONAL BULGER
DRIVER $600 1150 2250
Circa 1885-1895. Beech-head stamped "C. Gibson." Photo below.

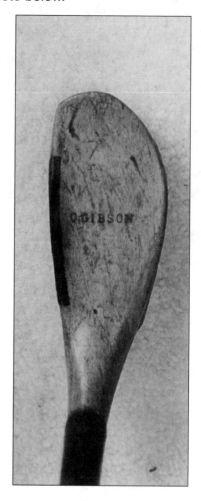

SOCKET WOODS $90 125 185
Circa 1900-1920. "C. Gibson" in block letters.

GIBSON, WILLIAM
KINGHORN, SCOTLAND

As one of the most prolific clubmakers during the wood-shaft era, Gibson began forging iron-head clubs in the mid-1890s in Edinburgh. Before the turn of the century, he relocated in Kinghorn on the northern shore of the Firth of Fourth. His maker's mark was a "Star" which varied in size and style during the nearly 50 years it was used.

He produced the first "flanged" back irons and the "Maxwell" drilled hosel irons in large quantities for a variety of clients who assembled clubs. He forged many patent clubs including the heel and toe weighted "Smith's Patent" anti-shank irons. Collecting only Gibson forged clubs would be a formidable task.

KINGHORN SERIES PUTTERS $55 90 150
Circa 1910. Emoried smooth-face straight blade.

BRAID SERIES PUTTERS $60 85 150
Circa 1915. Putting cleek.

STAR MAXWELL SERIES
PUTTER $50 65 100
Circa 1915. Blade putter, regular hosel.

STAR MAXWELL SERIES PUTTER $65 85 145
Circa 1915. Flanged back with Maxwell holes
drilled in hosel. Photo below.

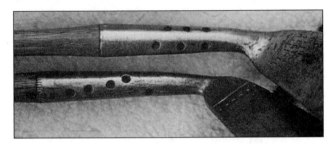

SAVILLE SERIES PUTTER $50 65 90
Circa 1930. Stainless steel blade putter.

FIFE GOLF CO. SERIES
PUTTERS $60 80 125
Circa 1930. Flanged back offset blade putter with
"Maxwell" holes drilled in the hosel.

ESKIT RUSTLESS PUTTER $50 65 90
Circa 1930-1935. Offset blade, dot-face. "G.
inside a Star" mark.

ORION PUTTER $125 190 350
Circa 1910-1920. Flanged back with flat hosel
and shaft.

GEM PUTTER $90 120 175
Circa 1920-1925. Stainless steel head.

BROWN-VARDON PUTTER $125 175 290
Circa 1910-1915. Crescent shaped steel head.
Oval hosel and shaft.

VARSITY PUTTER $125 200 325
Circa 1910. Crook in hosel. Bulge weight at toe.
Photo below.

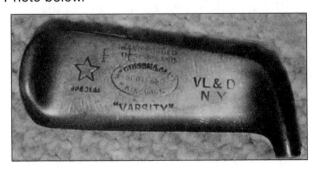

"G" IN CIRCLE MARKED
PUTTER $50 65 90
Circa 1930. Stainless blade. "Star" inside circle.
Photo below.

DOT-FACE GIBSON IRONS $50 60 85
Circa 1915-1920. 1 through 9 irons. Photo below.

AKROS MODEL IRONS $55 70 100
Circa 1915. All irons. Geo. Duncan signature.
Photo below.

BRAID SERIES IRONS $55 70 100
Circa 1915. James Braid signature mid-iron,
mashie, mashie-niblick, or niblick.

BRAID SERIES IRONS $55   75   120
Circa 1915. James Braid signature full or light irons. Photo below.

BRAID SERIES IRONS $140   175   250
Circa 1915. "James Braid Autographed Dreadnought" niblick.

GENII MODEL IRONS $50   60   100
Circa 1915-1920. Marked face irons with offset hosel.

GENII MODEL IRONS $60   75   125
Circa 1910. Smooth-face irons with offset hosel.

STAR MAXWELL IRONS $50   60   85
Circa 1915. Regular hosel.

STAR MAXWELL IRONS $60   80   125
Circa 1915. Maxwell holes drilled in hosel.

FIFE GOLF CO. SERIES IRONS $50   60   85
Circa 1925. Stainless steel head. All irons.

SAVILLE SERIES IRONS $50   60   85
Circa 1930. Stainless steel 1 through 9 irons.

STELLA SERIES IRONS $50   60   85
Circa 1925-1930. 1 through 9 irons.

KINGHORN SERIES IRONS $50   60   85
Circa 1930. "Star-in-Circle." All irons.

POWDER HORN SERIES $55   70   100
Circa 1925-1930. Stainless steel heads. 1 through 9 irons. Photo below.

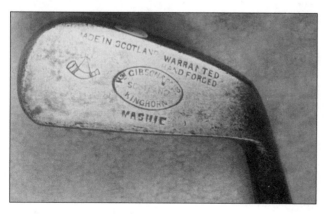

SUPERIOR SERIES IRONS $50   60   85
Circa 1925-1930. Stainless steel heads. 1 through 9 irons.

SUPERIOR SERIES IRONS $150   225   325
Circa 1925-1930. Anti-shank irons.

PIXIE SAMMY $75   90   125
Circa 1920. Line-scored face.

BAXPIN SERIES $120   170   235
Circa 1914-1922. Corrugated deep groove irons.

BAXPIN SERIES $125   180   250
Circa 1914-1922. Slot deep groove irons.

JERKO DEEP GROOVE IRONS $150   190   275
Circa 1920. Mashie, mashie-niblick or niblick.

ANTI-SHANK IRONS $150   190   275
Circa 1910. Fairlie style anti-shank irons. Various face scoring.

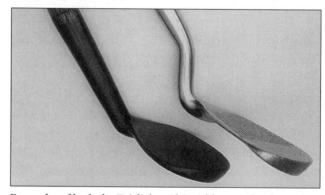

Examples of both the Fairlie's and Smith's anti-shank patent irons.

SKOOGEE SAND IRON $300   400   600
Circa late 1920s. Wide flat sole and deeply concave face.

RUT NIBLICK $450   650   1000
Circa 1895. Small rounded head. "Wm Gibson & Co, Kinghorn" in an oval with his "Star" mark inside.

GIANT NIBLICK $1400   1800   2500
Circa 1925. Big Ben Model.

GIBSON KINGHORN WOODS $90   110   170
Circa 1920s. Driver, brassie or spoon.

GOURLAY, JAMES
CARNOUSTIE, SCOTLAND

James Gourlay began forging clubs during the mid-1890s and continued into the Great Depression. He had a number of marks including an "Anchor," "Crescent and Star," "Crescent" and small circle, and a "Horseshoe"-type mark.

OFFSET BLADE PUTTER $50 60 90
Circa 1915-1920. "Crescent and Star" mark. Dot-punched face.

MUSSEL BACK PUTTER $60 75 110
Circa 1910-1915. Smooth-face. "Crescent and Star" mark.

DIAMOND BACK PUTTER $65 85 125
Circa 1905-1915. Smooth-face. "Crescent and Star" mark.

PARK STYLE PUTTER $95 125 190
Circa 1910. Severely bent neck. "Crescent and Star" mark.

BRASS-HEAD MALLET
PUTTERS $225 325 475
Circa 1915. Brass-head, steel face insert. "Crescent and Star" mark.

SWAN NECK PUTTER $400 600 900
Circa 1905-1910. P.A. Vaile Patent of 1905.

DIAMOND BACK IRONS $55 70 100
Circa 1905-1915. All irons. "Crescent and Star" mark. Photo below.

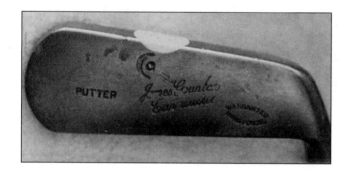

SMOOTH-FACE IRONS $60 80 125
Circa 1900-1910. Iron or lofter. "Crescent and Star" mark.

MAXWELL HOSEL IRONS $60 75 110
Circa 1910-1915. All irons. Smooth-face, flanged back. "Crescent and Star" mark.

SMOOTH-FACE CLEEK $65 85 135
Circa 1900-1910. "Crescent and Star" mark.

SAMMY IRON $70 90 135
Circa 1915. Dot-face. Rounded sole. "Crescent and Star" mark.

JUMBO NIBLICK $100 140 225
Circa 1925. Dot-punched face. Head size is 3-3/4 x 2-3/4 inches.

ANTI-SHANK IRONS $150 200 300
Circa 1905-1910. All irons. Fairlie's Patent. "Crescent and Star" mark.

RUT NIBLICK $175 275 450
Circa 1900-1910. Smooth-face. "Crescent and Star" mark.

PERFECT BALANCE IRONS $350 600 950
Circa 1910. All irons. "Lump" back weighting. "Patent No. 21307" and "R. Simpson, Carnoustie" at toe. "Crescent and Star" mark.

GRAY, JOHN
PRESTWICK, SCOTLAND

John Gray started as a blacksmith in Prestwick and began forging iron heads from about 1850 to the 1880s. He used at least two stampings to identify his clubs. "J. Gray," "Jn. Gray" and I've seen several simply marked "Gray." His clubs are very scarce and highly prized by collectors.

GENERAL PURPOSE IRON $850 1300 2800
Circa 1870-1885. Hooked face iron. Stamped "Jn Gray."

DISHED FACE LOFTER $900 1450 2950
Circa 1860-1875. Stamped "Gray."

SMOOTH-FACE CLEEK $950 1160 3500
Circa 1860-1880. Long blade, 5-inch hosel. Stamped "Jn Gray." Photo below.

RUT IRON $2000 3800 6500
Circa 1860-1880. Small cupped head. 5-inch hosel. Stamped "Jn Gray." Photo below.

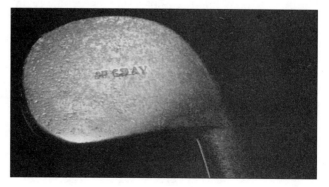

HACKBARTH, OTTO
CINCINNATI, OHIO

Circa 1920. Famous for manufacturing the bifurcated hosel putter commonly known as "The Hackbarth."

HACKBARTH PUTTER $400   650   950
Patented 1901. Bifurcated hosel. Photo below.

SPLICED-NECK CLEEK $175   250   500
Circa 1920. Wooden cleek marked "Otto Hackbarth."

HALLEY & CO., JAMES B
LONDON, ENGLAND

Halley & Co. began selling golf clubs about 1900, but did not make its own brands until much later. It had several marks: The "Pyramid" most often found on brass putters, a "Shell," "Circled 'H'" and a "Crossed Swords" mark.

SPECIAL PUTTER $55   75   100
Circa 1920. Offset hosel. "Crossed Swords" mark. Photo below.

RUSTLESS PUTTER $60   85   120
Circa 1925. Monel metal head. "Pyramid" mark.

BRASS-HEAD PUTTERS $60   80   120
Circa 1920s. "Pyramid" mark. Line-scored blade.

LINE-SCORED IRONS $50   65   85
Circa 1925-1930. All irons. "Crossed Swords" mark.

CONCENTRIC BACK IRONS $50   70   90
Circa 1915. All irons. Dot-punched face.

CIRCLE "H" MARKED IRONS $55   70   90
Circa 1920. All irons. "Diamond-dot" scoring.

MAXWELL HOSEL IRONS $60   85   120
Circa 1915. All irons. Circle "H" mark. Flanged back. Holes drilled in hosel.

DREADNOUGHT NIBLICK $75   110   160
Circa 1915-1920. Hyphen scored face. "Pyramid" mark.

PRETTY FACE WOODS $110   135   190
Circa 1920s. Ivorine pegs in circular configuration.

JUVENILE CLUBS $30   40   65
Circa 1920. Putter, iron, mashie or niblick. "Crossed Swords" mark.

JUVENILE CLUBS $75   100   150
Circa 1920. Juvenile wood. "Crossed Swords" mark.

HENDRY & BISHOP, LTD
EDINBURGH, SCOTLAND

Hendry & Bishop began producing clubs about 1910 and used the "Bishop's Hat" mark. They also made the "Cardinal" brand by which many of its clubs can be identified.

WRY-NECK PUTTER $50   70   100
Circa 1920s. Chromed head. "Bishop's Hat" mark.

THE SNIPER PUTTER $150   190   250
Circa 1920s. "Pencil" thin seven inch hosel. "Bishop's Hat" mark.

PER WIT PUTTER $500   750   1200
Circa 1920. "Patent No 247116." Hollowed out back and rounded face. The head gives the appearance of a pipe sawed lengthwise. "Bishop's Hat" mark. Photo below.

THE EAGLE PUTTER $55   70   100
Circa 1920s. "Bishop's Hat" mark. Photo below.

THE VIPER PUTTER $60   85   120
Circa 1920s. Long blade. "Bishop's Hat" mark.
Photo below.

CARDINAL SERIES IRONS $50   65   90
Circa 1925. All irons. Dot-punched face.

DEEP FACE MASHIE $50   65   100
Circa 1915. Dot-punched face. "Bishop's Hat"
mark.

LARGE-HEAD SPADE MASHIE $60   80   110
Circa 1915. Dot-punched face. "Bishop's Hat"
mark.

CONCENTRIC BACK IRONS $60   80   110
Circa 1915. All irons. "Mitre Brand" mark.

DREADNOUGHT NIBLICK $80   120   190
Circa 1920. Large head, dot-punched face.
"Bishop's Hat" mark.

PITCH-EM IRON $75   110   150
Circa 1915. Dot-punched face. "Bishop's Hat"
mark.

CARDINAL DREADNOUGHT
NIBLICK $100   170   250
Circa 1925. Head measures 3-1/2 x 2-5/8-
inches. "Bishop's Hat" mark.

DEEP GROOVE IRONS $100   175   275
Circa 1915-1922. All "Stopum" corrugated face
irons.

HIATT & CO.
BIRMINGHAM, ENGLAND

Made irons during the mid-1890s. They had at least
two marks, one "Hiatt's Mild Steel" in an oval configuration with very tiny lettering, and the other with slightly
larger lettering. Their irons are very scarce and desirable.

STEEL-HEAD PUTTERS $100   150   225
Circa 1895. Smooth-face blade. "Hiatt" stamped
on back.

BRASS-HEAD PUTTERS $125   175   275
Circa 1895. Smooth-face blade. "Hiatt" stamped
on back.

LOFTING IRON $120   160   275
Circa 1895. Smooth-face lofting iron. Marked
"Hiatt's Mild Steel." Photo below.

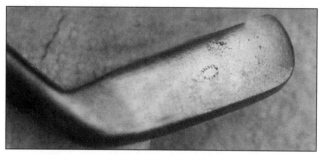

GENERAL PURPOSE IRON $125   175   300
Circa 1895. Stamped "Hiatt's Mild Steel."

SMOOTH-FACE CLEEK $150   200   325
Circa 1895. Long face. Stamped "Hiatt's Mild
Steel." Photo below.

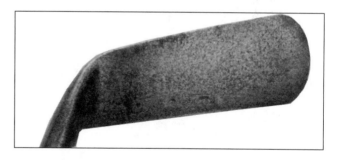

RUT NIBLICK $550   800   1350
Circa 1895. Small smooth-face head. Marked
"Hiatt's Mild Steel."

HILLERICH & BRADSBY
LOUISVILLE, KY

Began manufacturing clubs around 1915. Its early
"Invincible" series irons were smooth-faced. In 1918 it
patented a "Kork" grip for clubs. The "Deck of Cards,"
"Par-X-L" and "Lo-Skore" markings were the most
common on commercial quality clubs during the 1920s.

GRAND SLAM WOODS—Carnoustie Model

Steel shafts with black pyratone sheaths, red leather grips with aluminum tips.

No. 11/8—Driver. A Rakish English model with unusually long head. Natural finish with black band at point of contact. Special insert at point of striking with red bulls eye. Steel shafts only.............................$15.00
No. 12/8—Brassie to match.............15.00
No. 13/8—Spoon to match.............15.00

STANDARD MODEL

No. 11—Driver. The original Grand Slam model. Large head with medium lie. Medium deep and wide face provides large hitting surface. Ebony finish with natural band marking point of impact. Steel shaft, nickel plated.......$9.00
Hickory shaft...............................7.00

No. 12—Brassie to match. Steel shaft, nickel plated........$9.00
Hickory shaft...............................7.00

No. 13—Spoon to match. Steel shaft, nickel plated........$9.00
Hickory shaft...............................7.00

SPECIAL PUTTERS

No. 10P—Aluminum head with patented streamer line design. Runners on sole of club prevent lower edge from catching on grass and stopping stroke. Ebony finish with red arrow marking correct point of impact. Right hand only. Hickory shaft only. Price.........................$6.00

No. 10S—Aluminum head in hammer headed center shafted type. Ebony and nickle finish. Groove across head helps to line up club correctly. Steel shafts with satin nickle finish. No hickory shafts. Price.........................$7.50

INVINCIBLE GOLF CLUBS

For right or left hand players.

For those who wish serviceable clubs at a very moderate price, Invincible golf clubs offer a most satisfactory purchase. Second growth hickory shafts, leather grips. Standard, large size patterns with wide blades.

No. 51D—Driver............$2.00

No. 51B—Brassie............$2.00

No. 51D1—Driving Iron............$2.00

No. 51M1—Mid-iron............$2.00

No. 51M—Mashie............$2.00

No. 51MN—Mashie Niblick............$2.00

No. 51N—Niblick............$2.00

No. 51P—Putter............$2.00

GRAND SLAM IRONS

No. 6—PITCHING IRON
Full shot value 110 to 120 yards.
No. 6—Hickory shaft, chromium plated. $6.00
No. 6—Steel shaft, chromium plated.... $7.50
No. 6W—Ladies' right hand only, hickory shaft, chromium plated........ $6.00
No. 6X—Right hand only, stainless steel, hickory shaft......... $7.00

No. 8—TROUBLE IRON
Especially designed for bunker use. Can be used for fairway pitching shots 50 to 80 yards.
No. 8—Hickory shaft, chromium plated. $6.00
No. 8—Steel shaft, chromium plated.... $7.50
No. 8W—Ladies' right hand only, hickory shaft, chromium plated........ $6.00
No. 8X—Right hand only, stainless steel, hickory shaft......... $7.00

No. 10—PUTTER
No. 10—Hickory shaft, chromium plated. $6.00
No. 10—Steel shaft, chromium plated.... $7.50
No. 10W—Ladies' right hand only, hickory shaft, chromium plated........ $6.00
No.110X—Right hand only, stainless steel, hickory shaft......... $7.00

No. 5—PITCHING IRON
Full shot value 125 to 135 yards.
No. 5—Hickory shaft, chromium plated. $6.00
No. 5—Steel shaft, chromium plated.... $7.50
No. 5W—Ladies' right hand only, hickory shaft, chromium plated........ $6.00
No. 5X—Right hand only, stainless steel, hickory shaft......... $7.00

No. 7—PITCHING IRON
Full shot value 95 to 105 yards.
No. 7—Hickory shaft, chromium plated. $6.00
No. 7—Steel shaft, chromium plated.... $7.50
No. 7W—Ladies' right hand only, hickory shaft, chromium plated........ $6.00
No. 7X—Right hand only, stainless steel, hickory shaft......... $7.00

No. 9—CHIPPING IRON
For short run up approaches from just off the green.
No. 9—Hickory shaft, chromium plated. $6.00
No. 9—Steel shaft, chromium plated.... $7.50
No. 9W—Ladies' right hand only, hickory shaft, chromium plated........ $6.00
No. 9X—Right hand only, stainless steel, hickory shaft......... $7.00

GRAND SLAM IRON CLUBS

All standard Grand Slam irons are now chromium plated to resist rust and staining. While these clubs are not guaranteed to be rust proof, the chromium plating is the best protection yet devised for golf club heads.—Chromium plated heads should not be buffed. All that is necessary to keep them clean is to wipe them with a damp cloth. Do not permit them to be used on the wheel, since continued buffing will remove plating.

Hickory shafts in Grand Slam clubs are extra select. Steel shafts are the new true temper type. Grips are of calf skin with aluminum tip. Stainless steel heads can also be furnished us priced under each illustration.

No. 1—FAIRWAY IRON
Full shot value 185 to 195 yards for average good player. Lengths 38 to 39½ inches.
No. 1—Hickory shaft, chromium plated. $6.00
No. 1—Steel shaft, chromium plated.... $7.50
No. 1W—Ladies' right hand only, hickory shaft, chromium plated........ $6.00
No.1X—Right hand only, stainless steel heads, hickory shafts......... $7.00

No. 2—FAIRWAY IRON
Full shot value 170 to 180 yards for average good player. Lengths 37½ to 39 inches.
No. 2—Hickory shaft, chromium plated. $6.00
No. 2—Steel shaft, chromium plated.... $7.50
No. 2W—Ladies' right hand only, hickory shaft, chromium plated........ $6.00
No. 2X—Right hand only, stainless steel, hickory shaft......... $7.00

No. 3—FAIRWAY IRON
Full shot value 155 to 165 yards for average good player.
No. 3—Hickory shaft, chromium plated. $6.00
No. 3—Steel shaft, chromium plated.... $7.50
No. 3W—Ladies, right hand only, hickory shaft, chromium plated........ $6.00
No. 3X—Right hand only, stainless steel, hickory shaft......... $7.00

No. 4—FAIRWAY IRON
Full shot value 140 to 150 yards for average good player.
No. 4—Hickory shaft, chromium plated. $6.00
No. 4—Steel shaft, chromium plated.... $7.50
No. 4W—Ladies' right hand only, hickory shaft, chromium plated........ $6.00
No. 4X—Right hand only, stainless steel, hickory shaft......... $7.00

GRAND SLAM SERIES PUTTER $40   50   80
Circa 1920s. "Hand Holding Playing Cards" mark.
Photo below.

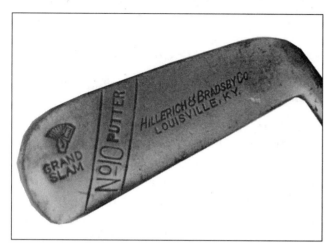

PAR-X-L SERIES IRONS $40   50   80
Circa 1920s. All irons. Photo below.

LO-SKORE SERIES PUTTER $40   50   80
Circa 1920s. Chrome plated head.

INVINCIBLE SERIES PUTTER $40   50   80
Circa 1925-1930. "Chromium" blade. Photo
below.

KERNEL SERIES IRONS $40   50   80
Circa 1920s. Flanged back. Photo below.

INVINCIBLE SERIES IRONS $45   70   100
Circa 1915. All irons. Dot "Ball" face. Photo
below.

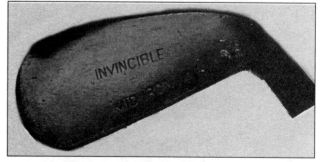

N-9 APPROACHING PUTTER $50   60   90
Circa 1920s. Lofted line-scored face.

ALUMINUM-HEAD PUTTER $80   110   170
Circa 1920s. "H & B Model H 50."

SCHENECTADY PUTTER $150   225   350
Circa 1920. Cork grip. "Par-X-L" mark.

GRAND SLAM SERIES IRONS $40   50   80
Circa 1920s. All irons 2 through 9. "Deck of
Cards" mark.

APPROACHING CLEEK $50   70   100
Circa 1915-1920. "Mussel" back. "Dot-Hyphen"
face scoring.

DIAMOND BACK IRONS $50   70   95
Circa 1920. "Stag-dot" face scoring. "Hand Made"
and "H & B Monogram" marks.

HAND MADE IRONS $50 70 95
Circa 1920. "Stag-dot" face scoring. "Hand Made" and "H & B Monogram" marks. Photo below.

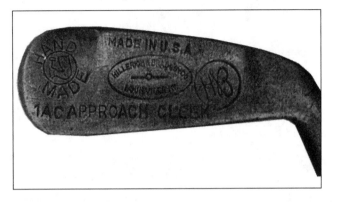

GRAND SLAM SERIES IRONS $55 70 95
Circa 1920s. #1 driving iron with the "Deck of Cards" mark.

INVINCIBLE SERIES IRONS $55 70 95
Circa 1915. All irons. Smooth-face.

CORK GRIP IRONS $60 80 120
Circa 1915. All irons. Patented 1914. "Hand Made" in circle mark.

DEEP GROOVE IRONS $90 150 225
Circa 1915-1922. All irons with corrugated face. Marked "Baxpin."

DEEP GROOVE IRONS $100 175 250
Circa 1915-1922. All irons with slot grooves.

DEEP GROOVE IRONS $125 175 250
Circa 1920. All Everbrite Monel metal slot groove.

SLOTTED HOSEL JIGGER $145 190 275
Circa 1920s. "S-C2 Jigger." Stag-dot-face scoring. "Hand Made" mark.

LO-SKORE SERIES IRONS $40 50 80
Circa 1920. All irons. Photo below.

INVINCIBLE SERIES WOODS $75 110 150
Circa 1920. Driver, brassie or spoon.

LO-SKORE SERIES WOODS $80 110 150
Circa 1920s. Driver, brassie or spoon.

PAR-X-L SERIES WOODS $85 110 150
Circa 1920s. Driver, brassie or spoon.

JUVENILE CLUBS $30 40 65
Circa 1920. Putter, Mid-iron or mashie.

JUVENILE CLUBS $60 80 120
Circa 1920. Juvenile wood.

HORTON, WAVERLEY
CHICAGO, IL

Clubmaker from Chicago whose major claim to fame was the patented "Wonder Club," with a metal-cased wooden head, made in 1920.

WONDER CLUB $400 700 1000
Circa 1920. Patented aluminum shell, wood face.

HUNT MFG. CO.
WESTBORO, MA

A turn-of-the-century manufacturer of rustless clubs. The clubs were made with a nickel alloy and had a greenish coloring. "Hunt" in script was their mark. All Hunt-marked clubs are highly desirable to collectors.

NON-RUSTABLE BLADE
PUTTER $150 200 300
Circa 1895-1900. Smooth-face blade. Photo below.

NON-RUSTABLE IRONS $100 150 250
Circa 1895-1900. All irons. Smooth-face.

HUNTER, CHARLES
PRESTWICK

Professional and clubmaker at Prestwick from 1868 to 1921. His clubs were marked "C. Hunter."

OFFSET BLADE PUTTER $60   75   110
Circa 1915-1920. Hyphen-scored face. Stamped "C & J Hunter, Prestwick."

DOT-FACE BLADE PUTTER $65   75   110
Circa 1910-1915. Offset hosel. Stamped "C & J Hunter, Prestwick."

LONG-NOSE PUTTERS $950   1600   2400
Circa 1885-1895. Transitional beech-head. Marked "C Hunter."

LONG-NOSE PUTTERS $1350   2450   4000
Circa 1870-1880. Beech-head shallow-face putter. Stamped "C. Hunter."

IMPERIAL GOLF
SUNDERLAND, ENGLAND

Made aluminum-head putters and fairway clubs similar to Mill's Standard Golf Co. Most of its clubs were cast during the late teens and early 1920s.

U MODEL $125   160   250
Circa 1910-1920. Aluminum mallet.

RM MODEL $150   200   275
Circa 1910-1920. Aluminum mallet.

THE VERDEN $175   225   350
Circa 1910-1920. Rounded-dome aluminum mallet.

XXX PUTTER $200   250   350
Circa 1915-1920. Long aluminum mallet. "Ivorine" sight line.

ALUMINUM-HEAD WOODS $125   200   350
Circa 1915-1920. All lofts. Marked "Imperial Golf Co., Sunderland, England."

ALUMINUM-HEAD NIBLICK $375   600   1000
Circa 1915-1920. Marked "Imperial Golf Co, Sunderland, England." Photo below.

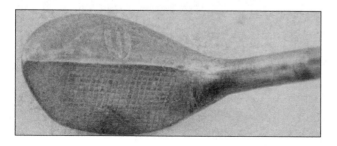

JOHNSON, FRANK A.
LONDON, ENGLAND

Used a skeleton "Key" as his mark. Made irons from about 1900 through the early teens.

PREMIER SPECIAL PUTTER $65   90   150
Circa 1910. Line-scored blade. "Key" mark.

SMOOTH-FACE IRONS $60   80   135
Circa 1900-1910. All irons. "Key" mark.

DOT-FACE NIBLICK $75   100   150
Circa 1910. "Key" mark. Photo below.

SMOOTH-FACE NIBLICK $125   175   275
Circa 1900-1910. Medium-size head. "Key" mark.

KROYDON
NEWARK, NJ

Began making clubs after WWI. The ball-face and the brick-face designs are popular collector clubs. The "Banner" series with the degree of loft on the face is also highly collectible although not expensive.

SHALLOW-FACE PUTTER $55   65   90
Circa 1920. Long blade, offset hosel. "Diamond-Dash" face scoring.

BALL-FACE PUTTER $65   80   125
Circa 1920s. "S-7" ball-face.

ALUMINUM MALLET PUTTERS $85   110   160
Circa 1920s. "Kroydon S 31 B Putter."

SCHENECTADY STYLE
ALUMINUM $100   150   250
Circa 1920s Model S-32-A

PENDULUM PUTTER $350   500   750
Circa 1920s. Center shafted. Hatched face scoring. Photo below.

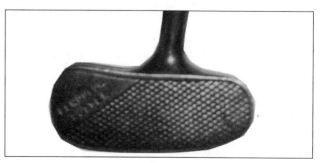

HEAT-TREATED IRONS $35   45   80
Circa 1920s. All irons.

ROYAL SERIES IRONS $35   45   80
Circa 1920s. All irons. Widely spaced line face scoring. Photo below.

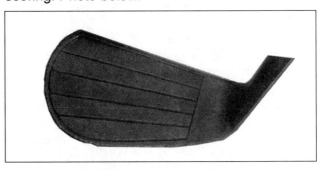

BALL-FACE IRONS $50   70   100
Circa 1920s. All irons. Photo below.

BANNER IRONS $45   65   90
Circa 1920s. All irons. Name and loft of iron at toe of blade. Photo below.

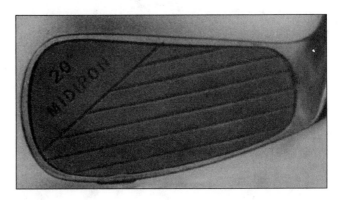

P SERIES IRONS $55   70   100
Circa 1925-1930. All irons. Alternating "Dashes" and tiny "Diamonds" face scoring.

WAFFLE-FACE IRON $85   130   190
Circa 1920s. About 400 tiny waffles on face.
Photo below.

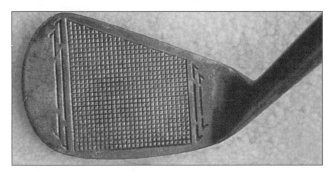

VERTICALLY-SCORED
NIBLICK $225   300   425
Circa 1920s. "R 2, 50 Degree Niblick" with verti-
cal deep groove face scoring. Photo below.

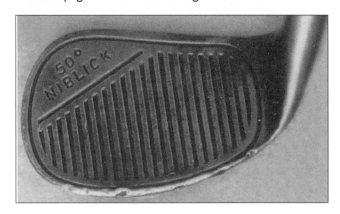

BRICK-FACE IRONS $375   500   725
Circa 1920. All irons. Photo below.

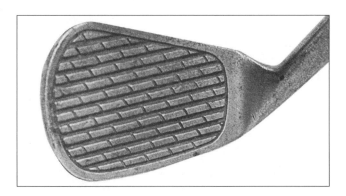

SOCKET WOODS $80   110   150
Circa 1920. All woods. Many have aluminum
back weights.

KROYDONITE SOCKET
WOODS $80   110   150
Circa 1920. Driver, brassie or spoon.

LEE, HARRY C.
NEW YORK, NY

Sporting goods retail business that began about
1900. Famous for marketing the "Schenectady" putter.
Most domestic clubs were made by Burke and marked
with the "Lee" stampings. Lee also imported clubs
from more than a dozen Scottish and English makers
including Jack White, Nicholl, Standard Mills, Spence,
and Hendry & Bishop.

DEXTER PUTTER $45   55   80
Circa 1920s. Offset blade. "Acorn" mark.

DOT-FACE BLADE PUTTER $45   55   80
Circa 1915. "Acorn" mark.

LINE-FACE BLADE PUTTER $45   55   80
Circa 1920-1925. "Acorn" mark.

SCHENECTADY PUTTER $175   325   550
Circa 1903-1915. Patent date "Mar. 24, 1903" on
back. Photo below.

CONCENTRIC BACK IRONS $45   55   80
Circa 1915. "Harry C Lee Co." mark. Photo
below.

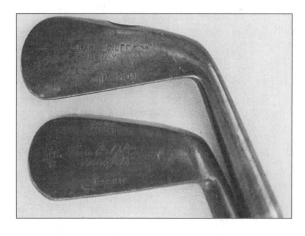

DOT-FACE NIBLICK $50   60   90
Circa 1915-1920. "Acorn" mark.

BALL-FACE IRONS $60   80   120
Circa 1910-1915. All irons. Dot ball-face scoring.
"Acorn" mark.

HAND MADE SERIES WOODS $80   110   150
Circa 1920-1925. Driver, brassie or spoon.

LEYLAND & BIRMINGHAM RUBBER CO.
Made many "Rustless" clubs during the late 1920s.

BRASS-HEAD PUTTERS $60 70 100
Circa 1925-30. Stamped "L L M B" inside a "Triangle."

MUSSEL BACK PUTTER $55 65 100
Circa 1930. "Rustless Putter."

MUSSEL BACK IRONS $50 60 100
Circa late 1920s. Rustless irons.

STAINLESS STEEL IRONS $50 60 90
Circa 1925-1930. "Goudie Bear" mark. Dot-punched face.

STAINLESS STEEL IRONS $50 60 90
Circa 1925-1930. "Leyland" mark. Dot-punched face. Photo below.

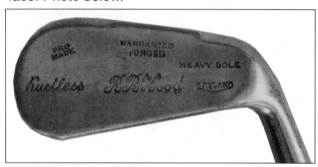

LOCKWOOD & BROWN
LONDON, ENGLAND

Although Lockwood & Brown did not forge its own clubs, it assembled and marked many heads with "Lockwood & Brown, London" in block letters and a monogrammed "LB" mark. It sold clubs from about 1920 through the early 1930s.

SPLICED-NECK PUTTER $500 650 900
Circa 1910. Persimmon head "Gassiat" style with the back squared off. Stamped "Lockwood & Brown, Lt'd., 2 Jermyn St S."

GIANT NIBLICK $1200 1800 2400
Circa 1920s. Rustless giant head. Stamped "Lockwood & Brown, Lt'd., 2 Jermyn St S."

SPLICED-NECK WOODS $150 225 350
Circa 1910-1920. Driver, brassie or spoon.

BULL DOG WOOD $100 135 190
Circa 1910. Well lofted wood with "Triangular" black face.

LOGAN, HUGH
Logan was a club designer credited with the famous "Cherokee" aluminum-head putter and the "Genii" model series made by William Gibson.

CHEROKEE PUTTER $250 375 550
Circa 1915. Round aluminum head marked "H Logan's, Cherokee," "T" sight line. Photo below.

MacGREGOR
DAYTON, OH

Crawford, MacGregor and Canby began making golf clubs shortly after 1895. Initially they made wood heads until the 1900s when Willie Dunn was hired to design clubs, including irons and putters. MacGregor's first iron-head clubs carried a mark similar to a bow tie with the monogram "W. D." Shortly after Dunn's departure, "J. MacGregor, Dayton, O." was the mark used along with a Condie-type flower mark. About 1910 "Par," "Peerless," and an economy line "Edgemont" were introduced. During the teens, "Superior," "Perfection," "Pilot," and "Bakspin" clubs were offered. During the late 1920s, "Duralite," "Superior" and "Nokorode" irons were the top-of-the-line clubs with "Popular," "Edgemont" and "Go-Sum" being the economy brands. Other marks were "Airway-o," "Bap," "Claymore," "Paragon," "Premier," "Pro iron," "Rob Roy," "Tomahawk," "Sink-it," "Down-it," and "Worldwin."

DUNN BOW TIE MARK
PUTTER $150 220 375
Circa 1900. Smooth-face.

DOUBLE CIRCLE MARK
PUTTER $100 150 250
Circa 1900. Smooth-face with "J MacGregor, Dayton, O" around a "Double Circle" mark with a shamrock inside.

J MACGREGOR SERIES PUTTER $55 80 140
Circa 1900-1905. Smooth-face putting cleek.

EDGEMONT SERIES PUTTERS $50 70 100
Circa 1910-1915. Blade putter with a "Diamond" marked face.

"O A" SERIES PUTTER $55 70 120
Circa 1915. With a flanged back.

POPULAR SERIES PUTTER $40 50 90
Circa 1915. "10X" with a hyphen-scored face.

GO-SUM SERIES PUTTERS $40 50 90
Circa 1915-1920. Blade putter.

PILOT SERIES PUTTERS $40 50 90
Circa 1915. Blade putter.

SUPERIOR SERIES PUTTERS $40 50 90
Circa 1915-1920. Offset blade putter.

ROB-ROY SERIES PUTTER $40 50 90
Circa 1920s. Mussel-back design. Photo below.

PERFECTION SERIES PUTTERS $45 55 90
Circa 1915. Offset blade putter.

RADITE SERIES PUTTER $50 60 100
Circa 1920. Offset blade.

DURALITE SERIES PUTTERS $45 55 90
Circa 1928-1930. Blade putter with the line and "Pyramid" dot-face.

CLIMAX-FIFE SERIES PUTTERS $55 65 90
Circa 1915-1920. Dot-face straight blade.

BRASS-FLANGED PUTTERS $65 80 140
Circa 1915. Flanged-back brass putter marked "60" or "90."

ALUMINUM-HEAD PUTTERS $80 120 190
Circa 1920s. "MacGregor, Dayton, 0." Photo below.

SEMI-PUTTER $90 120 175
Circa 1920. Anti-shank type offset hosel. Photo below.

J MACGREGOR SERIES
PUTTERS $175 250 400
Circa 1900. Willie Park style severely bent neck smooth-face blade.

SCHENECTADY PUTTER $140 200 300
Circa 1915. With "J MacGregor" markings.

"R A" PUTTER $225 350 550
Circa 1920. "Right Angle" putter. Persimmon head mallet with a black vulcanite T-shaped "sight line." Photo below.

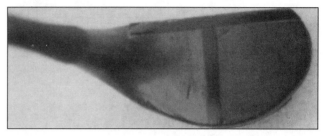

DOWN-IT 486 PUTTER $225 400 625
Circa 1915-1920. Wooden-head mallet putter. Brass face plate with hatched scoring.

WORLD WIN PUTTER $250 400 625
Circa 1920. Persimmon wood head, center shafted "Schenectady"-style putter. "Ivorine" sight line on head.

IVORA PUTTER $250 350 550
Circa 1915-1919. Brass-head with "Ivorine" face insert. Face marked similar to a sun with rays. Photo below.

DUNN BOW-TIE MARK
IRONS $150 200 350
Circa 1900. smooth-face cleek, iron and lofter.

DUNN BOW-TIE MARK
IRONS $350 475 900
Circa 1900. Rut niblick.

DOUBLE CIRCLE MARK IRONS $95 140 250
Circa 1900. Smooth-face with "J MacGregor, Dayton, 0" around a "Double Circle" mark with a shamrock inside.

RUT NIBLICK $325 475 850
Circa 1900-1905. Round concave face.

J MACGREGOR SERIES IRONS $50   75   110
Circa 1900-1905. Cleek with normal shafting. Photo below.

J MACGREGOR SERIES IRONS $70   100   190
Circa 1900-1905. Cleek with "Carruthers" through-hosel shafting.

J MACGREGOR SERIES IRONS $60   80   150
Circa 1900-1905. Smooth-face iron or lofter.

EDGEMONT SERIES IRONS $60   80   140
Circa 1910-1915. "Diamond" face. Photo below.

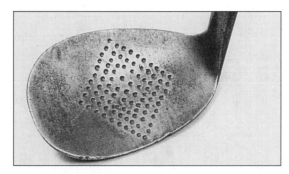

"O A" SERIES IRONS $55   70   120
Circa 1915. Flanged back.

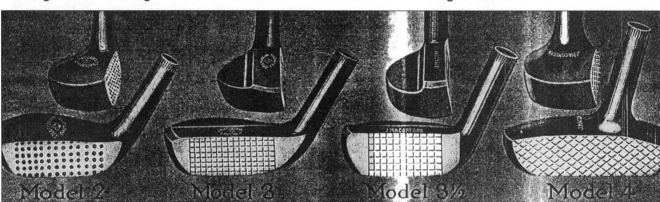

Model 2   Model 3   Model 3½   Model 4

Study your putting

You know—as does every Golfer—that more games are won on the greens than anywhere else.

The man who can putt **always** has his opponent worried. Can **you** putt?

Study your putting—and your putter. Get all there is out of the club—for the club has a lot to do with it. Does your putter fit you? Does it **feel** right? Are you comfortable and natural using it? We call your attention to the

1919

PEERLESS SERIES IRONS $40   50   80
Circa 1925-1930. Stainless steel heads.

GO-SUM SERIES IRONS $40   50   80
Circa 1915-1925. Hyphen and line-scored faces.

PILOT SERIES IRONS $40   50   80
Circa 1912-1920. Various face markings.

CLIMAX-FIFE SERIES IRONS $45   55   90
Circa 1915-1920. "Crown" mark. All irons.

TOMAHAWK BRAND IRONS $100   150   250
Circa 1920. "Shield" marked face. Photo below.

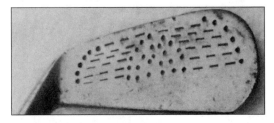

RADITE SERIES IRONS $45   60   90
Circa 1920-1925. A rustless metal head with line-scored face.

RADITE SERIES IRONS $100   150   250
Circa 1915-1920. Bakspin mashie, mashie-niblick and niblick.

SUPERIOR SERIES IRONS $40   50   80
Circa 1915-1920. Various face scoring.

SUPERIOR SERIES IRONS $100   140   225
Circa 1918-1920. Slotted hosel patented 1918. Photo below.

POPULAR SERIES IRONS $40   50   80
Circa 1915. Dot scored face. All irons.

POPULAR SERIES IRONS $40   50   80
Circa 1915. Mussel back irons. Photo below.

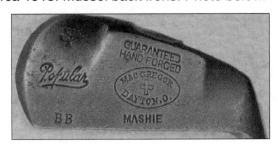

POPULAR SERIES IRONS $70   85   125
Circa 1915. "Popular C 1/2 Sammy Jigger."

POPULAR SERIES IRONS $55   65   90
Circa 1915. Photo below.

"G" SERIES IRONS $75   120   175
Circa 1915-1920., "J. MacGregor" stamp "G" with a weighted toe bulge similar to the "Smith" patented anti-shank irons. Photo below.

PERFECTION SERIES IRONS $65   85   125
Circa 1915-1920. "B-4 Perfection Mashie" with wrap around "Maxwell" holes drilled in the hosel.

DURALITE SERIES IRONS $40   50   80
Circa 1928-1930. Stainless steel heads with Pyramid dots over line scoring. 1 through 6 and 9 niblick.

DURALITE SERIES IRONS $50   80   120
Circa 1928-1930. #7 Pitcher.

DURALITE SERIES IRONS $125   150   250
Circa 1928-1930. #8 Jigger.

AIRWAY-O IRONS $80   100   150
Circa 1925. Concave face, "Goal Post" scoring.

BAKSPIN SERIES IRONS $110   150   250
Circa 1915-1920. Slot deep groove.

BAKSPIN SERIES IRONS $175   250   375
Circa 1915-1920. Large dot scoring on only half the face.

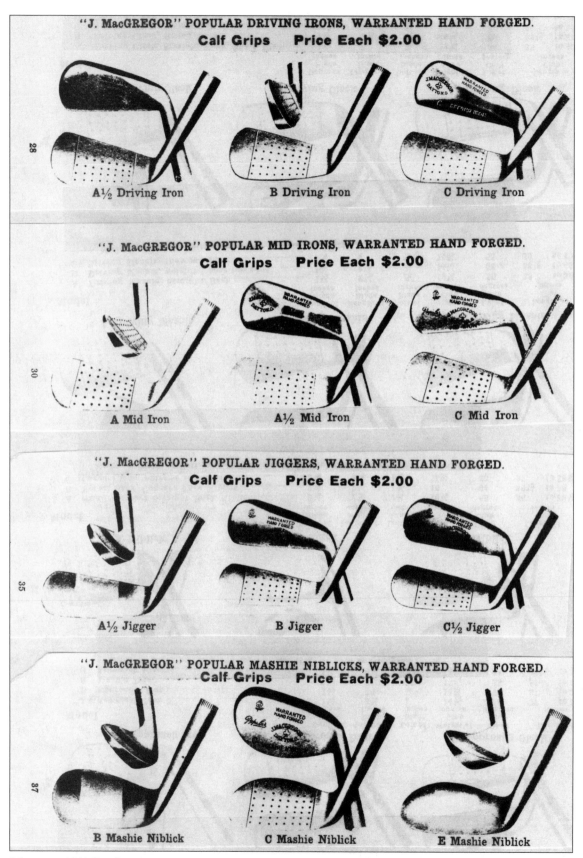

Macgregor 1913 Catalogue.

BAKSPIN SERIES IRONS $175   250   375
Circa 1915-1920. "Ribangle" face. Corrugated deep grooves with lines at an angle over deep grooves. Photo below.

PRETTY FACE WOODS $100   145   220
Circa 1920s. Small "Ivorine" inserts set around one large center insert.

SPLICED-NECK WOODS $200   325   575
Circa 1898-1905. Bulger driver with "J MacGregor, Dayton, 0" on the persimmon head.

"BAP" SERIES WOODS $85   110   175
Circa 1920s. Driver, brassie or spoon. Patented 1923.

WORLD WIN SERIES WOODS $85   110   175
Circa 1920s. Driver, brassie or spoon.

YARDSMORE SERIES WOODS $100   145   120
Circa 1925. Driver, brassie or spoon with a black face having one large round insert and four small inserts.

GO-SUM SERIES WOODS $80   110   170
Circa 1920s. Plain face.

DREADNOUGHT WOODS $95   120   180
Circa 1920s. Oversized heads. Driver, brassie or spoon.

GO-SUM SERIES WOODS $100   135   190
Circa 1920s with pretty face design.

BULL DOG WOODS $100   135   190
Circa 1915-1920. Rounded sole. Marked "MacGregor, Dayton, 0" and a black face insert.

EDGEMONT SERIES WOODS $100 135 195
Circa 1910-1915. Persimmon head driver, brassie or spoon.

ALUMINUM-HEAD WOODS $150 225 390
Circa 1915-1925. Various lofts.

SAMPSON FIBER FACE
WOODS $160 200 300
Circa 1915-1920. Driver or brassie.

ONE-PIECE WOOD $1500 2000 3200
Circa 1900. Driver or brassie one-piece hickory head and shaft. Has a leather face insert.

JUVENILECLUBS $35 45 80
Circa 1915. Edgemont putter, mid-iron or mashie.

JUVENILE CLUBS $70 100 175
Circa 1915. Edgemont driver.

McEWAN
MUSSELBURGH, SCOTLAND

The "McEwan" name was associated with clubmaking from about 1770 through WWII. The earliest marks were simply "McEwan" and a "Thistle." Subsequent family members used either "McEwan" alone or with their first initial. Clubs made by Douglas II from about 1895 were marked "D. McEwan & Sons" and are the most obtainable in today's marketplace.

BRASS-HEAD PUTTERS $150 250 375
Circa 1880-1890. "McEwan" in block letters. "Double Ringed" hosel knurling.

IRON-HEAD PUTTER $150 225 350
Circa 1890-1895. Straight blade. McEwan, Musselburgh mark.

BRASS-HEAD PUTTER $175 225 400
Circa 1890-1895. Straight blade. McEwan, Musselburgh mark.

LONG-NOSE PUTTERS $850 1500 2750
Circa 1885-1895. Transitional head style. "McEwan" mark.

LONG-NOSE PUTTERS $1400 2500 4000
Circa 1870-1880. Long head, large lead back weight. "McEwan" mark.

LONG-NOSE PUTTERS $1900 3500 6500
Circa Pre-1860 with Thorn head. Long head, large lead back weight. "McEwan" mark.

SOCKET WOODS $100 135 190
Circa 1905-1915. Persimmon head driver, brassie or spoon.

SPLICED-NECK WOODS $425 700 1450
Circa 1890-1900. Play club, brassie or spoon. Bulger face. Many have leather face inserts. Transitional head style. "McEwan" mark. Photo below.

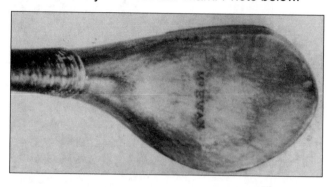

LONG-NOSE WOODS $1600 2950 5500
Circa 1870-1880. Play club or brassie. Long head, large lead back weight. "McEwan" mark. Photo below.

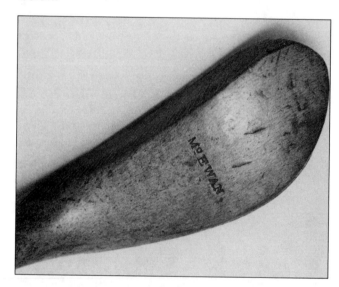

LONG-NOSE WOODS $2200 4250 8500
Circa Pre-1860 with Thorn head. Play club or brassie. Long head, large lead back weight. "McEwan" mark.

MILLAR, CHARLES
GLASGOW, SCOTLAND

Charles Millar began forging irons about 1895. He used several types of "Thistle Brand" marks to identify his clubs. He also marked his clubs "Glasgow Golf Co." and "Thistle Golf Co."

OFFSET BLADE PUTTER $55 70 110
Circa 1915. "Thistle Brand" and "The Glasgow Golf Company" marks.

SMOOTH-FACE BLADE $60 75 120
Circa 1900-1910. "Thistle" mark.

PUTTING CLEEK $60 75 120
Circa 1900-1910. Smooth-face blade. "Thistle" mark.

PREMIER BRAND PUTTERS $90 110 150
Circa 1920s. Brass-blade.

APPROACHING PUTTER $120 150 200
Circa 1915. Vertical line face scoring. "Thistle" mark.

RUSTLESS IRONS $50 60 85
Circa 1930-1935. All irons. Dot-punched face.

PREMIER BRAND IRONS $55 65 90
Circa 1915. Dot-punched face. "Thistle" mark. Photo below.

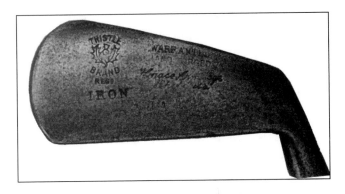

SMOOTH-FACE IRONS $60 80 120
Circa 1900-1910. All irons. "Thistle-In-Circle" mark.

SMOOTH-FACE IRONS $75 100 160
Circa 1895-1900. Cleek, iron or lofter. "C L Millar, Glasgow" mark.

D & T SPINNER $200 275 375
Circa 1915. All irons. "Patent #683488." Concave face, dot scoring on bottom.

MORRIS, TOM
ST. ANDREWS, SCOTLAND

Began making clubs in the early 1850s at Prestwick. He opened a shop in St. Andrews in 1864 across the street from the 18th hole and remained there until his death in 1908. The company continued to sell clubs until the Great Depression. His marks were "T. Morris" and "T. Morris, St. Andrews, NB" in oval. After his death "Tom Morris" in script and Old Tom's portrait were used. He purchased many iron heads from Tom Stewart and Robert Condie and added his marks on them. Many of his clubs can be found with shafts marked with "T. Morris, St. Andrews, N.B." The "N.B." was for North Britain.

IRON-HEAD PUTTER $190 300 550
Circa 1890-1900. Smooth-face usually made by Condie or Stewart.

SPLICED-NECK PUTTERS $400 650 1250
Circa 1905-1920. Long narrow head. Persimmon head.

LONG-NOSE PUTTERS $1100 2000 3650
Circa 1885-1900. Beech-head stamped "T Morris." Transitional head shape. Photo below.

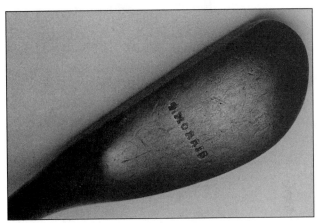

LONG-NOSE PUTTERS $1500 2900 5000
Circa 1860-1880. Beech-head stamped "T Morris." Long head with large lead back weight.

MORRIS MODEL IRONS $100 150 200
Circa 1915. All irons. Dot-punched face.

PORTRAIT IRONS $90 125 175
Circa 1920s. All irons. Morris' portrait stamped at toe. Most have line-scored face. Photo below.

SMOOTH-FACE IRONS $190 325 650
Circa 1890-1905. Cleek, iron or lofter. "T Morris, St. Andrews" with Condie's "Flower" or Stewart's "Pipe" marks.

RUT NIBLICK $325 600 1150
Circa 1890-1905. Smooth-face, round head. "T Morris, St. Andrews" and Condie's "Flower" or Stewart's "Pipe" marks.

SMOOTH-FACE IRONS $300   500   975
Circa 1880-1890. Cleek or General Purpose iron. "T Morris, St. Andrews" mark.

RUT IRON $1400   2500   4500
Circa 1880. Small round head. "T Morris, St. Andrews" mark. Photo below.

AUTOGRAPH SERIES WOODS $125   175   275
Circa 1915-1925. Driver, brassie or spoon. Two-tone head with "Tom Morris" in script.

SPLICED-NECK WOODS $275   450   750
Circa 1895-1910. Driver, brassie or spoon. Persimmon head stamped "T Morris."

LONG-NOSE WOODS $1750   3500   7500
Circa 1885-1900. Play club, brassie or spoon. Beech-head stamped "T Morris." Transitional head shape. Photo below.

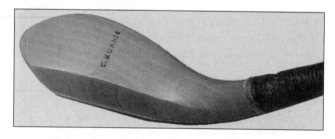

LONG-NOSE WOODS $2750   4500   9250
Circa 1860-1880. Play club, brassie or spoon. Beech or Thorn head stamped "T Morris." Long head with large lead back weight. Photo below.

NICOLL, GEORGE
LEVEN, SCOTLAND

A Partial Chronology of Nicoll Club Models

This list is not exhaustive; as soon as one claims to have seen all of the models, another new variety appears. (club model names in bold)

1881-1890: Large smooth-faced irons and putters with the circular mark and no hand.

1890-1905: Oval mark until 1898, then small crude hand. Patent leather face, Patent gutta face, smaller smooth-faced irons, Patent bent neck putter, irons for the Forth Rubber Company, Tait Cleek.

1905-1919: The black, smooth leather grip becomes standard **Zenith, Clinker, Excelsior, Trusty Putter, Nap, Gem** putter.

Early 1920s: **Stop-um, Viking, Park's Original Bent Neck** putter, **Cracker Jack, Able, Sure, Braid, Whippett, Recorder, Indicator, Sans Souci, Precision.**

Late 1920s, early 1930s: **Wizard Akurazy, Macdonald Smith, Plaklub, The Gray, Bigshooter, Big Ball, Compactum Blade, Roger Hill.**

1st Nicoll mark, 1880s-1890s.

2nd Nicoll mark, 1890s-1898.

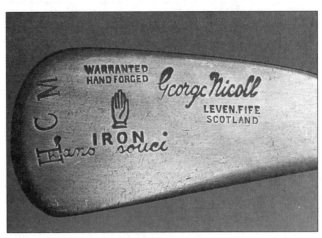

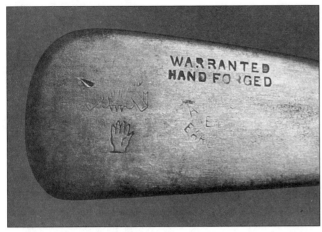

3rd Nicoll mark, 1st hand, 1898-1905. Scott Plume, 1902-1908.

5th Nicoll mark, 1910-1920.

4th Nicoll mark, 1900-1915. v.1.

6th Nicoll mark (or variation of 5th) 1910-1020.

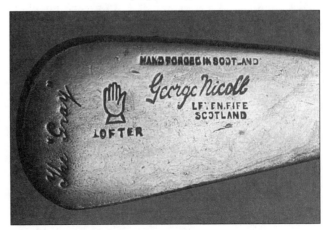

4th Nicoll mark, 1900-1915. v.2.

7th Nicoll mark, 1910-1920.

Nicoll 'O' Leven

By Roger Hill

Most collectors of antique golf clubs have probably come across an old club bearing the friendly upturned hand that is the cleek mark identifying a George Nicoll club. However, beyond initial identification, the collector has little to go on because much of the history of the George Nicoll Company of Leven, Fife, Scotland remains a mystery.

Beginning in the 1920s, Nicoll clubs became popular in the U.S., with both professionals and amateurs. In this market, Nicoll sold clubs directly to professionals and golf retailers. In addition, Nicoll iron heads were shafted and sold widely by the Burke Company of Ohio, as well as by the Link-Lyon company of Nashville, Tennessee. Most of these import clubs can be identified by the hand mark in the horizontal position on the back of the club, although there are exceptions. Many Nicoll clubs, mostly dating from the 1920s, are available to collectors in the U.S. today. When considering a Nicoll club made before the "Golden Age," the ambitious collector should be aware of what is known about this successful club maker's history.

The story of "Nicoll 'O' Leven" begins with blacksmith and bicycle-maker George Nicoll, who began to forge iron clubs in 1881. Mr. Nicoll was a large, strong man of gentle demeanor, a "hawky" character (a local Scots word meaning very astute and careful) according to his granddaughter. The cleeks, lofters and rut irons he made during these early years were of high quality and were the foundation for the company's excellent reputation for the next hundred years. Nicoll's famous leather-faced cleek of 1892 and the gutta percha-faced cleek that followed in 1893 are the prime, and most-prized, examples of this fine cleekmaker's early work. Nicoll's other patent of this period was the 1895 bent neck putter, with the hosel bent backward, toward the shaft.

Nicoll's manufacture of iron heads before 1895 has been brought into question by golf historian Aleck Watt. Citing his family's close relationship with the well-known Auchterlonie club-making family of St. Andrews and his conversations with both Laurie and Eric Auchterlonie, Watt reports that Tom Stewart made Nicoll's iron heads until 1895. Although Stewart started his own shop in 1895, he could have forged heads at Forgan's factory where he apprenticed prior to starting on his own. This idea could be supported by readily available evidence that many major cleek makers bought and sold iron and wood heads from each other. For example, Tom Morris bought many heads from the Tom Stewart firm; many Morris clubs display both the Morris and Stewart cleekmarks.

Watt also recounts that prior to 1895, Nicoll made only wood clubs. Golf historian, Pete Georgiady, disputes this claim, citing his contacts with the same sources. The fact that George Nicoll was a blacksmith by trade might suggest his manufacture of iron heads rather than wood; the lack of evidence of wood clubs attributable to Nicoll prior to the mid-1920s would seem to confirm his status as a cleekmaker only.

Early Nicoll smooth-faced irons can be identified by either a circular "G. Nicoll Leven" mark or a later, oval mark of the same legend. These high quality irons, in a wide variety of shapes and weighting patterns, are expensive and scarce collectibles today. Nicoll's early "The F.G. Tait Cleek" is a prize from this club maker's early years.

As Nicoll 'O' Leven entered the twentieth century and smooth-faced irons began to disappear in favor of face-marked irons, Nicoll introduced Zenith Irons, considered to be the company's top-of-the-line professional irons. Nicoll continued to experiment with head shapes and weighting patterns, introducing the toe-weighted Able Iron, the heel-weighted Sure Iron and the rounded (concentric) back Clinker Iron. In the early 20th century, Nicoll's most lasting original design was the famed Gem Putter, copied by most other makers for the next 50 years.

As was the fashion in Great Britain at the time, Nicoll made anti-shank irons and putters in both the Smith's and Fairlie's patterns. By 1926, George's son, Robert Nicoll, called a "proper gentleman" and "a lover of the game of golf" by a former employee, had assumed control of the company. However, George Nicoll was still actively involved and introduced Indicator Irons, the first iron clubs produced as a matched set. Also at about that time, Robert Nicoll moved the company into the manufacture of socket wood clubs.

Like most cleekmakers of the late 19th century, George Nicoll chose a "cleekmark" or trademark to identify his clubs. Sometime in the late 1890s, Nicoll chose the upturned hand as his mark. Later company records refer to the upturned, palm forward hand mark, which exists in 10 or more major designs as the "hand of friendship." One also has to assume the hand mark's connection with hand forging as well.

Great debate exists among collectors as to the chronology of these hand marks. While there is little debate about the fact that Nicoll's first two early hand marks (crude outlines) date from the period of 1898 to about 1905, it seems as if there is a middle period, roughly 1905-1920 where five or six distinct variations of the hand are noted. After about 1925, only two or three new hand marks appear. It seems that nine or 10 hand marks comprise the major designs.

Collectors often claim the existence of many more hand marks. It is likely that subtle variations in the designs were caused by the constant wearing of dies (stamps) and by the remaking of stamps. It is said that two brothers, the Nicholsons, were responsible for stamping Nicoll iron clubs. One brother was responsible for the face, and the other brother responsible for the back markings. Therefore, it is likely that many of the variations of the hand mark were created by these brothers. It is possible that changes were made when new stamps were ordered to replace worn stamps. Or perhaps the company made a conscious decision to change the mark, possibly as a marketing scheme.

Other explanations for the many variations in the hand cleek mark design have been offered. The practice of emorying clubs makes stampings difficult to distinguish from each other. There is also the possibility that the use of apprentices in the club making operation may have had an impact on the design and use of stampings and their variations. In any case, Robert Nicoll registered the hand as a trademark in 1922, but claimed continuous use back to 1898.

To complicate identification, the George Nicoll signature, found on many clubs, is of little use in determining the age of a club. At least eight variations of the signature exist, all but one only slightly different from each other. There appears to be loose correlation between the use of specific hand marks and particular signatures.

During its first fifty years, many golf professionals' names appeared on the backs of Nicoll clubs. Among them were F.G. Tait, James Braid, Tommy Armour and Macdonald Smith. Because of the absence of company records, it is unclear whether a formal business relationship existed between the company and these individuals. Several Nicoll clubs were in Bobby Jones' bag during his Grand-Slam year. Many famous club professionals, such as the Bradbeers, had irons especially made by Nicoll with their names centrally positioned on the back of their clubs. As was the practice at the time, many club professionals had Nicoll make irons without a Nicoll name stamp, leaving space for their personal stamp.

After the introduction of steel shafts in 1929, a new era began in club design and three Nicoll models that would become justly famous were introduced. The Wizard, Pinseeker and Pinsplitter models became instantly popular with amateurs and professionals alike. While the company ceased production at the outbreak of the Second World War, Nicoll resumed production in 1946 and continued for almost another 40 years. During the 1950s, Nicoll's association with Champion Henry Cotton became paramount. Cotton designed several successful Nicoll models while working as the company's "contract player."

Under the guidance of Robert Nicoll's son-in-law, the company prospered until the early 1980s—a one hundred year run, always under the guidance of the Nicoll family. Modern technology, marketing and the huge growth of American sporting goods conglomerates, as well as the growth of larger British golf companies, finally overtook the company, which closed its doors in 1983.

One further note for collectors: Nicoll continued to make in the old style, putters and possibly other special clubs with wood shafts, until its demise in 1983. I have seen a late giant niblick with a Nicoll mark and own several Gem and White Heather putters which can be documented as 1960s purchases. Most of the putters have wrapped leather grips with a plastic end cap secured by a screw. All of these later clubs have the last Nicoll hand mark and signature mark (known as the "sickle mark") which seems to date as early as the 1930s, and were used until the company's last days, further confusing accurate club dating. Any Nicoll club with these marks must be carefully considered before purchasing.

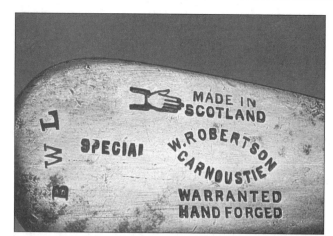

8th Nicoll mark 1910-1920.

9th Nicoll mark, worn into the "6 finger" mark. Hand is worn down-spaces between fingers become fingers 1925-1930.

9th Nicoll mark, 1920s. v.1.

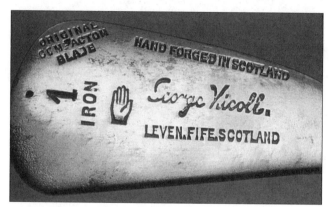

10th Nicoll mark, 1925-1930. v.1.

10th Nicoll mark, 1925-1983. v.2.

9th Nicoll mark, 1920s. v.2 or worn v.1.

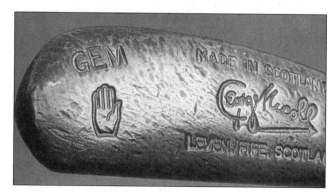

10th Nicoll mark, 1925-1983. v.3.

NICHOLSON, T.
PITTENWEEM, SCOTLAND

Tom Nicholson began forging irons in the old cleek-maker's style during the mid-1880s. Prior to winning the Gold Medal at the 1890 Edinburgh Exposition, he marked his clubs "T Nicholson, Pittenweem" in very tiny lettering. Most of these had the markings "emoried" away and are mistaken for much earlier forgings. After 1890 he used two oval marks on each club; one with "T Nicholson, Maker, Pittenweem," the other "Gold Medal Exposition, Edinburgh, 1890."

SMOOTH-FACE BLADE PUTTER $125 175 275
Circa 1890-1900. Straight blade. "T Nicholson, Maker, Pittenweem" football-shaped mark. Photo below.

GOLD MEDAL IRONS $85   125   225
Circa 1890-1900. All irons.

GOLD MEDAL CLEEK $100 150   250
Circa 1890-1900. Smooth-face cleek.

SMOOTH-FACE IRONS $125 175   300
Circa 1886-1890. All irons. "T Nicholson, Maker, Pittenweem" in tiny letters.

INDICATOR SERIES PUTTER $50   60   90
Circa 1925-1930. Straight blade, line-scored face. "Hand" mark.

WHIPPET PUTTER $50   65   95
Circa teens. Long narrow head, dot-punched face. "Hand" mark.

AGLAIA PUTTER $50   65   95
Circa 1920. Putting cleek. "Hand" mark.

GEM PUTTER $55   90   125
Circa 1930-1935. Rustless rounded back, offset hosel, line-scored face. "Hand" mark.

PRECISION PUTTER $60   100   150
Circa 1915. Flanged back and dot-punched face. "Hand" mark.

NAP PUTTER $60   70   100
Circa 1920. Offset hosel, line-scored face. "Hand" mark.

PREMIER PUTTER $100 135   200
Circa 1915. Wide sole similar to the Auchterlonie holing out putter.

PRE-1898 IRONS $100 140   290
Circa 1895. "G Nicoll, Leven" in block letters. Many made for "Forth Rubber Company, Dundee." Photo below.

PRE-1898 IRONS $125 190   325
Circa 1890. Cleek with "G Nicoll, Leven Fife" mark.

ABLE IRONS $50   75   125
Circa 1910. Irons with "Geo. Nicoll, Leven Fife" mark and early "Hand" mark. Photo below.

MAC SMITH SERIES IRONS $50   65   90
Circa 1920s. "Duplicate of Mac Smith's" with "Hand" mark. Photo below.

ZENITH SERIES IRONS $50   60   90
Circa 1925-1930. 1 through 9 irons. "Hand" mark.

PIN SPLITTER SERIES IRONS $50   60   90
Circa 1925-1930. 1 through 9 irons with flanged backs.

VIKING SERIES IRONS $50   65   90
Circa 1925-1930. 1 through 9 irons with large sailing ship on back.

INDICATOR SERIES IRONS $50   50   75
Circa 1925-1930. 1 through 9 irons. Line-scored or dot-face. "Hand" mark. Photo below.

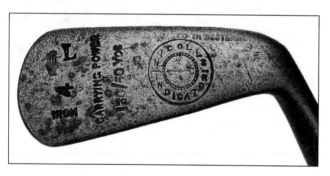

NICOLL SIGNATURE IRONS $50   65   100
Circa 1915. Dot-punched faces. Driving iron through niblick. Photo below.

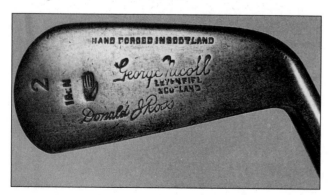

BRAID SIGNATURE IRONS $65   90   140
Circa 1915. "James Braid" in script. Many had flanged backs.

TAIT SIGNATURE IRONS $65   90   140
Circa 1915, "Freddie Tait" in script. Photo below.

CRACKER JACK SERIES IRONS $70   100   150
Circa 1925-1930. "Carruthers" through-hosel shafting. 1 through 9 irons.

SMITH ANTI-SHANK IRONS $120   190   300
Circa 1915-1925. Heel-and toe-weighted line-scored face. "Hand" mark.

CORRUGATED DEEP GROOVE
IRONS $125   160   275
Circa 1914-1920. "Zenith Pitcher." "Hand" mark.

ZENITH PRECISION JIGGER $60   90   150
Circa 1920s. Flanged back.

LEATHER-FACE IRON $1200   1800   3000
Patented 1892. Leather face insert. "G Nicoll, Leven Fife" and patent numbers. Photo below.

GUTTA-PERCHA FACE IRON $1500 2000 3200
Patented 1892. Gutta-percha face insert. "G Nicoll, Leven Fife" and patent numbers. About twice as rare as the leather face. Photos below.

DOT-PUNCHED IRONS $60 80 120
Circa 1910. All irons.

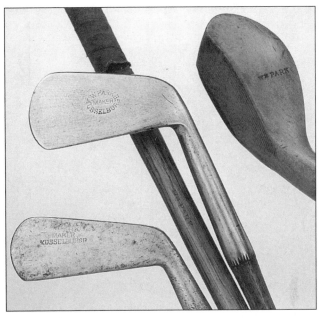

OKE, W. G.
FULWELL & LONDON, ENGLAND

William Oke began making clubs in the mid-teens and in 1923 registered the "Oak Brand" trademark of an "Oak tree."

LONG-HOSEL PUTTER $150 220 300
Circa 1920s. Blade putter with seven-inch pencil-thin hosel. "Oak Brand Registered" mark.

DEEP-FACE MASHIE $60 80 140
Circa 1920s. "W G Oke, Fulwell, G C" and the "Oak Brand Registered" mark. Photo below.

PARK, WILLIE
MUSSELBURGH, SCOTLAND

SMOOTH-FACE BLADE
PUTTER $135 195 350
Circa 1890-1900. "Wm Park, Musselburgh, Maker" oval mark.

BRASS-HEAD PUTTERS $150 250 425
Circa 1890-1900. Straight blade. "Wm Park, Musselburgh, Maker" oval mark.

APPROACHING PUTTER $65 90 150
Circa 1890-1898. Without the "Hand" mark. Smooth-face straight blade. Photo below.

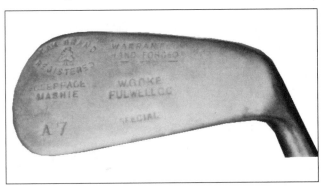

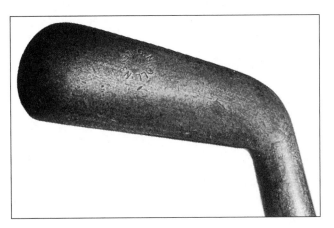

WILLIE PARK PUTTER $150 250 375
Circa 1920. Severely bent neck stamped "Willie Park's Original Bent Neck Putter."

SPECIAL PATENT PUTTER $175 225 350
Circa 1900. Severely bent neck smooth-face blade. Photo below.

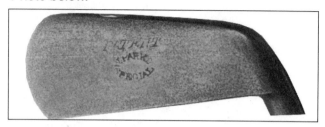

PARK'S PATTERN PUTTER $175 225 350
Circa 1900. Severely bent neck smooth-face blade. Made for Slazengers. Photo below.

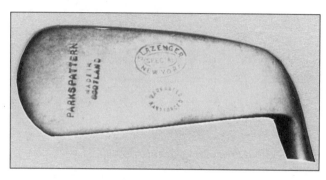

PATENTED BENT NECK
PUTTER $250 400 650
Circa 1895-1900. Severely bent neck. "Wm Park, Musselburgh, Maker" oval mark.

LONG-NOSE PUTTER $850 1500 2750
Circa 1895-1900. Transitional beech-head. "Wm Park" mark.

LONG-NOSE PUTTER $1500 2750 4450
Circa 1885-1895. Long head, large lead weight. "Wm Park" mark.

DOT-FACE IRONS $90 150 250
Circa 1910-1915. All irons. "Wm Park, Maker, Musselburgh" mark.

DIAMOND-BACK IRONS $100 160 300
Circa 1910. All irons. Smooth-face.

SMOOTH-FACE IRONS $150 250 425
Circa 1890-1900. All irons. "Wm Park, Maker, Musselburgh" mark.

PATENTED DRIVING CLEEK $250 450 675
Circa 1895-1905. Smooth-face compact head. "W. Park's Patent Driving Cleek" mark.

RUT NIBLICK $350 500 900
Circa 1900-1910. Smooth-face head. "Wm Park, Maker, Musselburgh" mark.

PARK PATENTED LOFTER $300 500 800
Circa 1890-1895. Concave face.

RUT IRON $700 1000 2250
Circa 1885-1895. Small smooth-face head. "Wm Park, Maker, Musselburgh" mark. Photo below.

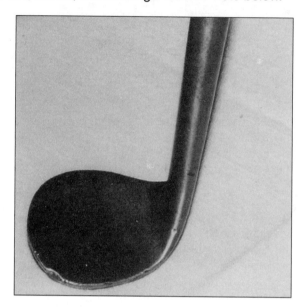

BULL DOG WOOD $150 250 500
Circa 1905-1915. Rounded sole, black triangular face insert.

SOCKET WOODS $150 250 400
Circa 1905-1915. Driver, brassie or spoon. "Wm Park" mark.

PICK-UP PATENT WOOD $300 450 700
Circa 1910. Metal sole with four runners. Well lofted head.

COMPRESSED-HEAD WOOD $400 600 1250
Circa 1895-1900. Spliced-neck. Driver, brassie or spoon. Spoon with "Park's Compressed Patent." Photo below.

PARK, WILLIE
MUSSELBURGH, SCOTLAND
by Pete Georgiady

William Park Jr. was undoubtedly the most versatile of all the great golfers of the 19th century. Young Willie, as he was known during his lifetime, used his golfing knowledge and skills to become a champion golfer, author, course designer, real estate developer, club and ball designer and, yes, even a clubmaker before he saw his fortieth birthday.

Born in Musselburgh in 1864, his father, "Auld" Willie, had already won two Open Championships before Junior could even walk. Literally born into the golf business, Young Willie had little choice but to follow in the footsteps of his father and uncles.

His first assignment, arranged by his Uncle Mungo (himself champion in 1874), was to lay out the course and serve as professional to the golf club at Ryton, Northumberland. While there he started entering professional competitions, winning his first at age 17.

Returning to Musselburgh in 1884, he took control of his father's firm, making his first splash in the business: inventing the bulger driver in 1885 and using it in the 1885 Open. Some years later, he was challenged by Sir Henry Lamb, the prominent amateur, who also claimed to have invented the bulger in the same time frame. Through some lengthy written communications, both men established they had devised similar clubs concurrently without knowing the other was involved in the same endeavor. Because Willie was a clubmaker and professional in the public eye, he received most of the acclaim for the bulger.

Over the next ten years, Willie was the best known clubmaker in the business. His victories in the 1887 and 1889 Opens set the stage for the introduction of four new clubs of his invention. He received much acclaim when he brought a new lofter to market. The club was at the forefront of a new development in the game—high approaching shots—and Willie created even more attention when he received a patent for his new implement in 1889.

The Patent Lofter was followed by the Patent Driving Cleek in 1891, the Patent Compressed Driver in 1893, and the most famous club of all, the Park Patent Bent Neck Putter in 1894. His success on the links as well as in the design, caused his business to swell and he was acknowledged to be the second largest manufacturer of golf clubs behind the firm of Robert Forgan. In later years, he brought out a patent groove-soled brassie called the Pik-up and a patent step-faced lofter for imparting backspin.

His patent clubs are easily recognizable because they are all marked as such. He did make many other regular clubs with three types of name stamps. The vast majority of these clubs are smooth-faced. It is very difficult to date these clubs accurately since they have minimal markings and were all made in the old style, even into the twentieth century. Since Park stamped his name on the shafts of all his clubs, many are still identifiable even if the club head markings are illegible.

The range of Park clubs available today is broad and deep. Small-headed niblicks, gunmetal-blade putters, Smith model irons, large-hosel lofters and short-bladed mashie irons are among the more unusual clubs from his output. Some can be found in lady's and children's models, as he was one of the first to cater to that growing segment of the market in the 1890s. Park's premium grade clubs are distinguished by his use of wood from greenheart, purpleheart, lemonheart or lacewood trees for the shafts.

Willie gradually lost interest in clubmaking and the retail business after 1910, concentrating instead in course layout. He spent a considerable amount of time in the United States and Canada, first setting up a retail outlet in New York City, and then course design offices in New York and Toronto.

He was a principal in the first modern residential resort golf community at Huntercombe in Oxfordshire, although the lack of rail access did not encourage its success. In 1896, Willie Park's *The Game of Golf* became the first published golf instruction book written by a professional. He followed up with *The Art of Putting*, a book that discussed the skill that made him most famous.

It was Willie Park who said, "The man who can putt is a match for any man." Not only was Willie a deft putter but he was the man to beat in club design, retailing and merchandising.

BULGER-FACE WOODS $450 700 1450
Circa 1890-1900. Driver, brassie or spoon. "Wm Park" mark.

LONG-NOSE WOODS $900 1900 3750
Circa 1895-1900. Driver, brassie or spoon. Transitional beech-head. "Wm Park" mark. Photo below.

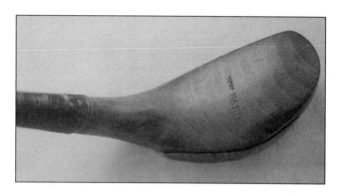

LONG-NOSE WOODS $1500 3950 5400
Circa 1885-1895. Play club, brassie or spoon. Long head, large lead weight. "Wm Park" mark. Photo below.

PATRICK, ALEX
LEVEN, FIFE, SCOTLAND

The Patrick family produced clubs from the late 1840s through the 1930s. On their wooden-head clubs the mark "A. Patrick" in block letters was used. They marked their irons and putters with "A. Patrick, Leven, Est. 1847." Shortly after the turn of the century they stamped a "Spur" mark on the backs of their irons, and about 1920 introduced the "Well-Made" horseshoe mark.

TWISTED-HOSEL PUTTER $80 110 190
Circa 1920. "Well-Made" horseshoe mark. Photo below.

BRASS-HEAD PUTTERS $150 250 375
Circa 1890-1895. "A Patrick, Leven" mark.

LONG-NOSE PUTTERS $1100 2000 3350
Circa 1885-1895. Beech-head driving putter. "A Patrick" in block letters.

HORSESHOE-MARKED IRONS $50 60 90
Circa 1920s. All irons. "Well-Made" horseshoe mark.

CONCENTRIC-BACK IRONS $75 100 150
Circa 1900-1910. Smooth-face. "A Patrick, Leven" mark.

SMOOTH-FACE IRONS $80 135 200
Circa 1895-1900. All irons. "A Patrick, Leven" mark.

SHALLOW-FACE CLEEK $125 200 350
Circa 1890. Smooth-face. "A Patrick, Leven" mark.

ACME WOODS $100 135 190
Circa 1920s. Driver, brassie or spoon.

BULL DOG WOOD $100 135 190
Circa 1910-1915. Rounded sole lofted face. Most have face inserts.

PRETTY FACE WOODS $100 135 190
Circa 1920. Black face insert.

VICTORY SERIES WOODS $125 175 250
Circa 1920s. Large-head driver, brassie or spoon. "Alex Patrick, Leven, Victory" mark.

SPLICED-NECK WOODS $175 250 375
Circa 1900. Driver, brassie or spoon. "A Patrick" stamping.

SPLICED-NECK WOODS $300   600   1100
Circa 1900. Bulger face. Driver, brassie or spoon.
"A Patrick" stamping. Photo below.

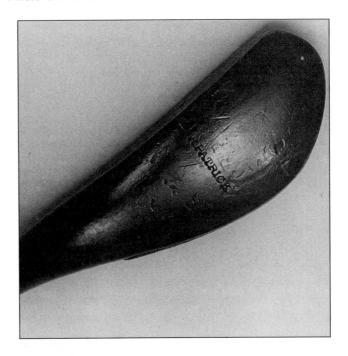

LONG-NOSE WOODS $1500   2750   6500
Circa 1866-1880. Long head with a large lead back
weight. "A Patrick" mark. Neck is more delicate than
later woods. Photo below.

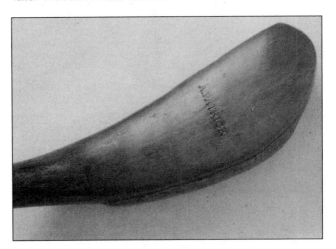

LONG-NOSE WOODS $650   1100   2250
Circa 1885-1895. Transitional head style. "A
Patrick" mark. Photo below.

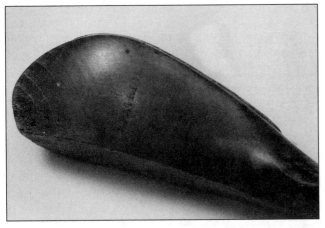

LONG-NOSE WOODS $1350   2450   5250
Circa 1880-1890. Large lead back weight. "A
Patrick" mark. Photo below.

PAXTON, PETER
EASTBOURNE, ENGLAND

Paxton became an apprentice with Tom Hood at Musselburgh. He began designing and forging clubs in the
early 1880s. His reputation for quality as a club and
ball maker was superb. He marked his clubs "P. Paxton, Eastbourne." He also used a "Crown" mark on
transitional style woods.

SMOOTH-FACE LOFTER $350   500   800
Circa 1890. "P Paxton, Eastbourne" mark.

SMOOTH-FACE CLEEK $350   550   900
Circa 1890. Smooth-face. "P Paxton, Eastbourne" mark. Photo below.

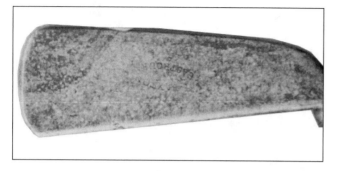

SPLICED-NECK WOODS $500   750   1350
Circa 1895. Bulger face. Driver, brassie or spoon. Photo below.

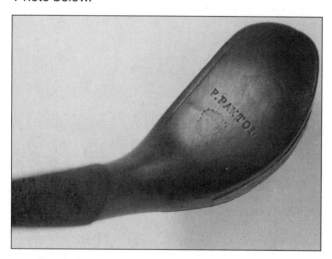

LONG-NOSE WOODS $950   1750   3000
Circa 1885-1895. Play club, brassie or spoon. Transitional head. "P Paxton" stamp.

LONG-NOSE WOODS $1250   2000   3750
Circa 1880-1890. Play club, brassie or spoon. Long head, large lead weight. "P Paxton" stamp. Photo below.

PHILP, HUGH
ST. ANDREWS, SCOTLAND

LONG-NOSE PUTTERS $2200   4800 10500
Circa 1840-1856. "H Philp" in block letters. Thorn head. Photo below.

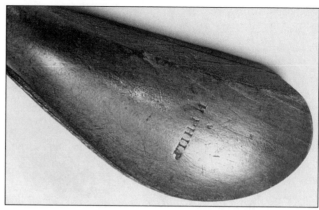

LONG-NOSE WOODS $4800 11000 22000
Circa 1840-1856. "H Philp" in block letters. Thorn head. Photo below.

LONG-NOSE BAFFIE SPOON $6000 15000 28000
Circa 1840-1856. "H Philp" in block letters. Thorn head. Photo below.

PHILP, HUGH
ST. ANDREWS, SCOTLAND
by Pete Georgiady

As with most other golfing notables who lived prior to 1850, very little is recorded on their lives and pursuits. Hugh Philp is no exception. Much of the information existent today comes in the form of reminiscences from forty or fifty years after his passing.

Philp was born in Cameron, Fife in 1782, the son of a farmer. As a teen he was apprenticed to a carpenter and subsequently pursued a career as a carpenter and joiner. Hugh was never known to have worked with any other club-maker and his bent towards that avocation apparently stemmed from his expertise as a carpenter and his love of playing golf. In time, these two skills obtained him an affiliation with the St. Andrews Society (later to be the Royal and Ancient Golf Club) for whom he repaired clubs beginning in 1812. The Society had a contract with McEwan's of Edinburgh to supply clubs for their semi-annual meetings. However, in 1819 they appointed Philp as their clubmaker, and did not sever their ties with McEwan until 1827. Also beginning in 1819, Philp served the Scotscraig Golf Club in the town of that name located between St. Andrews and Dundee.

With his new patronage, Philp moved from small quarters outside the town walls to a shop along the links adjacent to the Union Parlor, a popular gathering spot for golfers. Soon afterward he took up a position in a larger shop in the building that is today the Tom Morris shop. This shop would become a social center for golfers, congregating before and after their matches. Overhead in the shop were racks where his favored patrons could store their clubs between outings. The most remembered portion of his career was the last eleven years when he hired two assistants: James Wilson in 1845, and Robert Forgan in 1852. Forgan was his nephew and took over the Philp business when Uncle Hugh died in 1856.

Philp's clubmaking skills have been glorified to superior levels, though several contemporary sources say others like Peter McEwan and Alexander Munro were equally proficient. It could have been his mere presence in the town of St. Andrews and his service to the Royal & Ancient that gave Philps his reputation, by placing him in what little limelight could shine on such a craftsman. The gentleman and golf writer J.G. McPherson left us a romantic bit of insight saying, "The late Hugh Philp had polished an apple tree head for a whole afternoon when modern makers would have considered it quite finished."

His heads were made from apple, thorn and beech, long and slender, some straight in the face while others were hooked. Late in his life, he used hickory, though he never completely adopted it in making shafts. On chance, he bought an entire log in the 1850s wondering if he would ever use it all.

His reputation was again enhanced when the original Mills aluminum putters were patterned after some ancient Philp models. Obviously, the clubs' beauty and utility were still greatly admired fifty years after their heyday.

Historians have also recognized the fact that forgers were prone to producing Philp clubs. As early as the 1860s forged copies of Philp clubs were known to exist; forgeries for unwitting golfers who sought to use good clubs, not for collectors of a later age who would also covet Philp clubs. This legacy is not held by any other maker.

While he was the maker of superior grade clubs, much of the recognition he earned during his lifetime came from his play and his association with the scions of the golf community. A player he was; like the cracks of his day Philp was a supreme strategist, knowing at precisely which hole he should close out his opponent. He came to play infrequently, usually when he deemed the odds were in his favor. But it is also known that he would occasionally play a three ball with youthful Tom Morris and Allan Robertson.

Hugh Philp was a storyteller with a dry vein of humor. He came on in a crusty way, but in time his inner warmth would shine through. He wore silver spectacles through which he viewed the world with glittering black eyes. In 1859, three years after he passed away, his loss was lamented, "Hugh Philp, how full of bygone pleasant memories of golf land is thy name! Thou didst make clubs for our fathers, and didst mend them for their sons."

RANDALL, JOHN
BROMLEY, KENT, ENGLAND

Randall began making clubs shortly after 1900. He was most famous for his aluminum head putters with lead weighting in the face.

ALUMINUM HEAD PUTTER $175 300 475
Circa 1910-1920 with circular lead weights across the entire face. Photo below.

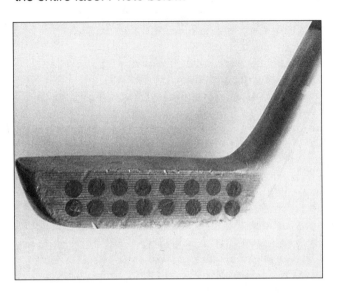

RODWELL, CHARLES
LONDON, ENGLAND

Charles Rodwell began selling clubs about 1905 and marked his clubs "Charles Rodwell, Lt'd."

IRON-HEAD PUTTER $90 125 190
Circa 1920. Long, shallow blade. Dot-punched face.

ALUMINUM-HEAD PUTTER $200 325 475
Circa 1920. Raised aiming circle. "The Rodwell New Standard Putter" stamped on the head. Photo below.

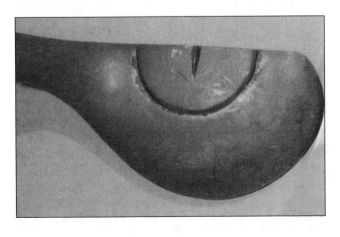

ROLLINS & PARKER
REDDICH, ENGLAND

Began selling clubs about 1910 and continued into the early 1930s. They used an "Eye" maker's mark. The firm was basically a wholesaler of heads to assemblers who stamped the clubs with their marks. Very few "Eye" stamped clubs carry the "Rollins & Parker" name.

EXCELSIOR SERIES IRONS $60 80 125
Circa 1915. All irons. Rounded back. "Eye" mark.

MAXWELL HOSEL IRONS $60 80 125
Circa 1920. Flanged back. "Eye" mark.

DEEP-GROOVE IRONS $100 170 220
Circa 1915-1922. All corrugated groove irons. "Eye" mark.

FLANGED-BACK IRONS $55 70 100
Circa 1915. All irons.

ANTI-SHANK IRONS $150 225 300
Circa 1910-1915. All irons. Fairlie's patent. Diamond-dot-face markings.

DEEP-GROOVE IRONS $120 180 250
Circa 1915-1922. All slot groove irons. "Eye" mark. Photo below.

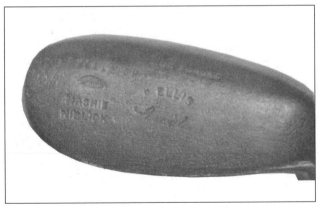

ANTI-SHANK IRONS $150 225 275
Circa 1920s. All irons. Smith's model. "Eye" mark.

RUSTLESS GOLF CLUB COMPANY
CHICAGO, ILLINOIS

The "RGCCO" began forging rustless metal heads about 1907 in Chicago. They used a "Sun" mark with a face spelling out "Rustless." Many of their clubs bear the PG Manufacturing "Anvil" mark.

ALUMINUM MALLET PUTTER $150 250 400
Mills type with "Rustless Sun" mark.

SMOOTH-FACE IRONS $60   85   140
Circa 1907-1910 with "Rustless Sun" mark. Photo below.

CARRUTHERS HOSEL IRONS $85   135   200
Circa 1907-1910 with "Rustless Sun" mark. Carruther's thru hosel shafting.

SAUNDERS, FRED
LONDON, ENGLAND

Fred Saunders first made clubs in Birmingham about 1896, then later moved to London.

ALUMINUM PUTTER $450   750   1200
Circa 1920. Elongated sight line. Photo below.

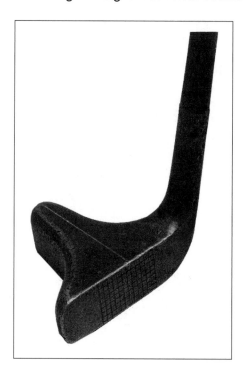

SAYERS, BEN
NORTH BERWICK, SCOTLAND

The Sayers family began their club business about 1890. They used the markings "B Sayers, N. Berwick" and about 1920 used a "Robin" cleek mark.

BENNY PUTTER $150   200   300
Circa 1930. Sole has 17 grooves. "Ben Sayers" in script. Photo below.

BRASS-HEAD PUTTERS $150   200   350
Circa 1890-1900. Smooth-face blade. "B Sayers" in block letters.

TARGET IRONS $50   65   90
Circa 1920s. All irons. "Target" sweet spot.

MAXWELL HOSEL IRONS $60   80   120
Circa 1915. All irons. Flanged back. "Ben Sayers" in script.

SMOOTH-FACE IRONS $75   95   150
Circa 1895-1905. All irons. "Ben Sayers North Berwick" marking.

DEEP-GROOVE IRONS $120   175   250
Circa 1915-1922. All irons. Corrugated face.

DEEP-GROOVE IRONS $130   180   275
Circa 1915-1922. All irons. Slot face.

SELECTED SERIES WOODS $100   135   190
Circa 1920s. All woods. Photo below.

DREADNOUGHT WOODS $100 135 190
Circa 1915-1920. Large-head driver, brassie or spoon. "Ben Sayers Dreadnought" stamp.

SPLICED-NECK WOODS $150 225 350
Circa 1900-1910. All woods.

GRUVSOL PATENT WOODS $150 225 325
Circa 1920s. All woods. "Gruvsol Patent #244925." Grooves on sole plate.

SCOTT, A. H.
EARLSFERRY, ELIE, SCOTLAND

Andrew Herd Scott began forging clubs about 1894. He was clubmaker to Prince Edward and used the "Plume" mark on his clubs during his reign. About 1910 he adopted the "Lion and Crown" mark.

STRAIGHT LINE PUTTER $100 160 225
Circa 1920s. Step down back design. Patent No 349407. "Lion-on-Crown" mark.

ALUMINUM MALLET
PUTTERS $125 175 250
Circa 1915. "Lion-on-Crown" mark. Photo below.

LION-ON-CROWN IRONS $60 75 120
Circa 1915. Smooth-face. "A. H. Scott, Elie, Earlsferry" marking. Photo below.

SMOOTH-FACE IRONS $75 100 160
Circa 1895-1905. All irons. "A. H. Scott, Elie, Earlsferry" marking.

LION AND CROWN WOODS $100 125 175
Circa 1915. All woods.

FORK SPLICED
PATENT WOODS $400 600 850
Circa 1895-1905. All woods. "A H Scott Patent No 21444." "Plume" mark. Photo below.

SIMPSON, ARCHIE
CARNOUSTIE, SCOTLAND

Began forging clubs during the mid-1880s. During the 1900s his clubmaking business became prominent because of the important clientele patronage. He marked his clubs "A Simpson, Carnoustie."

SMOOTH-FACE PUTTER $60 80 120
Circa 1900. Offset blade. "A Simpson, Aberdeen" mark.

BRASS-BLADE PUTTER $90 120 200
Circa 1900. "A Simpson, Aberdeen" mark.

DOT-FACE IRONS $55 70 100
Circa 1915. All irons.

RUT NIBLICK $225 350 600
Circa 1895-1905. Smooth-face. Medium-size rounded head. "A Simpson" mark.

BULGER-FACE WOODS $200 350 600
Circa 1895-1900. Driver, brassie or spoon. "A Simpson, Aberdeen" stamp.

SIMPSON, R.
CARNOUSTIE, SCOTLAND

Started forging irons about 1890 with the help of his brothers Jack and Archie. He marked his clubs simply "R. Simpson, Carnoustie." His most famous and highly collectible clubs were the ball-faced irons patented in 1903.

BRASS-HEAD PUTTERS $100   140   200
Circa 1900-1910. Smooth-face blade. "R Simpson, Maker, Carnoustie" mark.

PERFECT BALANCE PUTTER $300   450   650
Circa 1910. "Patent 21307." Simpson's circular mark. Bulge weight in center. Photo below.

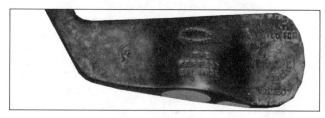

LONG-NOSE PUTTERS $800   1400   2400
Circa 1890. Beech-head putter stamped "R Simpson."

LINE-SCORED IRONS $50   60   85
Circa 1920s. All irons. "R Simpson, Carnoustie" with "S" and the "Anchor" mark.

SMOOTH-FACE IRONS $50   75   100
Circa 1900-1910. All irons. "R Simpson, Carnoustie" in a double circle.

PERFECT BALANCE IRONS $350   650   900
Circa 1910. All irons. "Lump" back weighting. "Patent No. 21307" and "R Simpson, Carnoustie" at toe. "Crescent and Star" mark.

GUTTA BALL-FACE IRONS $600   800   1350
Circa 1903. All irons. Line cut gutta ball-face. Photo below.

BALL-FACE IRONS $750   1500   2500
Circa early 1890s. All irons. Patent numbers on back.

SIMPSON SPECIAL WOODS $100   135   190
Circa 1910-1915. Driver, brassie or spoon.

PRETTY FACE WOODS $110   145   200
Circa 1910-1915. Driver, brassie or spoon. "Ivorine" face insert.

MALINKA SERIES WOODS $120   145   200
Circa 1920s. "Malinka No 367793." Driver, brassie or spoon. "R Simpson, Carnoustie" mark.

PRETTY FACE WOODS $110   145   200
Circa 1920s. "Diamond"-shaped face insert.

PERFECT BALANCE WOODS $125   190   275
Circa 1905-1910. Driver, brassie or spoon.

SIMPLEX WOODS $200   300   500
Circa 1900-1910. Spliced-neck. "Patent App. For No. 24835." "R Simpson, Carnoustie" stamp.

SEMI-LONG-NOSE WOODS $600   850   1250
Circa 1890-1900. Play club, brassie or spoon. Transitional head shape. "R Simpson" stamp.

LONG-NOSE WOODS $1300   2500   4000
Circa 1883-1890. Play club, brassie or spoon. "R Simpson" on a beech-head. Many have leather face inserts. Photo below.

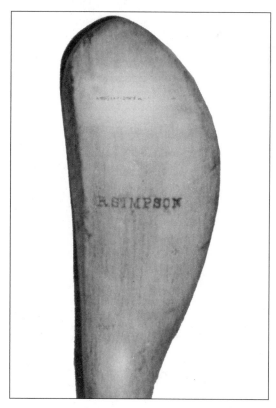

SLAZENGER AND SONS
LONDON, ENGLAND

Slazengers began marking and selling clubs and balls about 1890. It began by buying clubs from Tom Stewart and Robert Condie and other major makers of the time. During the wood shaft era it had outlets in London and New York and marked its clubs accordingly. The "Six-Pointed Star" was its London mark used during the late 1890s. The other mark was simply "Slazenger." It is presently making golf equipment as a subsidiary of Dunlop.

SLAZENGER, NEW YORK PUTTER $70   90   140
Circa 1900-1910. Smooth-face straight blade.

PUTTING CLEEK $100   160   225
Circa 1895-1900. Smooth-face straight blade. "Six-Pointed Star" mark.

SIX POINTED STAR IRONS $100   150   275
Circa 1895-1900. All irons. Smooth-face. Photo below.

RUT NIBLICK $350   475   700
Circa 1895. Small smooth-face head. "Six-Pointed Star" mark.

SLAZENGER NEW YORK IRONS $60   80   125
Circa 1900-1910. All irons. Smooth-face. Photo below.

SLAZENGER SPECIAL WOODS $100   135   190
Circa 1910-1915. Driver, brassie or spoon. "Slazenger Special, New York" stamp.

ALUMINUM-HEAD WOODS $150   250   375
Circa 1910. All lofts. "Carruthers" through hosel shafting.

SPLICED-NECK WOODS $175   250   400
Circa 1895-1910. Driver, brassie or spoon.

THREADED SOCKET PATENT $350   450   650
Circa 1901-1905. "Screw-in shaft" driver or brassie. "Patent No. 682,960 Slazenger" on the head. Photo below.

SPALDING
DYSART, FIFE, SCOTLAND

Spalding began operations in Great Britain about 1900. Clubs from the Dysart, Fife Works carried an "Anvil" mark. Others included "Baseball" mark stamped "Gt. Britain," "Gold Medal" series, "Tong" marked irons and "Argyle" clubs.

Jim Cooper has written the definitive work on Spalding, which is profusely illustrated. Every Spalding collector should have this reference in their library. It is available from Jim Cooper or Chuck Furjanic.

SMOOTH-FACE PUTTING
CLEEK $50   70   110
Circa 1905. "Made in Great Britain" baseball mark.

MORRISTOWN PUTTER $75   120   190
Circa 1898-1902. "Made in Gr. Britain" baseball mark.

FLANGED-BACK PUTTER $55   75   110
Circa 1920. "Anvil" mark.

THISTLE SERIES PUTTER $50   65   90
Circa 1920-1925. Line-face blade.

WRY-NECK PUTTER $50   65   90
Circa 1920-1925. Line face. "Thistle" mark.

ARGYLE SERIES PUTTER $50   65   90
Circa 1915-1920. Hyphen scored, offset hosel. "Thistle" marks.

GOLD MEDAL SERIES PUTTER $50   65   90
Circa 1915-1920. Calamity Jane type with "Wry Neck" with "Anvil" mark.

TONG BRAND PUTTING
CLEEK $175   250   400
Circa 1910. "Tong" mark. Photo below.

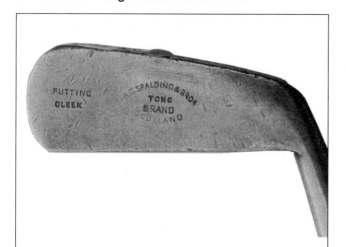

"S R" PUTTER $125   190   300
Circa 1920s. Long radial blade and 5-1/2 inch
hosel. "Anvil" mark.

SCHENECTADY PUTTER $150   275   450
Pre-1909. "A G Spalding, Makers" baseball trademark.

CALAMITY JANE PUTTER $225   400   600
Circa 1931. "Rustless Calamity Jane" with "Spalding Kro-Flite" mark.

STANDARD, LONDON IRONS $60   90   140
Circa 1910-1915. "Standard London" on back.
Smooth-face. Photo below.

CENTRA-JECT MASHIE $50   60   90
Circa 1910-1915. "Anvil" mark.

JIGGER $50   60   90
Circa 1910-1915. "Hammer" mark and "Diamond-
dot" face scoring.

HAND-FORGED IRONS $50   65   95
Circa 1915-1920. "Anvil" and "Dysart-Fife" marks.
Photo below.

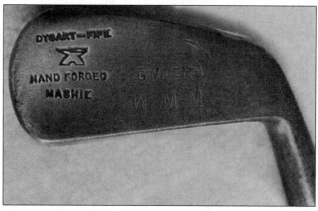

THISTLE SERIES IRONS $50   60   80
Circa 1910-1915. "Spalding" in large block letters.

GOLD MEDAL SERIES IRONS $50   60   90
Circa 1910-1915. "Dysart-Fife" and "Anvil" mark.

CRESCENT SERIES IRONS $50   75   125
Circa 1910-1915. Marked "Crescent" with the
"Hammer" mark. Photo below.

MORRISTOWN SERIES IRONS $70   100   160
Circa 1898-1902. "Made in Gr. Britain" baseball
mark.

TONG BRAND IRONS $125   175   300
Circa 1910-1915. "A G Spalding & Bros., Tong
Brand, Scotland" marks.

FOULIS PATENT $125   200   300
Circa 1905-1910. Concave, smooth-face. "Hammer" mark.

LEATHER FACE SOCKET
WOODS $100   150   225
Circa 1900-1905. "Baseball" mark.

LARGE-HEAD BRASSIE $75   100   160
Circa 1915-1920 marked "A G Spalding Bros."

SPALDING MEDAL 7 $75   115   165
Circa 1910-1915. Driver, brassie or spoon.

IVORINE FACE WOODS $100   140   200
Circa 1915-1920. Marked "A G Spalding Bros., Scotland."

BULLDOG TROUBLE WOOD $100   140   190
Circa 1915. Various markings.

SPALDING, A. G. & BROTHERS
USA

Spalding began importing clubs from Scotland about 1893. They were marked with "Spalding" in block letters. During 35 years of manufacturing wooden-shafted clubs, it used a multitude of cleek marks, including the baseball trademark, Morristown, Crescent, Spalding Special, Clan, Harry Vardon, SMCO and A. G. Spalding & Brothers model A, B, and C. From 1906 to 1918 various configurations of the Gold Medal was used. In 1919 the "F" Series irons were introduced including the famous Waterfall series. During the 1920s Spalding Medal, Spalding Forged, Dundee, and Kro-Flite were the dominant markings. In 1930 the wooden shaft Robert T. Jones, Jr. clubs were produced in very limited quantities.

As mentioned earlier, Jim Cooper has written the definitive work on Spalding, which is profusely illustrated. Every Spalding collector should have this reference in their library. It is available from Jim Cooper, or

Chuck Furjanic. Spalding Retail Catalogue reprints from 1899 to 1932 are also available from the author of this book.

"SMCO" PUTTER $300   450   800
Circa 1895. "Crescent Moon" mark on a straight blade putter.

CLAN SERIES PUTTER $125   225   450
Circa 1895. Blade putter marked "Clan" in large block letters.

SPALDING SPECIAL
SERIES PUTTER $150   225   375
Circa 1894-1896. Steel blade putter.

SPALDING SPECIAL
SERIES PUTTER $225   275   450
Circa 1894-1896. Brass-blade putter. Photo below.

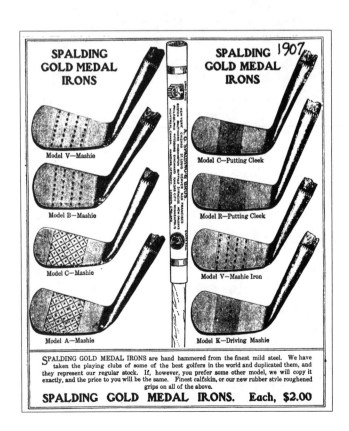

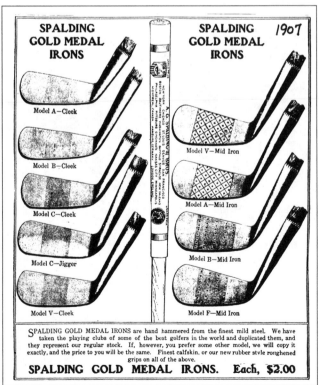

THE SPALDING SERIES
PUTTER $100   140   250
Circa 1898-1902. "Park" type severe bent neck putter.

THE SPALDING SERIES PUTTER $90   150   250
Circa 1898-1902. Brass-blade putter with a "Diamond" back.

THE SPALDING SERIES
PUTTER $150   225   350
Circa 1898-1902. Deep smooth-face, steel blade putter. Photo below.

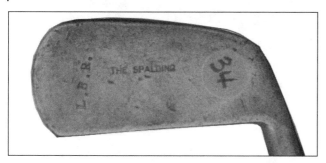

THE SPALDING SERIES
PUTTER $175   275   450
Circa 1898-1902. Deep smooth-face. Brass-blade putter .

MORRISTOWN SERIES PUTTER $65   90   150
Circa 1898-1900. Steel head blade. "Morristown" and "Baseball" marks.

MORRISTOWN SERIES PUTTER $75   100   175
Circa 1902-1905. Brass putter with "Baseball" mark.

MORRISTOWN SERIES PUTTER $80   120   200
Circa 1898-1902. Brass-head blade. "Morristown" mark only.

MORRISTOWN SERIES PUTTER $80   110   160
Circa 1898-1902. Steel-head approaching putter with "Morristown" stamp only.

HARRY VARDON SERIES
PUTTER $125   175   300
Circa 1900-1903. Gooseneck putter marked "A G Spalding & Bros, Makers."

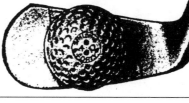

CRESCENT SERIES PUTTER $75 90 150
Circa 1902-1905. Diamond back with "Baseball" mark. Photo below.

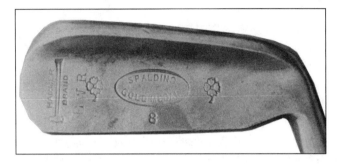

CRESCENT SERIES PUTTER $80 100 160
Circa 1902-1905. Brass-blade with "Baseball" mark.

GOLD MEDAL SERIES PUTTER $50 65 95
Circa 1906-1908 "Spalding Gold Medal 1" with dot ball-face.

GOLD MEDAL SERIES PUTTER $50 65 95
Circa 1906-1908. Brass-blade "Spalding Gold Medal."

GOLD MEDAL SERIES PUTTER $50 70 100
Circa 1912-1919. Ball-face.

GOLD MEDAL SERIES PUTTER $70 90 150
Circa 1912-1919. Flanged back, "Maxwell" drilled hosel.

GOLD MEDAL SERIES PUTTER $70 90 150
Circa 1912-1919. Flanged back, notched neck.

GOLD MEDAL SERIES PUTTER $75   90   135
Circa 1912-1919. Brass-head.

GOLD MEDAL SERIES PUTTER $90   135   175
Circa 1912-1919. Aluminum-head mallet #4.

GOLD MEDAL SERIES $40   60   95
Circa 1912-1919. "Gold Medal" in an oval with the "Hammer" mark at toe.

"F" SERIES PUTTER $55   75   120
Patented 1-3-1922. Blade putter with three deep scoring lines.

"M" SERIES PUTTER $45   60   80
Circa 1915-1922. "M-11, -12 and -16 all marked "Spalding Forged."

"MEDAL" PUTTER $45   60   85
Circa 1915-1920. Marked "Spalding Medal" between two "Thistle" marks.

KRO-FLITE SERIES PUTTER $45   60   80
Circa late 1920s. Blade putter marked "Spalding Kro-Flite" with "H" on the sole.

KRO-FLITE PUTTER $45   60   85
Sweet Spot "RF" putter with "Pat. Sept 13, 1927" date.

CALAMITY JANE PUTTER $175   290   450
Circa 1931. Marked "Robt. T Jones, Jr." Wood shafted. Photo below.

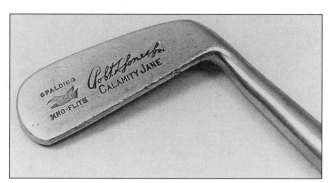

HEATHER PUTTER $40   55   80
Circa 1915-1920. Marked "Spalding Heather" between two "Rose" marks.

THISTLE PUTTER $40   55   80
Circa 1920s. Marked "Thistle."

SEMETRIC SERIES PUTTER $40   50   80
Circa mid to late 1920s. Chromed blade putter.

FLANGED-BACK PGA PUTTER $45   60   85
Circa late 1920s. Marked "Pro Golfers Assn" with "Crossed Clubs."

FLANGED-BACK PUTTER $45   60   90
Circa 1912-1919. Marked "Spalding Gold Medal 8."

FIRE BRAND PUTTER $60   75   100
One year only, 1923. "Arm & Torch" mark.

MONEL METAL PUTTER $80   150   300
Circa 1912-1913. "Ball-with-Wings" and "Baseball" marks. Photo below.

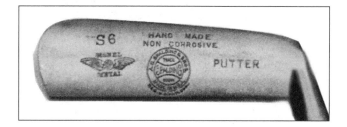

"B V" PUTTER $100   150   250
Circa 1910-1915. Crescent head shaped. Photo below.

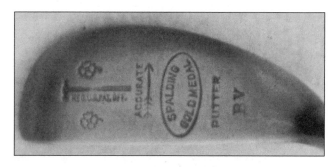

CHICOPEE PUTTER $75   100   150
Circa 1920 marked "Spalding Chicopee" on the brass-head. There are modern remakes with "Spalding" on the sole.

MAXWELL HOSEL PUTTER $125   175   275
Ten or twelve holes in hosel. Flanged back.

ALUMINUM MALLET PUTTER $70   100   150
Circa 1915-1920. "MR" on the sole. Marked "A G Spalding & Bros."

ALUMINUM MALLET PUTTER $90   120   175
Circa 1920. Marked "Reach" with a "Keystone" mark.

ALUMINUM PUTTER $75   100   150
Circa teens. "A G Spalding & Bros" and "AHP."

ALUMINUM PUTTER $90   135   200
Circa teens. "Gold Medal 4."

SCHENECTADY TYPE
PUTTER $125   175   350
Circa 1910-1920 marked "Spalding Gold Medal H H."

HOLLOW BACK PUTTER $200   350   550
Circa late 1920s. "HB" putter with hollowed-out back. Photo below.

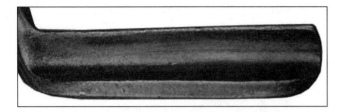

SPRING FACE PUTTER $375   600   1250
Circa 1897-1915. "The Spalding," Crescent" and "Gold Medal" marks.

TRAVIS PUTTER $500   700   1100
Circa 1905-1910. Center-shafted persimmon wood putter with a brass face and sole plate.

OLYMPIC PUTTER $500   800   1400
Circa 1914-1918. Square steel shaft. Pointed toe on the rounded head. Photo below.

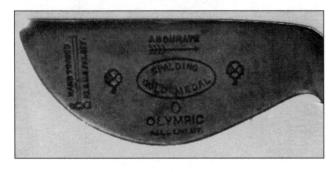

CLAN LOFTING IRON $150   225   350
Circa 1895. "Clan" in block letters on head and shaft.

"SMCO" SERIES IRONS $150   250   425
Circa 1895 Cleek, iron and lofting iron with the "Crescent Moon" mark. Photo below.

"SMCO" SERIES IRONS $450   700   1200
Circa 1895. Rut niblick with the "Crescent Moon" mark.

CLAN SERIES IRONS $125   225   400
Circa 1895. Iron and lofter marked "Clan" in large block letters.

SPALDING SPECIAL SERIES IRONS $90   150   300
Circa 1894-1896. Cleek, Mid-iron, lofting iron.

SPALDING SPECIAL SERIES IRONS $350   550   1000
Circa 1894-1896. Concave-face rut niblick.

THE SPALDING SERIES IRONS $50   85   140
Circa 1898-1902. Cleek, iron and lofting iron. Photo below.

THE SPALDING SERIES IRONS $80   150   275
Circa 1898-1902. Cleek with "Carruthers" through-hosel shafting.

THE SPALDING SERIES IRONS $90   150   300
Circa 1898-1902. Lofter with concave smooth-face.

THE SPALDING SERIES IRONS $300   500   950
Circa 1898-1902. Concave-face rut niblick.

MORRISTOWN SERIES IRONS $50   80   145
Circa 1898-1900. Steel head with "Morristown" stamping. Cleek, Mid-iron and lofting irons.

MORRISTOWN SERIES IRONS $50   75   135
Circa 1902-1905. Steel head with "Morristown" and "Baseball" marks. Cleek, mid-iron and lofting irons.

MORRISTOWN SERIES IRONS $175   300   600
Circa 1898-1900. Smooth-face niblick with "Morristown" stamping.

BASEBALL TRADEMARK IRONS $60   90   140
Circa 1902-1905. "Model B" lofting iron.

HARRY VARDON SERIES IRONS $60   100   175
Circa 1900-1903. Smooth-face cleek, Mid-iron and lofter marked "A G Spalding & Bros., Makers."

HARRY VARDON SERIES

IRONS $200 325 500
Circa 1900-1903. Smooth-face niblick marked "A G Spalding & Bros., Makers."

MODEL SERIES A, B, C IRONS $70 100 175
Circa 1899-1902. Cleek, mid-iron and lofting iron with "A G Spalding & Bros., Model" in very tiny letters.

MODEL SERIES A, B, C IRONS $300 600 1000
Circa 1902-1905. Rut niblick with concave face.

CRESCENT SERIES IRONS $50 75 125
Circa 1902-1905. Cleek, mid-iron, lofter and specialty clubs. Smooth-face with "Baseball" mark.

GOLD MEDAL SERIES IRONS $40 60 90
Circa 1909-1912. Various irons with ball-face designs. Photo below.

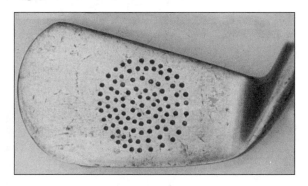

GOLD MEDAL SERIES IRONS $50 60 85
Circa 1912-1919. "Jigger."

GOLD MEDAL SERIES IRONS $50 75 135
Circa 1906-1908. "Gold Medal" in block letters. "C" lofter with "Diamond-dot" face scoring.

GOLD MEDAL SERIES IRONS $50 75 135
Circa 1906-1908. "Gold Medal 6" in block letters with a concave "Stag-dot" face.

GOLD MEDAL SERIES IRONS $60 85 125
Circa 1906-1908. "Gold Medal" in block letters. Iron, lofter and niblick. Photo below.

GOLD MEDAL SERIES IRONS $125 175 325
Circa 1906-08. Foulis concave mashie-niblick with "Gold Medal 3" in block letters.

CORRUGATED DEEP

GROOVE IRONS $100 150 225
C-54, C-67 and C-98. Mashie, mashie-niblick and niblick.

CORRUGATED DEEP

GROOVE IRONS $100 150 225
"F" series mid-iron, mashie, mashie-niblick and niblick.

SLOT DEEP GROOVE IRONS $110 160 250
"C-91, Dedstop mashie-niblick" on the sole.

A. G. SPALDING & BROS.

SERIES IRONS $40 50 80
Circa late teens-early 1920s. Irons 1 through 9.

A. G. SPALDING & BROS.

SERIES IRONS $60 80 120
Circa late teens-early 1920s. "Bobbie iron" on a "radial" sole.

"F" SERIES LINE GROOVES

IRONS $40 55 80
Patented 1-3-1922. 2 through 9 irons. "F" numbers marked on sole at toe. Photo below.

KRO-FLITE SERIES IRONS $40 50 80
Circa 1925-1930. Irons 1 through 7, and 19.

KRO-FLITE SERIES IRONS $50 75 110
Circa 1925-1930. Irons 8 Sky iron, 15 through 18, and 29 Sand dabber.

Spalding discovered

that *mild steel* banishes finger fatigue

So the heads of the world's most accurately matched golf "irons" are made of this superior metal

A STEEL clubhead hits a golf ball with a terrific impact. Where does the shock of the blow go? Spalding has discovered that it depends largely upon the kind of steel used.

Brittle steel resists the blow—transmitting the shock to your fingers. A succession of such blows often causes finger fatigue—that barely perceptible tiring of the finger muscles, which, by the end of a round, can effect the accuracy of your short game.

Mild steel absorbs the shock of the blow. Your fingers are relieved of the strain—a desirable condition in all your golf, a vitally important one in tournament play.

That is why the heads of all Spalding "Irons" are made of mild steel. You notice the difference in the sweeter feel of the impact as the mild-steel clubhead hits the ball.

Mild steel makes the "Sweet Spot" sweeter still

 The "Sweet Spot" is the one spot on the club face that gives greatest distance to the ball, and the sweetest feel to the shot. Every golf club has a "Sweet Spot." But it was Spalding who found that by planning the distribution of metal, it could be located in the same position on every club face. And Spalding has marked it there for you to see.

It was Spalding also who originated the idea of having golf clubs match each other. Spalding clubs are so perfectly related in balance and weight that they all *feel* exactly alike. You can time your swing the same for all of them. If you have analyzed the play of champions, you know that such uniformity is the secret of great golf. Spalding has put this uniformity into the clubs themselves.

These clubs have an exact relation of lie to lie. An exact graduation in the pitches of the blades. Even the torsion and resilience of the shafts is matched.

Your wood clubs should match too

You can buy Spalding wood clubs which are as accurately related as the Spalding irons. It is important that this relation exist, too!

Own a matched set .. Buy it complete

or *one club at a time*

YOU can now build up a perfectly related set of golf clubs, one by one if you wish. Spalding's new Kro-Flite Related Irons are sold one at a time.

There are three groups, or swinging weights, to choose from—indexed by one (.) two (..) and three (...) dots. The irons in each group are accurately related in pitch, lie, balance and feel. Buy one or two clubs of the index that suits you best. Add to them at any time by selecting additional clubs of the same index.

Each group includes a No. 1 iron (driving iron), No. 2 (mid-iron), No. 3 (mid mashie), No. 4 (mashie iron), No. 5 (mashie), and No. 6 (mashie niblick). The Kro-Flite Related Irons are $6.50 each. Kro-Flite Related Woods—Driver, Brassie and Spoon—are $12.50 each.

Spalding also offers the famous Registered Sets. These are the sets which first brought the matched club idea to golfers.

Eight perfectly matched irons comprise the Registered Kro-Flite Set, at $65. The Kro-Flite Registered Wood Set consists of twin driver and brassie, at $30. Spoon to match, made to order, is $15.

Registered Sets must be bought complete. Each set is registered by Spalding and a complete record is kept of every club. Therefore any registered club can be exactly duplicated at any time.

Ask your professional to outfit you—either one at a time with Kro-Flite Related Clubs, or all at once with a Registered Set. Spalding dealers also carry these clubs, and of course all Spalding Stores.

FREE— A GOLF CLUB BOOKLET that gives you a lot of information about clubs that you can apply to your own game. Simply request on a postal, "The First Requisite of Championship Golf" and mail to A. G. SPALDING & BROS., 105 Nassau Street, New York City.

© 1927, A. G. S. & B.

Spalding
KRO-FLITE
GOLF CLUBS
Registered sets— sold in sets only.   Related Clubs— sold one at a time.

At the left is shown an average set of golf clubs. The dotted line connects the centers of balance. There is little relation between them. Your swing and timing for each club would be a trifle different.

At the right are six Spalding clubs. Note that they are so accurately related that a line drawn through the centers of balance parallels the tops of the shafts. The clubs all feel exactly alike. The swing and timing is the same for every one of them.

Reading from left to right: BOBBY JONES
and the Spalding Clubs he designed

HERE is Bobby Jones examining the first set of golf clubs ever made which offer his idea of what perfect golf clubs should be!

From 8 to 1, is a set of the grandest Irons that the game has ever seen. Jones, now a Spalding Director, and the Spalding experts have, by redistributing weight, succeeded in designing an iron whose head tends to follow through naturally. As Jones himself expressed it, "the blade seems to flow through the ball."

This redistribution of weight—the heavier blade and lighter hosel—gives better control, too. The center of percussion is two inches lower than it is on hickory-shafted irons, and an inch lower than it is on other steel-shafted irons. This makes the clubhead easier to direct, and gives a more perfect instrument for shot control.

Another factor which contributes to control is the flange sole, which seats itself in back of the ball with the accuracy of a putter. This feature relieves the player of the distracting business of fussing with the lie of the blade, and lets him concentrate on the stroke itself.

In these clubs, Jones also cuts the number of stances right in half, by introducing the brand new idea of matching in pairs as to length and lie! This means that you need

master only *one* stance for every *two* clubs. And, every club is matched with every other club in swinging weight—so that one swing and one timing are correct for every club in the set!

"Poems in Wood"

Bobby Jones is recognized as one of the greatest wood players of all time. And his uncanny skill is reflected in the new woods which he designed. One famous expert, when first examining them, said—"They're poems in wood." When perfectly sane golfers get to talking like that about these clubs, they *must* be magnificent!

In addition to the customary woods, Jones contributes a new Senior Set of *Five* Graduated Woods—introducing two completely new woods to take the place of the Numbers 1 and 2 irons. Senior golfers will find, in this Set, a solution of the difficul-

ties they now have with their long iron shots.

Look! It's Calamity Jane!

That interesting looking club on the end is none other than Calamity Jane—an exact duplicate of the famous lady herself. Legend has it that Bobby Jones clings to this great putter because he considers it "lucky." In a way, that's true. Calamity Jane's magnificent balance and deadliness make it a lucky club in any golfer's bag.

Lower prices for all

The new Jones Clubs have the famous Spalding Cushion-neck. The sets are Registered, so that you can always get an exact duplicate of any club. And the prices are the lowest ever asked for Spalding fine clubs.

CUSTOM-BUILT REGISTERED IRONS
Set of 9 $75   Set of 8 $67   Set of 6 $50
(Cushion Shaft Irons, $5 each)
CUSTOM-BUILT DE LUXE
REGISTERED WOODS
Set of 4 $48   Set of 3 $36   Pair $24
CUSTOM-BUILT STANDARD
REGISTERED WOODS
Set of 4 $40   Set of 3 $30   Pair $20
(Autograph Woods, separately, $8 and $10 each)
Custom-Built De Luxe Senior Graduated Registered Woods, $60 for set of 5. Senior Graduated Matched Woods, $40 for set of 5. Calamity Jane Putter, $6.

Spalding
ROBERT T. JONES, JR.
GOLF CLUBS

R. T. JONES KRO-FLITE
IRONS $160   275   400
Irons 2 through 8. All wood shaft irons have a registration number preceeded by the letter "H." Irons that do not have the "H" prefix are metal shafted and have no real collectible value.

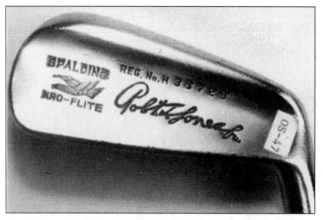

Spalding manufactured the Robert T Jones, Jr. irons with hickory shafts in very limited numbers. Each set has a Registration Number that begins with the letter "H" signifying "Hickory". During the 1930s through the 1950s, Spalding produced millions of sets with steel shafts, many coated with plastic and appear to be wood.

R. T. JONES KRO-FLITE IRONS $190   325   450
#1 Driving iron and #9 niblick.

R. T. JONES KRO-FLITE
IRONS $2200   3750   7500
Complete set 1-9 irons and Calamity Jane putter.

CUSTOM SERIES IRONS $50   65   100
Exactly the same as the Kro-Flite R. T. Jones, but marked "Custom."

CUSTOM SERIES IRONS $500   750   1400
Complete set 1-9 custom irons.

"M" SERIES IRONS $40   50   80
Circa early 1920s. Irons 1 through 9 with deep line scoring.

"F" SERIES IRONS $50   65   90
Patented 1-3-1922. #1 iron. "F" numbers marked on sole at toe.

SEMETRIC SERIES IRONS $40   50   80
Circa late 1920s. Irons 1 through 9.

FIRE BRAND SERIES IRONS $50   60   100
One year only, 1923. "Arm and torch," various irons.

MONEL METAL IRONS $50   65   95
Circa 1912-1913. "Ball with wings" and "Baseball" mark. Photo below.

MAXWELL HOSEL IRONS $60   90   135
Ten or twelve holes in hosel. Cleek, mid-iron, mashie, mashie-niblick and niblick all with flanged backs.

SPRING FACE IRONS $300   550   1000
Circa 1897-1915. "The Spalding," Crescent" and "Gold Medal" marks.

BALL BACK IRONS $400   650   1000
Circa 1905. Smooth-face cleek, iron and lofting iron with large protruding "Ball" back-weighting design.

WATERFALL IRONS $400   500   800
Circa 1920. Single waterfall "F" series. Photo below.

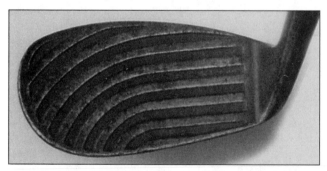

CRAN IRONS $500   950   1750
Circa 1897-1915. Wood face insert. "The Spalding," "Crescent" and "Gold Medal" marks. Photo below.

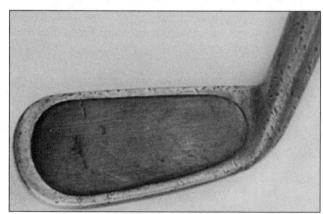

SEELY PATENT IRONS $500   800   1500
Circa 1912-1919. "Forked hosel" with "Gold Medal" marks. Photo below.

DOUBLE WATERFALL IRON $2000   2800   4500
Circa 1920. "F" series.

LARD PATENT IRONS $2200   3000   4500
Circa 1914-1920. Perforated steel shaft. Cleek, mid-iron, mashie, mashie-niblick and niblick. Photo below.

LARD PATENT IRONS $2750   3500   5500
Circa 1914-1920. Perforated steel shaft. Corrugated deep groove face scoring, any model.

THE SPALDING ONE-PIECE
WOOD $1200   1700   2600
Circa 1898-1902. Driver with leather face insert. Photo below.

THE SPALDING SERIES
WOODS $225   350   700
Circa 1898-1902. Pear-shaped driver, brassie and spoon. Heads were usually made from "Dogwood." Photo below.

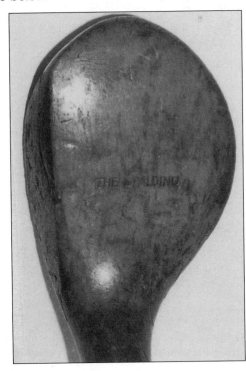

MORRISTOWN SERIES
WOODS $275   450   700
Circa 1902-1905. Spliced-neck, bulger-face brassie with "Morristown" and "Baseball" marks.

MORRISTOWN SERIES
WOODS $300   475   800
Circa 1902-1905. Spliced-neck semi-long-nose play club or brassie with "Morristown" mark.

HARRY VARDON SERIES
WOODS $200   375   700
Circa 1900-1903. Driver, brassie or spoon all with a leather face insert and stamped "Harry Vardon."

CRESCENT SERIES WOODS $90   135   200
Circa 1902-1905. Driver, brassie or spoon with "Baseball" mark. Photo below.

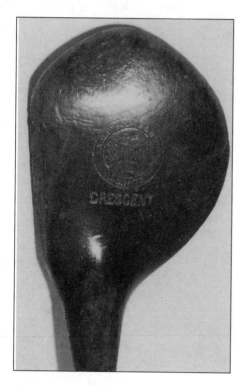

DUNCAN MODEL WOODS $85   110   160
Circa 1920. Patented one-piece sole and back weight.

FIRE BRAND SERIES WOODS $100   140   190
One year only, 1923. "Arm & Torch" mark.

SKOOTER PATENT WOODS $150   225   375
Patented August 22, 1911. Marked "A G Spalding & Bros." Driver, brassie or spoon.

ALUMINUM-HEAD WOODS $150   275   550
Circa 1915-1920. Aluminum-head driver and various loft fairway clubs marked "A G Spalding Bros., Makers."

MALTESE CROSS FACE WOODS $90   125   160
Circa 1920s. Red and black Maltese Cross plastic insert.

CROW FACE WOODS $125   175   275
Circa 1920s. Black flying "Crow" in an "Ivorine" insert.

TRIPLE SPLICE PATENT
WOODS $275   350   550
Circa 1920. Driver, brassie and spoon with a "Triple" splice affixing head to shaft.

JACOBUS PATENT WOOD $275   375   650
Circa 1910. Three Mahogany dowels arranged in the face. "A G Spalding Bros., Gold Medal" markings. Photo below.

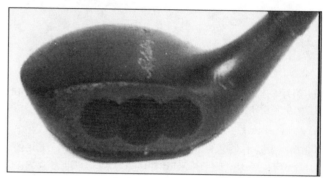

JUVENILE CLUBS $30   40   65
"A G Spalding Bros., Junior" smooth-face putter, mid-iron and mashie.

JUVENILE CLUBS $65   90   150
"A G Spalding Bros., Junior" driver.

SPENCE & GOURLAY
ST. ANDREWS, SCOTLAND

James Spence and George Gourlay went into partnership in 1895, and by 1908 they had built a great reputation and flourishing business. Their business came to an end in 1914 as a result of WWI. Their mark was a "Clover" with "S & G" inside.

OFFSET BLADE PUTTER $50   65   100
Circa 1920-1925. "S & G" inside a shamrock mark.

LONG HOSEL PUTTER $85   120   170
Circa 1920s. "Flag-in-hole." Hosel is 5-1/2 inches.

DOT-PUNCHED-FACE IRONS $50   60   85
Circa 1915. All irons. "S & G" inside a "Clover" mark.

DREADNOUGHT NIBLICK $75   95   150
Circa 1915. Dot-punched face.

ANTI-SHANK IRONS $120   175   250
Circa 1920. All irons. Smith's Patent.

SPENCE, JAMES
ST. ANDREWS, SCOTLAND

After the war, James Spence returned to the business previously operating under Spence & Gourlay. He changed the cleek mark and rebuilt a very successful company. In 1920 he sold out to Robert Forgan & Son. Forgan used the Spence trademark throughout the 1930s, and kept the James Spence (St. Andrews) Limited name for a while. He used the "Flag-In-Hole" and monogrammed "JS" marks.

BLACKWELL PUTTER $60   75   100
Circa 1920s. "Flag-in-Hole" mark on a beveled heel and toe, thick sole offset blade. Photo below.

DRIVING IRON $50   70   120
Circa 1915-1920. Dot-punched face.

SPECIAL APPROACHING CLEEK $55   75   110
Circa 1915-1920.

MAXWELL HOSEL IRONS $60   80   130
Circa 1915-1925. All irons. Flanged back, line or dot-faces.

LARGE HEAD NIBLICK $100   150   250
Circa 1915. Dot-punched face. Nearly "Giant" size.

ST. ANDREW GOLF CO.
DUNFIRMLINE & GLASGOW, SCOTLAND

Began making clubs after 1900. It used the "Running Stag" mark and "Stag." It produced many clubs made from "Hawkin's Never Rust," a silvery metal.

SMOOTH-FACE BLADE PUTTER $55   75   110
Circa 1900-1910. Deep-face, straight, compact blade. "The St. Andrew Golf Co., Ltd, Glasgow" stamping. Photo below.

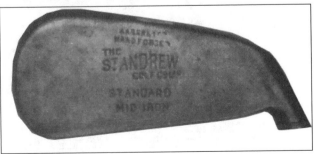

BLADE PUTTER $55   75   110
Circa 1910-20. "Stag" marking. Photo below.

STANDARD WRY NECK PUTTER $60   80   120
Circa 1920. Line-scored offset hosel blade.

HAWKINS NEVER RUST PUTTER $60   90   140
Circa 1920s. Monel metal flanged-back, offset hosel, line-scored blade.

STANDARD JIGGER $45   60   90
Circa 1915-1920. Hyphen-scored face.

HAWKINS NEVER RUST IRONS $55   75   110
Circa 1915-1920. All irons flanged back. "Running Stag" mark.

MAXWELL HOSEL IRONS $60   80   120
Circa 1915. Flanged back.

CONVEX FACE IRONS $60   80   120
Circa 1915-1920. "Running Stag" mark. Flanged back.

ANTI-SHANK IRONS $125   190   275
Circa 1920s. All irons. Fairlie's Patent. "Running Stag" mark.

ST. ANDREW SPECIAL WOODS $100   125   175
Circa 1915-1920. Driver, brassie or spoon with large heads.

STADIUM GOLF CO.
LONDON, ENGLAND

The Williamson family owned the Stadium Golf Manufacturing Company, Ltd., and Hugh Williamson was in charge of running the business with help from manager Jimmie Ross. They produced particularly modern clubs for that time, and in 1929 the company folded. They used an "Anchor" with a large "S" mark.

MUSSEL BACK PUTTER $60   80   120
Circa 1925. "Anchor & S" mark. Square punched face scoring. Photo below.

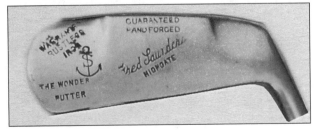

KORECTA PUTTER $175 250 400
Circa 1920s. "V" sight groove notched in the "Pagoda" shaped top of the blade. "Anchor and S" mark.

SCUFFLER SEMI PUTTER $175 275 400
Circa 1915-1920. "Rivers-Zambra" Approach putter "Reg'd no. 740870" on head.

DOT-PUNCHED-FACE IRONS $50 60 90
Circa 1915-1920. All irons with a dot-punched face. "Anchor & S" mark.

WHITCOMBE JIGGER $50 65 100
Circa 1915-1920. "Anchor" mark at toe.

ANTI-SHANK IRONS $125 190 275
Circa 1920s. All irons. "Anchor-S" mark.

STANDARD GOLF CO.
SUNDERLAND, ENGLAND

William Mills broke tradition in the mid-1890s when he made fairway woods and putters from aluminum. "Standard Golf Company, Sunderland, England" was his mark. The company used markings on the soles to indicate model names and the like. Many aluminum woods and putters were exported to America. The Harry C. Lee, Co. and B. G. I. were two of the agents that imported vast numbers of "Mills" aluminum clubs.

Peter Georgiady wrote a three-part series on Mills and Standard Golf in the author's monthly publications #88, 89 and 90. Any collector of Mills clubs should include these articles in their library.

Patrick Kennedy produced a reprint of the 1909 Mills Retail Catalogue and this, too, should be required reading.

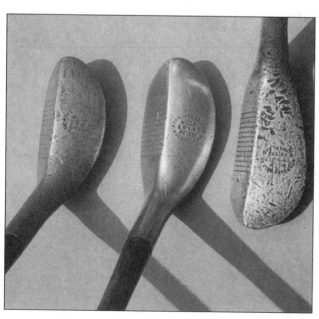

BRAID MILLS MODEL $50 85 150
Circa 1905-1915. Photo below.

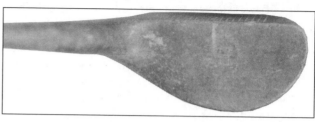

NEW RAY MILLS MODEL $50 85 150
Circa 1910-1915.

BRAID MILLS 1915 MODEL $55 85 150
Circa 1915-1920.

MILLS "SS" MODEL $75 120 175
Circa 1915-1920.

NEW MILLS "RNG" MODEL $75 125 200
Circa 1910-1915. "T" Bar sight line.

Mills

THIS IS THE PUTTER !! YOU ARE ENQUIRING FOR.

The "BRAID-MILLS"

ALUMINIUM PUTTER,

as used by the OPEN CHAMPION, JAS. BRAID, and all the leading Professionals and Amateurs.

Jas. Braid, Open Champion, 1901, 1905, 1906, and 1908, says:—I used the Putter manufactured by you throughout the Championships. I certainly putt more consistently with it than any other.

Harry Vardon, Open Champion, 1896, 1898, 1899, 1903, says:— Since I have taken to your Aluminium Putter, I must say I have been able to putt more accurately with it.

BEWARE OF SPURIOUS IMITATIONS.

None are genuine unless stamped on top thus ☞ STANDARD GOLF Cº MILLS PATENT SUNDERLAND and numbered above the word Patent. :: ::

This Putter (like all our Clubs) is made in any Weight and Lie to suit all players.

When the Leading Players find it an advantage to use our Putters, can you afford to be without one?

THEY INSPIRE CONFIDENCE.

Wonderful Clubs for long or short distances.

Particulars of Putters.

Marks on Sole.

On the Sole is stamped the Model, Lie, and exact Weight of the Head.

Angle of Lies for Putters.

No. 1.	Flat Lie	..	about 63°
No. 2.	Medium	"	67°
No. 3.	Upright	"	70.5°
No. 4.	Extra Upright	"	75°

Angle of Lies for Putters.

Loft of Putter Face.

The Loft is made to our Standard (see page 23) but is made more or less to Customers' special requirements, viz.:—The "Braid-Mills" Putter is made equal to Brassie Loft, see page 23.

Weights of Heads.

The Heads are made between the minimum and maximum weights given as stated with each illustration.

As it is impossible to keep on hand the exact weights to suit every requirement, orders will be supplied from the nearest in stock, but exact weights can be made by giving a few days' notice.

Shafts.

The Shafts are made to our Standard, as follows :— Flat, 36 in.; Medium, 35 in.; Upright and Extra Upright, 34 in., unless specially ordered otherwise.

The "MILLS" Patent Aluminium

PUTTERS.

In order to suit the physical and other requirements of different players, the "MILLS" Putters are made in various Shapes, Weights, and Lies, details of which are given herewith.

Y Model.

Face about 4" long by about ¾" deep. Weight from 9 to 10½ ozs.

Price 7/6 each.

YS similar in shape to Y, but smaller and lighter head. Face about 3¾" long by ¾" deep.

X an exact copy of the Putter used by Mr. H. H. Hilton at the Championship, 1901.

L. Model.

Face about 4" long by ¾" deep. Weight 9 to 11 ozs.

Price 7/6 each.

Z a Model between **Y** and **L**. This is a beautiful Model. We carry a full line of Left Hand Clubs in each Model. For Lie, Loft, &c., see page 22.

The "MILLS" Patent Aluminium

LONG, MID, BAFFY, AND BULGER

SPOONS

as used by all the Leading Players.

ADVANTAGES :

Combine all the advantages of WOOD SPOONS, without their disadvantages. Are impervious to wet and practically indestructible. Will not rust nor alter balance. There are no parts to come loose, such as horn, &c. Perfectly balanced and true. The ball will not skid from face. Inspires confidence in play.

Will play all the Strokes that can be played with irons. They are much easier to play with than Irons. Invaluable for Approaching.

THE PLAY CLUBS for the TWENTIETH CENTURY.

Prices :—
Finished Clubs, 7s. 6d. each.
Made in a variety of Shapes, Lies, and Weights, to suit all players

---

The "MILLS" Patent Aluminium

PUTTERS.

S S Model.

Face about 4" long by 1" deep. Weight 9½ to 11 ozs.

Price 7/6 each.

SB Model, shorter face than **S S**, almost like a Driver Head.

This is the shortest and broadest Putter Head we make.

K L Model.

Face about 5" long by ¾" deep. Weight 9¾ to 11 ozs.

Price 7/6 each.

K Model similar to **K L** but smaller and lighter Head. Face about 4¾" long.

LADIES' CLUBS A SPECIALITY.

Booklet, "HINTS ON PUTTING" sent post free on application.

The "MILLS" Patent Aluminium

Long Spoons equivalent to CLEEKS.

M S D 1 Model, with SHORT HEAD and Deep Face.

Price 7/6 each.

For Particulars of LOFTS & LIES, see page 22.

B S D 1 Model, with LONG HEAD and Deep Face.

Price 7/6 each.

Made in various Weights and Lies to suit all players.

The "MILLS" Patent Aluminium

MEDIUM LONG SPOONS equivalent to DRIVING IRONS.

M S D 1½ Model, with SHORT HEAD and Deep Face.

Price 7/6 each.

For Particulars of Lofts and Lies, see page 22.

B S D 1½ Model, with LONG HEAD and Deep Face.

Price 7/6 each.

Ladies' Clubs a Speciality, as supplied to H.R.H. The Duchess of Connaught.

The "MILLS" Patent Aluminium

MID-SPOONS equivalent to IRONS.

M S D 2 Model, with SHORT HEAD and Deep Face.

Price 7/6 each.

For Particulars of Lofts and Lies, see page 22.

B S D 2 Model, with LONG HEAD and Deep Face.

Price 7/6 each.

We carry a full line of Left Hand Clubs in each Model.

The "MILLS" Patent Aluminium

SHORT SPOONS equivalent to MEDIUM LOFTERS.

M S D 2½ Model, with SHORT HEAD and Deep Face.

Price 7/6 each.

For Particulars of Lofts and Lies, see page 22.

B S D 2½ Model, with LONG HEAD and Deep Face.

Price 7/6 each.

The Aluminium Spoons have a greater resiliency than Iron.

Examples of bottom markings on putters.

NEW MILLS "RM" MODEL $75   125   200
Circa 1910-1915. Photo below.

NEW MILLS "RBB" MODEL $90   135   250
Circa 1910-1915. Thick "sight line" on top.

**"MNB" MODEL ALUMINUM
HEAD** $100   150   250
Circa 1910. Offset hosel. "Blade" type aluminum head with 10 to 12 degrees of loft.

BENT NECK "JM" MODEL $100   175   250
Circa 1915.

MILLS "YS" MODEL $125   225   375
Circa 1905-1915.

NEW MILLS "RSB" MODEL $125   175   300
Circa 1910-1915. "Slanted Back" head.

MILLS "Y" MODEL $160   300   500
Circa 1900-1910. Long-nose aluminum putter.

MILLS "L" MODEL $160   290   450
Circa 1900-1910. "L" model indicated long-nose. Photo below.

SCHENECTADY-TYPE PUTTER $175   275   450
Circa 1903-1909. "Sunderland Golf Co" markings.
Photo below.

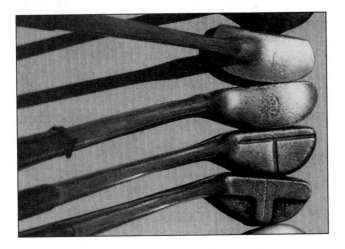

HILTON "X" MODEL $175   275   450
Circa 1910-1915. Long-nose head.

MILLS "RSR" MODEL $175   250   400
Circa 1910-1915. Two hollowed out sight bars on
either side of a hollowed out sight line.

MILLS "K" MODEL $200   450   750
Circa 1900-1910. Very long head.

MILLS "AK" MODEL $200   400   650
Circa 1910-1915. Rectangular head.

MILLS "RRA" MODEL $200   350   475
Circa 1910-1915. Raised right angle aiming sight.

MILLS "SB" MODEL $200   300   425
Circa 1910-1915. Head is nearly "D" shaped.

MILLS "Z" MODEL $200   350   500
Circa 1900-1910. Long-nose head.

"BSD" ALUMINUM
FAIRWAY WOODS $125   225   450
Circa 1895-1915. Long-head clubs. 1 cleek, 1-1/2
driving iron, 2 iron, and 2-1/2 medium lofter. "BSD"
on sole.

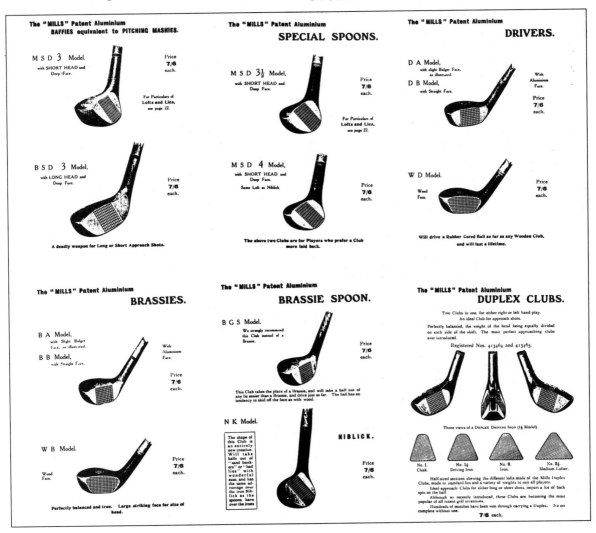

"MSD" ALUMINUM FAIRWAY

WOODS $125 225 450

Circa 1895-1915. Short-head clubs. 1 cleek, 1-1/2 driving iron, 2 iron, and 2-1/2 medium lofter. "BSD" on sole.

"CB" SERIES ALUMINUM

WOODS $150 250 450

Circa 1915-1920. All clubs.

"MSD" ALUMINUM FAIRWAY

WOODS $225 350 650

Circa 1895-1915. Short head. 3-1/2 BSD on sole.

ALUMINUM DRIVERS $250 375 575

Circa 1900-1915. "D A" bulger face or "D B" Straight face.

ALUMINUM BRASSIES $250 375 575

Circa 1900-1915. "B A" bulger face or "B B" straight face.

"MSD" ALUMINUM FAIRWAY

WOODS $275 450 750

Circa 1895-1915. Short head. 3 Pitching mashie. "BSD" on sole. Photo below.

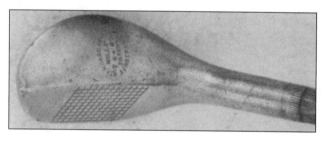

"BSD" ALUMINUM FAIRWAY

WOODS $275 450 750

Circa 1895-1915. Long head. 3 pitching mashie. "BSD" on sole.

DUPLEX ALUMINUM WOODS $375 600 1200

Circa 1900-1915. 1 cleek, 1-1/2 Driving iron, 2 iron, and 2-1/2 medium lofter. Photo below.

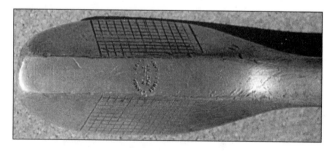

"MSD" NIBLICK WOOD $400 650 1300

Circa 1895-1915. Short head. 4 or "NK." "BSD" on sole.

STEWART, TOM
ST. ANDREWS, SCOTLAND

by Ralph Livingston

One of the most recognizable maker's marks is the "Clay Pipe"-shaped cleek mark of Thomas Stewart Jr. of St. Andrews, Scotland. The "Pipe of Peace" cleek mark is stamped into the back of the club head centered along the sole. From 1893 to 1904, Stewart used the pipe and also a "Serpent" (indicated a club for ladies) cleek mark. In July 1904, his registration mark was approved, and from thereafter, the stamping "T.S.St. A. REG. TRADEMARK" was added beneath the "Pipe" mark.

Stewart quickly gained a reputation for making clubs of the highest quality. Many of his clients were the top professionals and amateurs of that time. Today, he is best known for the clubs he made for Bobby Jones, Francis Ouimet, Harry Vardon and countless others.

When Stewart would personally supervise the making of a club, he would stamp a "Dot" into the toe on the back of the club. Approximately one in fifty clubs has Stewart's personal inspection mark. There are other inspection marks and these are attributed to his best associate clubmakers.

One of the most logical aspects of his business was that he sold only club heads. Most of his production was sold to professionals and retailers who would have their staff do the assembly. For a small fee, the club heads were personalized with the professional's name and golf course or the retailer's advertisement. Consequently, many "Pipe" marked irons have names other than "Stewart" stamped on their backs.

ORD PUTTER $50 65 100

Circa 1920. Line-scored blade. "Pipe" mark.

PUTTING CLEEK $55 85 125

Circa 1920. Line-scored faced. "Pipe" mark.

SMOOTH-FACE PUTTING

CLEEK $60 85 125

Circa 1910. Marked "Slazenger Special New York." "Pipe" mark.

GEM PUTTER $70 100 150

Circa 1915-1920. Rounded back. "Pipe" mark.

NEW ZEALAND CLUBS $75 125 200

Circa 1910. "Hood & Clements, Christchurch." Bent neck, smooth-face blade putter. "Pipe" mark.

BRASS PUTTER $100 175 300

Circa 1900. No registration marks under "Pipe" mark.

"R T J" PUTTER $150   275   550
Circa 1930. "Pipe" mark. Photo below.

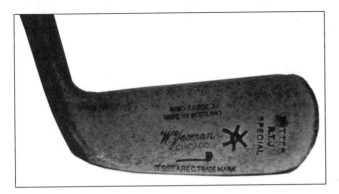

BRASS PUTTER $150   250   400
Circa 1895. "Serpent" mark.

"R T J" PUTTER $200   375   550
Circa 1930. "R T J" in block letters.

PATENTED "V" BACK
PUTTER $300   400   600
Circa 1920. "V" groove hollow back design. Photo
below.

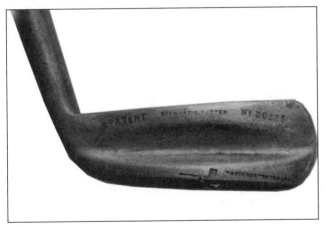

TWEENIE IRON $80   110   175
Circa 1920s. Rounded sole line-scored club. Similar
to a "Bobbie" iron. "Pipe" mark.

LARGE HEAD NIBLICK $150   200   350
Circa 1900. Smooth-face without registration marks
under the "Pipe" mark.

DIAMOND BACK IRONS $50   60   100
Circa 1910-1920. Dot-punched face. "Pipe" mark.

JIGGERS $50   70   120
Circa 1920. With broad flat sole, line-scored. "Pipe"
mark.

HARRY VARDON IRONS $60   95   150
Circa 1920. "Pipe" mark.

BOBBIE IRON $70   100   150
Circa 1920. Broad, rounded sole. Line-scored face.
"Pipe" mark.

SAMMY IRON $75   100   150
Circa 1915. Dot-punched face. "Pipe" mark.

T. STEWART MAKER IRONS $90   135   225
Circa 1895-1905. No "registration" stamp below the
"Pipe" mark.

T. STEWART MAKER IRONS $75   100   150
Circa 1910. Smooth-face cleek. "Pipe" mark. Photo
below.

T. STEWART MAKER IRONS $50   60   100
Circa 1915-1925. Dot-punched face. All irons

T. STEWART MAKER IRONS $50   60   95
Circa 1920-1930. Lined face. All irons

CONCAVE FACE LOFTER $75   125   200
Circa 1900. No registration marks under the "Pipe"
mark.

CLUBS FOR CAIRO, EGYPT $75   125   200
Circa 1915. All irons. "Pipe" mark.

TOM MORRIS IRONS $90   140   220
Circa 1920s. Line-scored face. "Pipe" mark.

"R T J" IRONS $100   140   225
Circa 1930. Line-scored face.

"F O, R T J" IRONS $120   175   250
Circa 1930. (Francis Ouimet, Robert T. Jones) initials at toe. "Pipe" mark. Photo below.

TOM MORRIS IRONS $100   175   300
Circa teens. Dot-punched face. "Pipe" mark.

Excerpts From Tom Stewart's 1930 Catalog

LIST OF GOLF IRON HEADS.

PUTTERS OR PUTT. CLEEKS.

1. Putters or Putt. Cleeks, Ordinary.
1. Do.   Round Back.
1. Do.   Diamond Back.
1. Do.   Deep Face.
1. Do.   'Accurate.'
1. Do.   „   Round Back.
1. Do.   „   Diamond Back.
1. Do.   Park Pattern.
1. Do.   Special—Blade bent at neck.
1. Do.   Sherlock Pattern.
1. Do.   F. G. Tait Pattern.
1. Do.   Rowland Jones Pattern.
1. Do.   Gun Metal.
2. Do.   Fairlie Pattern.
3. Do.   Logan Pattern.
3. Do.   Celtic Pattern.
1. Do.   R. T. J. Pattern.

3. Putters—Gem or '100.'
3. Do.   Gem 'Accurate' Bend.
4. Do.   Ballingall.
4. Do.   Smith—Hollow Back.
4. Do.   'Stewart' Patent.
4. Do.   Kinnell.
   Do.   Humphry.
6. Do.   'A.B.' Pattern, as used by Harry Vardon.
3. Do.   Auchterlonie.
6. Do.   'D.S.' Pattern.
   Do.   Aluminium.
4. Do.   Maxwell Pattern.
2. Do.   Citizen.

CLEEKS.

Cleeks—Ordinary, Driving and Approaching.
1. Do.   Ordinary, Long Head.

Sets of Iron Heads made similar to those used by the late Mr. F. G. Tait.

LIST OF GOLF IRON HEADS—Continued.

1. Cleeks—Ordinary, Short Head.
1. Do.   Bevel Heel.
1. Do.   „   and Toe.
1. Do.   Diamond Back.
1. Do.   Round Back.
1. Do.   Mussel Back.
1. Do.   Bulger Back.
1. Do.   Round Sole.
   Do.   Concentrated (Various).
1. Do.   The 'Nipper.'
1. Do.   Sammy.
2. Do.   Fairlie Pattern.
3. Do.   Braid or 'Auchterlonie' Pattern.
3. Do.   Logan Pattern.
3. Do.   Celtic Pattern.
4. Do.   Smith Pattern.
5. Do.   Smith Pattern—Hollow Back.
4. Do.   Carruthers Pattern.
4. Do.   Ballingall Pattern.
4. Do.   Maxwell Pattern.

IRONS.

Irons—assorted.
1. Do.   Mid.
1. Do.   Ordinary.
1. Do.   No. 1.
1. Do.   No. 2.
1. Do.   No. 3.
1. Do.   No. 4.
1. Do.   Bevel Heel.
1. Do.   „   and Toe.
1. Do.   Diamond Back.
1. Do.   Round Back.
1. Do.   Mussel Back.
1. Do.   Bulger Back.
1. Do.   Round Sole.
   Do.   Concentrated (Various).
2. Do.   Fairlie Pattern.
3. Do.   Logan Pattern.
3. Do.   Celtic Pattern.
4. Do.   Smith Pattern.

Sets of Iron Heads made similar to those used by the late Tom Morris.

LIST OF GOLF IRON HEADS—Continued.

5. Irons—Smith Pattern—Hollow Back.
4. Do.   Ballingall Pattern.
3. Do.   Auchterlonie Pattern.
4. Do.   Maxwell Pattern.

MASHIES.

Mashies—Assorted.
1. Do.   Deep Face.
1. Do.   Vardon Pattern.
1. Do.   Ordinary Pattern—Narrow Face.
1. Do.   Herd Pattern.
1. Do.   Kirkaldy Pattern.
1. Do.   Jamie Anderson Pattern.
1. Do.   Bevel Heel.
1. Do.   „   and Toe.
1. Do.   Diamond Back.
1. Do.   Round Back.
1. Do.   Mussel Back.
1. Do.   Bulgar Back.
1. Do.   Round Sole.

Mashies—Concentrated (Various).
1. Do.   Extra Deep Face.
1. Do.   Lofting.
2. Do.   Fairlie Pattern.
3. Do.   Logan Pattern.
3. Do.   Celtic Pattern.
4. Do.   Smith Pattern.
5. Do.   Smith Pattern—Hollow Back.
4. Do.   Ballingall Pattern.
3. Do.   Auchterlonie Pattern.
4. Do.   Maxwell Pattern.

JIGGERS.

Jiggers (Assorted).
1. Do.   Ordinary.
1. Do.   Round Back.
1. Do.   Diamond Back.
1. Do.   Hilton Pattern (in four different lofts, Nos. 1, 2, 3 and 4.
Do.   Concentrated (Various).

Driving Irons made similar to that as used by the late Jack Kirkcaldy.

LIST OF GOLF IRON HEADS—Continued.

2. Jiggers—Fairlie Pattern.
3. Do.   Auchterlonie Pattern (or ' Braid ').
3. Do.   Logan Pattern.
3. Do.   Celtic Pattern.
4. Do.   Smith Pattern.
4. Do.   Maxwell Pattern.

NIBLICKS.

Niblicks (Assorted).
1. Do.   Ordinary.
1. Do.   Deep Face.
1. Do.   Extra Large Heads.
1. Do.   Diamond Back.
1. Do.   Round Back.
2. Do.   Fairlie Pattern.
3. Do.   Logan Pattern.
3. Do.   Celtic Pattern.
4. Do.   Smith Pattern.
5. Do.   Smith Pattern—Hollow Back.
4. Do.   Maxwell Pattern.

MASHIE NIBLICKS, etc.

1. Mashie Niblick—Deep Face.
1. Do.   ' Benny Pattern.'
3. Do.   ' Young Benny ' Pattern.
1. Do.   Round Top and Straight Sole.
1. Do.   Egg Shape.
2. Do.   Fairlie Pattern—Deep Face.
3. Do.   Logan Pattern.
3. Do.   Celtic Pattern.
4. Do.   Smith Pattern
5. Do.   Smith Pattern—Hollow Back.
4. Do.   Maxwell Pattern.
1. Mashie Cleeks.
1. Do.   Irons—Deep Face.
1. Do.   „   Bevel Heel.
1. Driving Mashie.
1. Do.   Irons.
1. Push-Shot Irons.
1. Lofting Irons, etc., etc.
1. Spade Mashies.

Any pattern of head made to order.
Sets of Iron Heads made as used by Mr. Robert T. Jones.

STEWART'S PATENT PUTTER.

The chief feature of this club is in its broad sole, combined with a heavy top edge, which keeps the ball from 'jumping' when struck.

This pattern of putter is used by many professionals, also many prominent amateurs, including Mr. E. A. Lassen, Ex-Amateur Champion.

"SHERLOCK PUTTER."

This putter is a copy of Jas. Sherlock's own club (Pipe Brand). 'Sherlock' *Autograph* Putters can only be obtained direct from Mr. James Sherlock, Golf Club, Hunstanton.

"A. B." PUTTER.

The 'A. B.' Putter as *used* by Harry Vardon, Open Champion, is after the model of Gem Putter, having a heavy sole and a narrow face.

THE BALLINGALL PUTTER.

This pattern of putter, with a flange sole and invented by Mr. Ballingall, is the favourite style of putter in Ireland, and is used by Mr. Lionel Munn, Irish Amateur Champion, and most of the leading professionals of " Erin."

AUCHTERLONIE APP. CLEEK.

This Approaching Cleek, frequently called the 'Braid App. Cleek,' is the same as made for and played with by James Braid. (The Ex-Open Champion's club is '*Pipe*' *Brand*.) This club, which has a centre-balanced blade, is greatly praised by the Ex-Champion (see 'Braid's Book on Golf'), and has now a great hold on the market, both at home and abroad.

Nos. 1, 2, 3 and 4 Irons.

The professional kit does not seem to be complete now-a-days without this set of Irons, which range in loft from a driving Iron to that of a Lofting Iron.

This set of heads is used and played with (all 'Pipe' Brand) by Arnaud Massy, Alex. Herd, etc.

"VARDON" MASHIE.

The Vardon pattern of Mashie ('Pipe' Brand) is the most 'sought after' pitching club of the day, and is specially made to the direction of the Open Champion.

"SMITH HEADS."

A pattern of club which has received considerable attention of late is that known as the " Smith " pattern.

SERPENT MARK IRONS $125   175   300
Circa 1898-1902. Clubs marked "Slazenger Special New York" smooth-face. Photo below.

PIPE MARK AT TOE $125   200   350
Circa 1898. Smooth-face general purpose iron.

TOM MORRIS IRONS $125   250   400
Circa 1905-1915. Smooth-face. "Pipe" mark.

ANTI-SHANK IRONS $125   225   350
Circa 1915-1920. Smith's model. Dot-punched face. "Pipe" mark.

TOM MORRIS IRONS $200   375   650
Circa Pre-1905. Smooth-face. No registration marks below "Pipe" mark.

TOM MORRIS IRONS $175   350   600
Circa pre-1898. Smooth-face. "Serpent" mark.

RUT NIBLICK $200   350   600
Circa 1895. Medium-size round head. Smooth-face. "Pipe" or "Serpent" mark.

URQUHART, ROBERT

Robert Urquhart first patented an adjustable iron in 1892. His marks were a "U" in a circle and "Urquhart" in large letters on the face of the iron.

ADJUSTABLE IRON $950   1650   2750
Circa 1900-1905. "Urquhart" across face. Photo below.

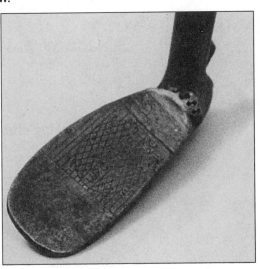

VICKER'S LIMITED
SHEFFIELD, ENGLAND

Vicker's Limited operated from 1924 to 1932. It made stainless steel heads sold under the name "Immaculate." Its market also included North America. It used a double "K" on either side of a "V" as a cleek mark.

IMMACULATE RUSTLESS
PUTTER $55   65   90
Circa 1925-1930. Double "K" mark. Photo below.

RUSTLESS IRONS $50   60   80
Circa late 1920s. All irons. "Double K" mark.

VULCAN GOLF CO.
PORTSMOUTH, OHIO

Began making clubs during the mid 1920s. Used "Vulcan" in a monogram as its mark. Made the "Burma" 7-inch-long pencil-thin hosel putter. "Septum" and "Pirate" were other markings.

LONG HOSEL PUTTER $100   150   190
Circa 1926-1930. 6-1/2 inch long hosel. "Burma 8 Putter" on back. Photo below.

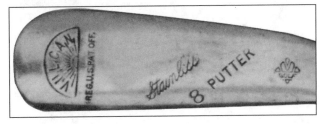

LONG HOSEL PUTTER $100   150   190
Circa 1926-1930. 6-1/2 inch long hosel. "Septum Putter" on back.

PIRATE SERIES IRONS $35   45   75
Circa 1930. All irons. Photo below.

SEPTUM SERIES IRONS $35   45   75
Circa 1927. All irons.

DRIVING IRON $50   60   90
Circa 1930. Stainless steel.

SEPTUM SERIES WOODS $75   95   135
Circa 1927. Driver, brassie or spoon.

WALTER HAGEN & L. A. YOUNG CO.

GETAWAY SERIES PUTTER $45   55   80
Circa late 1920s.

HAGEN AUTOGRAPH PUTTER $45   55   80
Circa late 1920s. Chromed blade.

THE HAIG ALUMINUM
PUTTER $150   200   250
Circa 1930-1935. Paddle grip.

LUCKY LEN PUTTER $250   350   450
Circa 1930-1935. Wooden-head mallet. Photo below.

STERLING SILVER PUTTER $700   900   1250
Circa 1930. "Sterling" marked on hosel. Photo below.

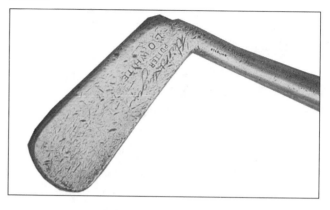

GETAWAY SERIES IRONS $35   45   70
Circa late 1920s. All irons.

HAGEN AUTOGRAPH IRONS $35   45   70
Circa late 1920s. All irons. Photo below.

IRON MAN SAND WEDGE $125   200   325
Circa 1930. Large flange. Dot-face.

CONCAVE SAND WEDGE $300   475   700
Circa 1930. Smooth concave face. Large flange. Photo below.

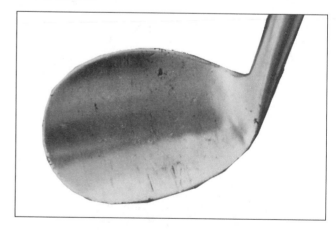

GETAWAY SERIES WOODS $75   95   150
Circa late 1920s. Driver, brassie or spoon.

HAGEN AUTOGRAPH WOODS $75   95   150
Circa late 1920s. Driver, brassie or spoon.

WALTER HAGEN & L. A. YOUNG CO.

by Pete Georgiady

If the truth were told, Walter Hagen never made a golf club in his life even though there are thousands that bear his name. His career as a professional and champion was radically different from any of his peers, and Hagen's style of living and playing left an indelible mark on the game of golf.

Born in upstate New York in 1892, he was first noticed by the golfing world as a dapper young U.S. Open champion at Midlothian in 1914, fast on the heels of Ouimet's sensational victory a year earlier. He was, at that time, the professional to Oak Hill Golf Club in Rochester, New York.

Following his win in 1914, Hagen went on a blitz through the next 13 years where he won every major championship at least once. He was twice the U.S. Open and twice the British Open champion, was a five-time American PGA champion (including four straight), he won both the Eastern and Western Opens, the North and South Opens, the French Open and a grand number of state championships.

But Hagen did more than win; he won with a style and flamboyance that golf had never witnessed before. He was not the typical pro, making clubs and giving lessons. Hagen passed time with royalty and the most celebrated people in society. He wore the finest clothes and drove the most luxurious autos. He lived on his terms, and his terms were that he was allowed in the clubhouse where the professional was formerly forbidden. His high style caused consternation in the ranks, but in the end it helped upgrade the lot of the club pro whose existence was generally less than honorable.

The never-bashful Hagen was the original endorsement magnet, and lent his image to many products. He was said to have carried 25 clubs in his bag at one time just to cover his endorsements. In the early 1920s, Hagen's primary golf club affiliation was with Burke, which manufactured the monel metal Walter Hagen autograph series. Walter also imported clubs for sale in his shop with Cochrane's of Edinburgh supplying many of the irons bearing Hagen's famous signature.

While he was at the Westchester-Biltmore in the mid-1920s, Hagen was enticed to leave New York and move to Red Run Country Club in Royal Oak outside Detroit. The auto business was making Detroit a city on the rise and this prosperity created some new opportunities for Walter.

Prior to this time, Hagen's involvement in the golf club business was minimal. He sold clubs through his shop at the various clubs that employed him but actually had little part in the clubmaking end, instead employing good workers for that job. He was one of the new breed of pros who sold the clubs of others, spending more time on the course playing competitively.

Hagen's reputation was based on an association with the best of everything. In 1925 he decided to market his own brand of clubs, striking a partnership with his friend, Detroit industrialist Leonard A. Young, owner of a wire and steel company. From 1926 onward, Walter Hagen brand clubs were made exclusively by the L. A. Young Co. Naturally, Hagen played his own brand, and to illustrate the change pervading the club business, he played a mixed set. His deluxe model N2 woods were available only with steel shafts, while his Walter Hagen De Luxe registered iron sets came with hickory shafts. The complete set of three woods and nine irons, including putter, cost $115, with the most expensive bag in his line priced at $100. Hagen's top-of-the-line goods were not for the economy-minded person.

There were also clubs priced more economically. The same iron sets were also sold in forged steel, in a non-registered series. Then came the Autograph brand followed by the Triangle brand and finally WH clubs, with all three brands available in woods and irons. The Getaway brand irons were for the beginner, at $27.50 for the 11-club set.

In premium woods, the Walter Hagen De Luxe models were fitted with steel shafts, but the Autograph models came with the choice of wood or steel. By 1930 additional mid-grade models included Arrow, Champion and Star-Line clubs.

The Hagen line contained two unique clubs. Capitalizing on the quality theme, the company produced a very limited number of sterling silver headed blade putters which could be engraved for use as trophies and awards. Made by Lambert Brothers in New York, they are rare today.

The club most associated with the firm is the notorious Hagen concave sand iron, designed and patented by Edwin McClain. It was the first production club with a "flange" on its sole for use in sand bunkers. It was also concave, which caused it to be banned from use in 1930. However, flat-faced clubs with the same flange followed and have been indispensable ever since. The next model sand iron, the "Iron Man," was also produced with a hickory shaft for a short time before the transition to steel.

Another popular club was the aluminum-headed putter called "The Haig." Many had the flat-ended paddle grip and today a few can be found with hickory shafts, though the vast majority was produced with steel.

WHITE, JACK
SUNNINGDALE, ENGLAND

Began making clubs in the early 1890s and continued through the late 1920s. Most of his clubs are marked Sunningdale with the "Sun" mark. Famous for making clubs for Bobby Jones.

AUTOGRAPH RUSTLESS
PUTTER $55 65 85
Circa 1925-1930. "Sun" mark. Photo below.

MUSSEL BACK IRONS $50 65 95
Circa 1920s. "Sun" mark.

DOT-PUNCHED FACE IRONS $50 60 90
Circa 1915-1920. "Sun" mark.

SUNNINGDALE WOODS $100 135 190
Circa 1920. Driver, brassie or spoon.

SPLICED-NECK WOODS $200 325 475
Circa 1900-1910. Driver, brassie or spoon.

WHITE, ROBERT
ST. ANDREWS, SCOTLAND

Began making clubs in the late 1870s. Marked his clubs with "R. White, Maker, St. Andrews" in an oval configuration. Clubs with full Robert White markings are scarce and command a premium.

BRASS-HEAD PUTTERS $250 375 700
Circa 1880-1890. Straight brass-blade. "R White, St. Andrews, Maker" mark.

SMOOTH-FACE IRONS $250 400 950
Circa 1880-1890. General purpose iron or lofter. "R White, Maker, St. Andrews" on back. Photo below.

SMOOTH-FACE CLEEK $275 425 875
Circa 1880-1890. Cleek. "R White, Maker, St. Andrews" on back.

RUT IRON $900 1800 3200
Circa 1880-1890. Small rounded head. "R White, Maker, St. Andrews" on back.

WILLIAMS, J. H. & CO.
BROOKLYN, NY

Began forging clubs prior to 1900 in Brooklyn, NY. Made iron heads for putters and irons marking them with a tiny "Diamond" and a "W" inside. The mark is found stamped into the hosel. "J H Williams Co, Brooklyn" in block letters was also used. They made fine-quality club heads.

SMOOTH-FACE BLADE $60 90 125
Circa 1895-1900. "Diamond in W" mark on hosel.

PARK STYLE PUTTER $125 175 250
Circa 1900. Severely bent neck blade. "W" in "Diamond" mark.

WILSON, R. B. (Buff)
ST. ANDREWS, SCOTLAND

Began making clubs in the late 1890s. Marked his clubs with "R B, Wilson, Maker, St. Andrews" in an oval configuration. He used the "OK" mark to signify irons exported or made in America.

SMOOTH-FACE BLADE
PUTTER $60 80 125
Circa 1900. "R B Wilson" in block letters.

GOOSE-NECK PUTTER $75 100 150
Circa 1900. "R B Wilson OK Special" mark.

OK SPECIAL IRONS. $60 90 125
Circa 1900. All irons. Smooth-face. Photo below.

SMOOTH-FACE IRONS $70 100 175
Circa 1900. All irons. Smooth-face.

RUT NIBLICK $250 400 650
Circa 1900. Smooth-face round head.

ONE PIECE WOOD $1200   1800   2500
Circa 1900. Smooth-face round head. Photo below.

WILSON, ROBERT
ST. ANDREWS, SCOTLAND

Began forging clubs about 1870 in St. Andrews and continued until about 1905. His marks were "R. Wilson, St. Andrews" and a bent "horseshoe" nail.

PUTTING CLEEK $300   450   950
Circa 1889-1890. "R. Wilson, Maker, St. Andrews" mark.

SMOOTH-FACE IRONS $250   400   750
Circa 1889-1890. All irons. "R. Wilson, Maker, St. Andrews" mark. Photo below.

SMOOTH-FACE CLEEK IRONS $300   450   800
Circa 1889-1890. "R. Wilson, Maker, St. Andrews" mark.

WILSON, THOMAS E.
CHICAGO, IL

CUP DEFENDER PUTTER $40   50   70
Circa late 1920s. Photo below.

WILSON, THOMAS E.
CHICAGO, IL

by Pete Georgiady

Ever since the first national championship unofficially pitted golfers from Chicago against the Boston/New York establishment, the Windy City was a hotbed for early golf in the United States. Its highly developed industrial manufacturing base quickly adapted, and the area became the home of several major golf manufacturing companies.

The Wilson Company, like so many of its contemporaries, entered the golf market as an adjunct to its primary product lines. In 1913 the group that would soon become Wilson was named the Ashland Manufacturing Company. Located on Chicago's Ashland Avenue it was a subsidiary of the meat packing firm of Schwartzchild and Sulzberger. Ashland was an outlet for goods made from meat by-products, namely intestines and entrails which they used to produce gut strings for banjoes, violins, tennis rackets and also surgical sutures. Looking to expand its fortunes, the company also began trading in tennis rackets, hunting and camping equipment, bicycles, phonographs and automobile tires.

Within a year, Ashland was in receivership and a New York-based bank assumed control. The bank chose a successful meat packing executive named Thomas E. Wilson to head its new investment because of his demonstrated managerial ability. In 1914, the name was changed to the Thomas E. Wilson Co., and the firm moved from its Ashland Avenue location to Chicago's south side. There was great irony in the hiring of Thomas Wilson because the owners of the company had already decided to name the firm the Wilson Company in an effort to draw upon the successes of the very popular President Woodrow Wilson. Still trading in diverse commodities, the rejuvenated Wilson Co. began manufacturing its own products in 1916.

Thomas Wilson was experienced with company acquisitions and charted a similar course for his new firm. Driven to make the company the best in the sporting goods field, he purchased an Ohio company already making leather balls, baseball gloves and harness gear, and moved it to Chicago. Next, the Indestructo Caddy Bag Manufacturing Co. was purchased and Wilson quickly entered the golf business in a big way.

In 1925, the young company underwent its first name change when it merged with Western Sporting Goods Manufacturing Co., also of Chicago. The newly merged company used the name Wilson-Western Sporting Goods Co. Finally, in 1931, the name changed to the familiar Wilson Sporting Goods.

Earliest Wilson golf clubs are actually marked with the Ashland Manufacturing Company's "A.M. Co." monogram in a circle. Most of these heads were obtained from MacGregor and were additionally stamped with retail or professional's names. The first clubs actually bearing the Wilson name were from the Plus Success series, with the model name in very small block letters dating from about 1916 or 1917. Slightly later were irons from the same series where the lettering is contained inside a large W. These irons all date from 1917-1918, although Plus Success clubs were available in several other variations continuing into the 1920s.

In the early 1920s, Wilson introduced its Aim Rite symbol, which would appear on many clubs during this decade. In one of these similar designs, the symbol was commonly placed on the face of the club at the sweet spot. Alternately, a mark of concentric circles was sometimes found at the sweet spot. Both of these marks were registered as trademarks and they also served to help golfers align the club face with the ball, useful since the vast majority of Aim Rite clubs were sold through stores to economy minded customers. But the golf market in the 1920s was booming just as the stock market was, and lower-end merchandise was selling very well to the new golfers learning the sport.

The all-time best selling Wilson series was the Wilsonian model of mid-priced clubs. Available throughout the 1920s, it was the mainstay of the company's club selection. All Wilsonian models were available in ladies weights and junior and juvenile sizes. Many of the early Wilsonian irons, as well as other models, were also stamped "Hammer Forged" with the mark of the ball peen hammer, the sign of a better quality product.

Wilson continued low priced domination throughout the post war era with many sets of clubs with names like Carnoustie, Cup Defender, Dixie, Lincoln Park, Linkhurst, Pinehurst, Skokie, Streak and Taplow. Because of their economical nature, most were configured with two woods, four irons (2, 5, 7, 9) and putter. In trying to complete a full set, collectors are often frustrated by searching for the in-between numbers which were never produced. In the late 1920s, brightly colored leather grips became fashionable and several lines were sold with bright red, blue or green leather.

One of the more uncommon Wilson clubs produced was the Baxpin model deep-groove mashie, which was also stamped for and sold to another Chicago manufacturer, Burr-key. Early deep-groove clubs can also be found with the old Ashland Manufacturing Co. markings, too. Another unique product is the Walker Cup set which featured rainbow pattern grooves on the faces of the irons. Introduced in the mid-1920s, the use of that name on a set of clubs is an indication of how important amateur competitions were during those times.

As the company became solidly established as a maker and seller of golf supplies, it also ventured into the country club market with higher grade equipment. Its Red Ribbon and Blue Ribbon sets were positioned for pro shop sales and were used by many tour golfers. Also in the prestige club category was Wilson's Harry Vardon "72" set with its readily identifiable green grips. Two collectible Wilson putter models from this period are the Amby-dex two-way putter and the Kelly Klub. In the 1940s, Wilson would begin its advisory staff program whose roots were established some fifteen years earlier with endorsements from young Gene Sarazen, Johnny Farrell, and the mature Ted Ray who won the 1920 U.S. Open at age 43. All three golfers lent their signatures to Wilson's first autographed lines of clubs.

WILSONIAN PUTTER $40 50 70
Circa late 1920s.

RED RIBBON PUTTER $40 50 70
Circa late 1920s.

WALKER CUP PUTTER $40 50 70
Circa 1925-1930. Offset blade with a five-inch hosel.

JOCK HUTCHISON MEDALIST
PUTTER $40 55 80
Circa 1925-1930. Offset blade. Photo below.

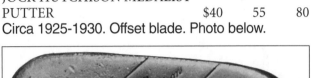

PINEHURST PUTTER $40 55 80
Circa 1925-1930. Dot-punched face.

TED RAY SEVENTY-TWO
PUTTER $40 50 70
Circa late 1920s.

SUCCESS PUTTER #2-1/2 $45 55 80
Circa 1920s. Bent neck line-scored blade. All original.

HARRY VARDON PUTTER $45 55 75
Circa 1926-1930.

FAIRVIEW PUTTER $50 60 90
Circa 1910-1915. Smooth-face blade.

TRIUMPH PUTTER $55 70 100
Circa 1925-1930. Flanged back.

WILSONIAN BRASS PUTTER $70 90 125
Circa 1925-1930. Ball-face scoring.

GENE SARAZEN PUTTER $125 175 225
Circa 1925-1930. "Pencil"-neck 7-inch long hosel. Photo below.

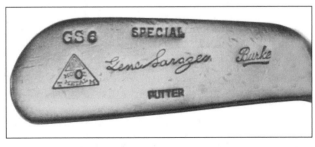

WALKER CUP RAINBOW
PUTTER $125 175 250
Circa late 1920s. Rainbow face.

SCHENECTADY PUTTER $150 225 325
Circa 1915-1920.

JOHNNY FARRELL IRONS $35 45 70
Circa 1930. "Matched Models D1002."

CREST IRONS $35 40 70
Circa 1930. All irons.

BOB MACDONALD IRONS $35 40 70
Circa late 1920s. All irons.

SUCCESS IRONS $35 40 70
Circa 1920s. All irons.

WALKER CUP IRONS $35 40 70
Circa late 1920s. All irons.

CUP DEFENDER IRONS $35 40 70
Circa 1930. All irons.

JOCK HUTCHISON IRONS $35 45 70
Circa 1930. All irons.

WILSONIAN IRONS $35 40 70
Circa 1920s. All irons.

TED RAY SEVENTY-TWO
IRONS $35 45 70
Circa 1930. All irons.

HARRY VARDON IRONS $40 50 75
Circa 1930. All irons.

PINEHURST IRONS $40 50 70
Circa 1925-1930. All irons. Photo below.

FAIRVIEW IRONS $50 65 95
Circa 1910-1915. All smooth-face irons.

DEEP GROOVE IRONS $100 140 225
Circa 1915-1922. All irons. Corrugated deep grooves.

DEEP GROOVE IRONS $110 150 240
Circa 1915-1922. All irons. Slot grooves.

WALKER CUP RAINBOW
IRONS $125   175   250
Circa 1930. All irons. Rainbow face design. Photo
below.

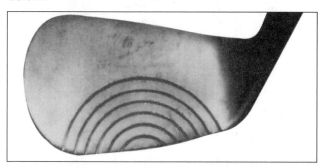

RED RIBBON IRONS $35   40   70
Circa 1930. All irons.

RED RIBBON IRON SET $375   500   750
Circa 1930. Mid-iron, mashie, mashie-niblick, niblick
and putter with 2 woods. Photo below.

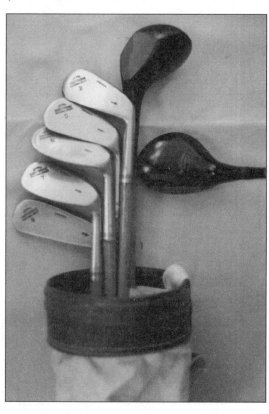

SUCCESS WOODS $75   95   140
Circa 1920s. Driver, brassie or spoon.

WILSONIAN WOODS $75   95   135
Circa 1920s. Driver, brassie or spoon.

RED RIBBON WOODS $75   95   135
Circa late 1920s. Driver, brassie or spoon.

PINEHURST WOODS $80   100   150
Circa 1925. Driver, brassie or spoon.

SEVENTY-TWO SERIES WOODS $85 110   160
Circa late 1920s. Harry Vardon or Ted Ray. Driver,
brassie or spoon.

GENE SARAZEN WOODS $85   110   160
Circa 1925-1930. Driver, brassie or spoon.

JUVENILE CLUBS $30   40   55
"Gene Sarazen 11-13" on a circa 1925-1930 line-
scored mashie. Appears all original.

WILSON, WILLIE
ST. ANDREWS, SCOTLAND

Willie Wilson began forging clubs about 1870 in St.
Andrews. He marked his clubs "W Wilson, St.
Andrews" and used the oval "St. Andrews Cross" mark
during the 1890s.

BRASS-BLADE PUTTER $275   450   875
Circa 1880-1890. "W Wilson St. Andrews, Maker"
mark.

SMOOTH-FACE IRONS $250   450   850
Circa 1880-1890. General purpose or lofting iron
with "W Wilson, Maker, St. Andrews" stamping.
Photo below.

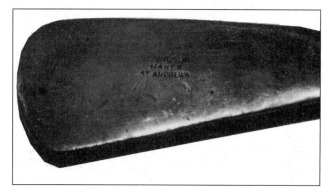

SMOOTH-FACE CLEEK. $275   500   900
Circa 1880-1890. "W Wilson, Maker, St. Andrews"
stamping.

RUT IRON $1000 1850 3250
Circa 1880-1890. "W Wilson, Maker, St. Andrews"
stamping.

WINTON, W. & CO., LTD
MONTROSE, SCOTLAND

The Winton family began forging irons about 1890 in
Montrose, Scotland. They later added outlets in London, and the club heads are marked as such. They used
a "Diamond" cleek mark. They also made Bobby
Jones' first "Calamity Jane" putters.

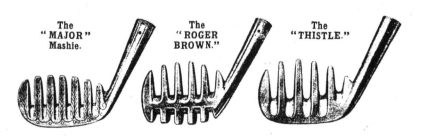

TAPLOW PUTTER $50 60 80
Circa 1920s. "Diamond" mark.

PICCADILLY BLADE PUTTER $50 60 80
Circa 1925. "Diamond" mark.

LINE-SCORED FACE PUTTER $50 60 80
Circa 1920-1925. Long blade putter. "Diamond" mark.

DOT-FACE RUSTLESS PUTTER $50 60 95
Circa 1925-1930. Offset blade. "Diamond" mark.

THE SPIELIN PUTTER $60 75 110
Circa 1925. Step down hosel. "Diamond" mark.

TWO LEVEL BACK PUTTER $75 120 190
Circa 1915-1920. "Diamond" mark.

DODO PUTTER $150 250 400
Circa 1925. Flanged back "Dodo, Little-Johnnie" putter. "Reg'd No. 353972." Photo below.

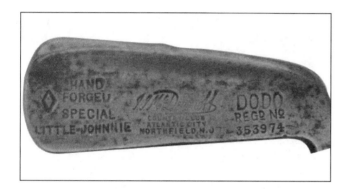

FINESSE PUTTER $175 275 400
Circa 1920. Shallow dot-face blade. Oval hosel and shaft.

THE MASCOT PUTTER $200 300 450
Circa 1920. Oval hosel and shaft. Large flange and rounded top line coming to a pointed toe.

JIGGER $50 60 90
Circa 1920. "Diamond" mark on toe.

HARRY VARDON SERIES IRONS $50 60 90
Circa 1920s. All irons. Line-scored face. "Diamond" mark.

WIN-ON NIBLICK $55 65 80
Circa 1925-1930. Flanged back.

HOYLAKE SPECIAL IRONS $55 65 95
Circa 1910-1915. All irons. "Criss-cross" face scoring.

SMOOTH-FACE IRONS $60 75 120
Circa 1900. All irons. "Winton, London" mark. Photo below.

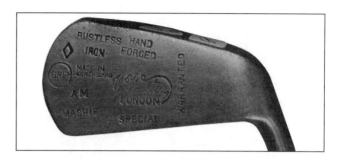

THE CERT SERIES IRONS $65 75 100
Circa 1920s. "Diamond" mark.

DREADNOUGHT NIBLICK $95 140 225
Circa 1920. Large head. "Diamond" mark.

ANTI-SHANK IRONS $125 225 300
Circa 1920s. All irons. Smith's Patent. Diamond mark.

POINTED TOE CANNON
PATENT $150 225 350
Circa early teens. "Ted Ray's Own." "Diamond" mark. Photo below.

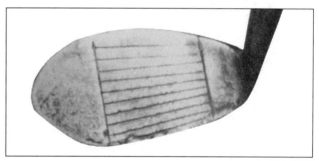

ANTI-SHANK IRONS $150 225 350
Circa 1910-1915. All irons. "Diamond" mark. "Fairlie's" Patent.

BOGIE SERIES IRONS $175 250 375
Circa 1920. Cavity back. "Bogie" stamped in the cavity. Photo below.

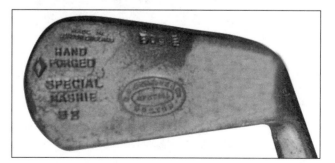

GIANT NIBLICK $1000   1600   2400
Circa 1920. Large head. "Diamond" mark. Photo below.

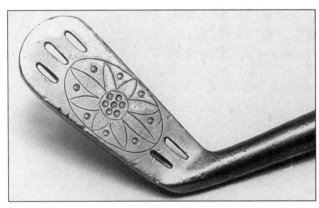

WATER IRONS $3500   5500   8000
Circa 1905. Horizontal slots perforating head at heel and toe. Fancy flower face.

Front of Water Iron.

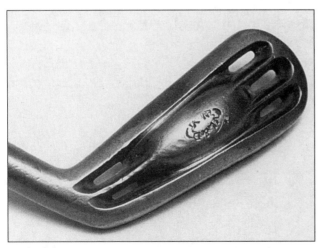

Back of Water Iron.

RAKE IRONS $4500   6000   8500
Circa 1905. "The Major." Seven pointed tines.

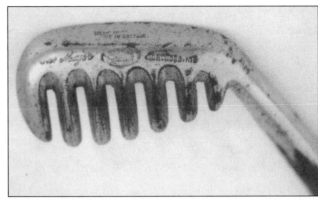

Back of Rake Iron

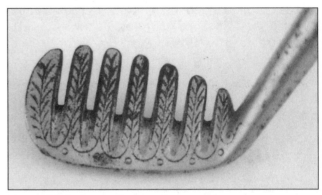

Front of Rake Iron

J. WINTON WOODS $90   110   160
Circa 1920. Driver, brassie or spoon.

SPLICED-NECK WOODS $150   225   350
Circa 1910-1920. All woods.

FLANGED BACK IRONS $65   75   100
Circa 1915. Diamond mark at toe. Photo below.

WRIGHT & DITSON
BOSTON, MA

Wright & Ditson began selling golf clubs at their Boston location about 1895. All clubs were purchased from A. G. Spalding & Brothers. Wright & Ditson added its own markings on the blank backs and wood heads for advertising purposes.

Jim Cooper has written the definitive work on Spalding, which is profusely illustrated. Every Spalding collector should have this reference in his or her library. It is available from the author, or Jim Cooper. There are also Wright & Ditson Retail Catalogue reprints from 1913, 1920, 1925 and 1930 available from the author of this book.

SEMI-CIRCLE W & D PUTTERS $200   350   600
Circa 1895-1897. Brass or steel smooth-face blade with "Wright & Ditson, Boston" mark in a semi-circle at the toe.

SEMI-CIRCLE W & D PUTTERS $350   650   1250
Circa 1895-1897. Brass or Steel smooth-face blade with "Wright & Ditson, Boston" mark in a semi-circle at the toe. Screw-in shaft. Photo below.

WRIGHT & DITSON SELECTED
PUTTERS $100   140   225
Circa 1898-1903. Severely bent neck in the "Park" style.

ONE SHOT SERIES PUTTERS $50   60   100
Circa 1915. Offset blade. Photo below.

ONE SHOT SERIES PUTTERS $70   100   150
Circa 1915. Smooth-face brass-blade.

ONE SHOT SERIES PUTTERS $80   120   190
Circa 1915. Flanged back with "Maxwell" holes drilled into the hosel.

"F" SERIES PUTTER $55   70   100
Circa 1922-1925. Deep scoring lines on bottom of face; top is smooth.

A. H. FINDLAY PUTTERS $60   75   120
Circa 1900-1905. Smooth-face, straight steel blade.

A. H. FINDLAY PUTTERS $70   90   135
Circa 1900-1905. Twisted neck gem-type wide-sole putter.

A. H. FINDLAY PUTTERS $75   95   140
Circa 1900-1905. Smooth-face straight brass-blade.

ST. ANDREWS SERIES PUTTERS $45   55   90
Circa 1910. Square punches on face. Photo below.

BEE-LINE SERIES PUTTERS $40   50   75
Circa 1920s. Offset hosel and a line-scored blade.

KRO-FLITE SERIES PUTTERS $40   50   75
Circa 1926-1930 Sweet Spot "R F Putter" with long hosel and offset blade. Patented Sept. 13, 1927.

VICTOR SERIES PUTTER $40   50   75
Circa 1920s. Blade putter.

RAINBOW SERIES PUTTERS $40   50   80
Circa 1920s. Dot-punched face. "Rainbow" mark.

ALUMINUM HEAD PUTTERS $100   140   200
Circa 1915-1920. "B M Wright & Ditson Special."

WRIGHT & DITSON, MAKERS,
ST. ANDREWS $70   90   150
Circa 1898-1903. All irons. Photo below.

WRIGHT & DITSON
SELECTED IRONS $55   75   125
Circa 1898-1903. All irons.

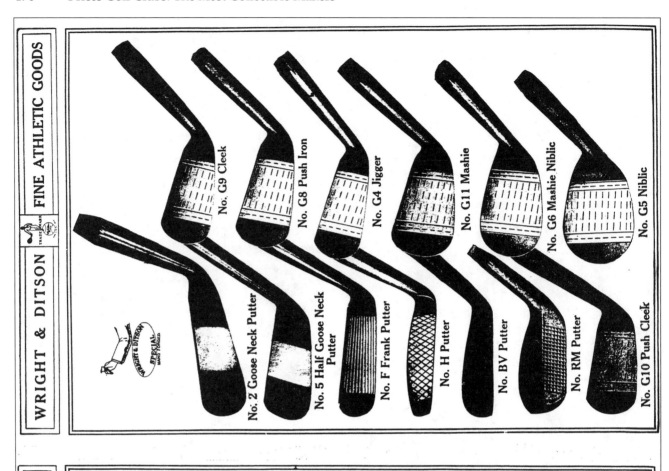

No. G9 Cleek

No. G8 Push Iron

No. G4 Jigger

No. G11 Mashie

No. G6 Mashie Niblic

No. G5 Niblic

No. 2 Goose Neck Putter

No. 5 Half Goose Neck Putter

No. F Frank Putter

No. H Putter

No. BV Putter

No. RM Putter

No. G10 Push Cleek

Wright & Ditson Golf Irons

PUTTERS

Putting is the most important part of Golf. A good putt will make up for many a poor shot, so it is well to have a putter adapted to the player's style.

No. 2 Goose Neck Putter. Has a longer and narrower blade than No. 1. Each, $2.00

No. 5 Half Goose Neck Putter. Same style as No. 1, only half goose neck. " 2.00

No. F. Frank Putter. Goose Neck, twist in neck enabling player to get full view of ball. Long, heavy, shallow blade and keeps ball close to the ground. Each, $2.00

No. H Putter. Goose Neck, with very heavy head and shallow straight face; a splendid club for heavy greens. . . . . Each, $2.50

No. BV Steel Putter. Has an oval bowl and shaft. Shaft is set in bowl in a straight line with the face, which prevents heeling. . . . . Each, $2.50

No. RM. Ray Mills Putter. Aluminum. Careful experiments prove a putter most easily placed in position if the head presents to the eye two long straight lines. This feature is found in the Ray Mills style. . . . . Each, $2.50

GOOSE NECK LINE

This line of clubs is made in a slight goose neck shape, same style as used by a former English champion, who claims it is the ideal shape for golf clubs. The back of each one of these irons is beveled at the bottom so that the sole will go well under the ball.

No. G10 Push Cleek. Has a short head, fairly deep face, and is a very long driving cleek. Extremely useful for long, low push shots against the wind. . Each, $2.00

No. G9 Cleek. Rather thin blade, light weight; medium deep face, with a slight loft; a splendid distance club out of bad lies. . . . . Each, $2.00

No. G8 Push Iron. Thin head, medium weight, mid iron loft. . . . . " 2.00

No. G4 Jigger. Long thin blade, well lofted; for long, high shots or short approaches. 2.00

No. G11 Mashie. Medium size head, with regular mashie loft. . . . Each, 2.00

No. G6 Mashie Niblic. Lofted a little more than the mashie. Sole projects in advance of the shaft, so that ball may be picked up cleanly without hitting socket. Each, $2.00

No. G5 Niblic. Well laid back, with the sole projecting in front of the shaft; capital club for playing out of bunkers, and short pitch shots from bunkers. . Each, $2.00

QUINT-ANGLE LINE

A set of irons, including No. 3 Cleek, No. 2 Driving Iron, No. 3 Mid Iron, No. 3 Mashie and No. 1 Approach Iron, all having the same lie, but with different lofts. These Irons have a fairly short hosel, and blade with a little extra weight behind the point of impact. Many poor shots are made because of a player using clubs of different lies. The Quint-Angle line eliminates this difficulty and gives the player added confidence. They are great favorites with professionals.

The shafts are steely and beautifully balanced, topped off with choice leather grips. All models made for right and left hand players. Ladies' clubs are the same as for men, but a little lighter in weight. When ordering state whether right or left hand clubs are wanted, and if for Ladies or Men.

RULE 27.

BALL IN CASUAL WATER THROUGH THE GREEN

(2) If a ball lie or be lost in casual water through the green, the player may drop a ball without penalty within two club lengths of the margin, as near as possible to the spot where the ball lay, but not make the hole.

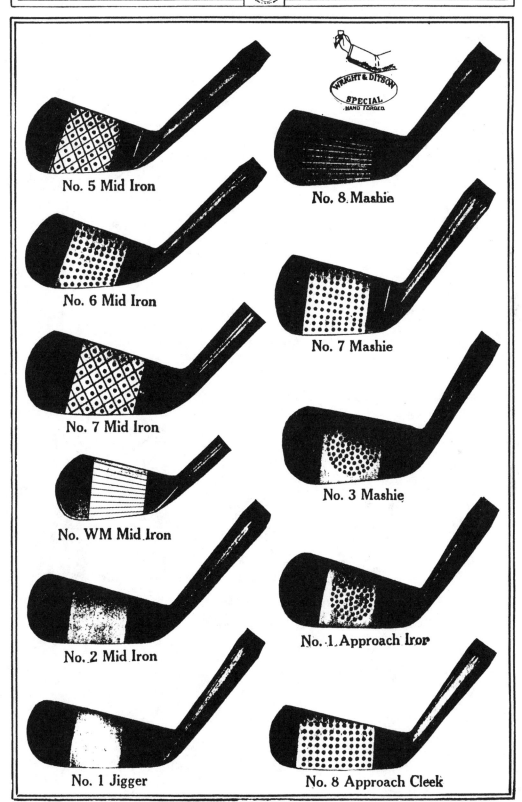

WRIGHT & DITSON FINE ATHLETIC GOODS

No. 5 Mid Iron

No. 6 Mid Iron

No. 7 Mid Iron

No. WM Mid Iron

No. 2 Mid Iron

No. 1 Jigger

No. 8 Mashie

No. 7 Mashie

No. 3 Mashie

No. 1 Approach Iron

No. 8 Approach Cleek

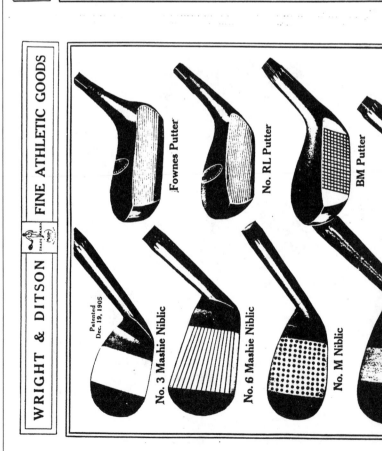

WRIGHT & DITSON $70   90   150
Circa 1898-1903. All irons. Photo below.

A. H. FINDLAY IRONS $75   90   150
Circa 1900-1905. Smooth-face cleek.

A. H. FINDLAY IRONS $60   75   125
Circa 1900-1905. Smooth-face iron or lofting iron.
Photo below.

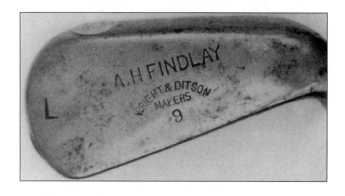

ONE SHOT SERIES IRONS $50   65   100
Circa 1910-1915. All smooth-face irons.

ONE SHOT SERIES IRONS $125   150   225
Circa 1920. Corrugated deep groove "Dedstop Jigger."

CRAN CLEEK $400   950   1700
Circa 1897-1915. Wood face insert. Photo below.

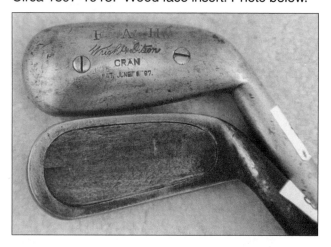

"F" SERIES IRONS $40   50   85
Circa 1922-1925. F-2 through F-7 or F-9 with deep
scoring lines on bottom of face, top is smooth.

ONE SHOT SERIES IRONS $45   60   90
Circa 1915. All marked face irons.

"F" SERIES IRONS $50   65   95
Circa 1922-1925. F-1 with deep scoring lines on
bottom of face, top is smooth.

ONE SHOT SERIES IRONS $50   65   95
Circa 1920. "#8" Sky-iron or Jigger.

"F" SERIES "SKY-IRON" $60   80   125
Circa 1922-1925. Deep scoring lines on bottom of
face, top is smooth.

ONE SHOT SERIES IRONS $100   135   190
Circa 1915-1922. Corrugated or slot-type deep
groove mashie, mashie-niblick or niblick.

BEE-LINE SERIES IRONS $35   40   65
Circa 1920s. All irons. Photo below.

KRO-FLITE SERIES IRONS $35   40   70
Circa 1926-1930. Sweet spot. 1 through 8 and 19.

ST. ANDREWS SERIES IRONS $35   40   70
Circa 1915-1925. All irons. Photo below.

VICTOR SERIES IRONS $35   40   70
Circa 1920s.

RAINBOW SERIES IRONS $35   45   75
Circa 1920s. Dot-scored face.

WATERFALL IRONS $400   500   800
Circa 1920. "Bee-Line" markings.

DOUBLE WATERFALL IRONS $2000   2800   4500
Circa 1920. "Bee-Line" markings.

SPLICED-NECK WOODS $150   250   450
Circa 1898-1903. "Wright & Ditson" in script. Driver, brassie or spoon. Some have leather face inserts.

SPLICED-NECK WOODS $250   350   700
Circa 1898-1903. Pear-shaped, persimmon head, bulger-face driver or brassie. Some have leather face insert.

A. H. FINDLAY WOODS $95   120   175
Circa 1900-1905. Driver, brassie or spoon. Many with leather face inserts.

A. H. FINDLAY WOODS $125   150   250
Circa 1900. Bulger driver or brassie with a leather face insert. Very thick, oval shaped socket hosel.

WRIGHT & DITSON WOODS $75   95   140
Circa 1910-1920. Driver, brassie or spoon.

BEE-LINE SERIES WOODS $75   95   140
Circa 1920s. Driver, brassie or spoon.

ST. ANDREWS SERIES WOODS $75   95   140
Circa 1920s. Driver, brassie or spoon.

ST. ANDREWS SERIES WOODS $95   120   175
Circa 1920s. Small head wooden cleek or Bull Dog head.

VICTOR SERIES WOODS $75   95   140
Circa 1920s. Driver, brassie or spoon.

ALUMINUM HEAD WOODS $125   160   275
Circa 1910-1920. Various lofts.

JUVENILE CLUBS $30   40   60
Circa 1920. "Y" Youth series. Putters or irons.

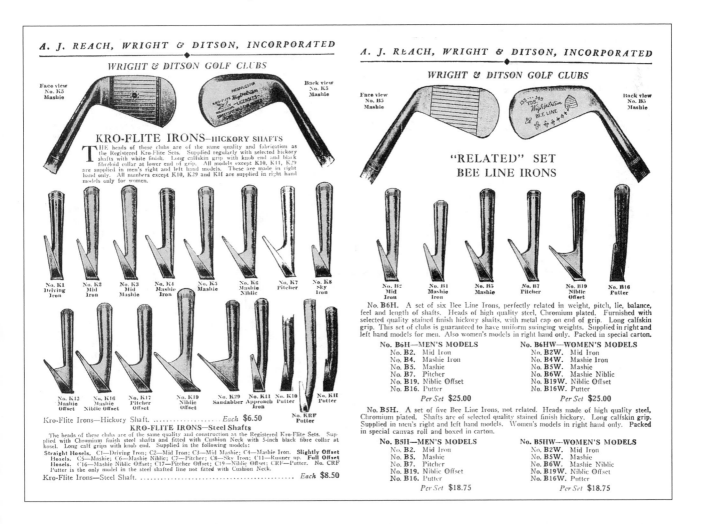

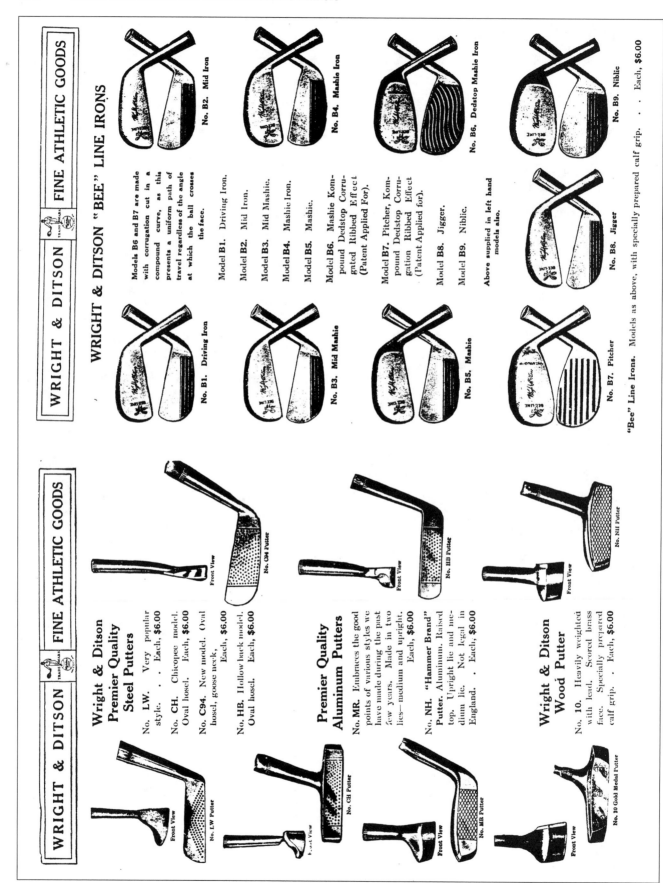

WRIGHT & DITSON — FINE ATHLETIC GOODS

WRIGHT & DITSON "BEE" LINE IRONS

No. B2. Mid Iron

No. B4. Mashie Iron

No. B6. Dedstop Mashie Iron

No. B9. Niblic

No. B1. Driving Iron

No. B3. Mid Mashie

No. B5. Mashie

No. B7. Pitcher

No. B8. Jigger

Models B6 and B7 are made with corrugation cut in a compound curve, as this presents a uniform path of travel regardless of the angle at which the ball crosses the face.

Model B1. Driving Iron.
Model B2. Mid Iron.
Model B3. Mid Mashie.
Model B4. Mashie Iron.
Model B5. Mashie.
Model B6. Mashie Kompound Dedstop Corrugated Ribbed Effect (Patent Applied For).
Model B7. Pitcher, Kompound Dedstop Corrugation Ribbed Effect (Patent Applied for).
Model B8. Jigger.
Model B9. Niblic.

Above supplied in left hand models also.

"Bee" Line Irons. Models as above, with specially prepared calf grip. . . Each, $6.00

WRIGHT & DITSON — FINE ATHLETIC GOODS

Wright & Ditson Premier Quality Steel Putters

No. LW. Very popular style. . . Each, $6.00

No. CH. Chicopee model. Oval hosel. Each, $6.00

No. C94. New model. Oval hosel, goose neck, Each, $6.00

No. HB. Hollow back model. Oval hosel. Each, $6.00

Premier Quality Aluminum Putters

No. MR. Embraces the good points of various styles we have made during the past few years. Made in two lies— medium and upright. Each, $6.00

No. NH. "Hammer Brand" Putter. Aluminum. Raised top. Upright lie and medium lie. Not legal in England. . Each, $6.00

Wright & Ditson Wood Putter

No. 10. Heavily weighted with lead. Scored brass face. Specially prepared calf grip. . Each, $6.00

Front View — No. CH Putter

Front View — No. HB Putter

Front View — No. NH Putter

Front View — No. LW Putter

Front View — No. CH Putter

Front View — No. MR Putter

Front View — No. 10 Gold Medal Putter

Chapter 5
GOLF BALLS

An assortment of individually wrapped and boxed balls.

Golfers through the ages have played with balls made from many different materials: wood, feathers stuffed into a leather cover, gutta-percha, wound rubber centers with celluloid covers, balls with "honey" centers, solid balls made of "space age" plastics, graphite windings, Cadwell Geer, syrlin, balata and zinthane covers.

The ball most people associate with pre-1850 golf is the "Feather" ball. A skilled worker took three pieces of leather, two round and one rectangular strip, and sewed the three together with heavy waxed thread. Before the last few stitches were completed, it was turned inside out to hide the seams. A quantity of boiled feathers, enough to fill a top hat, were stuffed through the tiny unsewn opening and the closing stitches finished the ball. Many ball makers soaked the leather in "Alum" and when the cover dried, it shrunk. At

the same time, the drying feathers inside expanded, making a surprisingly hard, very playable golf ball. The *Encyclopedia of Golf Collectibles* by Olman and *The Curious History of the Golf Ball* by Martin, provide lengthy descriptions of how the feather ball was made.

Only three or four good balls could be made in a day by a skilled worker and, as a result, the balls were rather expensive. It is thought that a feather ball in the early 19th century (expressing value in 1990s dollars) cost the golfer $50 or more! Only royalty and the very wealthy could afford these expensive balls.

In the 1840s, experiments making golf balls from gutta-percha transformed the ancient game that had been played for 400 years without hardly a change. Gutta-percha, dried sap of the Malasian sapodilla tree, was used during that time the same way we use styrofoam peanuts to pack fragile items. The gutta-percha was heated in boiling water and rolled into a sphere by hand, then left to "cure" for a few weeks before being painted. In a day's work, a skilled worker could make ten times as many "gutties" as he could featheries. The price of the gutties was about one fifth the price of the feather ball, with remade balls even less. Many who previously could not afford to play began to use this new inexpensive ball.

Smooth gutty mold with clamping device, ca. 1850.

This gutty ball was made by Allan Robertson, ca. 1853.

The transition from the feather ball to the gutta-percha ball was not as rapid as most golf writers and auctioneers make it out to be. Robert Forgan recalled: "..(in 1856) gutta-percha balls were just getting established, and as they were much cheaper than the feather ball, golf soon began to spread…" Featheries were most likely still played by many traditional Scotsmen well into the 1860s.

Gutta balls that had been scuffed and nicked during play were found to fly straighter and longer than the new smooth balls. Some players gave new balls to their caddies to "knock them around" before play began. Somewhere along the line, an enterprising ball maker used the "claw" of his hammer to nick the ball's surface. Patterns were cut into the ball using a chisel, until another enterprising maker decided a metal mold with raised markings could mold the gutta-percha into a uniform ready made "scored" ball.

A hand-hammered gutta ball, ca. 1855.

Golf was propelled into the modern game we know today by the Haskell Patent of April 11, 1899. Working for B.F. Goodrich of Akron, Ohio, Coburn Haskell and Bertram Works developed a process, in 1898, of winding thin rubber strips around a central core and covered these windings with a cover of gutta-percha. Again, everyone did not change from the guttie to the rubber-core balls overnight. In fact, the only player in the 1902 British Open field playing the new Haskell ball was Sandy Herd, the eventual winner. By 1910 though, only the diehards were playing gutties.

As the game grew during the later part of the 19th and early 20th centuries, golfers demanded a better ball, and hundreds of ball makers began molding balls with a variety of cover patterns. Covers had circles, dots, stars, swirls, crescents, squares in circles, triangles, hexagons, octagons, dimples, brambles

  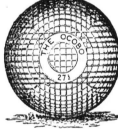        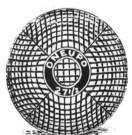 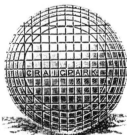   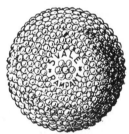 

THE NEW AMERICAN GOLF BALL.

THE MACGRIPPA: "Here's that Yankee again, blast him! I can't stand the fellow. There's nothing in him except bounce."

THE O'COBO: "O. I don't know, he's not such a bad sort. He's a bit of a bounder, I admit, and he can't putt for nuts; but he costs 2¡ dollars, so let's be charitable."

and were cut with lines. The "Pneumatic" ball was filled with air and there were some balls that emitted smoke or an odor to aid in finding it in the rough. There were also balls made to float on the water. Literally thousands of patterns and combinations of patterns were used by the manufacturers to single out their ball from all others available.

During the period from 1895 to 1940, most balls came in a wrapper with a paper seal that carried the advertisement and the ball's name. Many companies thought wrapping the ball justified the high prices for golf balls. We must understand that during the Great Depression balls were selling for 50 cents to $1.00 each. Balls were truly *expensive when considering the price of steak, potatoes and milk. Even in the bountiful "Roaring '20s," $1.00 was a large sum to pay for a golf ball.*

There are several good references on golf balls worth looking into, including *The Curious History of the Golf Ball, 1968, by Martin; The Encyclopedia of Golf Collectibles, 1985, by Olman; and Antique Golf Ball Reference Guide, 1993, by Kelly.*

My Passion for Old Golf Balls

by Jim Espinola

My first encounter with golf collectibles were the old wooden-shafted clubs. As my collection of clubs began to grow, I wanted examples of golf balls from different eras to display with the clubs. When I began to realize how many different types of balls were available, my collecting interests changed. My passion for ball collecting was fueled by the many different cover patterns I encountered. To me, looking at all these different patterns was like looking at a beautiful painting—a form of art.

Many new collectors I meet ask me why I collect balls, especially the odd cover patterns. I feel the golf ball *is the history of the game. It is through the ball's advancement that the game and its implements have progressed.*

There are literally thousands of different sizes, shapes, center cores and cover patterns, many yet to be discovered. If you join a golfing society, go to auctions and find dealers who publish catalogues—many golf balls will find their way into your collection. There are many fine balls that are not expensive and would make a great display for the collector on a limited budget.

As for advice on collecting balls, your personal taste and budget will be the primary factors. Personally, I began collecting everything regardless of quality and quantity, and condition did not matter. Eventually I realized it was a mistake and began to acquire only the best possible examples. It became evident, as I gained collecting experience, that quality and condition were most impor-

tant. There are exceptions, though; the rare ones or "one-of-a-kind" may not be available in top condition, and because of the scarcity factor, they are desirable. The best advice I can pass along is to collect what you like, in the best condition available that you can afford. It is not quantity, but quality that makes my collection meaningful to me.

Another exciting aspect of collecting is researching the history of golf and golf balls through books, auction catalogues, articles in old magazines, advertisements, and talking to old professionals and long time collectors. Developing a resource library and understanding the history of golf has helped me set collecting goals and given me insight as to availability and value. Without a library, my collection would not be complete.

With the prices of odd pattern balls, gutties, brambles and wrapped balls escalating at a brisk pace, many collectors cannot afford to purchase top quality examples. For those who want to collect balls in top quality, Signature Balls may be the answer. At present they are plentiful, most are priced under $50 and can be acquired in top condition.

In conclusion, I feel collecting and admiring the different pattern balls is a true form of art. They take me back to the past and bring the history of the game into focus.

Jim Espinola has been a collector of balls for many years. He has specialized in the odd, different and exceptional quality whenever possible. Many of the odd pattern balls pictured in this reference are from his collection.

Various molds for golf balls.

Collecting ball boxes can be as challenging as collecting balls.

PRICES
GOLF BALLS

G-5 G-7 G-9

<table>
<tr><td colspan="4" align="center">**GENERAL PRICING:**</td></tr>
<tr><td colspan="4">*The following pricing is by major type only. Prices are for the common balls of that type or cover pattern.*</td></tr>
<tr><td>FEATHER BALL</td><td>$3000</td><td>5000</td><td>8500</td></tr>
<tr><td>SMOOTH GUTTA-PERCHA</td><td>$1500</td><td>3000</td><td>6000</td></tr>
<tr><td>HAND HAMMERED GUTTA-PERCHA</td><td>$1500</td><td>2500</td><td>5000</td></tr>
<tr><td>LINE CUT GUTTA-PERCHA</td><td>$225</td><td>400</td><td>850</td></tr>
<tr><td>BRAMBLE GUTTA-PERCHA</td><td>$200</td><td>375</td><td>800</td></tr>
<tr><td>BRAMBLE GUTTA-PERCHA COVER WITH RUBBER CORE</td><td>$175</td><td>450</td><td>1150</td></tr>
<tr><td>BRAMBLE RUBBER OR CELLULOID COVER</td><td>$150</td><td>350</td><td>750</td></tr>
<tr><td>SQUARE MESH COVER</td><td>$45</td><td>80</td><td>225</td></tr>
</table>

FEATHER BALLS

NO MAKER'S NAME
FEATHER BALL $4500   6500   12,000
Circa 1800. Large size. Photo below.

NO MAKER'S NAME
FEATHER BALL $3000   5000   8500
Circa 1840-1860. Average size. Photo below.

GOURLAY, JOHN
MUSSELBURGH

FEATHER BALL $6500   9500   15,000
Circa 1840-1860. "J Gourlay" and size number. Photo below.

MORRIS, TOM, ST. ANDREWS

FEATHER BALL $8000 15,000 30,000
Circa 1840-1860. "T Morris" and size number.

ROBERTSON, ALLAN

FEATHER BALL $6500 12,000 20,000
Circa 1840-1850. "Allan" and size number. Photo below.

GUTTA-PERCHA BALLS

NO MAKER'S NAME

SMOOTH GUTTA-PERCHA $1500 3000 6000
Circa 1850-1860. White, brown or black usually with a "test" mark. Photo below.

HAND HAMMERED
GUTTA-PERCHA $1500 2500 5000
Circa 1850-1880. Hand marked with a chisel. Photo below.

REMADE, NO NAME

BRAMBLE GUTTA-PERCHA $200 375 600
Circa 1895-1905. No name, or maker's name not identifiable.

LINE CUT GUTTA-PERCHA $225 400 850
Circa 1880-1905. Photo below.

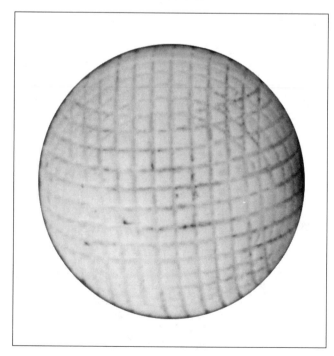

VARIOUS MAKERS
LINE CUT GUTTA-PERCHA $275   600   1800
Circa 1880-1905. Maker's name marked on ball. Photo below.

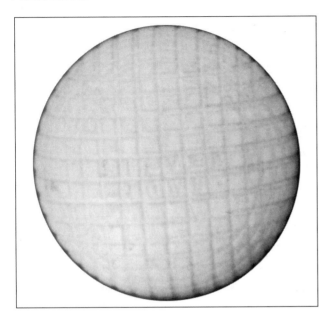

LINE CUT GUTTA-PERCHA $200   450   950
Circa 1895-1905. Maker's name marked on ball. Advertisement below.

BRAMBLE
GUTTA-PERCHA $225   450   950
Circa 1895-1905. Maker's name marked on ball.

UNKNOWN MAKERS
LINE CUT GUTTA-PERCHA $800   1200   2000
Circa 1895. "Allaway" in rectangular panel. Photo below.

BRAMBLE GUTTA-PERCHA $400   900   2000
Circa 1895-1905. "Maltese Cross," could have been sold by or made by F. H. Ayres, London. Photo below.

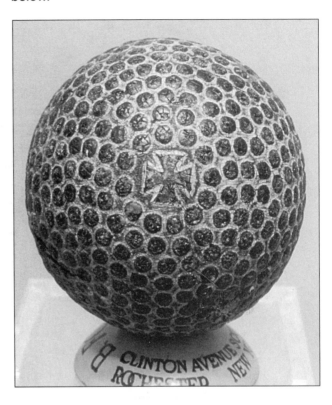

BRAMBLE GUTTA-PERCHA $400   800   1750
Circa 1895-1905. "The Finch." Photo below.

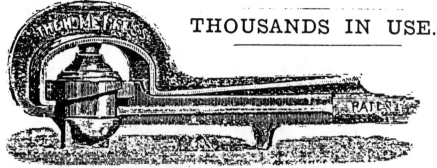

AUCHTERLONIE
ST. ANDREWS

BRAMBLE GUTTA-PERCHA $800   1200   2000
Circa 1895-1905. "Auchterlonie" at pole. (Notice the backwards "N" in the name.) Also collectible as a signature ball. Photo below.

COUNTY CHEMICAL CO.

CHEMICO DE LUXE $800   1500   3000
Circa 1900. "Horseshoe" type markings with "Dots." "Chemico De Luxe" at poles. Very scarce. Photo below.

DUNN, WILLIE
NEW YORK

LINE CUT GUTTA-PERCHA $500   1000   2500
Circa 1895. "Dunn's Record Ball 27." Photo below.

CLARK, J. & D.
MUSSELBURGH

LINE CUT GUTTA-PERCHA $400   850   2250
Circa 1900. "Musselburgh" across the equator. Advertisement below.

THE MOST POPULAR

GOLF BALL

THE  OCOBO

A LARGE STOCK OF WELL=SEASONED BALLS ALWAYS ON HAND

New B.G.I. Balls

═══NOW READY═══

Agrippas	New Eurekas
A1 Black	Silvertown

Craigpark Balls

MUSSELBURGHS A SPECIALTY

Copies of J. H. Taylor's celebrated mashys described in complete catalogue of clubs, balls, etc., free upon application, together with Instruction Book by John D. Dunn.

The BRIDGEPORT GUN IMPLEMENT CO.

313-315 Broadway, New York

Uptown Agency: JOHN D. DUNN, 17 West 42d Street

STARS AND STRIPES GUTTA $7500 15,000 40,000
Circa 1897. "Willie Dunn's Stars and Stripes" and "Patented July 27, 1897, No 27441" at the poles. Extremely RARE. Photo below.

FORGAN, ROBERT
ST. ANDREWS

HAMMERED
GUTTA-PERCHA $1500 3500 7500
Circa 1855-1880. Stamped "R Forgan" usually with size number.

GUTTA-PERCHA CO.
LONDON

EUREKA LINE CUT GUTTA $350 800 2250
Circa late 1890s. Widely spaced lines. "The Eureka 27 1/2" at poles.

HALLEY, J. B.
LONDON

LINE CUT GUTTA-PERCHA $400 800 1500
Circa 1895. "The Ocobo 27 1/2." Photo below.

HENLEY'S
LONDON

LINE CUT GUTTA-PERCHA $400 800 2000
Circa 1895. "Henley" in a rectangular panel. Photo below.

HUTCHISON MAIN
GLASGOW

SPRINGVALE GUTTA $200 450 1250
Circa 1900. Line cut.

SPRINGVALE SERIES BRAMBLE $200 400 1000
Circa 1900. "SVale" Hawk, Falcon, Eagle, Kite and others.

MORRIS, TOM
ST. ANDREWS

BRAMBLE GUTTA-PERCHA $1200 2500 4500
Circa 1895-1905. "The Tom Morris 27 1/2." Also collectible as a signature ball. Photo below.

PARK, WILLIE
MUSSELBURGH

LINE CUT GUTTA-PERCHA $1500 3000 5000
Circa 1890s. "Park" in rectangular panel. Also collectible as a signature ball. Photo below.

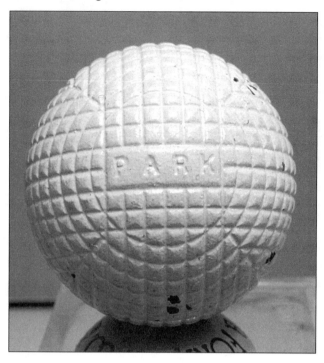

PARK ROYAL
HEXAGONAL FACES $9000 20,000 40,000
Circa 1896. Supposedly designed to minimize speed on downhill putts. RARE! Photo below.

SILVERTOWN

LINE CUT GUTTA-PERCHA $250 550 1500
Circa 1890-1905. Photo below.

SPALDING

BRAMBLE GUTTA-PERCHA,
VARDON FLYER $550 1150 2500
Circa 1900. "Vardon Flyer" at both poles. Also collectible as a signature ball.

WHIT & BARNES

THE DIAMOND GUTTA $1000   2000   3500
Circa 1895-1900. "Diamond W & B Co" at equator. "Diamond" pattern line cut gutta-percha. Very RARE. Photo below.

THE FALCON $800   1250   2500

Circa 1910. "The Falcon 27" at poles. Similar design to the "Diamond Chick." Photo below.

DIMPLE BALLS

UNKNOWN MAKER

THE RESILIENT $1000   2000   4000
Circa 1910. "The Resilient" at the poles. Ringed "Diamonds" pattern. Very scarce. Photo below.

CAPON HEATON $600   1200   2500
Circa 1910. "Capon Heaton" at poles. Five pointed stars inside a large dimple. Very scarce. Photo below.

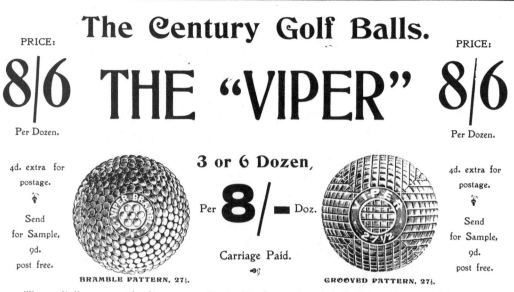

FAROID $2000   4500 10,000
Circa 1920. "Faroid, This End Up" at poles. Ringed pattern. Very scarce. Photo below.

CAPPER & CAPPER
CHICAGO

BLACK BUG DIMPLE $100   250   750
Circa 1920. No name, just a black bug at the pole. Advertisement below.

COCHRANE'S LTD.
EDINBURGH

STAR CHALLENGER $350   750   1500
Circa 1905-1910. "The Challenger" surrounding a "Star" on the poles. Joined stars circle the ball. Photo below.

THE GAMAGE
LONDON

GAMAGE'S ARIEL $300   650   1400
Circa 1920. "Gamage's Ariel" at poles. Large widely spaced dimples. Photo below.

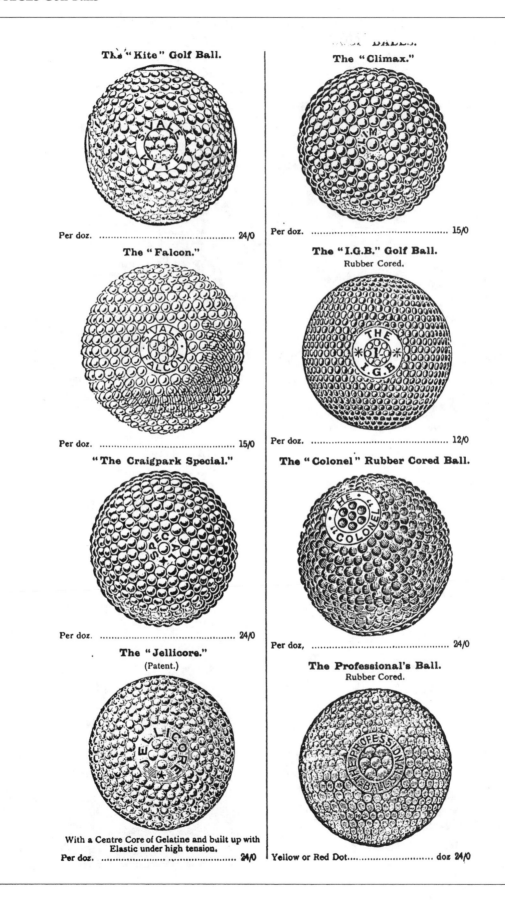

The "Kite" Golf Ball.

Per doz. 24/0

The "Falcon."

Per doz. 15/0

"The Craigpark Special."

Per doz. 24/0

The "Jellicore."
(Patent.)

With a Centre Core of Gelatine and built up with
Elastic under high tension.
Per doz. 24/0

The "Climax."

Per doz. 15/0

The "I.G.B." Golf Ball.
Rubber Cored.

Per doz. 12/0

The "Colonel" Rubber Cored Ball.

Per doz, ... 24/0

The Professional's Ball.
Rubber Cored.

Yellow or Red Dot............................. doz 24/0

HENRY, ALEX

HENRY'S RIFLED BALL $6000   15,000   40,000
Circa 1903. "Henry's Rifled Ball" at poles. Cover is a swirl pattern similar to a rifle barrel. Photo below.

HENRY C. LYTTON
CHICAGO

BLUE BIRD DIMPLE $40   90   250
Circa 1920s. No name, just a flying bird on pole. Advertisement below.

HENLEY'S
LONDON

HENLEY $3500   6500   12000
Circa 1920s. "Henley" at equator. Triple line pattern that resembles the British "Union Jack" flag. Very scarce. Photo below.

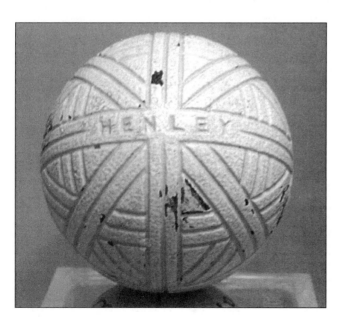

NORTH BRITISH
EDINBURGH

DIAMOND CHICK $1500   2500   5000
Circa 1910-1915. "Diamond Chick" at poles. A very odd pattern. Very scarce. Photo below.

SUPER CHICK DIMPLE $150   350   750
Circa 1920. "Super Chick 31" at poles. Large dimples. Very scarce. Advertisement below.

REACH, A. J.
PHILADELPHIA

REACH EAGLE DIMPLE $50   100   250
Circa 1920s. "Reach Eagle" at poles. Balls in boxes or wrappers are worth double. Advertisement below.

Keep your eye on the

SUPER-CHICK

The Latest and Best
Product of Scotland

Made by
NORTH BRITISH RUBBER CO.

BAKER, MURRAY & IMBRIE
DISTRIBUTORS
15 Warren St., New York

Announcing

Eagle <u>1</u> and Eagle <u>2</u>

TWO
NEW
REACH
GOLF
BALLS

Size 1.630 in. Weight 1.69 oz. High Powered—in that it is of small size and of heavy weight and built to arrive as nearly as possible by the air route. Certainly the equal of any ball of AMERICA or BRITAIN.

Both represent truly notable achievements in golf ball design and construction.

PRICE
Per Dozen
$12.00

at leading sporting goods stores, from club professionals.

or

Size 1.655 in. Weight 1.64 oz. It is easier to achieve greater durability in a ball of this kind —lighter—softer —sweeter—feeling—and the size, weight and winding more perfectly attuned for the average golfer, who seldom should attempt too much weight.

A. J. REACH CO.
PHILADELPHIA, PA.

APRIL 1920   Golfers Magazine.   19

Wright & Ditson Golf Balls

Made in different styles to meet the demands of all types of players and conditions of play

The Wright & Ditson VICTOR "75" is meeting with greater success than ever. We have had more favorable comments over its controllability, distance and durability than ever before. The "75" is the ball for all *expert* golfers.

The VICTOR "31" is the same quality, only larger.
The VICTOR "29", and all VICTORS—$1.00 each.

BLACK CIRCLE—90c each. THE BISK and BIRDIE —75c each. NATIONAL FLOATER— 75c each. The new NO. 19—60c each.

Have your Pro or Dealer show you the Victor and other Wright & Ditson golf balls. Give them a good trial and you will be delighted with the results.

In addition to our regular line of Irons, we are putting the BEE LINE Irons on the market. They are the last word in style, workmanship, quality of shaft, etc. Ten models in all. A club for every distance. Each $6.00.

Wright & Ditson balls and clubs for sale by all golf professionals and at

Wright & Ditson

Boston—Cambridge—Worcester
WRIGHT & DITSON—VICTOR CO.
New York—Chicago—San Francisco
Send for Golf Catalogue

VICTOR 75   VICTOR 29   BIRDIE   THE BISK   VICTOR 31   BLACK CIRCLE   NATIONAL FLOATER   NO. 19

REACH, WRIGHT & DITSON

DIMPLE BALLS $20   45   100
Circa 1930. Many names. Balls in boxes or wrappers are worth double. Fig. 1 and 2.

SPALDING, USA

DIMPLE COVER $50   125   375
Circa 1908-1925. Many markings including Midget Dimple, 40, 50, 60, Dot, Baby Dimple, Domino, Glory Dimple, Honor, and others. Photo below.

DIMPLE COVER $15   30   75
Circa 1920-1940. "P G A." Photo below.

ST. MUNGO, NEWARK & GLASGOW

HEAVY COLONEL $450   850   2000
Circa 1915. "Heavy Colonel" at poles. Large widely spaced dimples. Photo below.

STOW-WOODWARD

BURBANK $600   1000   2000
Circa 1930s. "Burbank" crossed vertically and horizontally at poles. An unusual swirl cover pattern. Very scarce. Photo below.

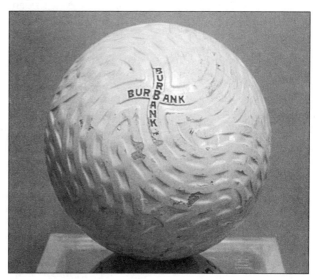

MESH BALLS

UNKNOWN MAKER

CUDAHY'S PURITAN MESH $50   100   300
Circa 1920s and 1930s. "Cudahys Puritan" at poles. Standard square mesh pattern.

WRIGHT & DITSON | FINE ATHLETIC GOODS

WRIGHT & DITSON GOLF BALLS

Made in different styles to meet the demands of all types of players and conditions of play.

VICTOR 75

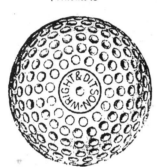

BLACK CIRCLE

BIRDIE

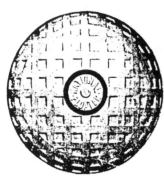

NATIONAL FLOATER

VICTOR "75." Small and heavy. Especially for the expert who requires a ball that he can control under all conditions. A wonderful ball for putting.
Each, **$1.00**   Dozen, **$12.00**
Compression average 4 1-2. Weight 1.69 ounces.

VICTOR "31." A larger size ball than the "75" and a trifle heavier. Especially adapted to players who desire a large heavy ball for play requiring distance under all conditions.
Each, **$1.00**   Dozen, **$12.00**
Compression average 4 1-2. Weight 1.70 ounces.

VICTOR "29." A truly wonderful ball. Same size as the "31," but a little lighter weight. The "29" is the best ball for sixty per cent of the golfers who prefer medium size and weight. Insures better lies, especially when the fair green is heavy.   Each, **$1.00**   Dozen, **$12.00**
Compression average 6. Weight 1.62 ounces.

BLACK CIRCLE. A size between the Victor "31" and "75" and is now, as it always has been, a ball of championship quality. An ideal ball in every respect.
Each, **90c.**   Dozen, **$10.80**
Compression average 6. Weight 1.68 ounces.

THE BISK. Mesh marking, with a lively center; the type ball best suited to players who drive low, depending upon the run for distance. The Bisk is medium size. Very dependable.
Each, **75c.**   Dozen, **$9.00**
Compression average 7. Weight 1.67 ounces.

NATIONAL FLOATER. A large light ball, floats in water, mesh marking, and is considered by a great many golfers to be the best floater ever produced.
Each, **75c.**   Dozen, **$9.00**
Compression average 8. Weight 1.44 ounces.

BIRDIE, or, Yellow Circle. Medium size and weight, has always been and always will be one of the most popular balls ever introduced, being suitable to all types of play.   Each, **75c.**   Dozen, **$9.00**
Compression average 7 1-2. Weight 1.52 ounces.

W. & D. No. 19. New this year. Large size, medium weight, recessed marking, and is beyond all doubt the very best for golfers who want a fine playing and durable ball at a low price.
Each, **60c.**   Dozen, **$7.20**
Compression average 7. Weight 1.63 ounces.

VICTOR 31

VICTOR 29

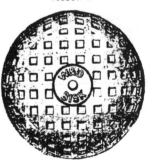

THE BISK

No. 19

ST. REGIS MESH $50   100   300
Circa 1930s. Standard square mesh pattern. There is a steel mold for this ball currently on the market. It sold for $700 in 1995.

ASSOCIATED GOLFERS

DARBY FLYER MESH $50   100   250
Circa 1920s. "Darby Flyer" at poles. Standard square mesh pattern. Advertisement below.

New Golf Balls
for
Old Ones

Send us twelve old golf balls—any make— together with your check for $5.00 — and we will send you postpaid — One Dozen "DARBY FLYER" Golf Balls — each ball guaranteed new and perfect — combining the maximum of Distance, Accuracy and Durability.

Look-up those old balls today and turn them in for brand new "DARBY FLYERS."

Introducing
"DARBY FLYER"
A New and Better
75c Ball

ASSOCIATED GOLFERS, Inc.
Makers of "Darbysteel" Golf Course Equipment

339 Brown Street   Philadelphia, Pa.

AVON

AVON DELUXE MESH $50   100   300
Circa 1920s. "Avon DeLuxe" at poles. Standard square mesh pattern.

BAKER & BENNETT
NEW YORK

GRAY GOOSE MESH $50   100   300
Circa 1920s. Standard square mesh pattern. They came in an individual box. A G-7 box will double the value. Advertisement below.

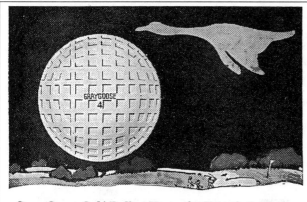

Gray Goose Golf Ball ⤙ Keeps the Friends It Makes

BAKER & BENNETT CO.

873 Broadway   New York, N. Y.

BURKE MFG. CO.
NEWARK, OH

BURKE 50-50 MESH $50   100   300
Circa 1920s. "Burke 50-50" at poles. Standard square mesh pattern.

COCHRANE'S LTD.
EDINBURGH

REX MESH $50   100   300
Circa 1920s and 1930s. Standard square mesh pattern

X L CHALLENGER $250   700   1250
Circa 1917. "X L Challenger" on equator. New basket pattern for 1917. Advertisement below.

THE WORLD'S BEST GOLF BALL

The X L CHALLENGER is the ball that will create a sensation in 1917. It will lead them off. It outdistances all others from the tee, keeps its shape, putts straight and keeps its paint.

When you buy an X L CHALLENGER you buy a quality which has given its makers the largest golf ball trade in the world.

XL CHALLENGER GOLF BALL
A NEW-COMER IN THE GOLF FAMILY

One peculiar merit about this ball, compared with any other make, is that it really improves in play. The X L CHALLENGER refuses to be knocked out of shape.

Like all champions, it will stand against the hardest hitter in the world.

Confidence is the possession of the golfer who plays with the X L CHALLENGER.

Tested and Proved to Go Further Than Any Other Golf Ball Ever Produced

PRICE $1.00 EACH. PER DOZEN $12.00   To be had from all leading Golf Professionals and Sporting Goods Stores.

R & A CHALLENGER—New Basket Pattern, 75c each. $9.00 per dozen. Medium size, 29 dwts, 31 dwts.
THE CHALLENGER—Bramble, Star and Mesh Marking, 65c each. $7.50 per dozen. Floating, 29 dwts and 31 dwts.
THE REX—Bramble and Mesh Marking, 50c each. $6.00 per dozen. Floating and Non Floater.
We have a large stock for immediate delivery of Challenger Brand, —Scotch Hand Forged Iron Heads.

J. P. Cochrane & Co., 95 Chambers St., New York City
EDINBURGH   CARNOUSTIE   LONDON
Chicago Distributors, Van Lengerke & Antoine, 128-132 So. Wabash Ave.

DRAPER-MAYNARD
PORTSMOUTH, NH

OWL MESH $50   100   300
Circa 1930. "D & M Owl" at poles. Standard square mesh pattern.

DUNLOP

DUNLOP ENGLAND MESH $45   80   225
Circa 1920s. "Dunlop" and "England" at poles. Pattern similar to the "Super Harlequin" pictured here.

Spalding Golf Balls
Season 1920

4 OUTSTANDING FEATURES Emphasized in the leading balls of the Spalding Golf Ball Family—the leading balls of the game.

Added DURABILITY in the 1920 productions.

DISTANCE, ACCURACY.

A Ball for Every Kind of Player.

FIFTY—A small ball. For expert play. Noted for extreme Distance. Controllability and Durability.......Each, $1.00

SIXTY—A trifle larger than the fifty and of unusual Durability. Recommended for light hitters.....Each, $1.00

FORTY—As the fifty, for expert play. A trifle larger and heavier.....Each, $1.00

THIRTY—A ball suitable for fully 85% of all Golfers—Expert as well as Novice. Weight, just right..........Each, $1.00

RED HONOR—A popular ball with a splendid record from past years. Weight and size suitable for all conditions of play ....Each, $0.90

BABY DIMPLE—Also one of the old-time favorites. Thoroughly reliable. For light hitters................Each, $0.75

GLORY DIMPLE—A floater. Excellent for all-around play. For women players, light hitters and beginners...Each, $0.75

BLACK DOMINO — A first-class ball. Large size, medium weight. A fine ball for the beginner............Each, $0.60

GREEN DOT MESH—Large size, slightly heavier than the Domino. An excellent practice ball.................Each, $0.60

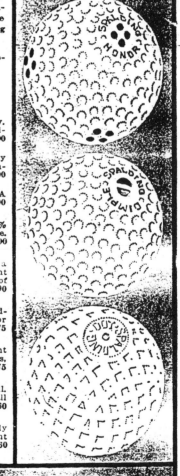

A. G. SPALDING & BROS
Stores in all Principal Cities

DUNLOP GOLD CUP MESH $50   100   250
Circa 1920s. "Dunlop" and "Gold Cup" at poles.
Standard square mesh pattern. Photo below.

GOLF DEVEL
BROMFORD MESH $50   100   250
Circa 1930s. Standard square mesh pattern.

TEE-MEE MESH $50   100   300
Circa 1930s. Standard square mesh pattern.

GOODRICH, B. F.
WHIZ MESH $50   100   300
Circa 1920s. Standard square mesh pattern.

WHIPPET MESH $50   100   300
Circa 1920s. Standard square mesh pattern.

MACGREGOR
DAYTON, OH
JACK RABBIT MESH $50   100   300
Circa 1920s. "Jack Rabbit" at poles. Standard
square mesh pattern.

NORTH BRITISH
EDINBURGH
NORTH BRITISH MESH $50   100   300
Circa 1920s-1930s. "North British" at poles. Stan-
dard square mesh pattern.

REACH, A. J.
PHILADELPHIA
REACH PARAMOUNT MESH $50   100   250
Circa 1920s. "Paramount" at poles. Standard
square mesh pattern.

REACH PARAMOUNT
TRIANGLE $75   175   450
Circa 1920s. "Reach Paramount" at poles. Triangle
pattern. Advertisement below.

REACH, WRIGHT & DITSON
MESH BALLS $50   100   300
Circa 1930. Many names. Fig. 3

SCOTTISH INDIA RUB
GLASGOW
MAXIM MESH $50   100   300
Circa 1920s. "Maxim" at poles. Standard square
mesh pattern.

SILVERTOWN
LYNX MESH $50   100   300
Circa 1930s. "Lynx" at poles. Standard square
mesh pattern. Photo below.

A. J. REACH, WRIGHT & DITSON, INCORPORATED

GOLF BALLS

THE WRIGHT & DITSON RECORD

Made for durability and distance. This ball is guaranteed not to cut or nick in actual play. Tests have proven it to be one of the longest distance balls ever made. We have produced in this ball a wonderful degree of durability without sacrificing its distance qualities. *Record* golf balls fully live up to the players' expectations in every kind of shot. Absolute dependability in the continuous uniformity of the *Record* ball will inspire confidence which improves the player's ability. Mesh marked. Also furnished with the new Multidot marking. Each ball is painted with twelve colored dots. This new marking gives the player greater visibility; easier to identify and easier to hit accurately. ....*Dozen* $9.00 Each .75

Wright & Ditson Record

Wright & Ditson Record With the New Multidot Marking

THE WRIGHT & DITSON BULLET
Dimple Marked

Approved Dimple marking. Made for distance. Special type of marking, and very high-powered. Golfers are surprised at the great distance to be obtained with it. Flies especially well into the wind and holds direction better than any ball we know of. In addition to its wonderful flight, it is very accurate in approaching and putting. Its durability is very satisfactory—more so than is usually found in a high-powered ball. These balls are also furnished with the new Multidot marking. *Dozen* $9.00 Each 75c.

Wright & Ditson Bullet Dimple

THE WRIGHT & DITSON BULLET
Mesh Marked

We furnish the Bullet with a mesh marking. Also with the new Multidot marking; Specify kind of ball. Otherwise our regular Dimple Bullet will be furnished on mail orders. ....*Dozen* $9.00 Each 75c.

Wright & Ditson Bullet Dimple With the New Multidot Marking

twelve colored dots painted on ball.

All the above golf balls can be supplied in either the 1930 size of 1.62 inches, weight 1.62 ounces or in the 1931 size of 1.68 inches, weight 1.55 ounces. Multidot golf balls are supplied in the following colors: Red, Blue, Green and Maroon.

Wright & Ditson Bullet Mesh

A. J. REACH, WRIGHT & DITSON, INCORPORATED

GOLF BALLS

THE REACH EAGLE

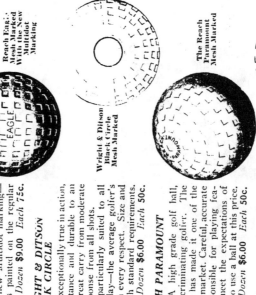

The essential qualities for which the Reach Eagle is noted are distance, control and durability. Eagle balls can be depended on for the full measure of distance in accordance with the power put into the stroke. No halting or lagging but straight and sure in flight or roll. When hit true, an Eagle ball flies true. On the green the accuracy of response inspires confidence in putting. The tough, lasting covers, stand terrific punishment yet remain in good playing shape for a remarkable length of time. Mesh marked. Also furnished with the new Multidot marking—twelve colored dots painted on the regular Eagle ball. ....*Dozen* $9.00 Each 75c.

Reach Eagle Mesh Marked

Reach Eagle Mesh Marked With the New Multidot Marking

THE WRIGHT & DITSON
BLACK CIRCLE

Mesh marked. Exceptionally true in action, remarkable for distance and durable to an extreme degree. Great carry from moderate blow and quick response from all shots.

These balls are particularly suited to all general forms of play—the average golfer's ball. Dependable in every respect. Size and weight conform with standard requirements.
Dozen $6.00 Each 50c.

Wright & Ditson Black Circle Mesh Marked

THE REACH PARAMOUNT

Mesh marked. A high grade golf ball, suitable for the discriminating golfer. The quality of this ball has made it one of the most popular on the market. Careful, accurate construction is responsible for playing features which fully meet the expectations of players who prefer to use a ball at this price.
Dozen $6.00 Each 50c.

The Reach Paramount Mesh Marked

All the above balls can be supplied in either the 1930 size of 1.62 inches, weight 1.62 ounces or the 1931 size of 1.68 inches, weight 1.55 ounces.

THE WRIGHT & DITSON NATIONAL FLOATER

Mesh marked. Due to its light weight construction, this ball is long in driving quality. Excellent for soft turf conditions. Especially good for ladies' use, for light hitters and beginners. As the name implies, this ball floats in water. The use of this type of ball for water holes reduces mental hazard. Standard floater size and weight. ...*Dozen* $6.00 Each 50c.

Wright & Ditson National Floater Mesh Marked

SPALDING BALLS, USA

MESH COVER $50   100   300
Circa 1920-1935. "PGA" made in both British and American sizes. Square markings. Photo below.

MESH COVER $50   100   300
Circa 1920-1935. "Spalding" and "Kro-Flite" at poles. Square markings. Photo below.

ST. MUNGO, NEWARK & GLASGOW

MESH COVER $50   125   350
Circa 1920-1935. "Arch Colonel" and "1.55," "1.62" or "1.68" at poles. Square markings. Photo below.

COLONEL MESH $50   100   275
Circa 1915-1920. Many names including "F S," "29," "31," "27," "Click" and others. Balls in boxes or wrappers are worth double. Advertisement below.

The D&M "OWL" GOLF BALL
50c

The outstanding feature of this ball is service. It will stand up and give complete satisfaction for general play. It is responsive to all shots, has good carry, and has a particularly tough but elastic cover that will not cut easily. The "Owl" is a wonderfully fine ball for the price. Available in new size and weight to conform to new requirements to be adopted by U.S.G.A. January 1, 1931 (1.68 in. 1.55 oz.) or in present standard size 1.62 in. and weight 1.62 oz.

Unless the new size and weight are specified, the present standard size ball ('1.62 in. 1.62 oz.) will be furnished on all orders.

No. 14M. Mesh. Price.....$0.50   No. 14D. Dimple. Price....$0.50

The D&M "BLUE FOX" GOLF BALL
75c

This ball represents a splendid combination of distance and durability. It has a speedy get-away, flies far and true and has a protective covering that will stand the gaff of hard usage. Marked in four colors and available in either mesh or dimple markings. Available in present standard size only (1.62 in. 1.62 oz.).

No. 12M. Mesh. Price.....$0.85   No. 12D. Dimple. Price....$0.85

PRACTO GOLF BALLS

These balls are very light and soft. Ideal for outdoor or indoor practice. They have a strongly knit cover that will stand up under many hard shots from wood and iron clubs.
No. P1. Practice Balls. Price..............$0.25

TURNER PRACTICE GOLF BALLS

The Turner practice balls are of thin hollow rubber. A flanged base is provided for teeing the ball up for practice shots. They are very soft, light and durable.
No. PT5. Turner Practice Balls. Price $0.25

[29]

U.S. RUBBER CO.
NEW YORK

U.S. ROYAL MESH $45   80   150
Circa 1930s. Standard square mesh pattern.

FAIRWAY MESH $45   80   225
Circa 1930s. "Fairway" on poles. Standard square mesh pattern.

NOBBY MESH $250   550   1250
Circa 1930s. Truck tire pattern. Advertisement below.

WALGREEN'S
CERTIFIED MESH $45   80   225
Circa 1930s. Standard square mesh pattern.

WANNAMAKER
NEW YORK

FLASH MESH $50   100   300
Circa 1920s. Several varieties marked "Flash." Blue, Yellow, Red, Long and others. Standard square mesh pattern.

WILSON, THOMAS E.
CHICAGO

WILSON MESH $50   100   250
Circa 1920s and 1930s. Many including Crest, "W," Top Notch, Success, Pinehurst and Hol-Hi. Standard square mesh pattern. Advertisement below.

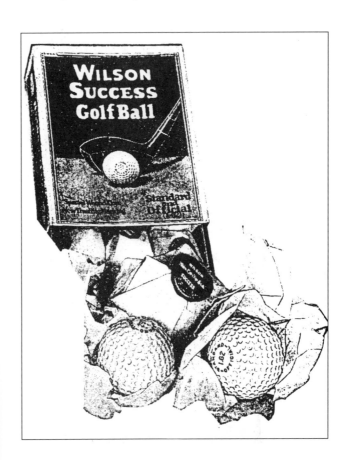

WORTHINGTON
OHIO

DIAMOND SERIES MESH $50   100   300
Circa 1920s. Diamond King, Jack, Four, Chip and others. Standard square mesh pattern.

RUBBER CORE

VARIOUS MAKERS
BRAMBLE, RUBBER CORE $175   400   850
Circa 1900. Gutta-percha cover.

BRAMBLE, RUBBER CORE $160   375   800
Circa 1905-1920. Celluloid or rubber cover.

The Crawford, McGregor & Canby Co.,
Dayton, Ohio, U. S. A.

The Crawford, McGregor & Canby Co.,
Dayton, Ohio, U. S. A.

THE ST. MUNGO COMPANY OF AMERICA, LINE OF GOLF BALLS.

ARCH COLONEL

Sunken Marking.
Small size. Sinks,
Price per Doz............$9.00

GREEN STAR COLONEL

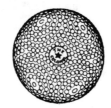

Pebble Marking.
Small size. Sinks.
Price per doz............$9.00

CRESCENT COLONEL

Sunken Marking.
Regular size. Floats.
Price per Doz............$9.00

THE COLONEL

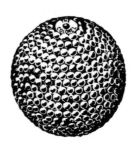

Pebble Marking.
Regular size. Floats.
Price per Doz............$9.00

LITTLE CRESCENT COLONEL

Sunken Marking.
Small size. Sinks.
Price per Doz............$9.00

HEAVY COLONEL

Price per Doz............$9.00

MAJOR RUBBER CORE

Pebble Marking.
Regular size. Floats
Price per Doz............$6.00

ST. MUNGO WATER CORE

Pebble Marking.
Price per Doz............$6.00

ST. MUNGO REMADES.

Excellent Practice Ball.   Regular size.
Pebble Marking.   Price per Doz..........$4.00

Taken from McGregor 1913 catalogue

UNKNOWN MAKERS

BRAMBLE, RUBBER CORE $250   450   1000
Circa 1905-1915. "The Resilient" at poles. Photo below.

BRAMBLE, RUBBER CORE $1500   3000   7500
Circa 1900-1905. "The Bruce Cored Center" with a "Spider" and "Web." Gutta-percha cover. Photo below.

HARRINGTON SPECIAL $100   250   550
Circa 1920s. "Harrington Special" at poles. Squares and rectangles in an odd design. Photo below.

COUNTY CHEMICAL CO.

CHEMICO TRIUMPH $75   175   450
Circa 1920. "Chemico Triumph" surrounding a "Cross" at the poles. Small concentric squares form the pattern. Photo below.

CRAIG PARK
GLASGOW

WHITE FLYER $500   1200   2250
Circa 1915. "White Flyer" at poles. Circles with a "Cross" inside. Very scarce! Photo below.

DUNLOP
BIRMINGHAM, ENGLAND

WARWICK $75   175   450
Circa 1925-1935. Alternating rows of square and dimple markings.

GOODRICH, B. F.
AKRON, OH

BRAMBLE, RUBBER CORE $750   1250   2250
Circa 1899-1905. "Haskell" and "Pat. Apr. 1, 1899" at poles. Gutta-percha cover. Photo below.

BRAMBLE, RUBBER CORE $325   550   1250
Circa 1899-1905. "Haskell" and "Pat. Apr. 1, 1899" at poles. Celluloid cover. Photo below.

LINE CUT RUBBER CORE $1800   3500   5500
Circa 1902. "Haskell" and "Pat. Apr. 1, 1899" in rectangular panels. Gutta-percha cover. Photos of front and back below.

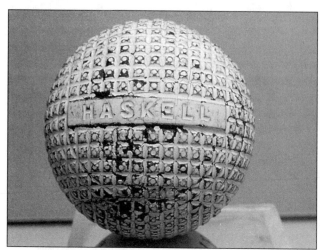

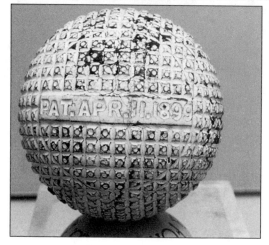

BRAMBLE, RUBBER CORE $400   800   1500
Circa 1910. "Haskell Royal" with a celluloid cover.
Photo below.

THE METEOR $250   500   1350
Circa 1920. "The Meteor" at poles. Concentric triangles. Photo below.

GOODYEAR RUBBER CO.
OHIO

BRAMBLE, RUBBER CORE $300   600   1500
Circa 1905. "The Pneumatic" at equator. These
were rubber cored with a center of compressed air.
Photo below.

BRAMBLE, RUBBER CORE $700   1250   2500
Circa 1905. "The Pneumatic" at poles. These were
rubber cored with a center of compressed air. Photo
below.

GOODYEAR A $75   150   400
Circa 1920. "Goodyear A" at poles. Odd pattern of
squares. Photo below.

HARLEQUIN
SUPER HARLEQUIN $150   350   850
Circa 1920s. "Super Harlequin" crossed at poles.
Unusual arrangement of squares. Photo below.

HENLEY'S
LONDON

WHY NOT BRAMBLE $175   350   900
Circa 1915. "Why Not" at both poles. Advertisement
below.

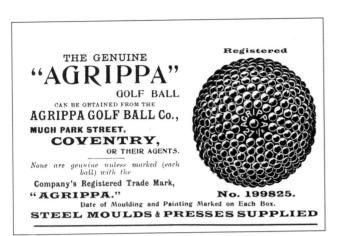

IMPROVED GOLF BALLS
LONDON

BRAMBLE, RUBBER CORE $250   500   1000
Circa 1902-1905. "I R" at poles. These were recovered "Haskell or other cored balls." Gutta-percha cover. Photo below.

KEMPSHALL
NEW JERSEY

RUBBER CORED BRAMBLES $175   375   900
Circa 1905-1920. Many, including: "Chick," "Flyer," Arlington," "League" and others.

DATED BRAMBLE $250   450   1200
Circa 1905-1908. Large numerals on one pole, patent date on other pole. Photo below.

MARTINS
BURMINGHAM

ZOME TWO $400   800   1750
Circa 1900-1910. "Zome Two" at poles. Large circles with a raised center.

NORTH BRITISH
EDINBURGH

CLINCHER CROSS $200   450   950
Circa 1915. "Clincher Cross" and size number at poles. Ball is lined into four sections. Triangles and rectangles make up the pattern. Photo below.

SILVERTOWN

BRAMBLE, RUBBER CORE $250   450   1000
Circa 1905-1915. "Silver King" at poles. Photo below.

SPALDING
USA

RUBBER CORED BRAMBLES $175   375   900
Circa 1906-1920. Many, including: "White," "Wizard," "Dot," "Blue Circle," "Spalding Bramble," "Spalding Bob" and others.

DIAMOND COVER $75   150   400
Circa 1920-1930. Entire cover with diamonds. "Spalding" at poles. Photo below.

ST. MUNGO, NEWARK & GLASGOW

CRESCENT COLONEL $175   350   800
Circa 1920s. "Crescent Colonel" surrounds a "Crescent." Pattern is opposing crescents. Photo below.

*The Crawford, McGregor & Canby Co.,
Dayton, Ohio. U. S. A.*

THE B. F. GOODRICH CO'S LINE OF GOLF BALLS.

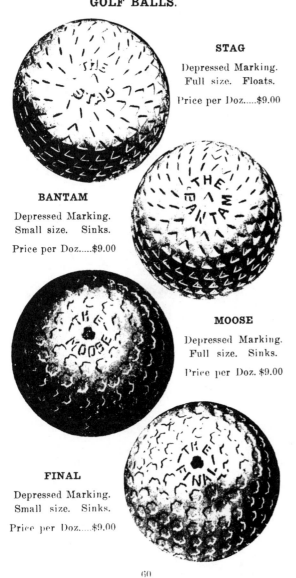

STAG

Depressed Marking.
Full size. Floats.

Price per Doz.....$9.00

BANTAM

Depressed Marking.
Small size. Sinks.

Price per Doz.....$9.00

MOOSE

Depressed Marking.
Full size. Sinks.

Price per Doz. $9.00

FINAL

Depressed Marking.
Small size. Sinks.

Price per Doz.....$9.00

60

*The Crawford, McGregor & Canby Co..
Dayton, Ohio. U. S. A.*

METEOR

Depressed Marking.
Full size. Floats.

Price per Doz.....$6.00

SCOTTY

Depressed Marking
Small size. Sinks.

Price per Doz.....$6.00

COMET

Pebble Marking.
Medium size. Floats.

Price per Doz.....$6.00

61

From the McGregor cataloge of 1913

U.S. RUBBER CO.
NEW YORK

U. S. TIGER $250   650   1500
Circa 1920. "U S Tiger" at poles. Large circles. Was made in white and yellow cover colors. Photo below.

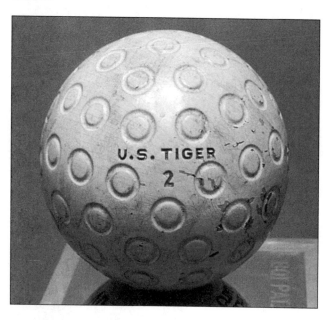

WILSON, THOMAS E.
CHICAGO

WILSON BRAMBLE $600   1200   2250
Circa 1920. "Wilson" at poles. Pattern is large flat brambles. Photo below.

WORTHINGTON
OHIO

WHITE FLAT BRAMBLE $600   1250   2250
Circa 1910-1915. "White Worthington" at poles. Large flat brambles. Very scarce. Photo below.

WRIGHT & DITSON
BOSTON, MA

CIRCLE SERIES,
RUBBER CORE BRAMBLE $175   375   900
Circa 1906-1915. "Wright & Ditson" and patent dates inside colored circles. Blue, Green, Orange Floater, Black and others. Fig. 4

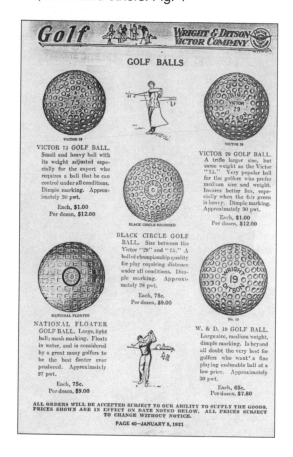

WRAPPED BALLS

Golf ball manufacturers began wrapping balls about 1895. Dunlop, Slazenger, Penfold, Spalding, Wilson and several other companies continued through the 1980s. The first wrappers were made of paper with an advertising seal; later wrappings were of colored cellophane.

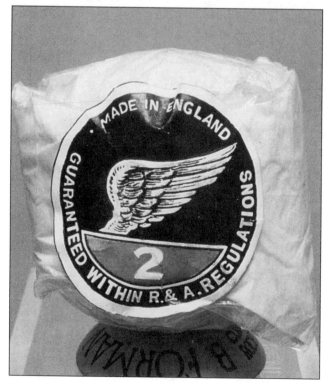

Wright & Ditson Golf Balls

$9.00
REG. U. S. PAT. OFF.

BABY BLACK CIRCLE

ALL the great tournaments of 1911 were won by players using the BLACK CIRCLE GOLF BALL. The National Open Championship, the blue ribbon event of American golf, in which all of America's greatest was won by a player using the Black Circle. In all the great open events of the North and South during 1912, the winners played with the Black Circle. In the National Open Championship of America, the first three prize winners played with the Black Circle, the Western Open Championship, the first four prize winners played with the Black Circle, and the Pacific Coast Open Championship the first two prize winners played with the Black Circle. ¶ It is a small heavy ball with Lynx style marking and sinks in water. It is a long driving ball, flys low and holds its direction against the wind. Its greatest qualities, however, are in its approaching and putting, and a good putt makes up for many poor drives. . . . . Per dozen,

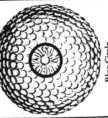
Purple Ringer

Red Circle

Blue Circle

ORANGE AND BLACK RINGER

Orange and Black Ringer

A new ball for 1913; made in the very popular marking that gives distance without great effort. Medium size, light weight, floats in water. . . . Dozen, **$9.00**

PURPLE RINGER

Also a new ball for 1913; made like the Orange and Black, only heavier, being medium size and weight; sinks in water. Fine ball to use in connection with the Orange and Black when playing against the wind. Dozen, **$9.00**

ORANGE "BABY" RINGER

Orange "Baby" Ringer

Size of the Purple ball; a little lighter in weight; sinks in water; a fine all-round playing golf ball. Per dozen, **$9.00**

RED CIRCLE

Made of the best rubber core center, covered with white gutta; heavy weight, which makes it a desirable ball against the wind. Long driving ball. Dozen, **$9.00**

GREEN CIRCLE

Green Circle
REG. U. S. PAT. OFF.

Floats in water. The players like it because they find it to be the most reliable ball for driving, approaching and putting. The marking is the popular 6-Pole style; is known to be the best for accurate flight. Dozen, **$8.00**

BLUE CIRCLE

Rubber cored; lynx style marking. Very popular. Dozen, **$6.00**

REALIZING the necessity that exists for a line of golf balls that shall satisfy not only the taste of every discriminating and critical golfer, but shall cover every variation of weather, season, turf condition, and in fact, any golfing emergency whatever, and firmly believing that these above conditions can be met only by a variety so comprehensive, we submit the following balls for the season of 1913, with recommendations as noted, regarding special merits of different sizes and weights. "Dimple" marking controlled by A. G. Spalding & Bros., under patent dated February 4, 1908. We can also furnish any rubber cored golf balls made under the Haskell patent.

LARGE SIZE BALLS

LIGHT—For moderate hitters, soft turf conditions, water holes.

HEAVY—For distance players, long roll, hard turf, use in wind, steadiness on greens.

No. 1
Spalding Red Dot
REG. U.S. PAT. OFF.
Floats in water. Light weight. Dozen, **$6.00**

No. 2
Spalding Glory Bramble
REG. U.S. PAT. OFF.
Red, White and Blue dot. Floats. Light. Dozen, **$8.00**

No. 3
Spalding Glory Dimple
REG. U.S. PAT. OFF.
Red, White and Blue dot. Floats. Light. Dozen, **$9.00**

No. 4
Spalding Domino Dimple
REG. U.S. PAT. OFF.
Four Black dots. Sinks in water. Heavy. Doz., **$9.00**

MEDIUM SIZE BALLS

HEAVY—For long distance, use in wind, fairly hard turf conditions, and for the player who wishes to combine the advantages of both extremes in sizes.

LIGHT—For ladies and light hitters generally, water holes, and the accurate "holding" of greens or short holes.

No. 5
Spalding Domino Bramble
REG. U.S. PAT. OFF.
One Black dot. Sinks in water. Heavy weight. Dozen, **$8.00**

No. 6
Spalding Domino Dimple
REG. U.S. PAT. OFF.
Four Light Blue dots. Sinks in water. Heavy weight. Dozen, **$9.00**

No. 7
Spalding Domino Dimple
REG. U.S. PAT. OFF.
Four Red dots. Floats in water. Very light weight. Dozen, **$9.00**

SMALL SIZE BALLS

MEDIUM—For the average distance man who prefers this size ball, good in wind and on almost any turf.

HEAVY—For extreme distance in carry and roll, for long players particularly, excellent in heavy wind and on smooth, hard courses.

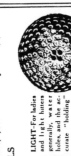

No. 8
Spalding Baby Bramble
REG. U.S. PAT. OFF.
One Blue dot. Sinks in water. Medium weight. Dozen, **$8.00**

No. 9
Spalding Baby Dimple
REG. U.S. PAT. OFF.
Two Red and two Blue dots. Sinks in water. Medium weight. Doz., **$9.00**

No. 10
Spalding Midget Bramble
REG. U.S. PAT. OFF.
Green, White and Orange dot. Sinks in water. Heavy weight. Doz., **$8.00**

No. 11
Spalding Midget Dimple
REG. U.S. PAT. OFF.
Two Green and two Orange dots. Sinks in water. Heavy weight. Doz., **$9.00**

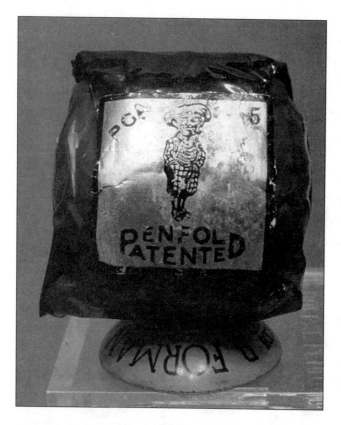

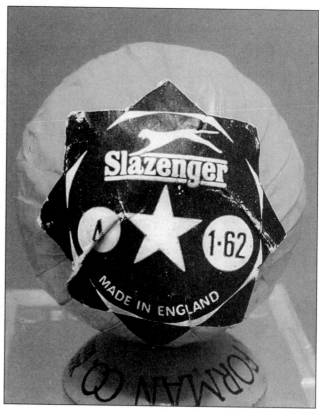

WANNAMAKER
NEW YORK

CIRCA 1924 DIMPLE BALLS $15   35   100
Circa 1925. Dimple patterns. Many names including "Red Flash," "Radio Crown," "Xray," "Taplow" and others.

BALL BOXES AND CONTAINERS

All prices given are for empty boxes and containers.

UNKNOWN MAKER

RE-MOULDED DOZEN BOX $50   90   175
Circa 1920s. Dozen box dimple or mesh.

VARIOUS MAKERS

INDIVIDUAL DIMPLE BALL
BOXES $5   20   50
Circa 1940s-1960s. Individual boxes for dimple
balls.

INDIVIDUAL DIMPLE BALL BOXES $15 35 75
Circa 1920s-1930s. Individual boxes for dimple pattern balls from the period pre-1935.

INDIVIDUAL MESH BALL BOXES $20   45   90
Circa 1920s-1930s. Individual boxes for mesh pattern balls from the period pre-1935.

DUNLOP

DUNLOP 65 BALL TUBE $10   25   60
Circa late 1930s-1950s. Three-ball screw-top tube sleeve. Photo below.

DUNLOP 65 BALL BOXES $20   50   100
Circa late 1930s-1950s. Boxes for dimpled Dunlop 65 marked "Recessed."

DUNLOP BALL BOXES $40   75   125
Circa 1920s-1930s. Boxes for mesh or dimple pattern balls.

DUNLOP BALL BOXES $75   125   250
Circa 1905-1920. Boxes for bramble pattern balls.

DUNLOP METAL DISPLAY BOX $300   500   1000
Circa 1920s. Metal box for displaying two dozen balls on countertop. Photo below.

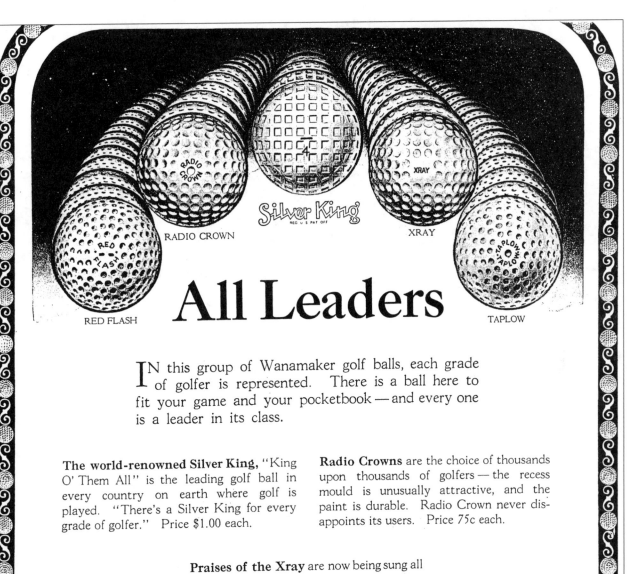

NORTH BRITISH
GLASGOW

NORTH BRITISH SLEEVE BOX $40   75   150
Circa 1920s. Cardboard sleeve box for three balls, mesh or dimple.

SILVERTOWN
SILVERKING DIMPLE
DOZEN BOX $75   150   300
Circa 1930. Balls encircling the globe, dozen box.

ST. MUNGO
GLASGOW

ONEUPO DOZEN BOX $100   225   500
Circa 1900. Box for gutta-percha balls. Photo below.

ST. MUNGO
NEW JERSEY

ARCH COLONEL MESH
DOZEN BOX $75   150   350
Circa 1920s. Colorful box picturing "The Colonel."

SILVERTOWN GUTTA
DOZEN BOX $100   225   450
Circa 1900. Slip case type dozen box.

U. S. RUBBER
NEW YORK

US 444 SLEEVE BOX $30   60   150
Circa 1930s. Cardboard sleeve box for three balls, mesh or dimple.

WORTHINGTON
OHIO

WORTHINGTON
DOZEN BOXES $35   60   100
Circa 1930s and 1940s. Dozen boxes for mesh or dimple.

WORTHINGTON
DOZEN BOXES $50   90   150
Circa 1920s. Dozen boxes for mesh or dimple.

A variety of collectible golf items.

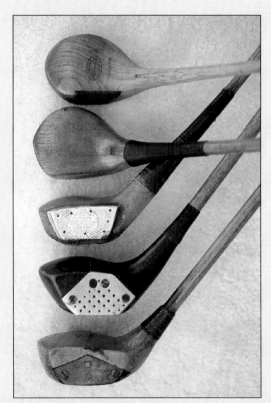

Some patent woods, circa 1895-1905.

A box of mesh balls, new, mint, circa 1930s.

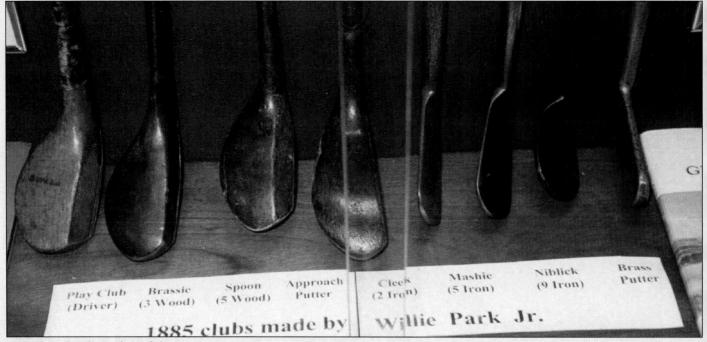

| Play Club (Driver) | Brassie (3 Wood) | Spoon (5 Wood) | Approach Putter | Cleek (2 Iron) | Mashie (5 Iron) | Niblick (9 Iron) | Brass Putter |

1885 clubs made by Willie Park Jr.

A display of Willie Park, Jr. clubs.

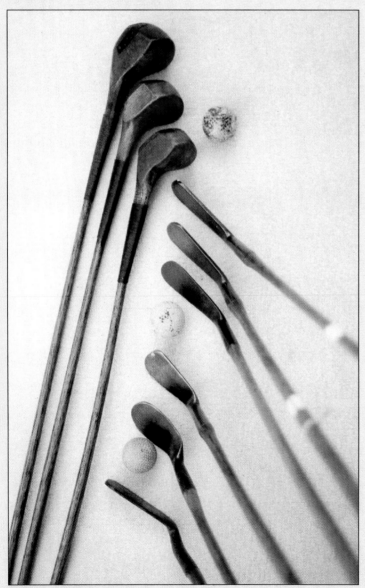

Typical gutta ball era set, 1890-1905. Driver, brassie, spoon, cleek, mid iron, mashie, lofting iron, niblick and putter.

Gutta percha balls. Line cut, molded line cut and molded bramble pattern, circa 1890-1905.

These golfers were important enough to be on the cover of Time magazine. These publications are highly sought after by collectors.

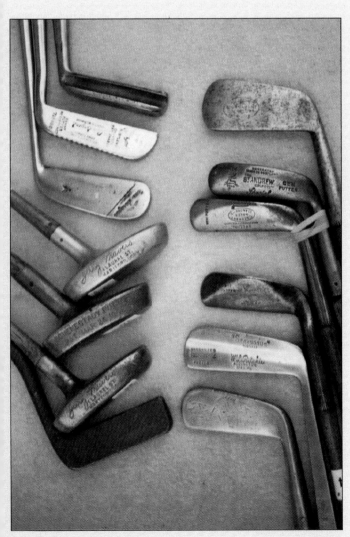

A collection of various putters.

Assortment of putters. Different strokes for different folks.

Original golf paintings are very valuable, both in terms of dollars, and in what they teach us about the history of the game.

Medals, badges, jacket patches, caddy badges and bag tags are all part of collecting golf.

Ceramics and pottery are quite scarce and highly sought after.

Ceramic collectibles made by Doulton, Lambeth, England, circa 1885. Hand painted, Burslem. Extremely valuable.

Ceramics not only make nice display items, they are also quite valuable.

A rut or track iron, circa 1860.

Golf balls were made from steel molds. These are from the 1930s.

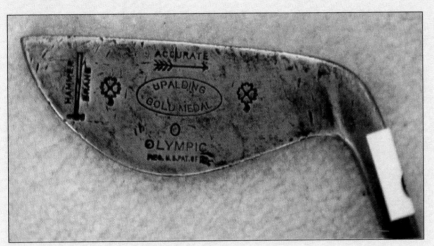

A rare Spalding olympic putter, circa 1917.

A giant niblick and a Spalding "waterfall" deep groove iron.

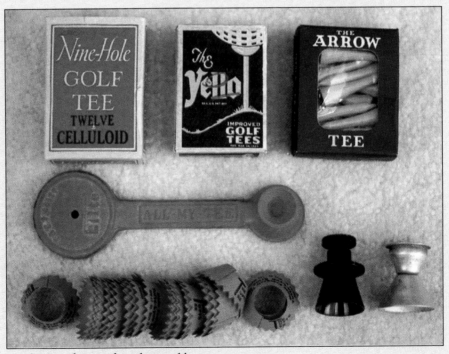

A selection of tees and sand tee molds.

Golf balls came in colorful boxes.

Golf certainly was not restricted to men! Picture dated October 24, 1926.

Caddy badges, circa 1930-1950.

Ball markers make a nice collection.

Collectible golf is more than clubs and balls.

A Tom Morris driver, circa 1900.

An assortment of putters.

Transitional long nose by Charles Gibson, circa 1885-1890. Westward Ho!

1923
WILLS

1924
WILLS

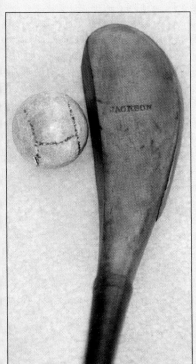

A rare Jackson short spoon, circa 1830-1840.

1928
J. MILLHOFF

Cigarette companies put cards depicting famous golfers in the packs as premiums. Today they are prized collectibles.

Signature ball boxes. Another way to collect golf balls.

The author standing in front of a "Spalding" building in Nashua, New Hampshire, dated 1883.

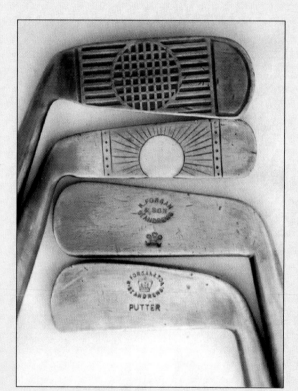

Some interesting gun metal (brass) putters.

Money clips are used for identification and tournament access on the professional tours.

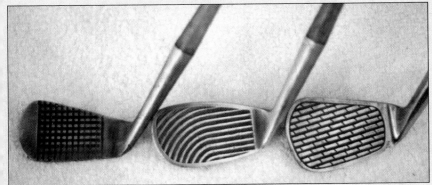

Face scoring on irons such as the waffle face, brick face and deep grooves (waterfall variety) were deemed illegal for play in 1921.

Irons with unusual face scoring are highly collectible.

Many collectors have a "golf room".

An assortment of square mesh pattern balls, circa 1920s-1930s.

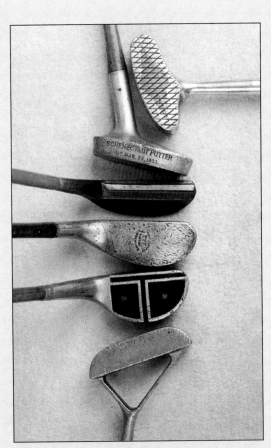

Putters came in various shapes and sizes.

Logo balls are becoming highly collectible; prices range from .50-$5.00.

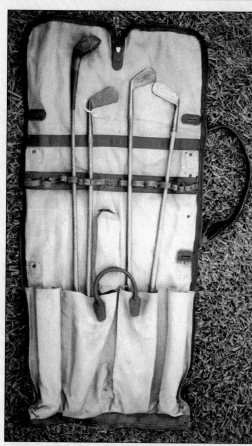

1920s golfers were affluent. This is a convertible golf bag, travel bag that holds 14 clubs.

Masters badges are highly collectible.

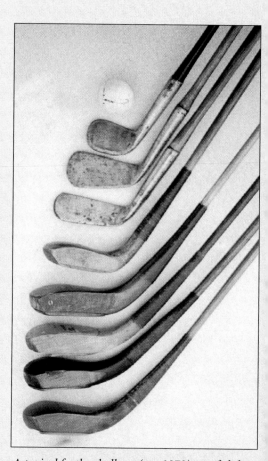

A typical feather ball era (pre 1870) set of clubs. Play club, long spoon, short spoon, baffing spoon, putter, cleek, banker or general purpose iron, rut/track iron.

Three Spalding rarities: The Cran, Seely and Spring face patented irons.

Ryder Cup program and player's shield from 1961. Ryder Cup memorabilia is highly collectible.

The author in period dress assisting the auctioneer.

Boxed tees and a weighted double rubber tee.

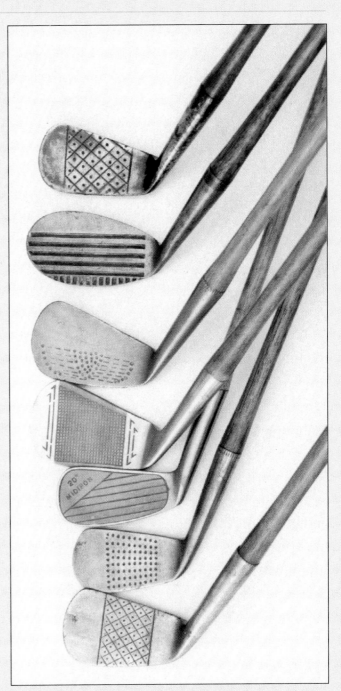

Today's clubs are boring compared to these circa teens and 1920s clubs!

A variety of collectibles, the old with the modern.

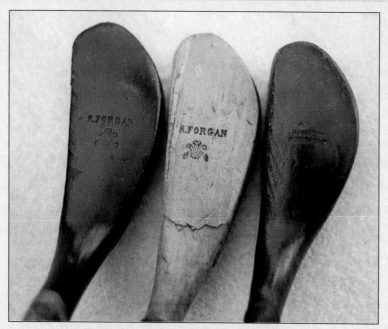
Long nose woods from the 1880s.

Two early McEwan play clubs.

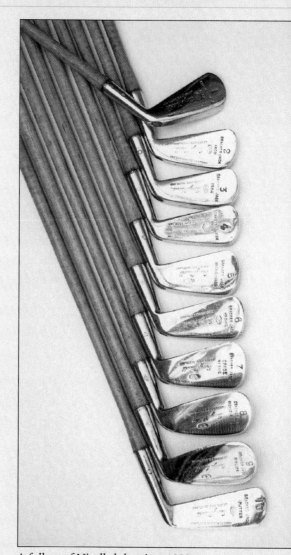
A full set of Nicoll clubs, circa 1930.

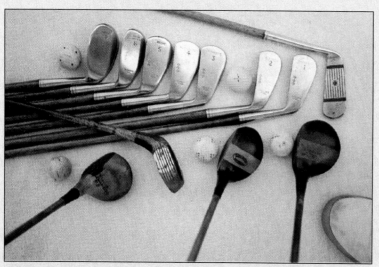
Typical set from the rubber core era, 1915-1930. Driver, brassie, spoon, bull dog trouble wood, driving iron, mid iron, mid mashie, mashie, spade mashie, mashie niblick, niblick and putter.

Turn of the century golf balls: a Vardon flyer and a Zodiak.

Aluminum putters were very popular from 1900-1930. A variety of head shapes and sizes were available.

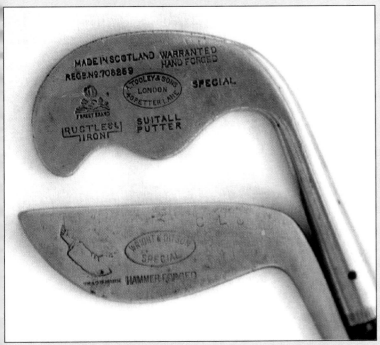

*And you thought some putters being made today were unusual!
The Wright & Ditson is from 1918, and the Tooley is from the 1920s.*

A collection of putters, circa 1920.

An assortment of tees, circa 1920.

Examples of grips on wood shaft clubs.

Three early Gutta Percha balls.

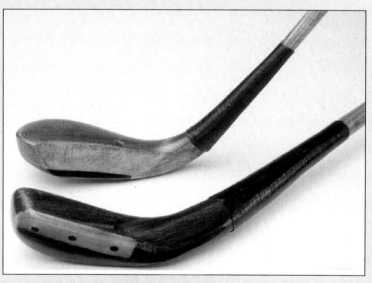

These two woods are replicas. Consult the experts before buying.

Wood tees replaced mounds of sand.

A good example of a circa 1850 Feather Ball.

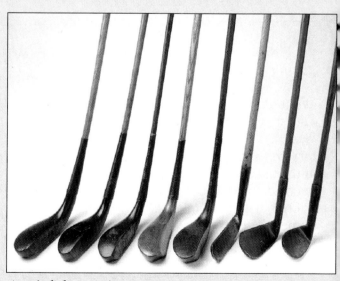

A typical play set prior to 1880.

Chapter 6
SIGNATURE BALLS

Examples of signature balls from the 1950's through the late 1970's.

One of the most asked questions by would-be ball collectors is, "What is a signature ball?" Signature balls are imprinted, at the time of manufacturing, with a professional's name. Golf balls signed, or autographed by a professional, president or celebrity (usually with a "Sharpie" felt tip pen) are NOT SIGNATURE balls, but autographed balls and classified as autographed items.

The first signature golf balls were feather balls. Willie Park, about 1890, made gutta-percha balls and simply marked them "Park." Harry Vardon was the first professional golfer to receive monetary compensation for the use of his name when, at the turn of the century, A. G. Spalding & Brothers made the "Vardon Flyer" gutta-percha ball.

Over the years, literally thousands of different named balls and varieties bearing those names have been collected singly, in sleeves or in original half dozen and dozen boxes. About 140 different varieties of the MacGregor-made balls marked with Jack Nicklaus' name have been classified.

Paul Biocini has authored the *Signature Golf Ball Collector's Guide, 1995,* and has been gracious enough to write the introduction to this chapter.

Collecting Signature Golf Balls

by Paul Biocini

It all started in Scotland when the names Morris, Gourlay, Allan (Robertson), etc., were imprinted on the feather balls they had made. Forgan, Park, Auchterlonie, etc. were the best ball makers during the gutta-percha period, 1860-1900, and they, too, imprinted their names on balls.

But why were the names put on the ball? Perhaps it was for recognition, posterity, a symbol of quality, sales promotion, or a way to honor their favorite professional, whatever the reason, it was here to stay.

Originally, many of the early American golf professionals were golf pros from Scotland and England. This was the case with John Dunn of New York, who when remolding used and damaged gutties, imprinted his name on the ball, thus creating the first signature ball made in the USA, circa 1898.

In 1900, A. G. Spalding & Bros. introduced the Vardon Flyer, with Bramble markings, which became the first manufactured signature ball. During 1905-1915 there were hundreds of newly formed golf ball manufacturing companies producing a variety of exotic balls, but only the J. H. Taylor Company's "JH" Bramble Ball (1915) and later the "JH" Mesh Ball (1925) were stamped with a professional's name.

Starting in the late 1920s, Worthington, Wilson and other companies produced both mesh and dimple design balls imprinted with the names of the stars who played them. As a result, collectors today ardently search for balls bearing the names of Walter Hagen, Gene Sarazen, Jock Hutchison,

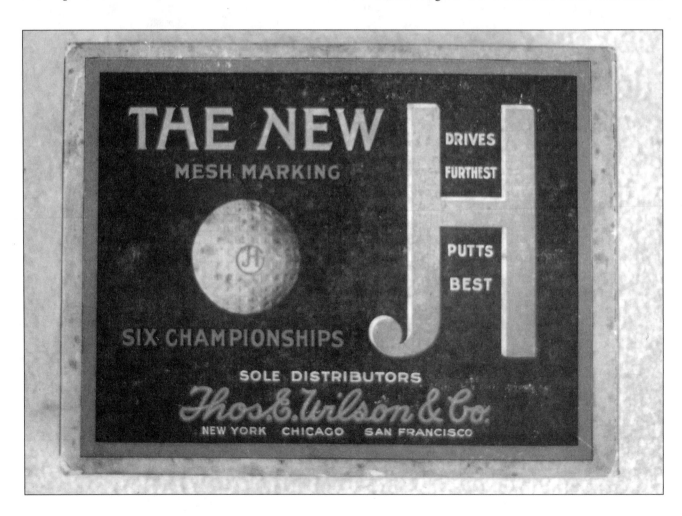

Johnny Ferrell, Tommy Armour and others. This was the first attempt by ball companies to create the "Professional Staff" concept.

Wilson was also the first company to sign a lady professional in 1933, and "Helen Hicks" became the first woman's name to appear on a manufactured ball. "Babe" Didrickson was the second, in 1935, when the Goldsmith Co. made a ball bearing her name. Wilson, in 1937, also made a "Didrickson" ball, but to my knowledge, no collector has reported having found one.

Around 1936, the larger golf companies started the "Sold in Pro Shop Only" line of more expensive "Professional" quality balls. This helped promote the sale of the lesser expensive signature balls sold only in retail, sporting goods and department stores.

During the period from the late 1930s through the 1960s, local golf pros like Wiffy Cox, George Buzzini, Andy Silva and others, began having specially made balls with their name imprinted as an advertising ploy (much like the logo balls imprinted with St. Andrews or Pebble Beach) which sold as inexpensive over-the-counter balls. Approximately 5,000 pros did so, and today more than 2,000 different names have been reported by various collectors.

Signature ball collecting is a relatively new specialty in golf collecting and the new or experienced collector can still find many treasures from local flea markets, garage sales, friends, old golf bags, professional tournaments, collectibles dealers, or trading with other collectors.

Which signature balls to collect, should be determined by where your interest lies. There are many who want to "collect them all" and have hundreds or even thousands of balls in their possession. Others may want to collect only winners of the Masters, or only winners of major tournaments. Presidential, ladies or celebrity balls are other collectible venues. I know of one individual who collects only signature balls of the pros he has seen play in person.

The field is limited only by your imagination, physical storage or display space, and your pocket book.

When placing a value on a signature ball, keep in mind the overall preservation, how much it has deteriorated from mint new, and the name clarity. If the signature name is scuffed or partially unreadable on a nearly new ball, the ball is technically uncollectible, unless it is very rare or the only example available.

THE G-5, G-7, G-9 PRICING VALUES WILL REPRESENT THE FOLLOWING CONDITIONS:

G-5

An average ball, with a good clear name, may have iron marks (no cuts), some paint loss, or may be slightly out of round.

G-7

An above average condition ball showing only the slightest evidence of play. The name and all markings are bold.

G-9

Mint new as made. No evidence of play.

Collecting Signature Ball Boxes

by Gary Hilgers

Gary Hilgers has been a long time collector of signature balls and signature ball boxes. He has graciously submitted a brief overview on collecting ball boxes.

The manufacture of signature balls reached its peak in the 1960s. During this time, the large golf ball companies such as Wilson, Spalding & MacGregor lead the way in finding those pros who were willing to have their name stamped on a ball and have it marketed "to the world." While ball performance was (and is) critical to ball sales, the ball companies realized that marketing played an equally key role. Golfers who bought these balls either wanted to emulate the play of a particular golfer or they simply liked the way the ball box looked on the store shelf. Today, the golf ball box collector graces his or her walls with colorful graphics of these golf ball boxes, and the result is a step back in time to an idea of what people saw on the golfing shelves of that era.

As one might imagine, it is getting more and more difficult to locate balls and boxes. The best sources are antique golf dealers, private collectors, collectibles shows, auctions and garage sales.

Golf ball boxes of the big name pros, Palmer, Nicklaus, Snead, Nelson, Sarazen, Hagen, and Hogan, are a must for the beginning collector. Discovering a scarce full-dozen box of signature balls stamped with a pro name such as Ted Makalena, Tony Lema, Patty Berg, Babe Zaharias, Porky Oliver or Wiffy Cox, would be a very enjoyable find!

One subtle point of signature ball collecting that goes unnoticed, is the very fact the collector is forced to learn more of the history of the game. With every new ball box (or ball) one acquires, one can't help wanting to find out a little history of the pro himself.

Most signature golf ball collectors seek those boxes which ideally meet four criteria:

1. Picture of the golf pro
2. Facsimile signature of the pro
3. Balls in their original packaging
4. At least a G-5 condition

In recent years, the trend for ball manufacturers has been to steer away from these pro-specific balls. While the Jack Nicklaus "Golden Bear" ball has been the top seller of all signature balls, over the past 15 years very few have found their way to store shelves. Balls endorsed by John Daly, Greg Norman, Ben Hogan and some by Tommy Armour, are a few that can currently be found on store shelves. This trend indicates that golf ball boxes will maintain their value and niche appeal as the supply becomes more and more limited.

Signature ball boxes make a colorful display in anyone's collection.

PRICES
SIGNATURE BALLS

G-5   G-7   G-9

TOMMY AARON

MADE IN JAPAN $10   15   25
Circa 1960-1965. Several varieties marked "Japan."

SPALDING, USA $10   15   25
Circa 1965. "Unicore."

TOMMY ARMOUR

WORTHINGTON BALL CO.
MESH $120   250   550
Circa 1931. "Tommy Armour" in black letters. "Great Lakes" monogram "GL" at poles. Photo below.

WORTHINGTON BALL CO. $30   60   100
Circa 1935. Small or large "Tommy Armour" in black letters. Four red and black dots at poles.

WORTHINGTON BALL CO.
DIMPLE $25   45   75
Circa 1937. "Tommy Armour" 50 or 60 with name in red block letters.

WORTHINGTON BALL CO. $10   15   30
Circa 1958. "Silver Scot."

LAURIE AUCHTERLONIE

DUNLOP $40   60   100
Circa 1957. Block letters on Dunlop 65 ball.

SEVE BALLESTEROS

SLAZENGER, UK $15   25   35
Circa 1980. Name in script.

LAURA BAUGH

WILSON, THOMAS E.,
CHICAGO $20   30   45
Circa 1975. Wilson "XK."

GEORGE BAYER

MACGREGOR $25   35   50
Circa 1958-1962. All varieties.

PATTY BERG

WILSON, THOMAS E.,
CHICAGO $45   65   100
Circa 1955-1960. Four balls about the same value: "Autograph," "Trophy," "Classic," or the "Patrician."

TOMMY BOLT

KROYDON $10   15   25
Circa 1955-1965. Photo below.

JULIUS BOROS

WILSON, THOMAS E.,
CHICAGO $20   35   60
Circa 1958. "100," "Zenith" and others.

BILLY BURKE

WORTHINGTON BALL CO. $30   45   75
Circa late 1930s. Three balls about the same value. "50," "Victory" and "75."

JACK BURKE

MACGREGOR $10   20   45
Circa late 1950s. Many varieties all about the same value.

BILLY CASPER

WILSON, THOMAS E.,
CHICAGO $25   35   50
Circa 1958. "Wilson Tournament" or "Super Power" with number at bottom.

WILSON, THOMAS E.,
CHICAGO $10   15   20
Circa 1960s-1980s. Most varieties found.

KROYDON $25   35   50
Circa 1958. "Wilson Tournament" or "Super Power" with number at bottom.

KROYDON $10   15   20
Circa 1960s-1980s. Most varieties found. Photo below.

HARRY COOPER

WORTHINGTON BALL CO.
MESH $120   250   550
Circa 1931. "Harry Cooper" in black letters. "Star" at poles. Photo below.

WIFFY COX

WORTHINGTON BALL CO.
MESH $125   275   550
Circa 1930. Square mesh pattern. Photo below.

WRIGHT & DITSON,
BOSTON, MA $60   90   125
Circa 1936. "Wright & Ditson" with four green dots.

BOBBY CRUICKSHANK

MACGREGOR $50   80   120
Circa 1936. Two dots, red and black.

WORTHINGTON BALL CO. $45   70   100
Circa 1938. Worthington cured cover.

JIMMY DEMARET

MACGREGOR $25   35   50
Circa 1958. All varieties.

BABE DIDRIKSON

GOLDSMITH CO., NEW YORK $250   350   550
Circa 1936. Wilson 35 and 50.

GOLDSMITH CO., NEW YORK $450   650   1000
Circa 1936. Wilson 75. Photo below.

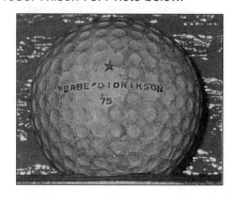

LEE ELDER

FAULTLESS $10   15   20
Circa 1962-66. Photo below.

JOHNNY FARRELL

WILSON, THOMAS E.,
CHICAGO $125   250   550
Circa 1930. Any mesh cover ball.

WILSON, THOMAS E.,
CHICAGO $45   70   100
Circa 1936. "50." Photo below.

WILSON, THOMAS E.,
CHICAGO $45   70   100
Circa 1936. "Autograph," "Champion," or "Supreme."

JACK FLECK

SPALDING, USA $70   100   150
Circa 1956.

AL GEIBERGER

SPALDING, USA $70   100   150
Circa 1977. "Mr. 59" with score card. Photo below.

RALPH GULDAHL

WILSON, THOMAS E.,
CHICAGO $75   100   150
Circa 1935. Radio Active 75.

WILSON, THOMAS E.,
CHICAGO $35   50   75
Circa 1936-1939. All varieties. Photo below.

WALTER HAGEN

HAGEN GOLF CO. $140   275   575
Circa 1930. Any mesh pattern.

HAGEN GOLF CO. $50   75   125
Circa 1935. "Bingo," "Playboy," "Vulcord," "Honey Bee, "It's A Honey," or "288 For Tournament Play."

HAGEN GOLF CO. $60   90   150
Circa 1935. "Hagen PGA" with Honey Bee. Photo below.

HAGEN GOLF CO. $20   35   50
Circa 1950-1965. "Sir Walter," "Speed-Flo," "Trophy Plus," or "International."

HAGEN GOLF CO. $10   15   25
Circa 1955-1965. "The Haig," "The Haig 80-90-100," or "TCW 80-90-100."

HELEN HICKS
WILSON, THOMAS E.,
CHICAGO $50   75   125
Circa late 1930s. All varieties.

JIMMY HINES
WORTHINGTON BALL CO. $40   75   150
Circa 1938. Dimple ball. "Victory" and "Jimmy Hines."

BEN HOGAN
MACGREGOR $35   50   90
Circa 1950. "Crown."

HOGAN $5   10   15
Circa 1970-1990. Most all varieties.

HOGAN $20   35   50
Circa 1955-1960. "River Run," "Hogan Construction" or red "Star." Photo below.

JOCK HUTCHINSON
WORTHINGTON BALL CO.
MESH $120   250   550
Circa 1930. Square mesh pattern. Photo below.

PEGGY KIRK BELL
SPALDING, USA $25   35   50
Circa 1965. Spalding Pinehurst.

JOE KIRKWOOD
WORTHINGTON BALL CO. $30   40   65
Circa 1940. All varieties.

KY LAFFOON
WRIGHT & DITSON, BOSTON, MA $40   85   175
Circa 1938. Two orange dots above and below name. Photo below.

TONY LEMA
KROYDON $35   60   90
Circa 1963. With champagne glass. Photo below.

KROYDON $15 25 40
Circa 1962-1965. Small or large signature in red or black.

NANCY LOPEZ
RAM GOLF CO. $15 25 40
Circa 1970-1972. All varieties.

TED MAKALENA
UNKNOWN MAKER $60 100 150
Circa 1960.

LLOYD MANGRUM
WILSON, THOMAS E.,
CHICAGO $25 50 95
Circa 1950. Name in block letters. Photo below.

DAVE MARR
WILSON, THOMAS E.,
CHICAGO $10 20 30
Circa late 1960s. "Stylist" under name. Also "Pinehurst," "Medalist" and "100," all about the same value. Photo below.

CARY MIDDLECOFF
WILSON, THOMAS E.,
CHICAGO $10 15 25
Circa 1960. Autograph 100. Photo below.

JOHNNY MILLER
WILSON, THOMAS E.,
CHICAGO $10 15 25
Circa 1969-1980. All varieties.

BYRON NELSON
MACGREGOR $40 70 120
Circa 1935-1938. All varieties.

NORTHWESTERN $25 35 50
Circa 1962-1968. Steel center.

NORTHWESTERN $15 25 45
Circa 1962-1968. All varieties. Photo below.

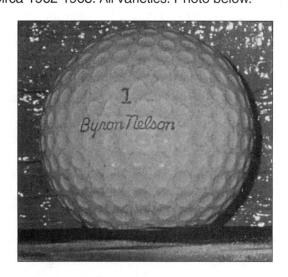

JACK NICKLAUS
MACGREGOR $25 45 75
Circa 1963. Gold colored Golden Bear.

MACGREGOR $10   15   35
Circa 1964. Three red crowns above name. Photo below.

MACGREGOR $15   25   40
Circa 1962-1968. "Champion," "Century," "Supreme," "Ambassador," "Embassy," "Diplomat," and "VIP 100."

MACGREGOR $10   15   20
Circa 1970s. Most all varieties.

PORKY OLIVER

WILSON $35   85   150
Circa 1958. "Autograph" below name. Photo below.

ARNOLD PALMER

WILSON, THOMAS E.,
CHICAGO $25   40   75
Circa 1960. "Personal," "Autograph," "Victory," "S T C," "100," and "Steel Center." Photo below.

SEARS, ROEBUCK $15   20   35
Circa 1963. Steel center.

PRO GROUP $15   20   35
Circa 1965. Steel center.

PRO GROUP $10   15   25
Circa 1977. Surlyn cover.

JOHNNY REVOLTA

WILSON, THOMAS E.,
CHICAGO $25   45   80
Circa 1936-1945. All varieties. Photo below.

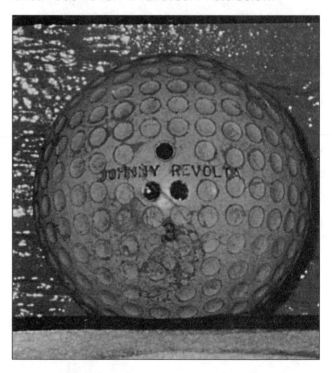

NORTHWESTERN $15   20   35
Circa 1963-1964.

CHI-CHI RODRIGUEZ

WILSON, THOMAS E.,
CHICAGO $12   18   35
Circa 1962. "Chi-Chi" signature. Photo below.

GENE SARAZEN

WILSON, THOMAS E.,
CHICAGO $125   250   550
Circa 1930. All mesh pattern balls.

WILSON, THOMAS E.,
CHICAGO $65   150   275
Circa 1932-1935. "50," "75," and "Flag." Tough or vulcanized covers.

WILSON, THOMAS E.,
CHICAGO $15   25   50
Circa 1940-1952. "Squire."

WILSON, THOMAS E.,
CHICAGO $15   20   30
Circa 1960. "Strokemaster" and "Autograph."

SARAZEN FIFTY

WILSON, THOMAS E.,
CHICAGO $25   40   75
Circa 1950. Dimple with "Sarazen" and a "Flag-in Hole" then "Fifty." Photo below.

DENNY SHUTE

WORTHINGTON BALL CO. $35   65   110
Circa 1940. "Medalist." Photo below.

WILSON, THOMAS E.,
CHICAGO $40   60   90
Circa 1939-1940. "Red 50," "Custom," "Medalist" and "Red 75."

SAM SNEAD

WILSON, THOMAS E., CHI. $35   50   75
Circa 1938-1939. "White Sulpher" and "Greenbriar."

WILSON, THOMAS E., CHI. $10   15   30
Circa 1950. Blue Ridge.

WILSON, THOMAS E., CHI. $10   15   30
Circa 1960s. "100." Photo below.

ALEX TAYLOR

ALEX TAYLOR CO., NEW YORK
MESH $120   250   550
Circa 1930. Two different mesh pattern balls. A "Taylor Ace" and "Alex Taylor Co" T 30 with a "T" at the poles.

ALEX TAYLOR CO., NEW YORK
DIMPLE $75   150   325
Circa 1930. "Taylor Imp, 31" at the poles. (Fig. X)

VARDON FLYER

SPALDING, USA $600   1200   2750
Circa 1900. Bramble pattern. Gutta-percha. "Vardon Flyer" at pole. Photo below.

CRAIG WOOD

DUNLOP, ENGLAND $50   90   150
Circa 1939. "Craig Wood" with "2 6 4" below name. Photo below.

LOU WORSHAM

MACGREGOR $20   30   50
Circa 1955-1958.

BABE ZAHARIAS

WILSON, THOMAS E., CHI. $175   275   475
Circa 1939. Wilson 75.

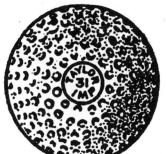

Chapter 7
COLLECTING AUTOGRAPHS

Signed photos of Ben Hogan and other golfing icons make great additions to any collection.

Autographed photographs, gum cards, books, golf balls, letters and other items are highly sought after by collectors. The first questions collectors pose are about authenticity and guarantee. There are only two sources from which you can confidently obtain signed items. The first is to get them signed IN PERSON. If you send balls, pictures, cards, etc. by mail to a golf pro, his wife, secretary or an aut2580 pen may do the signing, not the professional. Jack Nicklaus, Lee Trevino and several others use an auto pen to sign pictures. I've seen many "rubber stamp" Ben Hogan items, especially letters and 3 x 5 cards. Several others have their secretaries or family members sign items. Your best bet to get in-person signed items is to go to tournaments on *prac-*

tice days. Pros prefer not to sign anything but their official score card on tournament days.

The second, and most convenient source, is to purchase your signed items from a *reputable dealer or experienced collector who will guarantee the signed items for authenticity for LIFE. This means that anytime during the ownership of the signed item, it may be returned if there is a reasonable doubt the signature is not authentic. When a dealer or collector can give you this lifetime assurance, you can be confident it is an authentic signature. Many dealers will issue a "Certificate of Authenticity" that is, in fact, a worthless piece of paper unless backed by a LIFE guarantee. California law mandates all autographed items sold in or to a California resident for $50.00 or more must be* *accompanied by a certificate of authenticity. Many other states may have—or will have—similar laws. Just remember the certificate is only as good as the guarantee of the issuing dealer.*

Most auction houses offer no return of any item when purchasing in person at the sale. Make sure you know the signatures you are purchasing are authentic or hire the services of an expert to inspect signed items for you. Experience is great, but the opinion of an expert is almost essential when purchasing at auctions.

Be careful when purchasing autographed golf balls. (These are not to be confused with "signature" balls that are imprinted with a professional's name at the ball factory as a form of advertising.) The dimple pattern and the small size of a ball makes it difficult to sign and many signatures are hard to authenticate. Forgers are acutely aware of this and will take every advantage. Do yourself a favor, collect only autographed balls you have had signed in person, or again buy only from dealers who offer a life guarantee of authenticity.

Mark Emerson, a recognized expert and a long time collector of quality autographed items, has been kind enough to offer his perspective on collecting autographs.

Golfing Autographs: A Brief History

by Mark Emerson

The autograph hobby dates back about 1,000 years, and with the first British Open Championship in 1860, golf began to establish itself as a sport. As a result, autographs of golf's greatest players did not escape interest of collectors.

The first great impresario of the game was Old Tom Morris. Old Tom was the most outstanding player of his day—winner of four British Open titles (1861, 1862, 1864 and 1867)—was a fine clubmaker, golf ball manufacturer and architect. He also was a visionary, understanding the appeal and collectibility of signed material and, even at the turn of the century he was signing limited edition prints.

The emergence of "The Great Triumvirate," Harry Vardon, James Braid and J. H. Taylor, who between them captured 16 British Open titles, cemented interest in collecting autographs of golf's great stars in the United Kingdom. Signatures were mainly obtained in small leather-covered books designed for collecting autographs. Morris, Vardon, Braid and Taylor were responsible for creating the spark of collecting golf memorabilia overseas.

In the United States, the U.S. Open Golf Championship began in 1895. Initially it attracted small fields. It wasn't until Francis Ouimet stunned the golf world with his 1913 U.S. Open triumph over Ted Ray and Harry Vardon that Americans began to take note of golf heroes. Consequently, autographs of early U.S. Open winners are scarce. The boom in American golf was just around the corner when Gene Sarazen, Bobby Jones and the flamboyant Walter Hagen began winning numerous major golfing titles between 1914 and 1930.

In the late 1950s, Arnold Palmer's magnetism electrified galleries and television viewers. Crowds at P.G.A. tour events grew at a larger pace. Today, at nearly any event, players are hounded for signatures on just about anything imaginable.

WHY AUTOGRAPHS?

The appeal of autograph collecting generally falls into a few categories. First, collecting signatures in-person can be fun and exciting. "In-person" collectors say they enjoy the moment a famous person spends with them, and every once in a while a brief conversation ensues that makes it a life-long memory.

The aspect of collecting older autographed pieces, especially those from deceased individuals, seems to center around the "connection" of an item held by, and then signed by them.

In addition to the fun of autograph collecting, it can also become an investment that might pay off in time. Quality autographs, just like quality collectibles of all kinds, can appreciate in value.

Autographs can also become an outstanding piece of art that can adorn an office or home. As the collector, you can be the creator of that piece of art which can be fun and satisfying as well.

WHOM TO COLLECT

This is a topic every collector should try to come to grips with early on in the process. The best advice in any collecting pursuit is to develop a focus or goal. It is always up to the individual to make this decision, but collecting autographs of major championship winners seems to be the most logical.

COLLECTIBLE FORMATS

Once an individual decides whom to collect, it is wise to choose a preferred format for the collection. This is a matter of taste and value. Golf autographs can be on programs, pairing sheets, magazine covers, photos, letters, 3 x 5 cards, and golf balls, just to name a few.

CONDITION

The "quality"of autographs is an important aspect of collecting and involves several factors: the neatness of the actual signature, the boldness of the signature in relation to its background, the instrument with which the autograph is written, and what it's written on.

PRICES AUTOGRAPHED ITEMS

The following list identifies key players and current values for their autographs. Many autographs are found on pairing sheets, programs, score cards, 3 x 5 cards and autograph book album pages as well as towels, hats and golf gloves. Prices are for ink signatures pre-1975 or "Sharpie" post-1975. Pencil signatures are valued at 30- to 50- percent less.

	G-5	G-7	G-9

ISAO AOKI
ALL SIGNED ITEMS	$10	20	30

Sharpie signature.

TOMMY ARMOUR
SIGNED CARD OR PAGE	$100	175	350

Vintage fountain pen signature.

SIGNED BOOK	$175	250	450

Most commonly signed book, *How to Play Your Best Golf All the Time, 1953.*

SIGNED PHOTO	$225	400	675

Vintage fountain pen signature.

PAUL AZINGER
ALL SIGNED ITEMS	$10	20	30

Sharpie signature.

SEVE BALLESTEROS
ALL SIGNED ITEMS	$15	20	30

Sharpie signature. Signature below.

MILLER BARBER
ALL SIGNED ITEMS	$10	15	25

Sharpie signature.

JAMES BARNES
SIGNED CARD OR PAGE	$200	300	450

Vintage fountain pen signature.

SIGNED BOOK	$225	350	500

Most commonly signed book, *Picture Analysis of Golf Strokes, 1919.*

PATTY BERG
SIGNED PHOTO	$20	30	40

Circa 1950-1980.

SIGNED CARD OR PAGE	$10	15	20

Circa 1950-1980. Signature below.

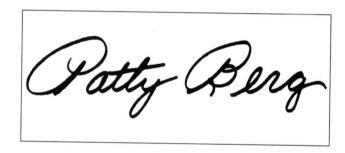

JULIUS BOROS
SIGNED PHOTO	$20	35	50

Ink pen signature.

SIGNED CARD OR PAGE	$10	20	30

Ink pen signature. Signature below.

JAMES BRAID
SIGNED CARD OR PAGE $350   600   1000
Circa 1900-1920.

SIGNED PHOTO $500   800   1500
Circa 1900-1920.

GAY BREWER
ALL SIGNED ITEMS $10   20   30
Sharpie signature.

BILLY CASPER
ALL SIGNED ITEMS $10   20   30
Sharpie signature.

JIM COLBERT
ALL SIGNED ITEMS $10   20   30
Sharpie signature.

GLENNA COLLETT
SIGNED CARD OR PAGE $125   225   400
Vintage fountain pen signature.

GLENNA COLLETT-VARE
SIGNED PHOTO $150   275   450
Vintage fountain pen signature. Signature below.

HENRY COTTON
SIGNED CARD OR PAGE $40   65   100
Vintage fountain pen signature.

SIGNED LETTER $75   125   200
Most letters by Cotton were handwritten in fountain pen.

SIGNED PHOTO $75   125   200
Vintage fountain pen signature.

FRED COUPLES
ALL SIGNED ITEMS $15   20   25
Sharpie signature. Signature below.

JOHN DALY
ALL SIGNED ITEMS $20   25   30
Sharpie signature.

JIMMY DEMARET
SIGNED CARD OR PAGE $50   75   100
Vintage fountain pen signature.

SIGNED PHOTO $100   175   275
Vintage fountain pen signature.

JIM DENT
ALL SIGNED ITEMS $10   20   30
Sharpie signature.

LEO DIEGEL
SIGNED CARD OR PAGE $100   150   250
Vintage fountain pen signature.

DAVID DUVAL
ALL SIGNED ITEMS $10   20   30
Sharpie signature.

ERNIE ELS
ALL SIGNED ITEMS $15   20   25
Sharpie signature.

CHICK EVANS
SIGNED CARD OR PAGE $125   225   400
Vintage fountain pen signature.

NICK FALDO
SIGNED PHOTO $10   15   25
Circa 1980s-1990s. Signature below.

JOHNNY FARRELL
SIGNED CARD OR PAGE $75   100   150
Vintage fountain pen signature. Signature below.

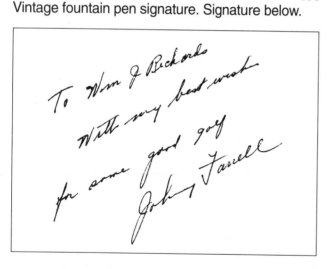

SIGNED BOOK $100   150   225
Most commonly signed book, *If I Were In Your Shoes*, 1951.

RAY FLOYD
ALL SIGNED ITEMS $10   20   30
Sharpie signature.

AL GEIBERGER (MR. 59)
ALL SIGNED ITEMS $10   20   30

JOHNNY GOODMAN
SIGNED CARD OR PAGE $125   200   350
Vintage fountain pen signature. As an amateur won U.S. Open and U.S. Amateur.

DAVID GRAHAM
ALL SIGNED ITEMS $10   20   30
Sharpie signature.

RALPH GULDAHL
SIGNED PHOTO $125   250   400
Vintage fountain pen signature.

SIGNED CARD OR PAGE $75   125   200
Vintage fountain pen signature. Signature below.

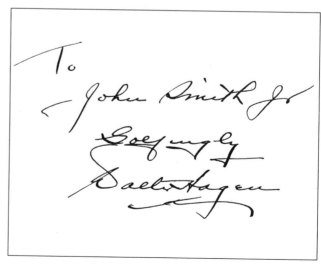

WALTER HAGEN
SIGNED PHOTO $500   850   1500
Vintage fountain pen signature.

SIGNED BOOK $325   450   600
The Walter Hagen Story, any edition. 1st addition add 20%.

SIGNED CARD OR PAGE $250   350   550
Vintage fountain pen signature. Signature below.

CLAUDE HARMON
SIGNED CARD OR PAGE $50   75   125
Vintage signature. Signature below.

BOB HOPE
GOLF RELATED ITEM $35   60   90
Pen or Sharpie signature. Signature below.

BEN HOGAN
SIGNED CARD $90   125   225
Circa 1960-1980. Signature not shaky.

SIGNED BOOK $200   275   450
Circa 1960-1980. Signature not shaky. Signature below.

HALE IRWIN
ALL SIGNED ITEMS $10   15   20
Sharpie signature. Signature below.

SIGNED PHOTO $200   300   450
Circa 1960-1980. Signature not shaky.

SIGNED PHOTO $300   500   950
Circa 1940-1950. Vintage ink pen signature. Photo below.

TONY JACKLIN
ALL SIGNED ITEMS $10   20   30
Sharpie signature.

LEE JANSEN
ALL SIGNED ITEMS $10   20   30
Sharpie signature.

ROBERT T. JONES JR.
SIGNED PHOTO $400   650   1000
Circa 1955-1970. Shaky ball point pen signature. Signature below.

SIGNED CARD OR PAGE $400   700   1200
Circa 1930-1950. Black fountain pen signature. Signature below.

SIGNED LETTER $750   1250   2000
Circa 1930-1950. Signed "Bob Jones." Black fountain pen signature.

SIGNED PHOTO $1500   2250   3500
Circa 1930-1950. Black fountain pen signature.

SIGNED PHOTO $1500   2250   3500
Circa 1930-1950. Signed "Bob Jones." Black fountain pen signature.

BERNHARD LANGER
ALL SIGNED ITEMS $10   20   30
Sharpie signature.

TOM LEHMAN
ALL SIGNED ITEMS $10   20   30
Sharpie signature.

TONY LEMA
SIGNED CARD OR PAGE $175   250   400
Ink pen signature.

SIGNED BOOK $300   500   700
Most commonly signed book, *Golfer's Gold, 1964.*

SIGNED PHOTO $350   500   750
Ink pen signature. Signature below.

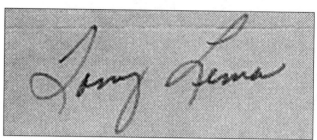

LAWSON LITTLE
SIGNED PHOTO $125   200   325
Vintage fountain pen signature.

SIGNED CARD OR PAGE $175   225   425
Vintage fountain pen signature.

BOBBY LOCKE
SIGNED CARD OR PAGE $50   75   125
Vintage fountain pen signature.

SIGNED PHOTO $75   125   200
Vintage fountain pen signature.

DAVIS LOVE III
ALL SIGNED ITEMS $10   20   30
Sharpie signature.

GARY MC CORD
ALL SIGNED ITEMS $10   20   30
Sharpie signature.

CARY MIDDLECOFF
ALL SIGNED ITEMS $15   25   35

COLIN MONTGOMERY
ALL SIGNED ITEMS $10   20   30
Sharpie signature.

TOM MORRIS

SIGNED CARD OR PAGE Circa 1900.	$1500	2000	3000
SIGNED PHOTO Circa 1900. Photo below.	$2250	3250	4750

BOB MURPHY

ALL SIGNED ITEMS Sharpie signature.	$10	20	30

BYRON NELSON

SIGNED CARD Circa 1960-1990s.	$10	20	30
SIGNED BOOK Circa 1980-1990s	$25	35	50
SIGNED PHOTO Circa 1960-1990s.	$30	45	60

SIGNED PHOTO	$75	125	225

Circa 1935-1950. Vintage fountain pen signature. Signature below.

LARRY NELSON

ALL SIGNED ITEMS Sharpie signature.	$10	20	30

JACK NICKLAUS

ALL SIGNED ITEMS	$60	75	90

Circa 1970-1990s. Beware of auto pen signatures.

ALL SIGNED ITEMS	$75	100	150

Circa 1960 vintage signatures. Signature below.

GREG NORMAN
ALL SIGNED ITEMS $20   25   30
Sharpie signature usually with flag-in-hole or word of wisdom. Signature below.

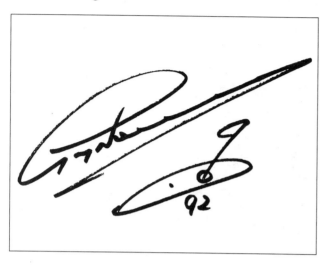

MARK O'MEARA
ALL SIGNED ITEMS $10   20   30
Sharpie signature.

JOSE-MARIA OLAZABAL
ALL SIGNED ITEMS $10   20   30
Sharpie signature.

FRANCIS OUIMET
SIGNED CARD OR PAGE $125   200   325
Vintage fountain pen signature.

SIGNED BOOK $200   300   450
Most commonly signed book was *The Rules of Golf, 1948. Signature below.*

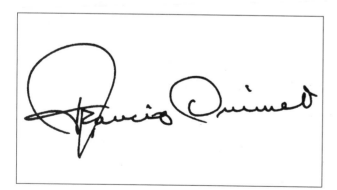

ARNOLD PALMER
ALL SIGNED ITEMS $30   40   50
Circa 1970-1990s.

ALL SIGNED ITEMS $40   60   90
Circa 1950s-1960s. Vintage signatures. Signature below.

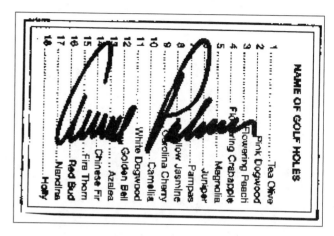

CORY PAVIN
ALL SIGNED ITEMS $10   15   20
Sharpie signature.

GARY PLAYER
SIGNED CARD OR PAGE $5   10   15
Circa 1960s-1990s.

SIGNED PHOTO $10   15   25
Circa 1960s-1990s. Signature below.

NICK PRICE
ALL SIGNED ITEMS $10   20   30
Sharpie signature.

JOHNNY REVOLTA
SIGNED CARD OR PAGE $60   90   150
Vintage fountain pen signature.

SIGNED BOOK $100   150   225
Short Cuts to Better Golf, 1949.

GENE SARAZEN
SIGNED CARD $10   20   30
Circa 1960-1990s.

SIGNED PHOTO $35   50   75
Circa 1960-1990s.

SIGNED PHOTO $75   125   225
Circa 1925-1950. Vintage fountain pen signature.
Signature below.

HORTON SMITH
SIGNED PHOTO $400   700   1200
Vintage fountain pen signature. Most sought-after
and most difficult Master's winner to obtain.

SIGNED CARD OR PAGE $250   400   600
Vintage fountain pen signature. Most sought-after
and most difficult Master's winner to obtain. Signature below.

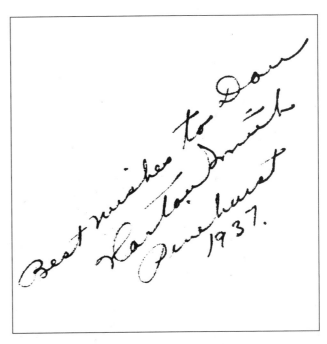

DENNY SHUTE
SIGNED CARD OR PAGE $100   150   225
Vintage fountain pen signature.

SIGNED PHOTO $125   200   300
Vintage fountain pen signature.

SAM SNEAD
SIGNED PHOTO $30   40   50
Circa 1980s-1990s.

SIGNED CARD $20   30   40
Circa 1980s-1990s.

SIGNED PHOTO $100   140   200
Circa 1940-1950. Vintage ink pen signature.

PAYNE STEWART
ALL SIGNED ITEMS $15   20   25
Sharpie signature.

J. H. TAYLOR
SIGNED CARD OR PAGE $350   550   950
Circa 1900-1920.

SIGNED PHOTO $450   750   1250
Circa 1900-1920.

PETER THOMPSON
SIGNED CARD OR PAGE $15   20   25
Vintage fountain pen signature.

SIGNED PHOTO $20   30   45
Vintage fountain pen signature.

LEE TREVINO
ALL SIGNED ITEMS $20   30   40
Sharpie signature. Beware of auto pen signatures.
Signature below.

HARRY VARDON
SIGNED CARD OR PAGE $300   500   800
Circa 1900-1920.

SIGNED PHOTO $500   950   1500
Circa 1900-1920. Photo below.

KEN VENTURI
ALL SIGNED ITEMS $10   15   20
Circa 1964-1990s. Signature below.

TOM WATSON
ALL SIGNED ITEMS $20   30   45
Sharpie signature.

JOYCE WETHERED
SIGNED CARD OR PAGE $70   120   200
Vintage fountain pen signature.

SIGNED PHOTO $100   200   350
Vintage fountain pen signature. Signature below.

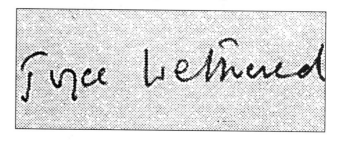

TIGER WOODS
ALL SIGNED ITEMS $35   50   80
Sharpie signature. Signature below.

MICKEY WRIGHT

SIGNED CARD OR PAGE $10   15   20
Vintage ink pen signature.

SIGNED PHOTO $15   20   30
Vintage ink pen signature.

BABE DIDRIKSON ZAHARIAS

SIGNED PHOTO $275   375   600
Vintage fountain pen signature.

SIGNED CARD OR PAGE $225   375   500
Vintage fountain pen signature. Signature below.

Chapter 8
TEES

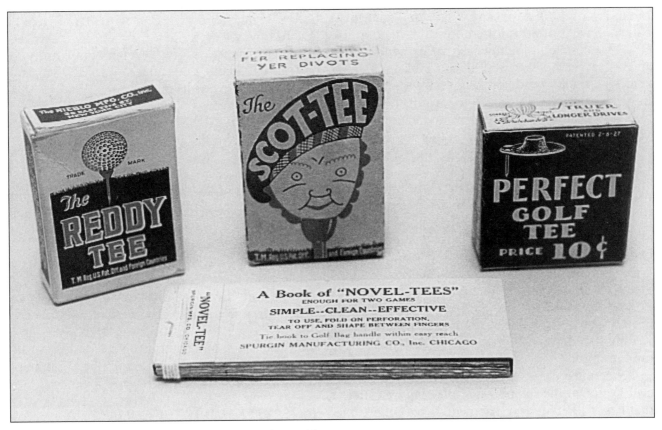

Tees come in boxes, booklets, match books, bags, packets and loose.

The "TEE" has played an important role since golf's inception over 500 years ago. Today we take them so matter-of-factly, we usually don't bother to pick them up after a tee shot.

It may surprise you to know tees were not always made of wood and one could obtain handfuls for free at the pro shop. They were made of aluminum, paper, plastic, steel, wire, zinc, rubber—anything that would raise the ball from the turf. Shapes and forms were stars, triangles, domes, tethers, spinners, molds, and just about anything imaginable and even some unimaginable.

They came individually, in boxes, string bags, paper bags, matchbooks, wheels, tins, and any other marketable containers. Pros stocked numerous varieties in their shops, and the greenskeepers lost their tempers when the new wire tees jammed their mowers. The poor tee was berated, bemused

and left on the teeing ground, until one day Walter Hagen was paid to use a particular tee, and as a gesture to his fans, left them on the teeing ground after a shot. When the last player in his group hit, and strolled down the fairway, a mad scramble ensued—by who else...the collector—to pick up the tee Hagen had just used!

Lee Crist has been a collector of tees for many years and has accumulated a vast collection and assortment. He was kind enough to provide the following for your collecting pleasures.

An Introduction to Golf Tees

by Lee Crist

Everyone knows golf tees are those little white trumpet-looking items approximately 1-7/8 inches long. In reality, golf tees have been around for more than one hundred years and, most likely, the first golf tee was a good swift stomp of a golfer's heel. This raised the ground from a common plain to a higher level, giving the player a type of launching pad.

After the heel print attempt, came forming a mound of moist dirt (or sand) that would give the ball somewhat of an elevated position, making it easier for contact. Molding each tee by hand constituted a very messy way of accomplishing the feat. Alas, the invention of the sand tee mold came into existence. This approach to forming a consistent tee became popular during the early 1890s. While this form of teeing the ball was not the ultimate, it was definitely a great improvement. Around 1893, more entrepreneurs were at work and individual tees were being developed. Prosper L. Senate of Philadelphia was given credit for inventing and patenting the first portable tee, although I suspect that individuals had made their own …"one-of-a-kind.".. long before this.

As golf became more popular in the United States, so did the quest to find a better way to present the ball for action. The poor golf tee has been the target of abuse ever since and, as of this writing, we have documented 31 variations of sand tee molds.

Collecting golf tees is not a matter of collecting every color in the rainbow or collecting every tee that has a different advertisement. A tee collector, a purist, is a person who has committed his every fiber to finding all the physically different shaped tees that were ever designed, every cloth tee bag ever made, every commercial box manufactured, every advertisement printed and, last but not least, how about patents? Probably none of the collectors started out that way, although it would be very nice to have a few odd looking tees around as a conversation piece.

HOW TO START A COLLECTION

It is recommended that you communicate with as many of your fellow golfers, friends, golf dealers and antique dealers as you can. Getting the word out and enlisting the help of others will go a long way. Letting people know that you are "looking" does wonders. It's human nature for people to want to help.

Designing your own business/collector card can also be very helpful and lots of fun. Flea markets and garage sales are a great source for finding tees; never pass up an opportunity to go through the pockets of an old golf bag.

Joining one of the antique golf societies, such as the Golf Collectors Society, is another way of finding fellow collectors who will be more than glad to have someone to correspond with. These people love to buy, sell or trade for something they need in their collection; if you have an opportunity to buy more than one unusual tee—buy it. It's always useful to have extras in trading.

HOW TO DISPLAY

Once you start accumulating tees, consideration should be given as to how you are going to sort, display, store, and transport your collection. There are numerous ways to display, as there are many categories of tees: old wooden tees, paper tees, plastic tees, metal tees, pencil tees, surface tees, height tees, novelty tees, tether tees, weighted tees, rubber tees, celluloid tees, swivel tees, and of course, sand mold tees.

Some collections are displayed in jewelry-type trays, others are mounted in styrofoam, some are mounted on plywood with very thin wire, and some use file cabinets, housing the collection in various zip lock bags. The latter is a little cumbersome if you plan to transport and show.

HOW EXTENSIVE IS TEE COLLECTING?

When talking to people about collecting, the one thing you always hear is "I had no idea that there were so many different tees." There have been more than 1,275 physically different tees catalogued and numbered; much of the credit for this belongs to Art Eden of Florida and Irv Valenta of North Carolina.

As far as "names" of tees, commercial and otherwise, 421 different names have been accounted for.

In the early 1900s, packaging to promote the merchandising of tees became an industry in itself. Tees were packaged in large and small boxes with very ornate designs. Boxes could hold 7, 9, 18, 25, 50, or 100 pieces. There are at least 64 different boxes that have been catalogued.

Another packaging concept was cloth tee bags, similar to a tobacco pouch, which held 50 or 100 tees. Walgreen Drug Co. and Sears Roebuck were two of the early suppliers of the bulk bags; 83 different ones have been catalogued. Paper bags were also used to hold 15 to 25 tees. Most bags were white with the printed advertisement of the golf companies.

Tee packets similar to matchbooks are also collectibles and have been produced since the early 1920s.

Tee advertisements have appeared as early as the 1890s in some sports magazines and are also collectibles.

PRICING

Pricing is a very subjective issue. Many individuals ask what a particular tee is worth. Obviously, the answer is, "Whatever someone is willing to pay."

The following entries and photos are an effort to help you identify some of the tees that you may find, and estimate their approximate value based on condition.

PRICES GOLF TEES

G-5 G-7 G-9

ALL-MY-TEE

VARIOUS $50   80   140

Circa 1920. Red rubber with weighted end. Photo below.

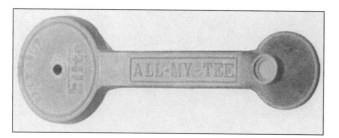

AVON DOUBLE ARM TEE

VARIOUS $75   100   150

Circa 1920s. Made in England of rubber with two tee heights. Approximately five inches long. Photo below.

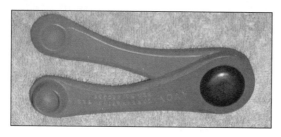

BOBBY TEES

VARIOUS $50   75   120

Circa late 1920s. Red wooden goblet-style tees in colorful box. Photo below.

BRASS DOUBLE GOLF TEE STAMP

RANSOME $600   800   1200

Circa 1900. Brass sand tee mold with a deep side for drives and shallow side for irons.

BREAK APART PLASTIC TEES

SPALDING, USA $70   100   190

Circa 1930s. Twenty red tees that break apart when needed. Photo below.

CRUICKSHANK STEEL TEES

VARIOUS $70   120   175

Circa 1930. Red wire tees with circular top. Green and red box with Bobby Cruickshank's picture. Photo below.

DOUGLAS SAND TEE GUN

VARIOUS $600   800   1200

Circa 1910-1920. Cylindrical plunger made of stainless steel. Made in England. Photo below.

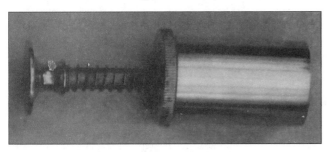

ETERNA TEE

VARIOUS $40   60   85

Circa 1950s. A three height plastic tee. Photo below.

G & S GOLF TEE

VARIOUS $65   90   150

Circa 1920s. Brass tee with rubber arm that swivels. Photo below.

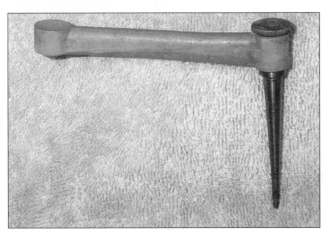

GOLD MEDAL GOLF TEE

VARIOUS $50   70   120

Circa 1930. Twenty wooden tees in box. Photo below.

INTERNATIONAL GOLF TEE

UNKNOWN MAKER $100   150   300

Circa 1917. Two rubber tees secured by a rubber tether. Illustration below.

A Good Drive Counts For a Lot

If your ball goes far and true from the tee the chances are you will make the hole in par. It is a good moral aid to your game—it maintains and increases your confidence.

The INTERNATIONAL GOLF TEE will improve your driving 100 per cent; you will learn to strike at exactly the same height each time you drive. You will never undergo the annoyance of having the ball roll off the tee just as you swing. You will no longer blame your caddie for not building the tee right.

The INTERNATIONAL GOLF TEE is made of soft rubber and there is not enough resistance to cause the ball to shoot off to one side when you strike it. Furnished in pairs of two different sizes, connected by a stout rubber band. Price, 25c. Agents wanted on every golf course in the world. Write for terms.

JOHN A. SETTLE & SON

Abingdon   -   -   -   Illinois, U. S. A.

Special Offer for May Only to Officers of Golf Clubs. Enclose this coupon with your order and we will ship 100 sets of our Tee's to any golf club in the U. S. for $15. Only 100 sets will be shipped to any one club at this price.

NAME...

G. M.   ADDRESS.................................

JUST PERFECT TEES

VARIOUS $45   70   120

Circa early 1930s. Eighteen wooden tees in pale green box. Photo below.

K-D SAND TEE MOLD

K-D MFG., LANCASTER, PA $400   600   800

Circa 1920s. Polished aluminum with spring

plunger. Photo and illustration below.

KEYSTONE SAND TEE MOLD

VARIOUS $300   400   500

Circa 1920-1930. Bakelite plastic with spring plunger. Photo below.

MATCH BOOK TEES

VARIOUS $15   25   50

Circa 1930s. Matchbook style with three to six tees. Matchbooks from the 1940s and later are worth considerably less. Photo below.

NO-LOOZ-TEE

VARIOUS $60   90   140

Circa 1950s-1960s. Weighted end. Made of rubber. Photo below.

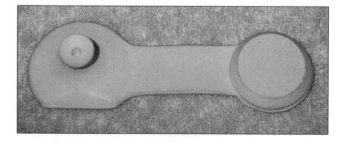

NOVEL TEES
VARIOUS $60   90   150
Circa 1930. Circular Handi-Pack of nine tees. Photo below.

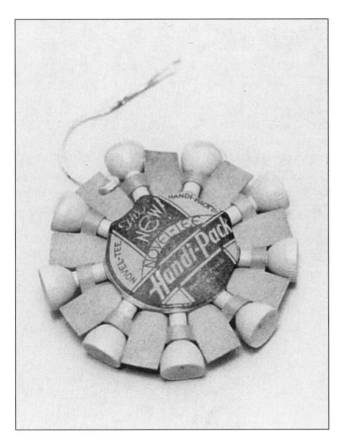

NOVEL-TEES
SPURGIN MFG., CHICAGO $50   80   140
Circa late 1920s. A book of eighteen paper tees. Photo below.

PEG GOLF TEE
VARIOUS $50   80   130
Circa 1930. Yellow box with twelve tees. (Original display boxes are quite valuable.) Photo below.

PERFECT GOLF TEE

VARIOUS $80   120   160

Patented 1927. Molded rubber tee secured in the ground by a nail. Photo below.

PERFEC TEE

UNKNOWN MAKER $65   100   180

Circa 1925. Illustration below.

PERMA TEE

VARIOUS $100   130   190

Circa 1930. Aluminum tee with steel arm that swivels. Photo below.

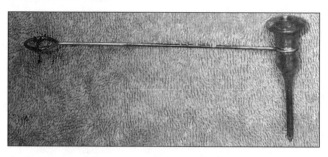

PRYDE'S ORANGE TEE

ORANGE MFG. CO. $60   100   150

Circa late 1920s. Carrot shaped wood tees. Blue and orange box. Photo below.

THE REDDY TEE

NIEBLO MFG. CO. $40   80   140

Circa 1930. Wooden tees in green, white and red box. Photo below.

REX ZINC TEES

THE REX CO., CHICAGO $60   100   150
Circa 1930. Red box. Zinc tees. Photo below.

RITE PENCIL TEE

WIMO SPECIALTY CO., NY $10   20   35
Circa 1927. Long tee with pencil lead at tip. Original boxes are scarce. Prices are for single tees. Illustration below.

ROUND CUPPED DOME METAL TEES

VARIOUS $40   60   90
Circa 1920s. Half-dollar sized "Cupped Dome"-type tee. Most had advertisements imprinted on them. Some were made of plastic and are valued less than the metal dome tees. Photo below.

RUBBER MANHATTAN TEE

VARIOUS $75   100   150
Circa 1920. Five-inch-long rubber tee with round weight at one end, tee at other. Photo below.

SAND TEE MOLD

VARIOUS $400   650   850
Circa 1890-1920. Brass with spring plunger.

THE SCOT-TEE

VARIOUS $65   100   150
Circa late 1920s. Box of eighteen wooden tees.

SELF-ADJUSTING GOLF TEE
MILLAR, GLASGOW $175   275   500
Circa 1900. Photo below.

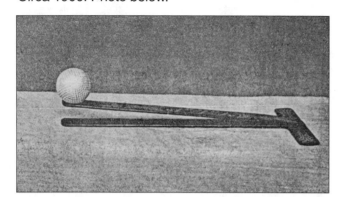

TOP NOT TEE
VARIOUS $50   70   120
Circa late 1920s. Made of both wood and steel. Orange and white box. Photo below.

TEES IN BAGS
VARIOUS MAKERS $30   60   90
Circa 1930s-1940s. Drawstring bags of 50 and 100 wooden tees. Photo below.

TETHER TEES

VARIOUS $75   100   140

Circa 1900-1930s. Many varieties with a cord or "Tether" between weight or colorful thistle and the tee.

TRIPLE-T GOLF TEE

SIMPLEX MFG.,
CLEVELAND, OH $10   15   25

Circa 1925. Made for adjusting to three heights. Original boxes are scarce. Prices are for single tees. Illustration below.

WALGREEN GOLF TEES

WALGREEN STORES $50   75   125

Circa 1930s. Yellow and black box of yellow-colored wooden tees. Photo below.

THE "YELLO" TEE

VARIOUS $50   70   120

Circa 1927. Black-and-yellow box of 18 yellow-colored wooden tees. Endorsed by Walter Hagen and Joe Kirkwood. Illustration below.

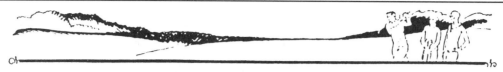

D&M GOLF TEES

White—
easy to find

Rock Maple—
hard to break

WRS

Single Tee

WRD

Double Tee

Made entirely of rock maple, the hardest, toughest wood possible to obtain. They are positively guaranteed not to chip and break like most tees on the market made of soft wood.

The two styles are scientifically designed for proper height, depth of cup and weight.

No. WRD. The Tee-Rite double tee which automatically adjusts itself to the right height. With this style the golfer is assured of the same even height on all tee shots. Packed 18 to the box. Price per box $0.25

No. WRS. The conventional single tee so popular with all golfers. Can be adjusted to any height. There are 18 White Rock tees packed in a convenient little box. Price, per box of 18 . . . . 0.25

No. YRSB.	Lucky Dog Tees, yellow. Bags of 1,000	$5.00
No. RRSB.	Lucky Dog Tees, red. Bags of 1,000 . . .	5.00
No. WRS5.	Lucky Dog Tees, white. Bags of 500 . . .	3.00
No. YRS5.	Lucky Dog Tees, yellow. Bags of 500 . . .	3.00
No. RRS5.	Lucky Dog Tees, red. Bags of 500	3.00

ZIP TEE HOLDER

No. Z1. No more need to worry which pocket your tees are in. Just slip a zip holder on your belt. Well made of tan belt leather and holds nine tees. Price, with nine tees $0.50

No. WRSB and No. WRDB. An assortment of 1000 white rock tees packed in a heavy canvas bag. By buying your golf tees in bulk considerable saving is made and you are always assured of a liberal supply in your locker. No. WRSB and No. WRDB Price per bag $5.00

REDDY TEES

No. RT. Turned from one piece of wood and stained a bright red or bright yellow to be easily seen against grass or dirt. This tee enables the golfer to tee his ball at any height he likes best. In ordering specify color desired. Price, per box of 18 . . . . $0.25

SCOT TEES

No. ST. The Scot Tee is very light and practical. It is conic in shape and well pointed for use on clay as well as grass tees. Bright yellow in color, which makes it easily seen against grass or dirt. Price, per box of 18 . . . . $0.25

[47]

Chapter 9
COLLECTING BOOKS ON GOLF

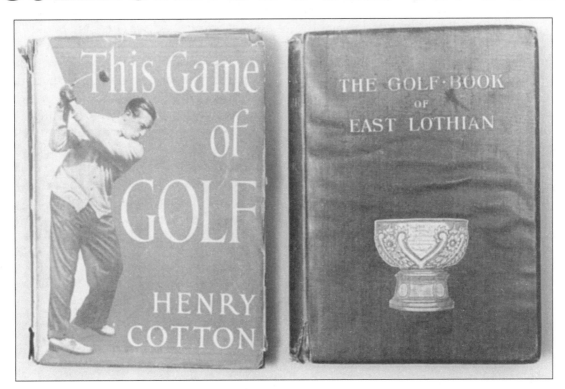

Golf books provide history, enjoyment and reference.

Golf books cover many categories. Instruction, architecture, history, rules and fiction are among the most popular with collectors. Some reference books, generally acquired for information and pricing, are highly collectible as well.

Scotland's King James II, in 1457, issued a decree outlawing golf because his soldiers were golfing more than practicing their archery skills. This decree became the first printed reference to the game of golf. It wasn't until the golf boom of the 1890s that books on golf were published in great quantities.

Richard E. Donovan and Joseph S. F. Murdoch collaborated to publish *The Game of Golf and the Printed Word (1988) which is a bibliography of golf literature in the English language. This is a highly regarded reference book, and a collectible.*

Joseph S. F. Murdoch, well known author, book collector and co-founder of the Golf Collectors Society, has kindly written an introduction to collecting books.

Collecting Golf Books

by Joseph S. F. Murdoch

The collecting of golf artifacts, a hobby that has a history going back several hundred years, has become a major collecting interest in recent years. Among the most popular collectible items are books that relate the history of the game, stories of great champions and, inevitably, books of instruction calculated to improve our skills. Some cynics may proclaim that no one ever learned to play the game from a book, although there are some notable examples of some who did. Walter J. Travis and Larry Nelson are two who come to mind.

Books of every description have been collected since the first book appeared about this hobby which has seized the mind of man throughout the ages. Golf books may not have the lineage of, say, a Gutenburg Bible or the famed poets of England, but for the man who loves the game and likes to read about it, there is a line of books calculated to intrigue him.

One of the many allures of book collecting is that one can select a subject or a subject within a subject, and spend a lifetime pursuing all of the books within this chosen field of interest. Books on golf can be divided and subdivided into many different categories, each of which may excite the interest of the collector. Books on golf history, the great champions of the game, the building of golf courses, golf humor, golf fiction, golf poetry, golf instruction, or other facets of the game have been written and published over the years, and the collector has the liberty of selecting that subject which is of his greatest interest.

One can, for example, choose books published in one country or by one writer and form a very nice library of such books. Perhaps a budding young collector may say to himself, "The game has only been played in America for 100 years, so I will collect books on the game which have been published only in America." In restricting himself to this one sphere, he will find great treasures and enough books to fill the shelves, floor to ceiling, of a fair-size room.

With the turn of the century, golfers and books proliferated and the books tumbled out of the publishing houses like bogeys from the clubs of a high-handicap hacker. There are books to interest every taste…those who strive for the ultimate par in books of instruction, history of the game, records of the great champions, fiction, poetry, the history of venerable clubs and, in more recent years, about the sport of golf collecting.

All of these books, now numbering in the thousands, are testimony to man's addiction to the game and a desire to read about it (if fog, sleet and snow conspire to keep him in the house). Should you be of a persuasion to read and to accumulate a few books on the game you love, you will find great treasures in the library of golf.

Determining Condition and Value of Books

by George Lewis

There have been well over 8,000 golf books published in numerous languages, and it would be almost impossible to list prices for them all. Therefore, to help you determine relative values, the following list of about one hundred books includes a few representative titles for each category, such as instruction, history, biography, architecture, essays, reference, etc. Although most of the books listed are still available today, a few of the cornerstone scarce and rare works are also included so that you can get a better feel for the range of pricing.

Prices of books, like so many other collectibles, are determined by condition, edition, scarcity and desirability. More recent books are not listed, because their value has not yet had a chance to fluctuate significantly from the published price. Also not included are rare works which are out of reach of most collectors, such as The Goff by Thomas Mathison, first published in 1743, last auctioned for over $30,000.

Books that are generally in poor condition (missing pages, broken cover or contents damaged, badly soiled or stained), or library books are not rated. These can be useful for information, but usually are not worth recording as part of your library.

Underlining, margin notes, repair or rebinding all reduce the value of a book. A book which has been beautifully rebound in leather may or may not be worth more than it is with the original binding; most serious collectors would prefer the book in its original state. A leather binding might enhance the value of an inexpensive book, but why spend the money to rebind it? Buy one in very good original condition instead! First printings of first editions command higher prices than later printings.

Lowest price shown is for a first printing in good condition (moderate cover wear, some fading and/or staining, considerable foxing, speckling or browning to pages).

Mid-range price is for a very good copy of a first printing (light signs of age, former owner's neatly inked name, date or brief inscription, perhaps a little foxing or speckling to pages) and if a post-1950 book, in a dust jacket (if it was issued with one).

Highest price is for a first printing which is fine (looks like it is virtually new, with no inscriptions, soil, stain or wear, with dust jacket if issued with one). It is usually quite hard to find pre-1950 books in fine condition, so they may command a significant premium, especially with a dust jacket. Very good or fine condition of the dust jacket may also increase the price, in some instances even doubling the value of the book if the dust jacket is very scarce.

If you want to form a golf library of any significance, it is suggested that you discuss your goals with a reputable and knowledgeable dealer who can advise you and assist you to put together a more meaningful collection.

George Lewis, PGA Master Professional, is one of the largest golf book, ephemera and collectibles dealers in the world. Established in 1980, George Lewis/Golfiana can be reached at PO Box 291, Mamaroneck, NY 10543, or www.golfiana.com.

Depending upon one's definition of a book, there are two early American prizes to be found, although some would describe them as pamphlets. The first, published in 1893, is Spalding's Golf, a thin, paper-covered booklet of 24 pages written by J. Stuart Balfour; the second, a booklet published by the Overman Wheel Company, was written by James Dwight. Both, or either of them, are very difficult to find.

The first book, commonly accepted as such, is by James P. Lee and entitled Golf in America. Published by Dodd, Mead and Company in Boston, it describes the game, recites a short history of the game in the United States and is blessed with a number of photographs of early clubhouses. In recent years it was reprinted in the Rare Book program of the United States Golf Association in an edition of 1900 copies.

There were only a handful of golf books published in the United States before the turn of the century and one of these, How To Play Golf, was the first book of golf instruction published here. It was written by one who was quite qualified to offer advice: H. J. Whigham was a native of England but settled here as a newspaperman in

Chicago. Whigham was the winner of our national Amateur Championship in 1896 and 1897. His book was illustrated with the very first action photographs taken of a golfer swinging a club; all previous pictures had been posed.

Considering the scarcity of books published in this country prior to 1900, 1898 saw a veritable flood of books for the relatively few golfers who had taken up the game here. Our annual publication on cricket saw fit to include golf in its summary of activity. This is The American Cricket Annual & Golf Guide, edited by Jerome Flannery. It is not easily obtained, but is an interesting record of early golf in this country.

Based on our personal experience, one of the scarcest books in the entire library of golf is Through The Green & Golfer's Year Book, edited by Prosper L. Senat and published in Philadelphia. Considering the paucity of information about early golf, this is a gold mine of information and a great prize to be won should it be found.

Two illustrated books are of interest; the first, The Golfer's Alphabet was published by Harper (New York), with delightful illustrations by the early golf illustrator, A. B. Frost; and An A.B.C. of Golf by "A Victim" (Blanchard, New York), both of which were, as the titles indicate, a letter of the alphabet given to describe the game of golf.

That same year, the first book of fiction on golf published in this country was published by Harper and written by the same W. G. VanTassel Sutphen who was an early (and verbal) supporter of the game. It is a collection of short stories under the title The Golficide & Other Tales.

To complete the list of books published here before 1900, 1899 saw another book of fiction, Drives and Putts by Walter Camp and Lilliam Brooks (published by L. C. Page in Boston), and a delightfully illustrated poem by Samuel Peck called The Golf Girl. The illustrations were done by Maud Humphrey, a popular child's illustrator of the time and, of some distinction, because she was the mother of Humphrey Bogart, who played golf but won greater fame in the motion pictures.

As the record indicates, although golf had now been played with ever-increasing popularity for some fifteen years, the book publishers were slow to find a market for books on the game. On the other side of the Atlantic, many books had already been published and, indeed, there were already collectors of them, but the publishers ignored the American public. There was one exception and if it is elusive, it remains a target for the collector who may want a complete collection of American-based books. This was The Art of Golf by Sir Walter G. Simpson, published in Edinburgh in 1887 and released in an American edition in New York in 1892.

"Buy the BOOK before the collectible" is a statement heard by most beginning collectors.

PRICES GOLF BOOKS

	G-5	G-7	G-9

ALLEN, PETER
FAMOUS FAIRWAYS $60 125 150
Architecture. 1968.

ARMOUR, TOMMY
HOW TO PLAY YOUR BEST GOLF
ALL THE TIME $8 25 35
Instruction. 1953. Many later editions. Photo below.

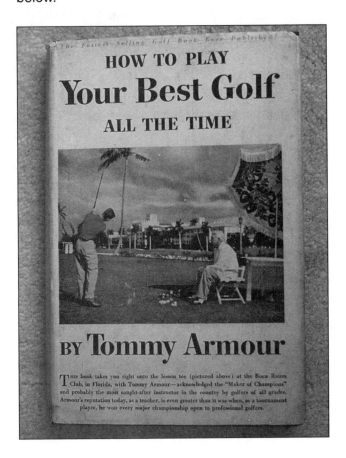

BAMBERGER, MICHAEL
THE GREEN ROAD HOME $15 25 40
Biography. 1986.

BARNES, JAMES M.
PICTURE ANALYSIS OF GOLF
STROKES $50 125 200
Instruction. 1919.

BOOMER, PERCY
ON LEARNING GOLF $20 40 60
Instruction. 1942.

BROWN, KENNETH
PUTTER PERKINS $50 80 100
Fiction. 1923.

BROWNING, R. H. K.
A HISTORY OF GOLF $190 275 325
History. 1955. An important addition to any library.

CLARK, ROBERT
A ROYAL AND ANCIENT
GAME $800 2500 3000
A library cornerstone. 1875. Many later editions.

COCHRAN, A. & STOBBS, J.
THE SEARCH FOR THE PERFECT
SWING $40 75 100
Instruction. 1968. Reissued.

COLLETT, GLENNA
LADIES IN THE ROUGH $100 150 250
Autobiography. 1928. Photo below.

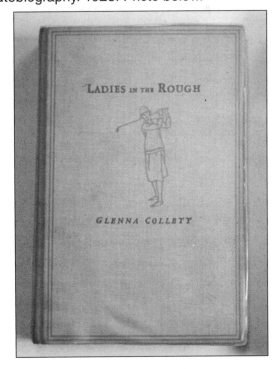

CORNISH, G. & WHITTEN, R.
THE GOLF COURSE $30   50   75
Architecture. 1979.

COTTON, HENRY
THIS GAME OF GOLF $25   50   90
Instruction. 1948. Photo below.

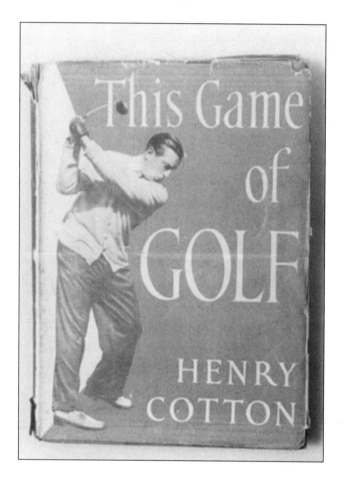

COUSINS, GEOFFREY
GOLFERS AT LAW $40   55   75
Rules. 1958.

DANTE, J. & ELLIOTT, L.
THE FOUR MAGIC MOVES TO
WINNING GOLF $20   35   50
Instruction. 1962. Reissued.

DARBYSHIRE, L. CLAUGHTON
GO GOLFING IN BRITAIN $35   50   67
Architecture. 1961. Photo below.

DARWIN, BERNARD
BRITISH GOLF $25   50   75
History. 1946.

GOLF BETWEEN TWO WARS $40   80   100
History. 1944.
GOLF COURSES OF THE BRITISH
ISLES $550 1100 1500
Architecture. 1910. A library cornerstone.

GREEN MEMORIES $250   450   650
Autobiography. 1928. Reissued.

DARWIN, BERNARD, ET AL
HISTORY OF GOLF IN
GREAT BRITAIN $175   275   400
History. 1952.

DAVIES, PETER
DAVIES' DICTIONARY OF
GOLFING TERMS $20   40   50
Reference. 1980.

DEMARET, JIMMY
MY PARTNER, BEN HOGAN $75   140   175
1954. Books signed by Demaret are worth about
a $150 premium.

DOBEREINER, PETER
THE GLORIOUS WORLD OF
GOLF $20   40   75
History. 1973.

DONOVAN & MURDOCK
THE GAME OF GOLF AND THE
PRINTED WORD $40   80   100
Reference. 1988.

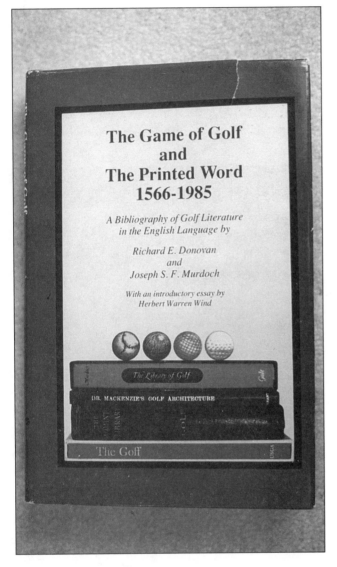

DUNCAN, G. & DARWIN, B.
PRESENT DAY GOLF $40   90   165
Anthology. London, 1921.

EVANS, CHICK
CHICK EVANS' GOLF BOOK $75   175   225
Autobiography. 1921. Also limited edition.

FLAHERTY, TOM
THE U.S. OPEN 1895-1965 $12   20   35
History. 1969.

GIBSON, NEVIN
ENCYCLOPEDIA OF GOLF $15   32   40
Reference. 1958.

GRAFFIS, HERB
THE PGA $35   55   80
History. 1975. Photo below.

HAGEN, WALTER
THE WALTER HAGEN STORY $35   60   80
Autobiography. 1956. Books signed by Hagen are worth about a $350 premium. Photo below.

HAULTAIN, A.
THE MYSTERY OF GOLF $90   150   250
Instruction. 1910. Reissued; also 1908 limited edition.

HENDERSON & STIRK
GOLF IN THE MAKING $50   80   125
Reference. 1979.

HILL, DAVE
TEED OFF $10   20   35
1977.

HILTON, HAROLD
ROYAL AND ANCIENT GAME
OF GOLF $1000   2500   3000
Anthology. 1912. Also large paper edition.

HOGAN, BEN
POWER GOLF $15   35   50
Instruction. 1948. Books signed by Hogan are worth about a $250 premium.

FIVE LESSONS, THE MODERN
FUNDAMENTALS OF GOLF $10   30   40
Instruction. 1957. Photo below. Reissued.

HOUGHTON, GEORGE
CONFESSIONS OF A GOLF
ADDICT $10   20   35
Humor. 1952.

HUNTER, DAVE
GOLF SIMPLIFIED $10   20   35
Instruction. 1921. Photo below.

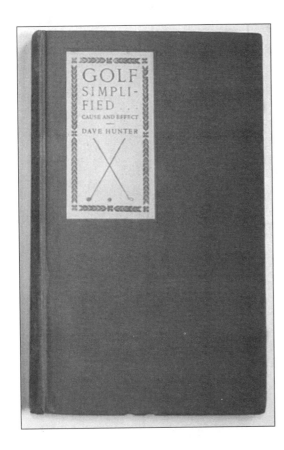

HUNTER, ROBERT
THE LINKS $400   650   950
Architecture. 1926. Reissued.

HUTCHINSON, HAROLD
FIFTY YEARS OF GOLF $200   400   600
Biography. 1919. Reissued.

HUTCHINSON, HORACE
GOLF, THE BADMINTON
LIBRARY $125   275   375
Anthology. 1890 and many later issues. Large paper edition.

JACOBS, JOHN
GOLF $25   40   50
Instruction. 1963.

JENKINS, DAN
DOGGED VICTIMS OF INEXORABLE
FATE $25   40   60
Humor. 1970. Reissued.

JEROME, OWEN FOX
THE GOLF CLUB MURDER $50   100   150
Mystery. 1929. Photo below.

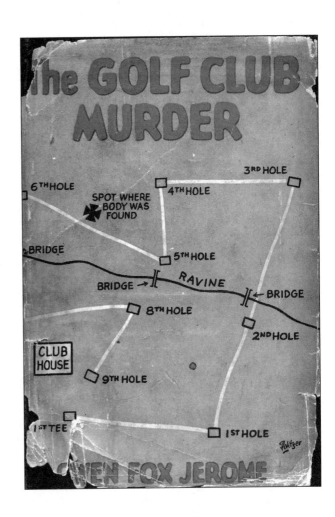

JONES, ERNEST
SWING THE CLUBHEAD $20   30   45
Instruction. 1952.

JONES, ROBERT T., JR.
DOWN THE FAIRWAY. $125   300   600
History. 1927. Signed books by Jones are very scarce and are valued between $500 and $1,500.

GOLF IS MY GAME $35   60   90
History. 1960. Reissued.

BOBBY JONES ON GOLF $35   60   90
Instruction. 1966. Reissued. Photo below.

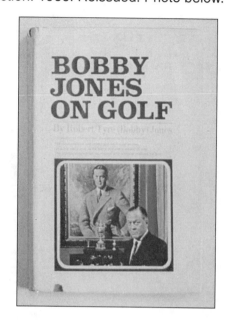

KERR, JOHN
GOLF BOOK OF EAST LOTHIAN
                  $800   1200   1500
History. 1896. Also large paper edition.

LEMA, TONY
GOLFER'S GOLD $20   35   50
History. 1964. Photo below.

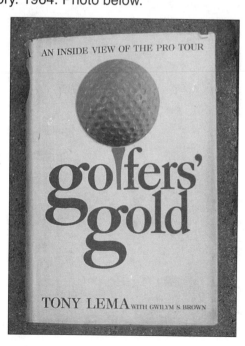

LOCKE, BOBBY
BOBBY LOCKE ON GOLF $40   60   75
Instruction. 1953.

LONGHURST, HENRY
TALKING ABOUT GOLF $40   60   80
Essay. 1966.

ONLY ON SUNDAYS
                 $40   60   75
Essays. 1964.

MacDONALD, C. B.
SCOTLAND'S GIFT; GOLF $300   600   750
History. 1928. Reissued. Limited edition.

MACKENZIE, ALISTER
GOLF ARCHITECTURE $400   750   1000
Architecture. 1920. Reissued.

MARTIN, H. B.
FIFTY YEARS OF AMERICAN GOLF
             $250   400   650
History. 1st edition, 1936.

MARTIN, JOHN STEWART
CURIOUS HISTORY OF THE
GOLF BALL $150   275   325
Reference. 1968.

MORRISON, ALEX
A NEW WAY TO BETTER GOLF $20   30   45
Instruction. 1932. Many reprints.

BETTER GOLF WITHOUT PRACTICE
             $25   35   45
Instruction. 1940.

MURDOCK, JOSEPH S. F.
THE LIBRARY OF GOLF,
1743-1966 $350   500   650
Reference. 1968.

NELSON, BYRON
WINNING GOLF $20   30   45
Instruction. 1946. Books signed by Nelson are
worth about a $40 premium.

NICKLAUS, JACK
MY 55 WAYS TO LOWER YOUR
GOLF SCORE $10   20   30
Instruction. 1964. Books signed by Nicklaus are
worth about a $60 premium.

GOLF MY WAY $10 20 30
Instruction. 1974.

THE GREATEST GAME OF ALL;
MY LIFE IN GOLF $25 40 60
Instruction. 1969.

NORWOOD, JOE
JOE NORWOOD'S GOLF-O-METRICS
$20 40 60
Instruction. 1978. Photo below.

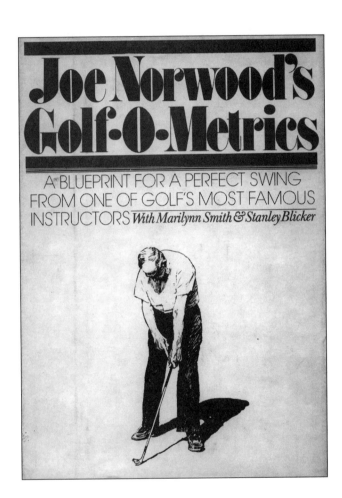

OLMAN, JOHN & MORTON
ENCYCLOPEDIA OF GOLF
  COLLECTIBLES $10 20 40
Reference. 1985.

OUIMET, FRANCIS
A GAME OF GOLF $125 190 250
Autobiography. 1932. Photo below of later edition.

PALMER, ARNOLD
MY GAME AND YOURS $10 20 30
Instruction. 1965. Books signed by Palmer are worth about a $35 premium. Photo below.

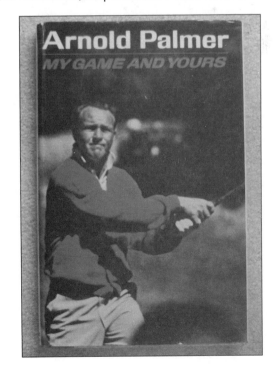

PARK, WILLIE
THE GAME OF GOLF $200   400   600
Instruction. 1896.

PLAYER, GARY
GARY PLAYER'S GOLF SECRETS $10   20   25
Instruction. 1962. Books signed by Player are
worth about a $25 premium.

PLIMPTON, GEORGE
THE BOGEY MAN $10   15   25
Essay. 1968.

PRICE, CHARLES
THE WORLD OF GOLF $35   50   75
History. 1962. Photo below.

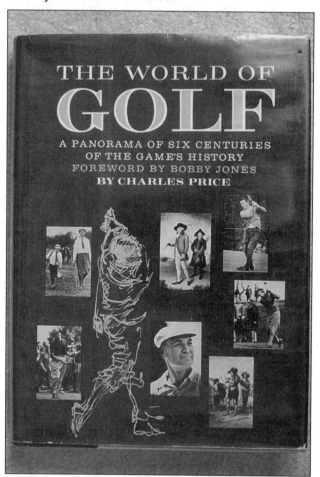

THE AMERICAN GOLFER $30   50   70
Anthology. 1964. Reissued.

REVOLTA, JOHNNY
SHORTCUTS TO GOOD GOLF $10   20   30
Instruction. 1949. Books signed by Revolta are
worth about a $75 premium.

RICE, G. & BRIGGS, C.
THE DUFFER'S HANDBOOK
OF GOLF $100   175   275
Humor. 1926. Reissued; also limited edition.

RICE, G. & KEELER, O. B.
THE BOBBY JONES STORY $40   65   125
Biography. 1953. Photo below.

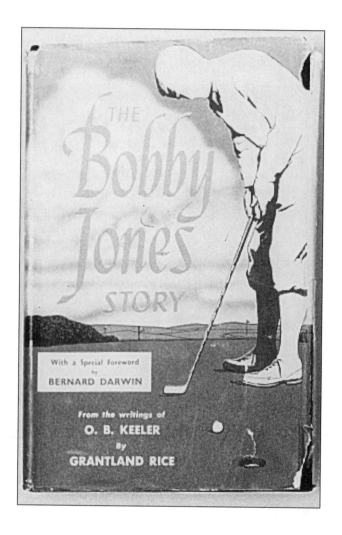

ROBERTS, CLIFFORD
THE STORY OF AUGUSTA
NATIONAL GOLF CLUB $45   75   125
History. 1976. Photo below.

SCHAAP, DICK
MASSACRE AT WINGED FOOT $8   15   25
History. 1974.

SHAW, JOSEPH T.
OUT OF THE ROUGH $25   60   80
Fiction. 1934. Reissued.

SIMPSON, SIR WALTER G.
THE ART OF GOLF $600   750   900
Instruction. 1887, 1891. Reissued.

SMITH, H. & TAYLOR, D.
THE SECRET OF …HOLING PUTTS!
$12   25   40

Instruction. 1961.

SNEAD, SAM
THE EDUCATION
OF A GOLFER $20   30   45
History. 1962.

HOW TO PLAY GOLF $10   20   30
Instruction. 1946, 1952. Photo below.

ROTELLA, ROBERT J.
MIND MASTERY FOR
WINNING $20   30   40
Instruction. 1981.

SAMPSON, CURT
HOGAN $10   12   15
Biography. 1996.

SARAZEN, GENE
BETTER GOLF AFTER FIFTY $8   15   25
Instruction. 1967. Books signed by Sarazen are
worth about a $40 premium.

THIRTY YEARS OF CHAMPIONSHIP
GOLF $30   60   90
History. 1950.

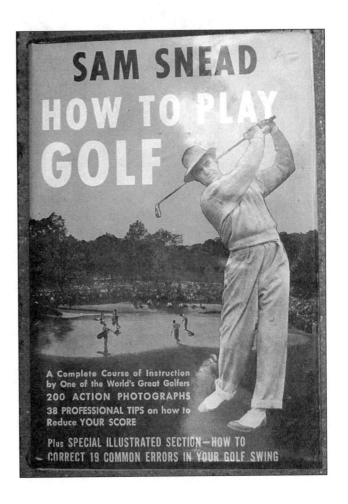

STANLEY, DAVE
A TREASURY OF GOLF
HUMOR $15   30   45
Humor. 1949. Photo below.

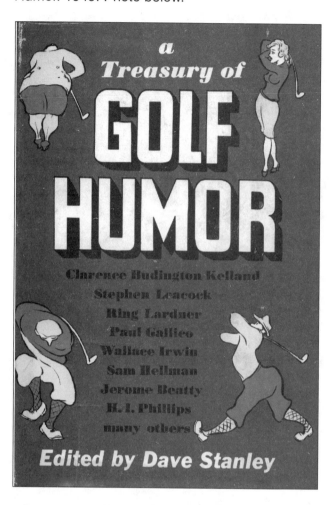

STANLEY, LOUIS T.
THIS IS GOLF $20   30   40
Instruction. 1954.

STEEL, DONALD & RYDE & WIND
THE ENCYCLOPEDIA OF GOLF $60   100   125
Reference. 1975.

STEELE, C. K.
THE GOLF COURSE MYSTERY $60   100   200
Fiction. 1919.

SUGGS, LOUISE
GOLF FOR WOMEN $10   20   30
Instruction. 1960. Books signed by Suggs are
worth about a $25 premium.

TAYLOR, JOHN HENRY
TAYLOR ON GOLF $200   350   450
Instruction. 1902.

THOMAS, GEORGE G., JR.
GOLF ARCHITECTURE IN
AMERICA $350   650   800
1927.

TRAVIS, WALTER J.
PRACTICAL GOLF $150   250   350
Instruction. 1901. Photo below 1902, 1909 edi-
tions.

TUFTS, RICHARD S.
THE PRINCIPLES BEHIND THE
RULES OF GOLF $75   120   150
Rules. 1960, 1961. Reissued.

TULLOCH, W. W.
LIFE OF TOM MORRIS $800   1200   1450
Biography. 1908. Photo below.

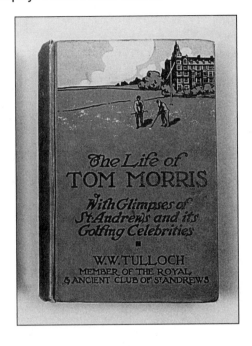

VAILE, P. A.
THE NEW GOLF $30   50   70
Instruction. 1916.

VARDON, HARRY
HOW TO PLAY GOLF $50   80   140
Instruction. 1st American edition 1912.

THE COMPLETE GOLFER $50   100   200
Instruction. 1905. Photo below.

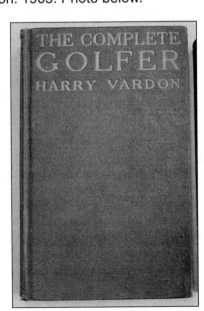

WETHERED, JOYCE & ROGER
THE GAME OF GOLF $100   150   200
Anthology. 1929.

WHIGHAM, H. G.
HOW TO PLAY GOLF $175   225   300
Instruction. 1897.

WHITLATCH, MARSHALL
GOLF FOR BEGINNERS & OTHERS
                $30   60   100
Instruction. 1910. Photo below.

WIND, HERBERT WARREN

| COMPLETE GOLFER | $25 | 50 | 75 |

Anthology. 1954. Reissued.

| THE STORY OF | | | |
| AMERICAN GOLF | $125 | 250 | 350 |

History. 1st ed. 1948. Reissued. Photo below.

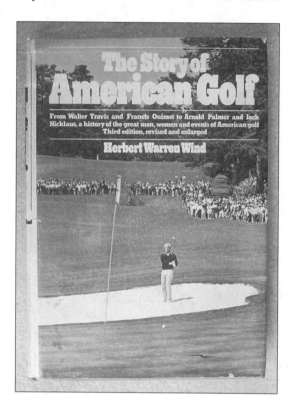

WODEHOUSE, P. G.

| GOLF OMNIBUS | $40 | 65 | 90 |

Fiction. 1973.

| GOLF WITHOUT TEARS | $75 | 150 | 300 |

Fiction. 1924.

WOOD, HARRY B.

| GOLF CURIOS AND THE LIKE | $900 | 1400 | 2000 |

Reference. 1910.

| GOLF CURIOS AND THE LIKE | $35 | 40 | 45 |

Reference. Reprint 1980.

ZAHARIAS, BABE D.

| THIS LIFE I'VE LED | $30 | 50 | 70 |

Biography. 1955.

Chapter 10
COLLECTING GOLF ART

Watercolor by Harry Rowntree "Bembridge Golf Course" featured in The Golf Courses of the British Isles.

The Pictorial History of Golf: A Suggestion for Collectors

by Martin Hardie

We are indebted to David White (GCS, London) for the article that follows, reprinted from THE CONNOISSEUR, July 1902. It appeared in the Golf Collectors Society Bulletin No. 21, January 1975.

At some moment in every student's career the question arises whether he shall know a little about everything or everything about something. So for the collector, there comes the time when he, too, must decide whether he will continue in his pleasant dilettante ways, or devote his research to some special branch of art. Is he to wander at ease in the low-lying meadows, plucking a flower here or there as they please his fancy, or is he to climb the heights in search of edelweiss and the rare blooms? Yet, even when he is drawn to some particular branch of study, be it pictures, or china, or books, or even postage stamps, the possibilities before him are too infinite, and he will feel at once the need of further limitation.

To give an instance from the book world, there is a well-known editor of the present time who devotes his energies to the collection of books of the year 1598.

To suit our present theme, let us suppose that prints are the subject elect for specialization. The study of engravings is endlessly elaborate and complicated, and in making his further limitation, the specialist has an unlimited variety of choice. Shall it be a master, a period, or a method? He may give his lifetime to the countless states of Rembrandt, or the two thousand prints of Hollar. He may choose a period, that of Durer and the Little Masters, or the engravers of the eighteenth century. He may be attracted by a method-etching or mezzotint, or the color-prints of Japan. As he faces the subject, there are innumerable pleasing vistas of choice.

Now to the collector who is fond of any manner of sport, we would suggest that in tracing its pictorial history he has a new and interesting subject ready at hand, and our present purpose is to show the attraction offered by the game of golf. And surely every collector ought to be a golfer. Both collecting and golf are games in which the individual depends on himself alone. Both have their glorious possibilities, their successes and disappointments, their moments of fortune, their bunkers of despair. It is a serious question for one who plays both games to decide whether he would prefer a hole in one, or to pick up for five schillings in a country village, a first proof, say of the Salisbury Cathedral by Lucas. Let him search his heart and decide whether he would rather be a better golfer or a better collector.

First it may be pointed out that the collection of golf prints may be of the greatest value in settling disputes in the history of the Royal Game. For the origin of golf, like that of Mr. Yellowplush, is "wropt in mistry" and it is still a moot point whether Scotland or the Low Countries can claim to be the incunabula of the modern game. For its early literary history, the only sources are the Scottish Acts of Parliament and records of Kirk Sessions. "The fut ball and golf be utterly cryit dune" is the stern behest of the Parliament in 1457. So also, a century later in 1593, two golfers were prosecuted by the Town Council of Edinburgh for "playing of the Gowff on the Links of Leith every Sabbath at the time of the sermones."

But, while Scotland can produce this documentary evidence, it is to the Low Countries that we go for the pictorial history of the game. Without any doubt, as our illustrations will show, golf was in vogue in Holland in the sixteenth century, being played on ice as well as on grass. Indeed, early in the seventeenth century, golf balls were imported to Scotland. For in a letter of 1618, the writer says that "no small quantitie of golf and silver is transported yearlie out of his Hienes' Kingdome of Scotland for bying of golf balls." For pictorial records of the earliest period of the game in the Low Countries, one has to search manuscripts of the fifteenth and sixteenth centuries.

Perhaps the earliest representation of golf, or of a game which must be the ancestor of golf, is to be found in a manuscript in the Chantilly Collection, and shows figures putting both to a post and to a hole. Mr. W.H. Weale, the well-known authority on Flemish painting, has dated this for me as between 1460 and 1470. Another Flemish "Book of Hours" in the British Museum Library, executed at Bruges between 1500 and 1520, shows distinctly that in this period the golfer putted to a hole. The home green in front of the clubhouse, the red coat of the player, and the steel-faced club, are all curiously modern. Hidden away among collections of manuscripts must be many a treasure which would throw light on the early history of the game.

By the seventeenth century, golf in Holland had become almost entirely a winter game. The Dutch painters of the period seem to have found a peculiar fascination in winter scenes, with their clear, bright atmosphere, and the moving crowds of figures in their various occupations of sledding, skating or golf. As might be expected, many a golfing scene is to be found in the pictures of Van de Velde, Van der Neer, Avercamp, Van Goyen, and others of their school. Several drawings of this period showing single figures or small groups, give perhaps a better idea of golf at the time.

Two such drawings by Avercamp in the Royal Collection at Dresden, of about the year 1610, are obviously character studies from life, and show us players that, except for their costumes, they exhibit a startling modernity. How often have we seen a golfer stand in the pose of this stout Dutchman; pipe in hand, club held loosely - resting on the ground, as he surveys a difficult "lie" and swithers for a moment between this club and that. We wonder who the present owner is of the drawing that fetched 18 schillings at the William Esdaile Sale of 1840, catalogued as "Lot 1178, H. Avercamp: Figures playing at Kolf on the ice—capital?"

For the ordinary collector, however, whose aspirations are limited by the length of his purse, the engravings of the period offer the happiest hunting grounds. Juys, Van Schoel, Jan and Adomen Van de Velse, Van Sichem and R. de Hooghe are some of the artists whose engraved work contains golfing scenes. A rare etching by Hendrik van Schoel shows a reservoir with skaters and golfers, particularly noticeable is a small boy at the top of his swing. The connoisseur will appreciate the fact that neither Bartsch nor Nagler chronicle the existence of van Schoel's etching. Another interesting feature of the picture is the group of curlers in the middle distance on the right. The stones, the kneeling attitude of the player, and the "skip" giving directions with outstretched arm, all show that here we have an early picture of the "roaring game." Several etchings by Jan Van de Velde, from sets representing the twelve months, show figures of golfers playing on ice. Of the late seventeenth century is an engraving by Romeyn de Hooghe, giving us perhaps the best presentment of a golfer with club in hand that can be found among these Dutch prints.

From France we have an engraving by J. Aliament of about 1750, after a picture in our National Gallery by Adriaen Van de Velde. It is interesting to note that the plate is reversed, with the result of the player seeming to be left-handed. A thrill runs through the collector when he notices for the first time in a catalogue of Rembrandt's etchings, the entry "A Kolfer." He is, however, doomed to disappointment, for the Kolf there depicted is the modern Dutch indoor game, only remotely connected with our golf.

In Scotland of the sixteenth and seventeenth century, our "rude fore-fathers" had no Van de Velde or Avercamp to chronicle with brush the annals of the game. Records of Kirk Sessions tell of the chastisement of offenders against the Sabbath laws; club minutes relate the winning of casks of wine; but of pictures we have nothing until the end of the eighteenth century, when there begins a series of excellent portraits of golfers with caddie and clubs. These are interesting to the collector because many have been translated into the beautiful mezzotints for which the period is famous.

Bruntsfield Links Golf Club painted by Sam Bough. Presented by Captain Alexander Whyte for 1871 competition, won by Andrew Usher.

For the player, their value also lies in their historic associations and in the representation they give us of the baffies and spoons and other disused weapons of the game.

One of the best known of these mezzotints is the portrait of William Innes by Val. Green, after L. F. Abbott, dedicated to "the Society of Golfers at Blackheath." No trace can be found of the original picture. It may be presumed that it was destroyed in the fire which burned down the Blackheath Clubhouse at the end of the eighteenth century. Another beautiful mezzotint is that by J. Jones, after the portrait by Raeburn, of James Balfour, an early secretary of the Honourable Company of Edinburgh Golfers. This mezzotint carries the inscription: "Published by Wm. Murray, Bookseller, Parliament Close, Edinburgh, October 1796."

An interesting etching is one of Kay's portraits, dated 1803, showing Alexander M'Keller, a well-known character of the Bruntisfield Links, Edinburgh. The engraving by Wagstaffe, of the picture by Charles Lees, R.S.A., "A Grand Match at Golf" 1850, is of great historical interest. It depicts a foursome in which Sir David Baird and Sir Ralph Anstruther are matched against Major Playfair and John Campbell, of Saddell. In the group of onlookers are many distinguished Scotchmen of the day, and in the background are seen the towers and spires of St. Andrews. Many similar engravings of championship meetings have been published of late years, but scarcely of sufficient merit to attract the connoisseur.

The collector of wood engravings of "the sixties" will find two interesting golf illustrations by Doyle of "Punch in London Society" for 1863. In more modern times, capital photogravures have been published by the Fine Arts Society after "The Sabbath Breakers," "The Stymie" and other paintings by J. C. Dollman, R.I., and for those clever prints by Mr. Nicholson and Mr. Cecil Aldin, without which the golf collection will be incomplete.

In the case of most collectors, the length of their purse is an important consideration. "Non cuivis contingit adire Corinthum"—not everyone is fortunate enough to dream of acquiring the "Hundred Guider" print, the "Melancholia", the "Abside" or the "Ladies Waldegrave." But these golf prints can, for the most part, be purchased at a reasonable price. To the connoisseur who is a golfer as well, their acquisition will add a new interest to his game.

Olman's Guide to Golf Antiques, by John and Mort Olman, 1991, provides the most complete reference on art available to collectors.

PRICES
GOLF ART

G-5   G-7   G-9

THE BLACKHEATH GOLFERS

ABBOTT, L.F. $350   500   750

Circa 1900. A colored engraving of the original from 1790.

THE BLACKHEATH GOLFERS

ABBOTT, L.F. $1400   1800   2200

A mezzotint. Original 1790. Many later reprints. Photo below.

THE DRIVE

ADAMS, DOUGLAS $200   300   450

Circa 1960. Approximately 16 x 24. Colored engraving from the original oil painting circa 1894.

A DIFFICULT BUNKER

ADAMS, DOUGLAS $200   300   450

Circa 1960. Approximately 16 x 24. Colored engraving from the original oil painting circa 1894.

THE PUTTING GREEN

ADAMS, DOUGLAS $200   300   450

Circa 1960. Approximately 16 x 24. Colored engraving from the original oil painting circa 1894.

THE PUTT

BROCK, CHARLES EDMOND $1200   1800   2500

An engraving, circa 1894. Photo below.

THE DRIVE

BROCK, CHARLES EDMOND $1200   1800   2500

An engraving, circa 1894. Photo below.

1ST INTERNATIONAL GOLF MATCH

BROWN, MICHAEL J. $500   750   1000

1903. 1st International Golf Match, England vs. Scotland at Hoylake, 1902. Michael Brown was famous for his "Life Ass'n of Scotland Calendars".

DEDICATED TO THE FIELD MARSHALL

CHAMBERLAIN, J. $250   350   500

Engraving. Frost & Reed, publishers, 1955. Photo below.

THE RULES OF GOLF

CROMBIE, CHARLES $150   225   300

A humorous series published in 1905 by Perrier. Many reprints. Prices listed are for reprints. Photo below.

GOLF PLAYERS

DE HOOCH, PETER $60   80   100

Contemporary prints. Photo below.

THE SABBATH BREAKERS

DOLLMAN, J. $175   200   300

Circa 1896 black and white engraving. The original sold for $1,320. in 1992. Prices listed are for circa 1977 lithographs in color.

PUTTING

DOLLMAN, JOHN CHARLES $1200   1800   2500

An engraving, circa 1900. Photo below.

FAIRWAY SHOT

DOLLMAN, JOHN CHARLES $1200   1800   2500

An engraving, circa 1900. Photo below.

ST. ANDREWS CADDIE

EARLE, L. $100   200   300

Original, 1908, second printing 1928 and also 1979.

OLD SCOTCH CADDY

EARLE, L.C. $110   150   300

Circa late 1920s. Approximately 16 x 20. Colored print of the circa 1904 oil painting.

THE TRIUMVIRATE

FLOWER, CLEMENT $300   450   600

1913 painting, prints 1914 and later. Photo below.

PLAYING OUT OF HEATHER

DOLLMAN, JOHN CHARLES $1200   1800   2500

An engraving, circa 1900. Photo below.

GARY PLAYER

FORBES, BART $40   60   90

1980 watercolor reprints. Photo below.

VARIOUS WATERCOLORS

FROST, A.B. $20   30   50

Circa 1900 including, "By Sheer Strength", "Temper", "Stymied" and others. Prices are for reprints.

JOHN WHYTE MELVILLE

GRANT, SIR FRANCIS $300   450   600

Circa 1970. Color print, London, limited edition of 750.

JOHN WHYTE MELVILLE

GRANT, SIR FRANCIS $75   100   150

Circa 1988 color print of the original.

HISTORY OF GOLF IN AMERICA SERIES

GUSTOVSON, LELAND $400   500   600

Circa 1960s. Six color prints. "The First Clubhouse in America, Shinnecock", "The Old Apple Tree Gang", "Awarding The First USGA Trophy", "Rober Tyre Jones", "Ouimet Wins The Open" and "Playoff For Masters Championship", Snead and Hogan. Singles are $50-100 each.

THE GOLFERS

LEES, CHARLES $150   250   350

Circa 1920. Hand colored. Approximately 21 X 33. Print of the circa 1849 engraving.

BEN HOGAN

MILOSEVICH, PAUL $20   30   40

1980s. Prints in sepia. Photo below.

CRENSHAW WINS 1984 MASTERS

MILOSEVICH, PAUL $150   175   225

1985. Limited edition of 600.

SLAMMIN' SAMMY

MILOSEVICH, PAUL $20   30   40

1980s. Prints in sepia. Photo below.

COPE'S TOBACCO

PIPESHANK, GEORGE $20   30   40

Circa 1900 humorous advertisement print for Cope's Tobacco. Reprints 1870s. Photos below.

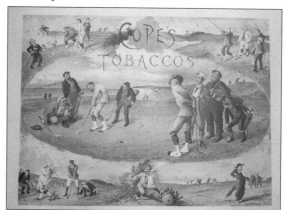

TOM MORRIS

REID, SIR GEORGE $4000 6000 8000

A gravure. 1903. Photo below.

A LITTLE PRACTICE

SADLER, W.D. $300 450 650

Original print, black and white, 1915. Many reproductions worth less than $50.

A WINTER EVENING

SADLER, W.D. $300 450 650

Original print, black and white, 1915. Many reproductions worth less than $50.

CARICATURES OF FAMOUS GOLFERS

SIR LESLIE WARD, 'SPY' $200 300 400

1890s to 1910. Various amateur and professional golfers. Ward used the pseudonym "Spy".

ST. ANDREW'S HELL'S BUNKER

SMART, JOHN $250,000

Watercolor, 1889. Photo below.

THE BLACK SHED AT HOYLAKE

SMITH, GARDEN G. $20,000

A watercolor, 1897. Photo below.

BOBBY JONES

STEVENS, THOMAS E. $250 350 500

1952. Limited edition prints. Signed prints can bring as much as $3,500.

DUTCH TILES

UNKNOWN MAKER $200 300 500

Circa 1800. Photo below.

WALTER HAGEN

VAIL, ARNOLD $500

1993 original oil. Mr. Vail painted famous golf immortals at the request of Chuck Furjanic. Seventeen were done from 1993 until his death in Feb. 1995. Fourteen of his seventeen works are pictured in the "Linda Craft Auction" catalogue, May 7, 1995, conducted by Chuck Furjanic, Inc. Photo below.

JIMMY DEMARET

VAIL, ARNOLD $500

1993 Original oil. Mr. Vail painted famous golf immortals at the request of Chuck Furjanic. Seventeen were done from 1993 until his death in February 1995. Fourteen of his seventeen works are pictured in the "Linda Craft Auction" catalogue, May 7, 1995, conducted by Chuck Furjanic, Inc. Photo below.

A FROST SCENE

VAN DE VELDE, ADRIAEN $75   125   250

Prints circa 1920s made from originals circa 1600. Photo below.

MAURITS de HERAUGIERES, AGE 2

VAN DER LINDE, ADRIAEN $45,000

1595. Oil-on-panel. Photo below.

WINTER LANDSCAPE

VAN DER NEER, AERT $75   125   250

Prints circa 1920s, made from originals circa 1650. Photo below.

ST. ANDREWS

WATSON, J.F. $400   500   650

1977. Limited edition print.

OLD TOM MORRIS

WEAVER, ARTHUR $200   300   400

Late 1980s.

YOUNG TOM MORRIS

WEAVER, ARTHUR $200   300   400

Late 1980s. Photo below.

Chapter 11
COLLECTING GOLF CERAMICS & GLASS

Libations were an integral part of golf-especially after the round.

Wayne Aaron has collected golf ceramics for 25 years and has assembled a very extensive collection. He offers his insight to both the beginner, as well as advanced collector of golf ceramics.

Golf Ceramics

by Wayne Aaron

One of the wonders of collecting golf antiquity is the diversity of fields represented. While clubs, balls and books dominate the hobby as collecting themes, there is now a heightened level of interest in golf ceramics.

One reason for this growing popularity may be because many are rapidly discovering that while all fields of golf collecting have intrinsic value, ceramics offers additional aesthetic value. Another reason may be the realization that the true social impact of the game can be better understood by studying (and collecting) the artistic artifacts that evolved with the game—such as ceramics, glass, silver, jewelry, art, toys, statuary, medals and numerous advertising memorabilia items. All of these "aesthetic" categories in their own way help to document, as well as visibly demonstrate, the significant influence golf had on the world around the turn of the century—as it does today.

As one contemplates the joys of collecting golf ceramics, it is wise to recognize at the outset that this endeavor invariably will become a "journey," and as such, never a "destination" that is ultimately reached.

First and foremost, before embarking on this journey it is best to acquire as much knowledge as possible. Only through knowledge can you truly understand what is possible. Also do not be tempted to become a "consumer of quantity" rather than a "collector of quality." A good working definition of quality should not stop at discerning the condition of a potential collectible, it should also encompass historical significance and rarity.

Perhaps the best advice a collector can follow is to always seek out and acquire the very best you can afford. The very scarce items will command a premium price and will appreciate in value at a higher rate than mid to lower-end examples. High-end items may even become prohibitively expensive in the future and therefore out of the realm of affordability for many collectors.

It is also helpful to establish clear goals before running head long into the world of golf ceramic collecting. In fact, this is sound advice for any field of golf collecting. In summary, acquire knowledge, define your budget, set your goals, collect only quality and buy the best when you see it.

While it is academically interesting to possess an encyclopedic level of knowledge covering the history of pottery and porcelain, including supporting terminology techniques, styles, artists, makers and country of origin, this level of proficiency is not a mandatory prerequisite to becoming a knowledgeable collector of golf ceramics. While the history of pottery goes back to primitive man, and Chinese porcelain dates to 3000 B. C., ceramics featuring golfers or golfing scenes did not appear until the seventeenth century when they were used as decoration for Delft tiles. For those that do not subscribe to the "Dutch School" origin of golf, you can jump forward to around 1880 onwards when golf clubs gave golf ceramics as prizes. There was also an increased use of golfing subjects as embellishments for vases, pictures, tumblers, bowls, steins, plates and numerous other functional, as well as decorative items. Focusing on a period running from 1880 to 1940 makes the breadth of knowledge you need to acquire a lot more manageable.

Collectors, dealers and even auction houses are often confused by terminology. In its simplest form you need to remember the following:

- **Ceramics** is a general term for the study of the art of pottery.
- **Pottery** in its widest sense includes all objects fashioned from clay and then hardened by fire.
- **Porcelain** should only be applied to certain well-marked varieties of pottery. It is usually opaque white and is fired at 1,450 degrees centigrade. Also known as Bone China.
- **Stoneware** is vitrified clay fired at temperatures of 1,200 to 1,300 degrees centigrade, which makes it very hard and is tan or gray in color.
- **Earthenware** is not vitrified, retains a porous texture, is fired at no more than 1,200 degrees centigrade and is usually tan in color.

While some may be driven to become an expert on ceramics and submerge themselves into the world of *technique*, which encompasses materials, firing, glazes, colors and metals, it may be best to just understand what is available to collect.

The most definitive discussion to date for golf ceramics can be found in the Olmans' *Guide to Golf Antiques*. Another excellent reference is *Decorative Golf Collectibles* by Shirley and Jerry Sprung. In both of these recommended references you will find dates of production by manufacturer, including their marks, country of origin, and illustrations of objects.

Where do you start to find collectible golf ceramics? If you are not already a member, by all means join the Golf Collectors Society. (See page XX for membership information.) After you meet the requirements for membership you will be provided a directory of all members. Each member indicates their collecting interests. Look for the letter "C," which denotes ceramics. Start both your education (pursuit of knowledge) and search here. Call 10 or 15 people and you will identify through referrals the serious collectors of golf ceramics. They are the ones to contact because they may have duplicates for sale or trade. They will also get you headed in the right direction to other sources.

I have often been asked why I collect ceramics. It is because I have been stricken by an 18th century imagination. During this period it was a popular belief that porcelain was not just another exotic, but a magical and talismanic substance— the substance of longevity, of potency, of invulnerability—now you know why I collect ceramics.

The following listing is presented as an overview of golf ceramic collecting opportunities and is comprehensive for the majority of desired acquisitions, but is by no means all inclusive.

An introduction on collecting golf ceramics would not be complete without a brief discussion of what is an acceptable condition (cracks, chips, scratches, repairs, missing parts) before considering an object. The following suggestions are offered:

- If the item is truly very rare and you may never see it on the market again, this becomes an issue of price and personal taste. The more the damage, the lower the price. Do not pay a premium for poor quality. Be disciplined enough to walk away, but do not hesitate to purchase if the price is commensurate with condition. A rare item with some damage is a good candidate for a "museum" quality restoration.
- Do not be afraid to acquire an item that has undergone a "museum" level repair. The quality will be so high that only the restorer and the individual that paid for the repair will understand the true condition. If the repair is obvious to suggest the restorer was an amateur, walk away from mid to lower end items at any price. You will never be proud of owning junk and you probably will not be able to trade or sell it either.

United States

Ceramic Art Company (Pre Lenox)
Warwick
Lenox
American Beleek
Weller (Dickensware II)
Enfield Pottery
Rookwood
Buffalo China
Owens (Utopian)
Hanes (Little Arthur)
O'Hara Dial (Waltham Clock Co.)
Viktor Schrechengost (Cowen)
Robinson Clay Products
Sleepy Eye Indian Mugs
Taylor, Smith & Taylor

England

Doulton Burslem
Doulton Lambeth
Foley
Wedgewood
Minton
W. H. Goss
Royal Worcester
Taylor Tunnecliffe
MacIntyre Burslem
Arthur Wood
Willow Art
Grimwades
Royal Doulton (1902 and after)
- Kingsware
- Series Ware (Charles Crombie) "Pilgrim figures & Proverb sayings"
- Queensware
- Airbrush Brown
- Gibson Series
- Uncle Toby
- Bateman
- The Nineteenth Hole
- Morrissian
- Bunnykins
- Colonel Bogey
- Old English
- Copeland Spode
- Carleton Ware
- Arcadian
- Bridgewood
- Crown Staffordshire
- Dartmouth
Shelly
Williamson & Sons
Aonian
A. F. C.
Ambassador
A. Rogers
Burleigh
Cresan
Crown Ducal
Jasperware
Radfords
G. & S. Ltd.

Germany

Rosenthal
Royal Bonn
Simon Peter Gerz

Hohr-Grenzhausen
Hauber & Reuther
Royal Bayruth
Schwarzburg
Goebel
Villeroy & Boch (Metlach)
Frumper Ware
Schaffer and Vater

Austria

Amphora (Turn-Tepliz, Bohemia, Riessner)

Italy

Richard Ginori

Japan

Noritake
Nippon
Chikaramachi

France

Limoges
Sevres
Robj

Spain

Lladro (after 1940)

Netherlands

Dutch Delft Tiles (17th century)

Ireland

Irish Beleek

Collectible Glass

by Jerry Sprung

In the waning days of the Victorian period, through the art nouveau and art deco periods, most items of a personal nature carried some complex design, depicting an event or an item in a representational theme; American Indians for instance, were often depicted on pottery, silver, or bronze.

Ever since golf came to the United States in the late 19th century, it became the subject of many media designers who wished to capitalize on the latest fad. Workers in silver and gold took many of their popular sellers, such as cuff links, tie pins, watch fobs and match safes for men, hat pins and compacts for women, and added a golf motif. This was done either by depicting a figure playing golf, or an implement, golf stick, golf ball or tee.

In addition, silversmiths created trophies with a golfing motif as part of the design. This was done to supply the growing market for tournament prizes. Such makers as Unger Brothers had elaborate catalogs showing a golfer or a caddy as the center figure in all of their silver mounted items, from ashtrays to hair brushes to whiskey flasks.

Most bronze golf figures came from Austria. Karl Hagenauer was especially known for his art deco golf figures in the 1920s. Bronze was also used to make decorative humidors and cigarette boxes. Heintz Art Metal Shop and Smith Metal Arts (Silvercrest) of Buffalo, NY were two of the main suppliers of these items.

Most glass golf items were either produced in England or the United States. One of the popular glass designs involved a sterling silver golfer overlay that was attached to the glass bottle, goblet, or pitcher with an adhesive. The same figure is seen in many sizes, adorning glassware made by various manufacturers. Another method was to etch or engrave a golfer or golfing scene directly into the glass. Such companies as Hawkes, Cambridge Glass, and Pairpoint were well-known suppliers of these wares.

PRICES
GOLF CERAMICS

G-5 G-7 G-9

PORCELAIN HUMIDOR
AONIAN $1600   1800   2000
ENGLAND

Circa 1900s. Comical golf scene. Photo below.

WOOD & WOOD BISCUIT BARREL
ARTHUR WOOD & SON $2000   2500   3000
ENGLAND

Circa 1900. Hand painted porcelain with silver rim, bail, and ornate lid. Photo below.

EARTHENWARE MATCH BOWL
CARLTONWARE $150   250   375
ENGLAND

Circa 1920s. Photo below.

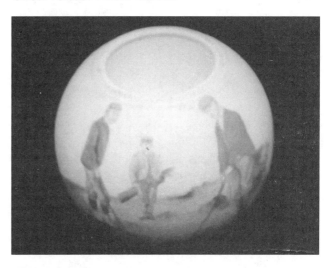

EARTHENWARE HUMIDOR
CARLTONWARE $450   600   900
ENGLAND

Circa 1920s. Photo below.

PORCELAIN ASHTRAY

CHIKARAMACHI $400 600 800

Circa 1930s. Six pieces. Hand painted. Photo below.

STONEWARE PITCHER

COPELAND SPODE $600 800 1200

Circa 1900. Golfers in relief, white on blue or green background. Photo below.

STONEWARE JARDINIERE

COPELAND SPODE $700 900 1400

Circa 1900. Golfers in relief, white on blue or green background. Photo below.

STONEWARE EWER

COPELAND SPODE $700 850 1200

Circa 1900. Golfers in relief, white on blue or green background. Photo below.

CHINA PITCHER AND CUPS

CRESANT $1200 1500 1800
ENGLAND

Circa 1900s. "Brownie" chocolate pitcher measuring 12-1/2 inches, with matching mugs. Photo below.

STONEWARE PITCHER

DOULTON $1800 2200 2800
LAMBETH, ENGLAND

Circa early 1900s. Golfers in white relief. Photo below.

PORCELAIN SPILL VASES

DOULTON $700   850   1100
   LAMBETH, ENGLAND
Circa early 1900s. Photo below.

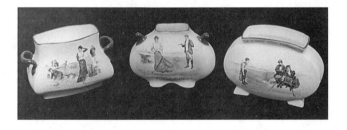

CREAMER

DOULTON $600   800   1000
   LAMBETH, ENGLAND
Circa early 1900s. Uncle Toby Series. Photo below.

TRIVET

DOULTON $600   800   1000
   LAMBETH, ENGLAND
Circa early 1900s. Uncle Toby Series. Photo below.

HAND PAINTED VASE
DOULTON $20,000
LAMBETH, ENGLAND
Circa 1885. Burslem. Photo below.

FLUTE NECK VASE
DOULTON $20,000
LAMBETH, ENGLAND
Circa 1885. Hand painted, Burslem.

HAND PAINTED HUMIDOR
DOULTON $12,000
LAMBETH, ENGLAND
Circa 1885. Burslem. Photo below.

OPEN NECK VASE
DOULTON $12,000
LAMBETH, ENGLAND
Circa 1885. Hand painted, Burslem.

ROYAL BONN "DELFT" STEIN
FRANZ ANTON MEHLEM $15,000
Circa 1890. Photo below.

THE BROWNIES PITCHER
GRIMWADES $1000   1200   1400
    STOKE-ON-TRENT
Circa 1910. Porcelain. Photo below

THE BROWNIES CUP AND SAUCER
GRIMWADES $400   500   600
    STOKE-ON-TRENT
Circa 1910. Porcelain. Photo below.

TOBACCO JARS
HANDLE WARE $1000   1500   2000
    MERIDEN
Circa late 1800. Photo below.

SILVER LID TANKARD
LENOX $1800   2200   2600
LAWRENCEVILLE, NJ
Circa 1905. Lady and gentleman golfers on blue background. Photo below.

SILVER RIM TANKARD
LENOX $1200   1500   1800
LAWRENCEVILLE, NJ
Circa 1905. Lady and gentleman golfers on green background. Photo below.

HOTEL DINNERWARE
LIMOGE $400   500   600
PARIS, FRANCE
Circa 1900. Hotel dinnerware "Golf Hotel Le Couquet". Photo below.

PORCELAIN FIGURINE
LLADRO $300   400   500
VALENCIA, SPAIN
Circa 1950s. Figurine. Photo below.

PORCELAIN CHINA
NORITAKE $600   700   800
JAPAN

Circa 1930s. Hand painted jar. Photo below.

PORCELAIN MUG
NORITAKE $400   500   600
JAPAN

Circa 1900s. Hand painted mug marked Nippon. Photo below.

PORCELAIN HUMIDOR
NORITAKE $400   500   600
JAPAN

Circa 1900s. Hand painted humidor marked Nippon.

PORCELAIN VASE AND ASHTRAY
RICHARD GINORI $600   800   1000
ITALY

Circa 1920s. Art deco golfers. Photo below.

PORCELAIN BOWL
ROYAL BAYRUTH $600   800   1000

Circa 1900s. Bowl measuring 10-3/8 inches, signed Brown. Photo below.

PORCELAIN BOWL
ROYAL DOULTON $400   600   800
ENGLAND

Circa 1930s. Bunnykins, Royal Doulton.

PORCELAIN PLATE
ROYAL DOULTON $200   300   400
ENGLAND

Circa 1930s. Bunnykins, Royal Doulton.

PORCELAIN CREAMER

ROYAL DOULTON $400   600   800
    ENGLAND

Circa 1930s. Bunnykins, Royal Doulton. Photo above.

ROYAL DOULTON, GOLF SERIES WARE

ROYAL DOULTON $1500   -   10,000
    ENGLAND

Circa 1900. Decorated with Charles Crombie figures. Photo below..

ROYAL DOULTON WHISKEY BARREL

ROYAL DOULTON $8000
ENGLAND

Circa 1900. Whiskey barrel with 19th hole scene at one end and The Club House, St. Andrews, on the other; it has silver spout and bucket. Photo below.

THE NINETEENTH HOLE PLATE

ROYAL DOULTON $400   600   800
ENGLAND

Circa 1900. Photo below.

HOTEL DINNERWARE

WARWICK $300   500   600
WHEELING, W. VA

Circa 1930. Hotel dinnerware depicting Bobby Jones. Photo below.

SUGAR BOWL WITH LID

WEDGEWOOD $650   850   1250
BURSLEM, ENGLAND

Circa early 1900s. Golfers in white relief. Photo below.

CREAMER

WEDGEWOOD $450   650   900
BURSLEM, ENGLAND

Circa early 1900s. Golfers in white relief. Photo below.

HIGH GLAZE VASE
WELLER $2500
ZANESVILLE, OH
Early 1900s. Dickinsware pottery. Photo below.

TEA SET
WILLIAMSONS & SONS $3000
ENGLAND
Circa 1900-1910. Porcelain tea set depicting golfers of the period—Vardon, Braid, Taylor and various caddies. Photo below.

PRICES
GLASS COLLECTIBLES

G-5 G-7 G-9

CRYSTAL DECANTER
WATERFORD $1500   2000   2500
Circa 1920. Sterling silver hallmarked neck. Hand painted golfing scene. Photo below.

DECANTER
UNKNOWN MAKER $250   350   550
Circa 1920s. Sterling silver golfer overlaid on blue glass. Photo below.

DECANTER
UNKNOWN MAKER $300   450   650
Circa 1920s. Sterling silver golfer overlaid on blue glass. Photo below.

COCKTAIL SET

UNKNOWN MAKER $1250   1600   2250
Circa 1920s. Shaker, six tumblers and six goblets. Sterling silver golfer overlaid

on blue glass. Photo below.

COCKTAIL SET

UNKNOWN MAKER $225   350   475
Circa 1920s. Shaker and four glasses. Sterling silver cap and sterling overlaid golfers on frosted yellow glass. Photo below.

COCKTAIL SET

UNKNOWN MAKER $550   750   1000
Circa 1920s. Shaker and six glasses. Sterling silver cap and sterling overlaid golfers. Photo below.

TANTALUS DECANTER SET

ART DECO CO. $300   500   750
Circa 1920s. Holder and caps are silver plated. Sterling silver golf scenes overlaid on clear glass. Photo below.

WINE DECANTER

UNKNOWN MAKER $250 400 600

Circa 1920s. Sterling silver golfer overlaid on clear glass. Photo below.

HAND PAINTED BOTTLE

UNKNOWN MAKER $200 275 375

Circa 1930. 8 inches high. Photo below.

AFTER SHAVE BOTTLE

A. R. WINARICK CO. $100 125 175

Circa 1920. 9-1/2 inches high. Photo below.

HAND PAINTED GLASS

UNKNOWN MAKER $50 75 100

Circa 1930.

ICE BUCKET

T. G. HAWKES & CO. $200 275 400

Circa 1900. Sterling silver handle. Golf scene engraved on glass. Photo below.

COCKTAIL SHAKER

T. G. HAWKES & CO. $450   600   850
Circa 1900. Sterling silver lid. Golf scene engraved on glass. Photo below.

WINE BOTTLE

T. G. HAWKES & CO. $225   300   400
Circa 1900. Sterling silver cap. Golf scene engraved on glass.

CLUB SODA BOTTLES

UNKNOWN MAKER $25   35   50
Circa 1920s. Milk glass. Various flavors.

ETCHED GLASSES

HEISSEY $450   650   900
Circa 1920s. Shot glass with etched golfers. Photo below.

ETCHED GLASSES

HEISSEY $450   650   850
Circa 1920s. Tumbler with etched golfers. Photo below.

COOKIE JAR

HEISSEY $2000   2750   3750
Circa 1920s. Silver overlay golfers on cut glass.

GLASS SET

CAMBRIDGE $150   200   300
Circa 1920s. Four pink tumblers and carrying tray with handle. Acid etched golfing scenes.

LOCKER BOTTLE, ENGRAVED GLASS

T. J. HAWKES & CO. $275   375   650
Circa 1910. 19th Hole design. Photo below.

CLAIRET PITCHER

UNKNOWN MAKER $800 1200 2000
Circa 1920. Sterling on glass. 16 inches tall. Photo below.

HAND BLOWN PITCHER

UNKNOWN MAKER $500 750 1000
Circa 1910. Two inch sterling silver neck band. Photo below.

CRYSTAL HUMIDOR-STERLING LID

UNKNOWN MAKER $1250 1750 2250
Circa 1900. Photo below.

CRYSTAL STEIN-STERLING LID

UNKNOWN MAKER $1250 1750 2250
Circa 1900. Golfer in relief on lid. Photo below.

PERFUME BOTTLE

UNKNOWN MAKER $450   600   900
Circa 1900. Sterling stopper with golfer. Photo below.

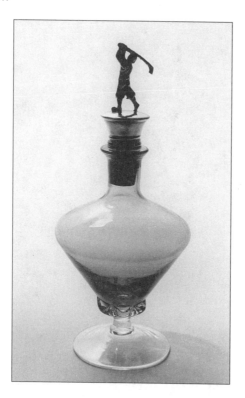

PERFUME BOTTLE

ART DECO $450   600   900
   CZECHOSLOVAKIA
Circa 1930. Cut glass with golfer. Photo below.

TUMBLER

DE PASSE MFG. CO. $60   90   150
Circa 1915. Sterling overlay. Photo below.

ASHTRAY

H. HOFFMAN $200   300   400
Circa 1920s. 5-inch x 3-inch intaglio cut. Photo below.

ASHTRAY

UNKNOWN MAKER $40   70   100

Circa 1940s. 2-1/2-inch x 2-1/2-inch acid etched glass. Photo below.

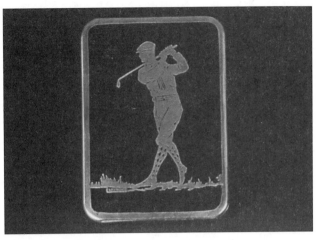

ASHTRAY

UNKNOWN MAKER $70   100   175

Circa 1940s. 4-inch x 3-inch acid etched glass. Photo below.

ASHTRAY

UNKNOWN MAKER $100   150   200

Circa 1940s. Sterling on glass.

CIGARETTE BOX

UNKNOWN MAKER $150   225   300

Circa 1940s. Sterling on glass. Photo below.

CIGARETTE BOX

UNKNOWN MAKER $200   300   400

Circa 1920s. Sterling on glass. Photo top right.

Chapter 12
GOLF MEDALS AND TROPHIES

Trophies are of many shapes, sizes and metals.

Collecting Medals

by Art Di Prospero

One of my favorite collectibles is medals. There is very little written about them and usually the only sources for obtaining them are the various world-wide auctions. They come in all shapes and sizes, and are made of bronze, brass, copper, pewter, silver and gold. Most of the silver medals are sterling. The gold medals may vary; the British used mostly 9kt., while Americans used 10kt., 14kt. and .900 fine. Some medals are also silver-plated and 12kt. gold filled.

I have been drawn to medals for several reasons. The initial visual impact is the artwork. Many are in fine detail, both recessed and in relief. The variety of emblems, golfers, clubs, balls, clubhouses and golfing scenes are sometimes breathtaking.

The pre-1900 British and Scottish medals are not only pieces of art, they tell the history of the game. The names of players, golf course emblems, dates of competition and other engravings help to identify the better players, where and when they played, and the varied types of competitions of that era.

The early American medals can help "put together" golf in a historical perspective. One of the greatest thrills I can have as a medal collector is to acquire a *documented* piece from Shinnecock, The National, Merion, Baltusrol, Oakmont or any of the other great circa 1890-1910 courses. It gives the collector a humbling feeling to know that Willie Anderson, Horace Rawlins, Walter Travis, Walter Hagen, Gene Sarazen and Bobby Jones competed over these hallowed links.

The feeling is purely spellbinding to hold in my hand a medal won by Walter Hagen, or one of my favorites: the medal presented to Olin Dutra upon winning the 1932 PGA Championship. It contains over two ounces of gold and has a 1kt. diamond inset. The strike and artwork were absolutely incredible! When holding it, I can almost feel Mr. Dutra's euphoria from winning the PGA and being presented with his well-earned medal.

The USGA at Far Hills, N.J., has an awesome display of Bobby Jones medals. Chuck Furjanic's home course, The Four Seasons Resort and Club at Las Colinas, where the Byron Nelson Tour event is held, has on display all eighteen medals won by Nelson during 1945, which include those from his incredible eleven straight wins and the PGA Medal.

When collecting medals, you begin to recognize their historical importance and the part they played in giving the recipients something tangible to remember their "moment of glory." It also gives us a way to identify with the winner's feeling of importance upon being presented with a medal.

Golf Trophies

by Henry Alperin

A trophy or "prize" for the winner of a competition surely must date the origins of golf. Most notable are the British Open Championship Belt and the British Open Claret Jug, which date from 1860. The original Open Championship Belt was retired by the famous young Tom Morris. The Claret Jug is still being awarded at the end of the championship, with a replica of the original Claret Jug given to the champion. Similar major trophies are awarded for the British and United States amateur, and the United States Open Championships and are well known. At the Masters, a replica of the original trophy (depicting the Augusta National Clubhouse) is presented to the Masters champion.

Many annual golf events in the United States and abroad have individual characteristic trophies, some are glass and others are silver. Medals are still presented in the amateur championships and to the low amateur at the Masters Championship.

A golf trophy may be any item ranging from the classic silver cup, bowl or plate, to the engraved ribboned medals of gold and silver. Etched and engraved glass trophies are often given at current golf championships, particularly in the United States. Golf trophies have been made using many different materials such as pewter, brass, bronze, plated silver, and ceramics.

Many types of objects have been used for trophies: traditional cups, golf clubs with engraved plaques, mugs, ashtrays, statues, humidors, inkwell sets, decanters, jewelry, cigarette lighters, and mechanical devices such as clocks or watches. All of these items are both collectible and decorative and while they may cost only a few dollars, they can become a significant investment. There are many collectors within the Golf Collectors Society who specialize in one particular type of trophy; for example items from a certain era, or particular championships. Some individuals may collect only sterling pieces or ceramics, others might collect items pertaining to a certain golfer. Still others may collect a variety of trophies with no particular theme other than the fact it was presented to a winner of a golf tournament. The prices of these items, like other collectibles, relate to the rarity, condition, and demand.

It is always recommended that collectors buy from reputable dealers who will verify the authenticity, particularly of the more expensive items.

There are many specialized texts available that relate to this field of collecting, particularly relating to artifacts of ceramic, silver, and other metals. Previous major auction house catalogs, and prior catalogs from golf collectible dealers are also very helpful. The old catalogs, with their prices realized, are good guides for the collector in need of prices of specific trophies.

Where do collectors find trophies? The smaller silver cups and some of the ceramic items can be found in antique shops and flea markets. Sometimes, watches and jewelry or smoking-related items such as ashtrays, and engraved lighters, may also be found at these locations. Many golf collectible dealers carry various trophies, and collectors at golf shows display golf trophies for sale. The large golf auction houses both in the United States and Great Britain often carry many trophies, especially important medals and significant trophy cups. Occasionally an entire collection belonging to a famous golfer may be offered, such as the recent "Bobby Locke" collection, or the large collection of items from the Walter Travis Estate.

The joy of trophy collecting may be in obtaining an item from one's favorite golfer, but many enjoy the history behind the trophy relating to the winning golfer, or the golf society that presented it.

At the United States Golf Association Library, one may research some of the inscriptions as to the particular tournament and the correct date. If the inscription does not contain the name of the golfer winning the trophy, it can be obtained here. Often, the trophy was presented with the date and tournament name, but the winner's name had to be engraved by the recipient.

Sterling silver from Great Britain can be dated as to its manufacturer to see if the date of the presentation and the manufacturer correspond. Sterling silver in the United States is marked with the maker of the company and a sterling mark, but no definite date can be attributed.

Medals and Trophies

by Bob Burkett

MEDALS

From the start of my collecting career in golf, I have always had a special fondness for medals. Unlike clubs, behind each medal there is a story, which can sometimes be found with a little research and imagination. Always, though, these medals represent man's triumph over an opponent, a golf course, and more importantly, himself.

Medals come in all sizes, shapes, materials and, of course, values. The value rests on a number of factors, the first being composition. A plain brass medal is usually worth less than one made of 18kt. gold. However, if the brass was won by, say, Horace Hutchison in a British Amateur Championship, and the gold by a local businessman, the values change.

Beauty, as well as content and history, play a part in the value of medals. Some of the best art in the game of golf is depicted on high quality golf medals and most of these have found their way into collections.

Like most collectibles, medals come in vastly different qualities and price ranges. They may vary in price from $40-50 for a 1950s base metal item, and up to $50,000 or more for a medal from an important championship such as the British Open or other majors. Each item is individual, and should be judged as such. Obviously, other factors such as age, wear, engraving and place of origin are to be considered.

The beginning collector should find a focus to his collection. For example, find a specific golf course, a specific time period, famous golfer, or type of medal. Usually your first category choice will be too broad. I started out collecting pre-1930 medals and within a short time it was narrowed to pre-1920 and then, again, to pre-1920 American. It took me 15 years to finally focus on pre-1920 American women's medals.

One last thought: It doesn't matter if you accumulate ten unrelated medals or one hundred related medals, as long as it gives you collecting pleasure. Taking time to research the recipients and places related to your medals may enhance the enjoyment of your collection. On the other hand, you may just want to display them, and that's great too. Remember, the enjoyment of collecting is paramount.

TROPHIES

Trophies come in a wider range of styles and materials than perhaps any other collectible in golf. The oldest known trophy is a silver golf club from the Edinburgh Burgess Golfing Society. Since then, trophies have appeared in every variation the golfer's twisted mind can conceive. China, crystal, gold, silver, wood, leather, pewter, bronze, and only God knows what else has been fashioned into some sort of symbols of achievement—in the addiction we call golf.

As a broad general statement, trophies are more commonly American than British, while medals are more commonly British than American. Having collected both, I will also make the broad general statement that trophies take up an awful lot more space.

Trophies are very visual and come in a wide variety of sizes and shapes. After 15 years of collecting, I have long since given up trying to find an example of each. Unlike medals, trophies can be striking in appearance and somewhat more modest in cost, owing to the materials being more diverse, and in many cases less expensive.

While some of the early high quality trophies will run easily into thousands, many unusual and decorative trophies from the Art Deco 1920s and 1930s can still be found at a relatively modest price. Find a style, period and price that fit your taste and budget.

Please avoid the classic beginner mistake of buying *any* trophy you find at a yard sale, flea market, or antique shop just because it is *golf related*. There are lots of later (1950s and newer) low quality golf items for sale that have little value now and little hope of appreciation in value.

Having said that, I would also advise that you buy what pleases you. Also, buy the best available. It doesn't matter if you have $50 to spend. Buy the best $50 trophy you can find. If you have $5,000 to spend, the rule is the same. Buy the best $5,000 trophy you can find.

The old saying is still true. The bitterness of poor quality remains long after the sweetness of a cheap price has vanished.

PRICES GOLF MEDALS

G-5   G-7   G-9

BRONZE COIN-SIZE MEDALS

VARIOUS MAKERS $35   50   75

Circa 1900-1930. Nickel to quarter size with club name and date. Medals with ribbons add 50 percent. Photo below.

BRONZE COIN-SIZE MEDALS

VARIOUS MAKERS $60   100   150

Circa 1900-1930. Half-dollar to dollar size with club name and date. Medals with ribbons add 50 percent. Photo below.

STERLING COIN-SIZE MEDALS

VARIOUS MAKERS $125   175   250

Circa 1900-1930. Nickel to quarter size with club name and date. Medals with ribbons add 50 percent. Photo below.

STERLING COIN SIZE MEDALS

VARIOUS MAKERS $200   300   400

Circa 1900-1930. Half-dollar to dollar size with club name and date. Medals with ribbons add 50 percent. Photo below.

HOLE-IN-ONE MEDALS

VARIOUS MAKERS $20   35   50

Circa 1920s through 1960s. Mostly made of bronze. "Royal" is most common. Photo below.

BRITISH AMATEUR CHAMPIONSHIP

WALKER AND HALL, SHEFFIELD $6000   8000   10,000

Circa 1900. 18kt. gold medal in presentation case. Price is for unmarked or unknown winner. Popular winners command a substantial premium. Photo below.

1924 BELGIAN OPEN GOLD MEDAL
UNKNOWN MAKER $7500
14kt. gold medal. Won by Walter Hagen. Sold at public auction in 1991 for $1750. Medals won by less popular players are worth substantially less. Photo below.

STERLING ST. ANDREWS MEDAL
FRICK JEWELERS, NY $2000
Circa 1900. Presented to members of the golf team at St. Andrews Golf Club, New York. Photo below.

BRITISH OPEN MEDAL
UNKNOWN MAKER
$45,000
"Open Golf Championship, 1949" gold medal won by Bobby Locke. In red leather presentation case. Sold at public auction in 1993.

BRITISH OPEN MEDAL
UNKNOWN MAKER
$40,000
"Open Golf Championship, 1950" gold medal won by Bobby Locke. In red leather presentation case. Sold at public auction in 1993.

BRITISH OPEN MEDAL
UNKNOWN MAKER
$45,000
"Golf Champion Trophy, 1885" gilt medal won by Robert Martin. With blue ribbon and in the original box. Sold at public auction in 1996.

U.S. OPEN GOLF MEDAL
UNKNOWN MAKER
$32,000
1955 won by Jack Fleck. Sold at public auction in 1993.

PGA CHAMPIONSHIP MEDAL
UNKNOWN MAKER
$45,000
1921. Won by Walter Hagen. Sold at public auction in 1991 for $8000.

CANADIAN OPEN GOLD MEDAL
UNKNOWN MAKER $8000
1931. Won by Walter Hagen. Sold at public auction in 1991 for $2000.

2-INCH STERLING RELIEF MEDAL
WM. DUNNINGHAM, ABERDEEN $2000
1921 from the Caldonia Golf Club, Carnoustie. Photo below.

WOMEN'S AMATEUR CONTESTANT MEDAL

VARIOUS MAKERS $250
Circa 1920-1935. Quarter size and enameled in different colors through the years.

MEN'S AMATEUR CONTESTANT MEDAL

VARIOUS MAKERS $300
Circa 1920-1935. Quarter size and enameled in different colors through the years.

MEN'S US OPEN CONTESTANT MEDAL

VARIOUS MAKERS $350
Circa 1920-1935. Quarter size and enameled in different colors through the years.

MEN'S WESTERN OPEN CONTESTANT MEDAL

VARIOUS MAKERS $150
Circa 1920-1935. Quarter size and enameled in different colors through the years.

VICTORY GOLF MEDAL

VARIOUS MAKERS $500
A number of medals 2-1/2 inches in diameter were minted to be gifts to participating Golf Clubs in a tournament to raise funds for the United War Work Drive. John D. Rockefeller presented the medals. Photo below.

1897 U.S. OPEN GOLD MEDAL

JOHN FRICK, NEW YORK $50,000
Won by Joseph Lloyd. Sold for $21,000 at public auction in 1990.

PRICES
GOLF TROPHIES

G-5 G-7 G-9

STERLING SILVER LOVING CUP

VARIOUS MAKERS $125   175   275

Circa 1910-1930. Two-handled sterling loving cup without golfing scene. 5 to 6 inches tall. Photo below.

STERLING GOBLET

VARIOUS MAKERS $100   150   250

Circa 1900-1920. Without golfing scene. 5 to 6 inches tall. Photo below.

STERLING SILVER CUP

GORHAM $200   375   450

Circa 1900-1920. Two-handled cup without golfing scene. 5 to 6 inches tall. Photo below.

STERLING SILVER CUP

GORHAM $600   800   1000

Circa 1900-1920. Two-handled cup with golfing scene or crossed clubs and ball. 7 to 8 inches tall. Photo below.

STERLING SILVER CUP

GORHAM $300   400   500

Circa 1900-1920. Two-handled cup without golf-ing scene. 7 to 8 inches tall. Photo below.

STERLING CHALICE

UNKNOWN MAKER   L   5000

Circa 1850. 7 inches tall with golfing scene. Pre-1890 trophies are very rare. Photo below.

HUMIDOR WITH STERLING LID

VARIOUS MAKERS $1000   1500   2000

Circa 1900. Glass or crystal with a sterling lid. 6 to 7 inches tall. Photo below, left.

STERLING GOLFER ON IVORY BASE

UNKNOWN MAKER $2000   2500   3000

Circa 1910. Six inches high including base. Photo below, right.

STERLING TEA POT

UNKNOWN MAKER   2500

Circa 1890-1900. 8 inches tall with ornate engravings. Very scarce. Photo below.

STERLING SILVER LOVING CUP

VARIOUS MAKERS $375   500   750

Circa 1910-1930. Two handled sterling loving cup without golfing scene. 10 to 12 inches tall. Photo below, left.

STERLING SILVER LOVING CUP

VARIOUS MAKERS $1000   1500   2000

Circa 1910-1930. Two-handled sterling loving cup with golfing scene or crossed clubs and ball. 10 to 12 inches tall. Photo below, right.

STERLING LOVING CUP MADE IN SCOTLAND

J. LAING $600   800   1000

Circa 1920s. 6 inches tall with golfing scene and fine detail. Photo below.

CERAMIC AND STERLING TROPHY

LENOX $3000   4000   5000

Circa 1900-1910. Opaque green ceramic pitcher with silver overlay. Very scarce. Photo below.

BLUE CERAMIC TROPHY

LENOX $750   1000   1250

Circa 1900-1920. Three-handled trophy with golfing scene. 7 to 9 inches tall. Photo below.

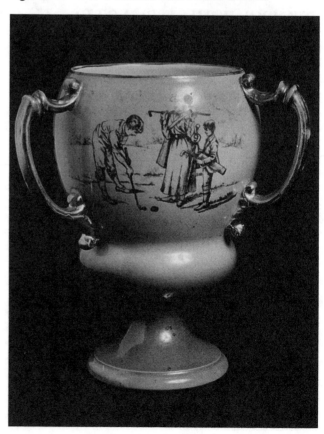

STERLING AND BRONZE TROPHY

PAIRPOINT $800 1000 1200

Circa 1900-1920. Three-handled trophy on legs.
Sterling on bronze. Photo below.

BRONZE GOLFER ON BASE

VARIOUS MAKERS $250 400 600

Circa 1900-1930. Bronze golfer on wood, bakelite
or marble base. 8 to 10 inches tall. Photo below.

BRONZE GOLFER ON BASE

VARIOUS MAKERS $125 200 300

Circa 1900-1930. Bronze golfer on wood, bakelite
or marble base. 5 to 7 inches tall. Photo below.

Chapter 13
GOLF TRADING CARDS

Examples of golf cards from the turn of the century to modern players.

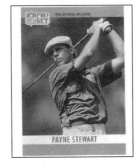

Although card collecting has been around for more than one hundred years, golf card collecting is still relatively new or unknown to many collectors. Most of us as youngsters collected baseball cards and even though we played golf, we had never seen a golf trading card. We hope that the next few pages will give you additional information and insight into this wonderful and untapped area of golf collectibles.

The History of Golf Cards

by Mike Daniels

Trade and cigarette cards were the first of the collectible cards. Trade cards were handed out by shop owners and manufacturers. These cards depicted the manufacturer's products and were printed with the name and address of the shop or shopkeeper. It was hoped that if they made these cards attractive, the customer would retain them as an informal business card.

The next step was to produce cards in a series with a particular theme. Flowers, fashion, children, pets or country scenes were the first series produced.

If you were to review scrap albums from the middle to the late 1800s, you would find evidence of the success of this new marketing strategy both in the United States and Europe. Hence, the card collecting craze began.

About this same time, 1870-1880, a change was taking place in the tobacco habits of people. Cigarettes were taking over from pipes and chewing tobacco. The cigarettes were usually packed in the same fragile packets of their ancestors. This idea of combining a cardboard type of stiffener with the current collecting craze started first in the United States and soon spread to Australia, Britain, and the rest of the world.

In the period from 1880 to about 1940, sets of cigarette cards were issued in profusion. Thousands of sets were made and the foundation was laid for the continuing card collecting hobby.

Since the majority of smokers prior to 1900 were men, subjects were chosen to appeal to men—military, sports, and women were popular choices.

In the United States, Kinney issued a military series in the late 1880s, Allen & Ginter issued its 50-card great generals set, and Duke did a 45-card famous ships series.

A year or two later, Allen & Ginter offered its first sport series called World Champions, which was a 50-card set. About the same time, Goodwin and Co. issued a 50-card Champions set and Kimball & Co. offered its 50-card Champions of Games and Sport set. Yet, in not one of these sets was there a golf card.

Around the turn of the century in England, the first golf cards were produced. Felix Berlyn and Cope Bros. and Co., Ltd. produced 25- and 50-card sets of golf scenes and strokes rather than of players. Original complete sets produced by these companies are extremely rare and sell for thousands of dollars. Do not despair, reprints of these and several other early sets were produced during the 1980s and sell for a fraction of the cost of originals.

The earliest American set to depict a golfer or golf scene was the American Tobacco Series of Champion Athletes and prize fighters of 1910—commonly referred to as the Mecca cigarette set. This set had six famous American golfers of the time: Finley Douglas, Alex Smith, Gil Nicholls, George Low, Jack Hobens and Fred Herreshoff. These are not exactly household names today, but several of these gentlemen had distinguished careers in American golf.

About the same time in England, Odgen's produced its Guinea Gold cigarettes issue of 18 photographic golf cards. This set included Old Tom Morris, Harry Vardon, James Braid, etc. and six scenic cards from an early match played between Harry Vardon and James Braid, two of the greatest golfers from this period. By the late 1920s Churchman felt that there was enough interest in the game, and a sufficient number of well-known players, to issue its "famous golfer" 50-card series of photographic cards. Over the next several years many other golf sets were produced by Churchman and other tobacco companies.

The success of the cigarette cards became the model for other types of commodities. Cards began to be inserted with newspapers, chocolates, magazines, cereal, tea, and gum packets. Then came a slow and gradual change from a situation where with every stick of gum you were given a few cards, until the time when every pack of cards came with a free stick of gum. Then, finally, why bother putting the gum in the packets at all? We are now in a world of trading cards where series are produced on a commercial basis and sold in packets or as complete sets. Thousands of cards are now produced each year.

Golf cards have gone through a series of cycles over the years with cards and sets being produced for a few years then going into a form of hibernation with only a few cards produced annually. Donruss produced two PGA tour sets of 66 cards each in 1981 and 1982. The PGA tour continued to produce sets from 1983 to 1990. These were very similar to the Donruss sets in style and layout. These sets have become quite scarce in their own right since only a few thousand sheets were produced each year and many of these were destroyed. Only a few collectors knew of their existence and managed to save some sets.

The Pro Set company began producing sets for the PGA tour in 1990 and produced sets for three years. The first set consisted of 100 cards, 75 regular PGA tour cards and 25 senior tour cards. These sets were well received by the collecting public and were quite popular by autograph seekers on the American tour.

These sets are no longer being produced and once again the only new sets available seem to be coming out of England. Most of these sets are of one theme or small sets of the 1993 or 1995 Ryder Cup Teams. Hopefully the cycle will continue with the ever increasing popularity of golf among young people throughout the world. Maybe new sets again will be produced in the U.S. to satisfy the collecting interests of golfers. These miniature storybooks tell us much about the history of the game and hopefully some of you will expand your collecting interests into golf cards.

Recommended Reference Books

The following new reference books and price guides have been printed in the last few years. These are excellent checklists, and list all known golf cards in the world through 1994.

A Century of Golf Cards by Bruce Berdock and Michael Baier, 1993.

The Price Guide to Golf Cards, Part I, Tobacco Cards, by Philip Smedley and Bruce Berdock, 1994.

The Price Guide to Golf Cards, Part II, Non-Tobacco Cards, by Philip Smedley & Bruce Berdock, 1995.

PRICES
GOLF CARDS

G-5 G-7 G-9

AMERICAN TOBACCO CO.
CHAMPION ATHLETES SERIES $30 55 100
Circa 1910. "Mecca" cigarettes. Six cards: A. Smith, F. Douglas, J. Hobens, F. Herreshoff, George Low and Gil Nicholls. Photos below.

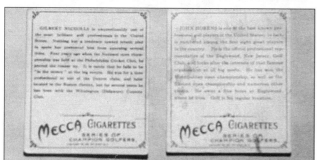

COLLEGE SERIES $20 35 60
Circa 1914. Seven cards.

COLLEGE SILKS $25 50 100
Circa 1910. Two sizes of colorful silks. 25 colleges included. Small size 5-1/2 x 3-1/2 inches; large size 7-3/4 x 5 inches. Photo below.

BERLYN, FEXIS S.
ENGLAND
BURLINE MIXTURE GOLF CARDS,
FULL SET $5500 12,000 20,000
Circa 1910. 25 small-size cards.

BURLINE MIXTURE GOLF CARDS,
ONE CARD $250 450 800
Circa 1910. 25 small-size cards.

BURLINE MIXTURE GOLF CARDS,
ONE CARD $400 1000 1500
Circa 1910. 25 large-size cards.

BURLINE MIXTURE GOLF CARDS,
FULL SET $9500 22,000 35,000
Circa 1910. 25 large-size cards.

CHURCHMAN
CAN YOU BEAT BOGEY AT
ST. ANDREWS $400 700 1000
Circa 1934. Complete set of 55 cards.

FAMOUS GOLFERS
SMALL SIZE $600 1250 1850
Circa 1927. Complete set of 50 cards.

FAMOUS GOLFERS
LARGE SIZE $700 1350 2000
Circa 1927. Complete set of 12 cards.

MEN OF THE MOMENT
IN SPORTS $300 500 800
Circa 1928. Set of 10 golf cards numbering 24 to 33.

PROMINENT GOLFERS
SMALL SIZE $500 1000 1600
Circa 1931. Set of 50 golf cards.

PROMINENT GOLFERS
LARGE SIZE $550 950 1400
Circa 1931. Set of 12 golf cards.

SPORTING CELEBRITIES $100   150   250

Circa 1931. Set of 7 golf cards, numbering 30 to 36. Photo above.

DONRUSS

PGA TOUR CARDS $25   35   50

1981. Complete set of 66 cards. All are considered "Rookie" cards. Photo below.

PGA TOUR CARDS $30   40   60
1982. Complete set of 66 cards. Photo above..

MEULLER ENTERPRISES, INC.
GOLF'S GREATEST $25   30   60
1992. Complete set of 30 cards.

MILLER PRESS
PRO TOUR CARDS $90   150   300
1983 and 1984. Uncut sheet of 66 cards.

PRO TOUR CARDS $65   100   200
1985, 1986 and 1987. Uncut sheet of 66 cards.

PRO TOUR CARDS $50   75   120
1988. Uncut sheet of 66 cards.

PRO TOUR CARDS $25   45   75
1989 and 1990. Uncut sheet of 66 cards.

NATIONAL EXCHANGE BANK
THE SEVEN AGES OF GOLF $850   1300   2250
Circa 1902. Seven card set. Photo at right..

OGDEN'S LIMITED
ENGLAND

OGDEN'S GUINEA GOLD $25   50   100
Circa 1901. Unnumbered cards. The Tom Morris card is worth about double.

OGDEN'S CHAMPIONS OF 1936 $10   22   35
Pam Barton, A. H. Padgham and H. Thomson. Photo below.

LIVERPOOL & LONDON

COPE'S GOLFERS $1500   3500   7000
Circa 1900. 50 numbered cards.

B. MORRIS
LONDON

GOLF STROKES
BY ARTHUR HAVERS $175   250   400
Circa 1925. 25 numbered cards.

PRIMROSE CONFECTIONARY

POPEYE 2ND SERIES $25   45   70
1961. Card #29.

POPEYE 4TH SERIES $8   10   20
1963. Cards #24 and #32. Photo below.

PRO SET, INC.

PGA TOUR INAUGURAL SET $5   6   10
1990. Complete set of 100 cards.

ARNOLD PALMER
HOLOGRAM CARD $50   55   60
1991.

BEN HOGAN
HOLOGRAM CARD $80   90   100
1992.

NFL FOOTBALL CARDS $10   20   40
1990. Payne Stewart special card. Photo below.

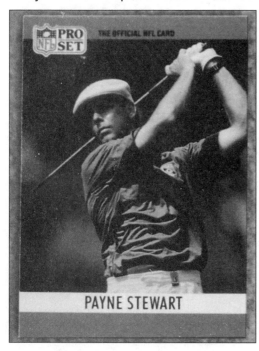

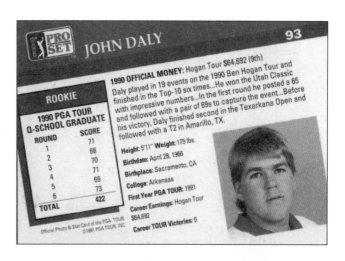

PGA TOUR CARDS $10   15   25
1991 and 1992. Complete sets of 285 and 300
cards. Photos below.

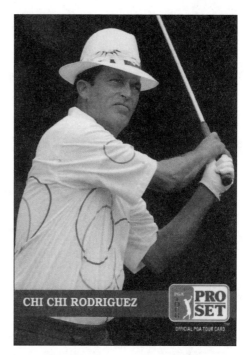

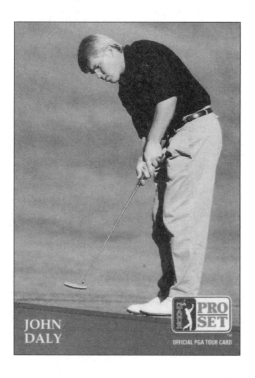

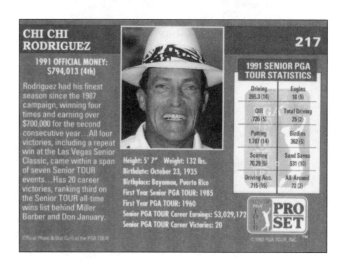

SHERIDAN COLLECTIBLES

THE BOBBY JONES STORY $5   7   12

1993. Complete set of 12 cards. Photos below.

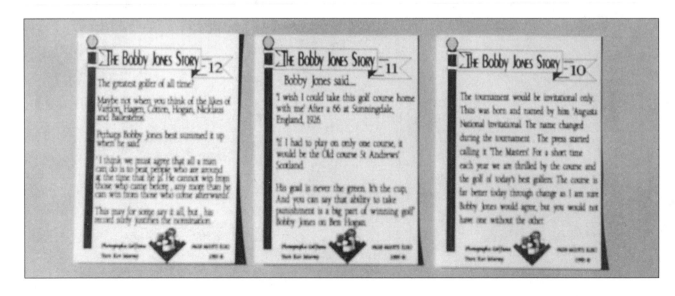

WILLS
ENGLAND

FAMOUS GOLFERS $500 800 1300
Circa 1930. 25 card set. Photo below.

FAMOUS COURSES $250 400 650
Circa 1924. 25 card set. Photo below.

Chapter 14
SILVER AND GOLD GOLF COLLECTIBLES

An assortment of silver whiskey flasks.

Precious metals were used to make many collectible golf items. Here we will discuss and evaluate those made from gold and silver.

Gold came in various qualities ranging from 9kt. to 18kt., and was mainly used for smaller items such as jewelry, in the form of cuff links and tie clasps for men, and brooches, pins and charms for women.

Silver items were very popular around the turn of the century and were either sterling or silver plated. Many of these were for ladies and the home. They included toast racks, knife rests, salt and pepper shakers, coffee and tea servers, various utensils, serving trays, hair brushes, coin purses, and pin cushions. Souvenir spoons were also made for both trophies and the tourist trade at famous course

locations like St. Andrews, Troon, etc. For the men there were whiskey flasks, cocktail items, match safes, cigarette cases, watch fobs, inkwells, tie clasps, cuff links, and scoring devices. Some of the prominent manufacturers included: Unger Brothers, Tiffany, Gorham, Wm. Kerr, and Whiting.

PRICES
SILVER AND GOLD
COLLECTIBLES

G-5 G-7 G-9

BELT BUCKLE - STERLING
UNKNOWN MAKER $300   400   600
Circa 1900. Photo below.

BLOTTER
UNGER BROS. $500   750   1100
Circa 1905. Golfer on front. Photo below.

BOOKMARK - STERLING
UNKNOWN MAKER $225   325   450
Circa 1900-1920. Caddy with bag. Photo below.

CIGARETTE CASE - STERLING
UNKNOWN MAKER $375   575   900
Circa 1900-1920. Golfing scene on cover.

CIGARETTE CASE - STERLING
NAPIER CO. $200   375   575
Circa 1930. Golfer on front. Knickers in black enamel. Photo below.

CIGARETTE CASE - STERLING
THE THOMAS CO. $200   375   575
Circa 1930. Golfer on front. Photo below.

CIGARETTE CASE - STERLING

NAPIER CO. $200   375   575
Circa 1930. Golfer on front. Place for initials at
right front. Photo below.

COCKTAIL SHAKER, TRAY AND CUPS

DERBY SILVER CO. $1200   1500   2000
Circa 1920. Silver plated. Mesh ball handled tray,
six cups and a 13-inch-tall pitcher. Photo below.

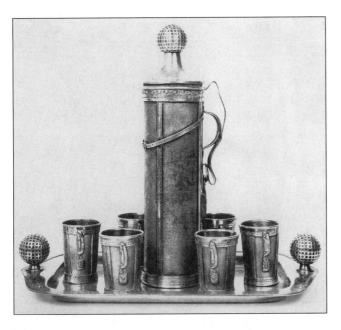

EGGCUP - STERLING

UNKNOWN MAKER $60   100   150
Circa 1920s. Made in England. 3-1/2 inches tall.

GOLD GOLF BALL CUFF LINKS

DUNLOP, NEW YORK $125   175   250
Circa 1920. Nickel-size 10kt. gold mesh golf ball
cuff links.

GOLF BAG PIN - STERLING

UNKNOWN MAKER $75   125   200
Circa 1910-1920s. 1-1/2 inches. Bag and clubs.
Photo below.

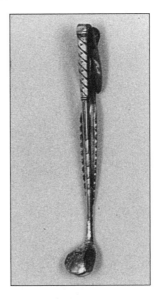

HAT PIN - STERLING

UNKNOWN MAKER $75   100   150
Circa 1900-1920s. Wicker basket at top. Photo
below.

HAT PIN - STERLING

UNKNOWN MAKER $50   75   100
Circa 1900-1920s. Iron head at top. Photo below.

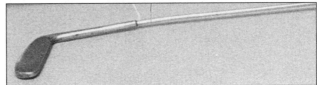

HAT PIN - STERLING

UNKNOWN MAKER $60   90   125
Circa 1900-1920s. Sterling, wood at top. Photo
below.

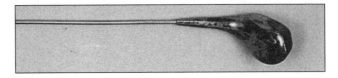

HAT PIN - STERLING
UNKNOWN MAKER $60   90   125
Circa 1900-1920s. Crossed clubs at top. Photo
below.

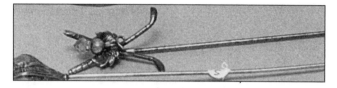

INKWELL - SILVER-PLATED
F. BRS. LTD. $475   600   900
Circa 1890. 6 x 11 inches. Two golf ball inkwells,
golfer in center. Photo below.

KNIFE RESTS
UNKNOWN MAKER $250   350   450
Circa 1900-1920. Silver plated. Photo below.

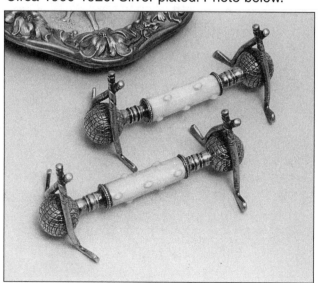

LADY'S COIN PURSE - SILVER-PLATED
UNKNOWN MAKER $200   300   450
Circa 1900-1920s. Caddy on front. Photo below,
bottom right.

LADY'S COIN PURSE - STERLING
UNKNOWN MAKER $350   450   650
Circa 1900-1920s. Lady golfer on front. Photo
below, top left.

MATCH SAFE - STERLING
UNGER, NEWARK, NJ $400   650   850
Circa 1900-1910. Caddy with bag. Photo below.

MATCH SAFE - STERLING
ART NOUVEAU $400   650   850
Circa 1900-1910. Woman golfer in backswing.
Photo below.

MATCH SAFE - STERLING
UNKNOWN MAKER $400   750   1000
Circa 1890. Woman golfer addressing golf ball.
Photo below.

MATCH SAFE - STERLING
UNKNOWN MAKER $300   450   675
Circa 1900-1910. Ball and crossed clubs. Photo
below.

MATCH SAFE - STERLING
GORHAM $300   450   675
Circa 1900-1910. Bag of clubs, flagstick and
large thistle plant. Photo below.

MATCH SAFE - STERLING

LA PIERRE MFG. CO. $300   450   675

Circa 1890. Male golfer in backswing. Photo below.

MATCH SAFE - STERLING

LA PIERRE MFG. CO. $250   375   575

Circa 1900. Small size with crossed clubs and ball. Photo below.

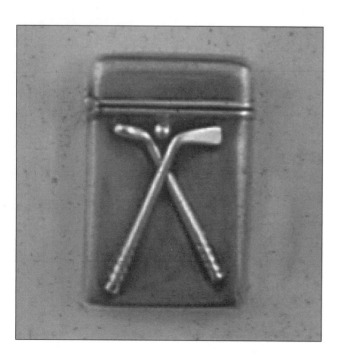

MATCH SAFE - STERLING

H. W. LTD, BIRMINGHAM $450   675   950

Circa 1900-1910. Golf ball-shaped with line cut guttie markings. Photo below.

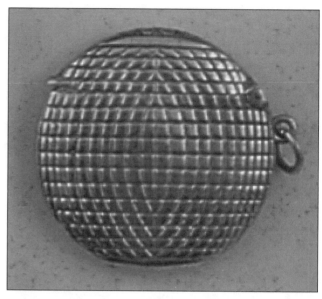

MATCH SAFE - STERLING

UNKNOWN MAKER $300   450   650

Circa 1900. Golf clubs and ball. Photo below.

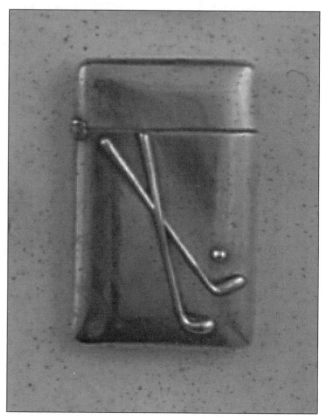

NUT TRAY - STERLING

UNKNOWN MAKER $400   500   600
Circa 1900-1910. 5-1/2 inch diameter. Golfer in center. Photo below.

PIN - STERLING

UNKNOWN MAKER $100   150   225
Circa 1910-1920s. 3 inches. Bag and clubs. Photo below.

PIN CUSHION-HAT PIN HOLDER - STERLING

UNKNOWN MAKER $300   450   600
Circa 1910-1920. Golf bag pin holder. Photo below.

PIN CUSHION-WATCH - STERLING

UNKNOWN MAKER $600   800   1100
Circa 1915-1925. Pin cushion with Swiss watch inside mesh ball cover. Photo below.

SALT DIP

UNKNOWN MAKER $175   250   375
Circa 1900. Silver plate. Gutta ball design with crossed clubs. Photo below.

SPOONS - STERLING SILVER

VARIOUS MAKERS $60   80   100
Circa 1900-1930. Golfers on handle. Photo below.

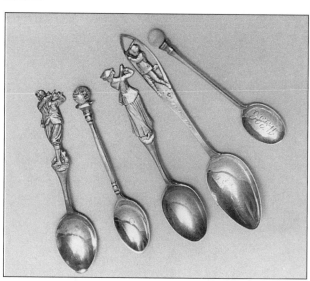

SPOONS - STERLING SILVER

VARIOUS MAKERS $60   80   100
Circa 1900-1930. Various handle designs. Larger ornate spoons command double the prices listed below. Photo below.

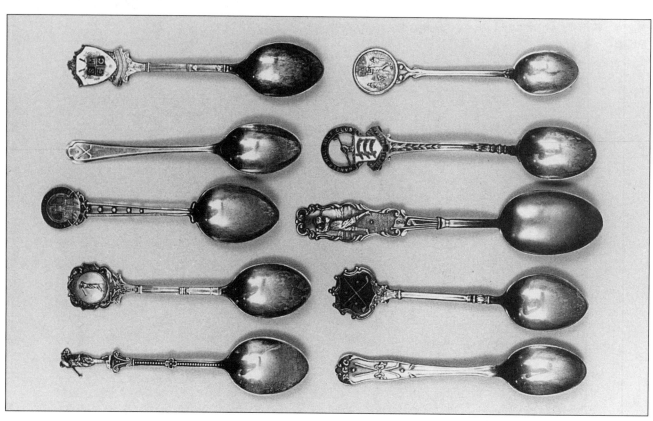

TABLE SCRAPER
UNKNOWN MAKER $225   325   450
Circa 1900-1920. Sterling handle, celluloid blade.
Photo below.

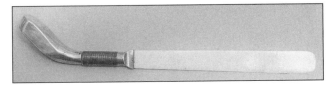

TEE INFUSER - STERLING
WATROUS,
WALLINGFORD, CT $175   300   450
Circa 1910-1915. Shaped like a driver.

TIE CLASP - STERLING
UNKNOWN MAKER $60   90   125
Circa 1910-1920s. 3 inches. Golf club. Photo
below.

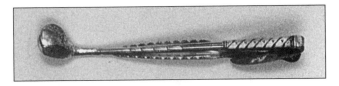

TOAST RACK
DERBY SILVER CO. $350   500   700
Circa 1900-1910. Four-slice rack.

TOAST RACK
DERBY SILVER CO. $400   550   800
Circa 1900-1910. Six-slice rack.

WHISKEY FLASK - STERLING
KERR & CO., NEWARK, NJ $500   800   1100
Circa 1920s. 4 x 8 inch pint size. Knickered golf-
ers on front. Photo below.

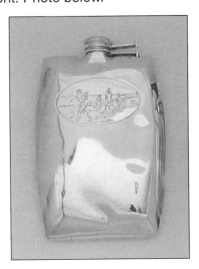

WHISKEY FLASK - STERLING
WATROUS MFG. CO. $350   500   750
Circa 1920s. Half-pint size. Golfing scene on
front.

WHISKEY FLASK - STERLING
UNGER BROTHERS $650   900   1250
Circa 1905. Small flask. Caddy with bag. Photo
below.

WHISKEY FLASK - STERLING
INTERNATIONAL SILVER CO. $350   500   750
Circa 1920. Small flask in oval shape. Ball and
club on front. Photo below.

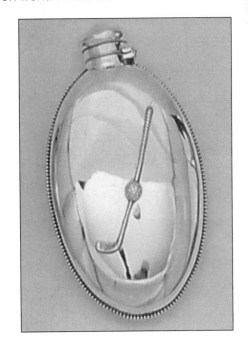

WHISKEY FLASK - NICKEL STERLING

EVANS CO. $100   200   350

Circa 1920. Golfing scene. Photo below.

Several photos were graciously provided by Glentiques, Ltd.

Chapter 15
MISCELLANEOUS GOLF COLLECTIBLES

During the 1920's and 30's a variety of golf ball companies made advertising pieces. They are highly collectible today.

Many collectors have wide and varied interests that are not limited to clubs, balls and books, and extend their search for golf-related collectibles in antique shops, flea markets and garage sales, as well as fixed price lists, auctions and dealer offerings.

This chapter will include items such as tournament badges from PGA events, U.S. Opens and the Masters. It also includes watches, score keepers, ball washers, drink serving trays, bookends, cigar boxes, games, practice devices, molds, tins, advertising items, golf course equipment, and one-arm bandits.

PRICES MISCELLANEOUS GOLF COLLECTIBLES

G-5 G-7 G-9

ACCESSORIES

BALL WASHERS

HALLEY & CO., LONDON $40   60   90
Circa 1920. Rectangular rubber holder for sponge. Photo below.

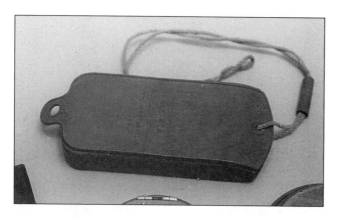

BALL WASHERS

NORTH BRITISH, EDINBURGH $30   45   75
Circa 1920. Square rubber holder for sponge. Photo below.

BALL WASHERS

UNKNOWN MAKER $150   225   375
Circa 1920. Round silver-plated holder for sponge. Golfing scene on lid. Photo below.

BALL WASHERS

UNKNOWN MAKER $125   200   300
Circa 1920. Round brass holder for sponge. Photo below.

BOTTLE GOLF PRACTICE DEVICE
UNKNOWN MAKER $150 225 350
Circa 1920s. Bottle-shaped device with mesh ball at end of long twine tether. Photo below.

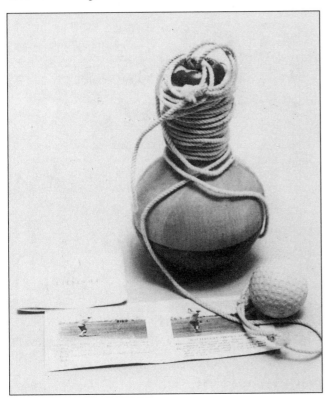

GOLF BALL PAINT
VARIOUS $150 225 375
Circa 1900-1920. Photo below.

GOLF SHOE SPIKES
UNKNOWN $50 75 100
Circa 1920s. "Black Boy" cricket and golf spikes. Colorful red, green and white box. Photo below.

GOLF SHOE SPIKES
UNKNOWN $50 75 100
Circa 1920s. "Goffix" golfers cleat that attaches to street shoes. Add 50 percent for original box. Photo below.

SMAKBAK PRACTICE DEVICE
MADE IN ENGLAND $75 90 125
Circa 1925. Long metal spike with heavy twine attached to golf ball. In colorful advertising box.

SCORE KEEPER

VARIOUS MAKERS $150   225   450

Circa 1920s. Pocket watch size. Photo below.

SCORE KEEPER

VARIOUS $150   225   350

Circa 1920s. Wristwatch style. Photo below.

SPOOL OF PITCHED LINEN

VARIOUS $150   225   375

Circa 1900-1930. For repairing golf clubs. Both British and American makers. Photo below.

HOGAN BELT WATCH

DUNLOP $300   400   550

Circa 1950s.

POCKET WATCH

U.S. ROYAL $100   150   250

Circa 1920s. Open face with mesh ball background. Photo below.

POCKET WATCH

DUNLOP $300   400   550

Circa 1920s-1930s. Sterling case in mesh ball pattern.

BADGES

TOURNAMENT MEDIA BADGES

VARIOUS MAKERS $15   20   30
1960s-1980. 2 to 4 inches, in various shapes: round, rectangular, oval, etc. Made of metal and plastic. Photo above.

U.S. OPEN MEDIA BADGES

VARIOUS MAKERS $20   30   50
1960s-1970s. Press arm bands. Made of felt with elastic band. Various colors. Photo above.

CADDIE BADGES

VARIOUS MAKERS $75   100   150
1910-1930. Brass or steel. Golf course name and caddie number. Silver-dollar size.

TOURNAMENT CADDIE BADGES

VARIOUS MAKERS $20   30   45
1960s-1980. 2 to 4 inches, in various shapes: round, rectangular, oval, etc. Made of metal and plastic.

MASTERS PRESS BADGES

VARIOUS MAKERS $50   60   75
1960s-1970. Rectangular and round. Made of metal. Photo below.

TOURNAMENT ENTRANCE BADGES

VARIOUS MAKERS $8   12   20
1960s-1980. 2 to 4 inches in various shapes: round, rectangular, oval, etc. Made of metal and plastic.

U.S. OPEN BADGES

VARIOUS MAKERS $15   25   45
1960s-1980. 2 to 4 inches in various shapes: round, rectangular, oval, etc. Made of metal and plastic.

GAMES

LAWN GOLF GAME

UNKNOWN MAKER $250   300   350
Circa 1920s. Four wooden-head clubs, "holes" with discs, one rubber bramble pattern ball, and a wooden storage box.

MASTERS SERIES BADGES

Year	Winner			
1934	Horton Smith	$6000	8000	12,000
1935	Gene Sarazen	$4000	5000	6500
1936	Horton Smith	$2500	3500	5000
1937	Byron Nelson	$2500	3500	5000
1938	Henry Picard	$1200	1800	2500
1939	Ralph Guldahl	$700	850	1200
1940	Jimmy Demaret	$750	900	1250
1942	Craig Wood	$650	750	1000
1943-45	Tournament was not held because of WWII			
1946	Herman Keiser	$450	650	850
1947	Jimmy Demaret	$450	650	850
1948	Claude Harmon	$400	575	700
1949	Sam Snead	$450	650	850
1950	Jimmy Demaret	$400	600	700
1951	Ben Hogan	$500	750	1100
1952	Sam Snead	$400	550	675
1953	Ben Hogan	$475	700	1000
1954	Sam Snead	$375	475	650
1955	Cary Middlecoff	$350	450	550
1956	Jack Burke, Jr.	$325	425	525
1957	Doug Ford	$325	425	525
1958	Arnold Palmer	$500	600	750
1959	Art Wall	$300	375	475
1960	Arnold Palmer	$400	500	650
1961	Gary Player	$325	425	525
1962	Arnold Palmer	$400	500	650
1963	Jack Nicklaus	$400	500	650
1964	Arnold Palmer	$325	425	525
1965	Jack Nicklaus			750
1966	Jack Nicklaus			350
1967	Gay Brewer			190
1968	Bob Goalby			190
1969	George Archer			175
1970	Billy Casper			160
1971	Charles Coody			160
1972	Jack Nicklaus			225
1973	Tommy Aaron			135
1974	Gary Player			135
1975	Jack Nicklaus			160
1976	Raymond Floyd			110
1977	Tom Watson			120
1978	Gary Player			100
1979	Fuzzy Zoeller			100
1980	Seve Ballesteros			90
1981	Tom Watson			100
1982	Craig Stadler			75
1983	Seve Ballesteros			70
1984	Ben Crenshaw			85
1985	Bernhard Langer			65
1986	Jack Nicklaus			160
1987	Lary Mize			60
1988	Sandy Lyle			50
1989	Nick Faldo			50
1990	Nick Faldo			40
1991	Ian Woosnam			40
1992	Fred Couples			50
1993	Bernhard Langer			40
1994	Jose Maria Olazabal			40
1995	Ben Crenshaw			45
1996	Nick Faldo			40
1997	Tiger Woods			100
1998	Mark O'Meara			40
1999	Jose Maria Olazabal			40

GOLF AROUND THE CLOCK GAME

P.S.P., INC., NEW YORK $125   200   325

Circa late 1920s. Cast-iron numerals and hole in an advertising tin. Photo below.

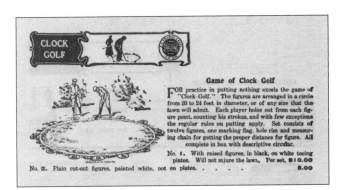

"PLAY GOLF" GOLF GAME

FERDINAND STRAUSS, NY $125   200   350

Circa 1910. Metal wind-up game. Photo below.

SPINGOFF GOLF GAME

UNKNOWN $125   175   250

Circa 1920s rainy day golf game. Photo below.

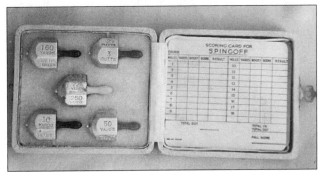

ROLA-BOLA GOLF GAME

VARIOUS $125   200   350

Circa 1920s. Putting game. Photo below.

HAND-HELD GOLF GAMES

MINIATURE GAME CO.,
PHILADELPHIA $100   150   225
Circa 1940s. Pocket golf and other hand-held games. Photo below.

KARGO CARD GOLF GAME

CASTELL BROS., LONDON $50   70   100
Circa 1920s. Card game. Photo below.

PAR-IT GOLF GAME

PAR-IT SALES, MILWAUKEE $25   40   65
Circa 1930s. Card game. Photo below.

ZWEIFEL CARD GOLF GAME

GROVER C. ZWEIFEL,
TULSA, OK $50   65   90
Circa 1930s. Card game. Photo below.

GOLF BALL SLOT MACHINE

VARIOUS MAKERS $2500   3750   5500
Circa 1930s-1950s. Jennings and Mills brands. Standing model. Photo previous page..

MILLS GOLF BALL VENDER

Built exclusively for Golf Clubs and locations catering to golf players, it's the first machine of its kind to do everything a golf ball vender should do.

It's a full fledged Vender but it pays out, not in mints or checks, but strictly in Golf Balls.

Every coin played in is registered. Every ball paid out is registered.

Capacity 114 Golf Balls. It saves you excessive service, protects you against a needless waste of time and effort.

It is entirely automatic, works just like a Mills Mystery. It comes in a beautiful cabinet, and through a large merchandise display window, shows the Golf Balls, all of them nationally advertised.

If the machine runs out of balls, it may be reloaded without unlocking the rest of mechanism. Each ball thus inserted is then registered.

This brand new Mills machine opens up a brand new market for coin machine amusement. Customers everywhere are reporting cash intakes of $40, $50 and more each day.

GOLF BALL SLOT MACHINE

VARIOUS MAKERS $2500   3750   5500
Circa 1930s-1950s. Jennings and Mills brands.
Countertop model.

GOLF COURSE EQUIPMENT

GOLF COURSE EQUIPMENT

VARIOUS MAKERS $50   75   100
Circa 1900-1910. Hole or cup liner made of steel.
Photo below, top left.

GOLF COURSE EQUIPMENT

VARIOUS MAKERS $150   250   400
Circa 1900-1910. Hole cutter. Photo below, left.

GOLF COURSE EQUIPMENT

VARIOUS MAKERS $200   300   450
Circa 1900-1910. Green aerifier. The tines were
hollow. Photo below, center.

GOLF COURSE EQUIPMENT

VARIOUS MAKERS $200   300   450
Circa 1900-1910. Sod mover. Photo below, right.

GOLF COURSE EQUIPMENT

VARIOUS MAKERS $100   175   275
Circa 1920-1930. Fringe mower. Photo below.

GOLF COURSE EQUIPMENT
VARIOUS MAKERS $100 175 275
Circa 1900-1930. Sand tee box. The box pictured was in use at the 11th tee, Baltusrol. Photo below.

MAGAZINES

MAGAZINES
GOLFING MAGAZINE $25 40 65
Circa 1930s.

AMERICAN GOLFER $60 80 120
Circa 1905-1916. Edited by Walter Travis.

GOLF ILLUSTRATED $50 70 110
Circa 1920s. Large size.

AMERICAN GOLFER $50 70 100
Circa 1920-1930. Large size. Photo below.

GOLFER'S MAGAZINE $60 80 125
Circa Teens. Photo below.

TINS & BOXES

COUNTRY CLUB CIGAR TIN
VARIOUS MAKERS $125   225   350
Circa 1920s. Colorful cigar tin. Photo below, left.

BISCUIT TIN
ROBERTSON BROS.,
TORONTO $200   300   450
Circa 1920s. Hand painted. Approximately 10 inches tall. Photo below, round tin.

SPICE TIN
VARIOUS MAKERS $50   70   100
Circa 1920s. Small 1-1/2-inch x 3-1/2-inch tins for spices. Photo below, small tin.

TIN BOX
SPALDING, DYSART, FIFE $150   250   350
Circa 1920s. Large tin box with colorful golfing scenes. Photo below, right.

TOMATO CAN
ROYAL BRAND $50   70   100
Circa 1920s. Lady golfer on label. Photo below, bottom right.

COUNTRY CLUB CIGAR BOX
VARIOUS MAKERS $40   70   100
Circa 1920s. Wooden cigar box.

HANDKERCHIEF BOXES
UNKNOWN MAKER $50   75   100
Circa 1920s. Hinged wooden boxes with colorful men and lady golfers on lid. Photo below.

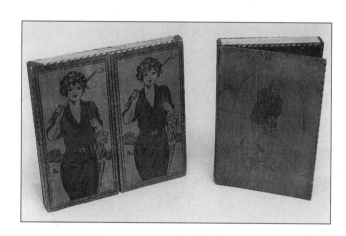

MISCELLANEOUS

BOOKENDS
UNKNOWN $100   125   150
Circa 1950s. Heavy granite, 7 inches tall with crossed clubs and ball. Photo above.

WHITE METAL BOOKENDS
VARIOUS MAKERS $100   125   150
Circa 1920s. Golfer in plus fours. Photo below.

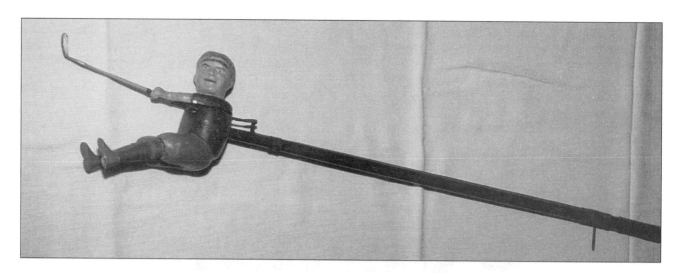

TOMMY GREEN SCHOENHUT GOLFER

SCHOENHUT CO. $350   450   600
Circa 1920s. Five-inch wooden golfer at end of control rod. Photo above.

SISSY LOFTER SCHOENHUT GOLFER

SCHOENHUT CO. $450   600   800
Circa 1920s. Five-inch wooden golfer at end of control rod.

ICE CREAM MOLDS

VARIOUS MAKERS $100   150   200
Circa 1910-1920. Made of pewter. Many shapes including a mesh golf ball mold not pictured. Photo below.

SILVER KING ADVERTISING FIGURE

SILVERTOWN $300   450   650
Circa 1920s. Papier-mache with mesh ball head. Approximately 10 inches tall. Photo below, left.

PENFOLD OR BROMFORD MAN

PENFOLD $250   400   600
Circa 1920s. Papier-mache golfing figure with large "Hogan"-type hat. Stand marked "He Played a Penfold, or Bromford". Approximately 22 inches tall. Photo below, center.

SCOTTIE DOG ADVERTISING FIGURE

NORTH BRITISH,
EDINBURGH $250   375   550
Circa 1920s. Made in both metal and pottery. Advertising for the North British Ball. Photo below.

SILVER KING ADVERTISING FIGURE

SILVERTOWN $300   450   650
Circa 1920s. Papier-mache with mesh ball head. Approximately 8 inches tall. Photo below, right.

DUNLOP MAN

DUNLOP $250 400 600

Circa 1920s. Papier-mache colorful golfing figure with golf bag. Stand marked "We Play Dunlop". Approximately 18 inches tall. Photo below.

PLASTER ADVERTISING PAPERWEIGHT

UNKNOWN MAKER $250 400 600

Circa 1920s. Whiskey advertisements made of plaster. Usually with golfer and mesh pattern ball. Photo below.

METAL SERVING TRAY

VARIOUS MAKERS $50 75 100

Circa 1930s. Many with beer advertisements. Photo below.

CAST-IRON DOORSTOPS
VARIOUS MAKERS $175   250   400
Circa 1920s. Colorfully painted. Photo above.

DESKTOP THERMOMETER
UNKNOWN MAKER $250   325   450
Circa 1910. 6 inches tall with golfer on top. Made of white metal with dark brown patina. Photo at right.

Chapter 16
A SHORT HISTORY OF GOLF BAGS

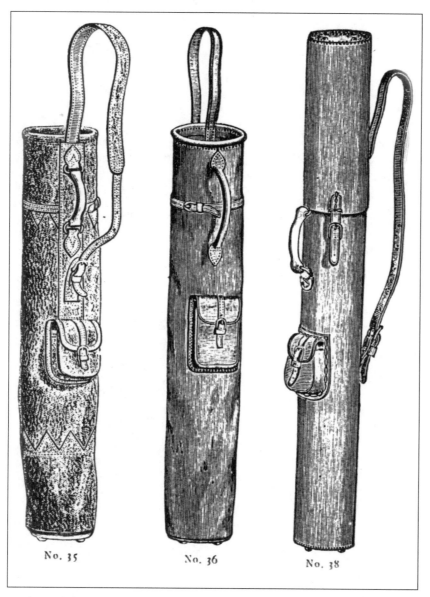

No. 35   No. 36   No. 38

Leather golf bags Circa 1900.

The number of years that golfers have used bags or other carrying devices for their clubs is greatly outnumbered by the years that clubs were simply carried under the arm. That is to say, golf bags are a fairly recent innovation in the history of the sport. There are two separate groups of implements to be examined: bags, or as they were once known, 'covers,' and carrying devices of another nature.

This match took place at St. Andrews, 1847. Notice the caddies carried the clubs under their arms as bags and other carrying devices were not used until the 1890's.

GOLF BAGS

Going back through centuries of golf, players carried their clubs under their arm without the assistance from any device. It might be said that golfers really never had a need for such devices because it was their caddies that actually did the carrying, however uncomfortable or awkward it might have been.

There was a second reason for the lack of requirement for a carrying valise or bag, and that was the relatively small number of clubs each player carried. Seven clubs was considered a large number, and four or five was often the selected set. Many players carried only three clubs, at a time when a man inventing a shot was more important than having a club that specialized in a particular loft of distance of shot.

Eventually, the bag, or cover, came into use primarily as a device for keeping club handles (grips) dry during the frequent and unpredictable rains that Britain is known for. The first of these covers were simply cloth sacks, long and tubular in shape like a long burlap pillowcase. There were no carrying handles or straps, no ball pockets or towel clips.

All leather bags are quite scarce in above average to superb condition.

They covered the handles and most of the wood shafts to keep them dry. Clubs were still just tucked under a player's or caddie's arm and carried as before. The lone characteristic to separate one bag from another, was the use of stenciled initials or a monogram on the fabric.

The first person recorded to have utilized a bag cover for his clubs is Mr. David Stocks of Edinburgh who allegedly did it to amuse his friends on the links in 1862. Whether or not he is responsible for other golfers adopting this new trend is not known, but they must have seen some merit in it, for Stocks's company later made a good business out of manufacturing golf bags. The popularity of such accouterments rose in the 1880s. Because of the primitive nature of these covers, few, if any, have survived today. They can, however, be seen in period photographs. While the advent of the club cover occurred in the 1880s they were not universally accepted for at least two decades. Period pho-

tos show caddies with unprotected bundles of clubs under arm as late as 1900.

The natural outgrowth of these early covers was a more advanced cover with new features. Leather was used to cover the base, so the bag could be rested on the ground without the fabric absorbing moisture. Leather was also added to the open end of the bag with a large circular metal ring allowing the opening to accept the insertion of clubs without difficulty. A handle was applied to the bag for easier carrying and this was ultimately joined by a shoulder strap. These deluxe covers began appearing in the early 1890s. The final parts would come in the form of the ball pocket and stays to keep the bag rigid in its length and prevent it from folding or collapsing. The ball pocket feature eventually grew to accept everything from balls to wardrobes of clothes.

By the mid 1890s the humble cloth cover had been supplanted by the new golf club bag made of leather. It was rigid with a strong base, had heavy

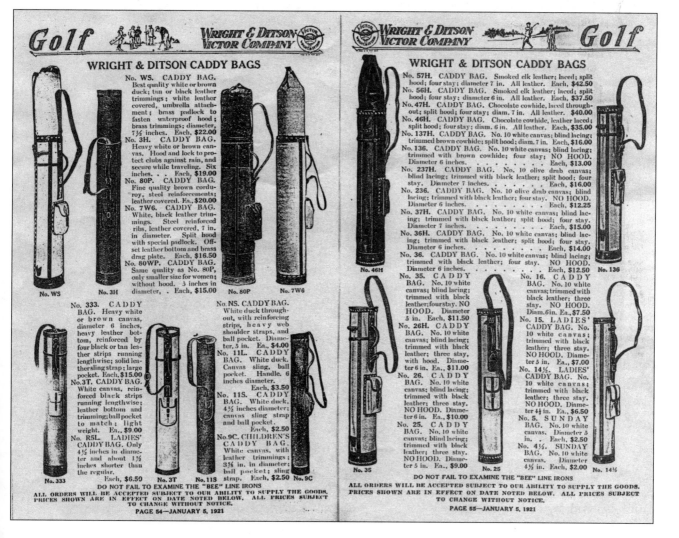

duty shoulder straps and handles and growing pockets. At a time when the sport was rapidly growing in both America and Great Britain, the large golf manufacturers like Spalding, MacGregor, Burke, Wright & Ditson, B.G.I. and Forgan were offering a complete line of golf requisites, including golf bags. Many of these are marked with their company names, although they were outsourced from saddlers and luggage manufacturers. Firms entering the golf bag manufacturing business came from the ranks of leather tanneries, luggage makers and golf grip manufacturers, as well as the golf club makers themselves.

By about 1910, the form of the modern bag was fairly well established. Most of these early bags were circular in shape, now often called quiver bags because of their resemblance to an archer's arrow-holder, though their size was growing from an opening diameter of three inches to four inches to six inches and larger. Eventually, the amount of leather in the larger bags made them so heavy that canvas sides were joined with leather top, bottom and straps to make a lighter weight kit.

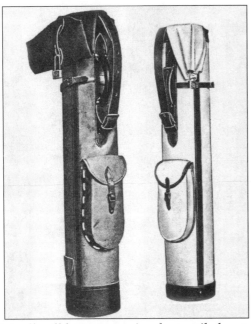

Virtually all bags were circular until about 1930 when oval bags entered the market. This was in reaction to the number of clubs being carried, often over 15. A circular bag large enough to accommodate this number of clubs was becoming barrel-sized and cumbersome. Oval or flat-shaped bags were easier to carry while walking four to five miles per round.

COLLECTING BAGS

So far, the collecting of golf bags has been primarily for the display of old clubs. The criteria for aesthetic display includes good preservation of the leather, the ability to stand upright, size—usually the smaller the better, and completeness of straps and accessories. Leather has a tendency to begin to rot after fifty years, especially when not conditioned with oil on a regular basis. The most prevalent problem with most old bags is that the carrying strap or its fixtures have broken. If they can stand upright they can still be used for static display, but a complete bag is more desirable and will be worth more over time.

Wicker bags were popular circa 1900. Original examples are quite scarce and bring prices between $600-1200. Be careful when purchasing as there are several good reproductions that were made during the 1970s and 1980s.

DESIRABILITY

In order of importance, collectors should seek these varieties of golf bags. Values are approximate.

CLOTH SACK OR CLUB COVER
PRE-1900. $500-1500
This earliest of all golf bags is very scarce. Examples extant today show they were usually made of brown sack cloth or canvas, finished at the opening and stenciled with the owners initials.

EARLY CLOTH BAG
CIRCA 1890-1900. $200-600
This type of bag was usually fitted with leather around the opening and at the base. They were fitted with one small ball pocket, a cinch strap, a carrying handle and a shoulder strap that was so lightweight it indicated that this sort of bag only carried six or seven clubs at most. Many early bags were made without stays to keep the barrel rigid, similar to the old cloth club cover.

THE "QUIVER" BAG
CIRCA 1895-1925.

3-INCH BAGS, ALL LEATHER	$300-800
4-INCH BAGS, ALL LEATHER	$150-400
4-INCH BAGS, CANVAS TRIMMED WITH LEATHER	$75-250
5-INCH BAGS, ALL LEATHER	$125-350
5-INCH BAGS, CANVAS TRIMMED WITH LEATHER	$50-200

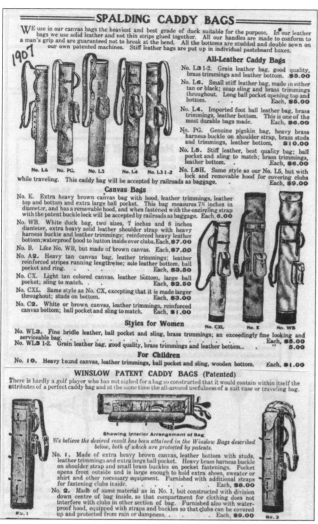

These larger bags reflect the increase in the number of clubs carried. Bags came in 6", 7" and 8" diameter sizes. Other details reflect on the quality of the bag when new. Different grades of leather were used in leather bags. At the upper end were materials like smoked elk hide and stiffer bag leathers. Softer kid leather and suede were good. Canvas or duck were usually at the lower end of the price range, although the tartan plaid canvas was the most expensive of the cloth bags.

This is the quintessential wood shafted golf club bag stereotypically included in any graphical representation of old golf. Smallest was the 3 inch bag. Most common wasthe 4 3/4" diameter bag. Relative age can often be seen in the size and style of pockets, the quality of straps and closure devices, rain/dust hood, metal base reinforcements, the use of side stays and decorative additions. These bags were popular for many years and it is often difficult to tell the age of the bag from its workmanship alone.

LARGE DIAMETER CIRCULAR BAG
CIRCA LATE TEENS AND 1920s ONWARD.

6-INCH BAGS, FULL LEATHER	$100-300
6-INCH BAGS, CANVAS TRIMMED WITH LEATHER	$40-175
7-INCH BAGS, FULL LEATHER	$90-250
7-8-INCH BAGS, CANVAS TRIMMED WITH LEATHER	$30-125

THE *Burke* GOLF COMPANY
NEWARK, OHIO, U.S.A.

No. 8 Smoked Elk Bag

An attractively designed bag of high grade smoked elkhide with mahogany leather trim. Padded fold handle. Padded sling. Nickel hardware. Rawhide bottom. Split hood.

6" size $40.00
7" size 45.00

No. 9 Spanish Leather Bag

Made of attractive green Dualtone Spanish leather, trimmed with mahogany strap leather with padded sling. Five steel stays. Nickel trim. Metal bottom, lock pocket and split hood. White rawhide lacing on ball pocket and up back of bag.

It is one of the most serviceable leather bags sold today.

6" size $25.00
7" size 30.00

Page Thirty-six

THE *Burke* GOLF COMPANY
NEWARK, OHIO, U.S.A.

No. 10 Cowhide Leather Bag

This is a very attractive bag of elephant grain cowhide trimmed in the same leather. It has a new padded fold handle and sling with nickel hardware and rawhide bottom. Split hood. This bag is not only an exceptionally serviceable one but very attractive in appearance.

6" size $25.00
7" size 30.00

No. 19 Chrome Tanned Leather Bag

A beautiful and serviceable leather bag—Burke's leader for years. Heavy mahogany leather, beautifully made up. Metal bottom. Split hood.

5" size, no hood $18.00
6" size, with hood 22.00
7" size, with hood 25.00

Page Thirty-seven

The J. Goudie Company of Glasgow (purchased by Leyland, Birmingham Rubber Company in 1920), a factory for golf equipment as early as the 1870s, was another pioneer in the manufacture of golf bags. Goudie was the first company to utilize the "zipp fastener" (zipper) in a golf bag, about 1925 and the oval shaped bag in about 1930.

Good quality bags had features like a wooden reinforcement plate in the bottom, a lock on the ball pocket flap and hood, a blocked or double blocked ball pocket and decorative leather trimming. Approximate values of these bags—$50-150.

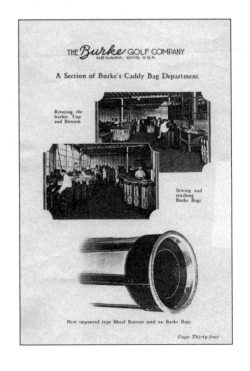

THE *Burke* GOLF COMPANY
NEWARK, OHIO, U.S.A.

A Section of Burke's Caddy Bag Department

Riveting the leather Top and Bottom

Sewing and stitching Burke Bags

New improved type Metal Bottom used on Burke Bags

Page Thirty-four

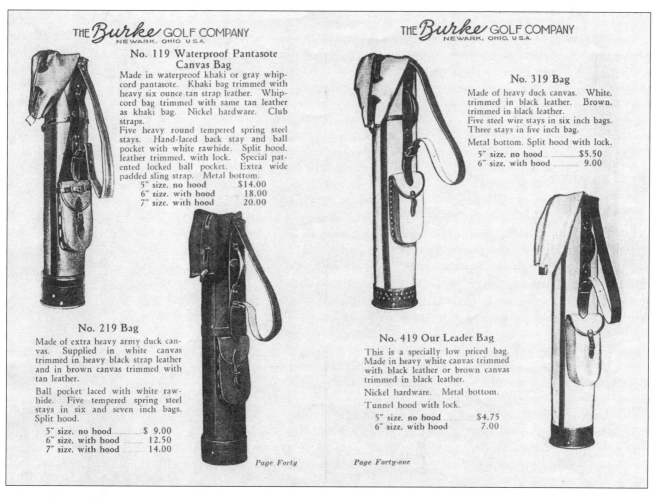

THE Burke GOLF COMPANY
NEWARK, OHIO U.S.A.

No. 119 Waterproof Pantasote Canvas Bag

Made in waterproof khaki or gray whip-cord pantasote. Khaki bag trimmed with heavy six ounce tan strap leather. Whip-cord bag trimmed with same tan leather as khaki bag. Nickel hardware. Club straps.

Five heavy round tempered spring steel stays. Hand-laced back stay and ball pocket with white rawhide. Split hood, leather trimmed, with lock. Special patented locked ball pocket. Extra wide padded sling strap. Metal bottom.

5" size, no hood	$14.00
6" size, with hood	18.00
7" size, with hood	20.00

No. 219 Bag

Made of extra heavy army duck canvas. Supplied in white canvas trimmed in heavy black strap leather and in brown canvas trimmed with tan leather.

Ball pocket laced with white rawhide. Five tempered spring steel stays in six and seven inch bags. Split hood.

5" size, no hood	$ 9.00
6" size, with hood	12.50
7" size, with hood	14.00

Page Forty

THE Burke GOLF COMPANY
NEWARK, OHIO, U.S.A.

No. 319 Bag

Made of heavy duck canvas. White, trimmed in black leather. Brown, trimmed in black leather.

Five steel wire stays in six inch bags. Three stays in five inch bag.

Metal bottom. Split hood with lock.

5" size, no hood	$5.50
6" size, with hood	9.00

No. 419 Our Leader Bag

This is a specially low priced bag. Made in heavy white canvas trimmed with black leather or brown canvas trimmed in black leather.

Nickel hardware. Metal bottom.

Tunnel hood with lock.

5" size, no hood	$4.75
6" size, with hood	7.00

Page Forty-one

Many whole bags and portions of golf bags were granted patents. Unusual patent bags include bags wider at the base than the top to provide more stability while standing, bags with spikes or supports to give similar stability and bags with uniquely shaped pockets and club holding accessories.

CLUB CARRIERS

A second group of club carrying devices includes all items not classified as golf bags. There are dozens of these implements including club caddie stands, club holders, straps, stands, rings and satchels.

AUTOMATIC CADDIES

In the 1890s and early 1900s several inventors tried to perfect a golf bag with bipod legs in an effort to dispense with the services of a caddie. Most sought-after of this variety of carrier equipment is Osmond's Patent. It is the most widely known, but there are another half dozen of similar age and stature that appeal to collectors.

OSMOND'S PATENT	$700-2000
OTHERS - SIMILAR	$500-1500

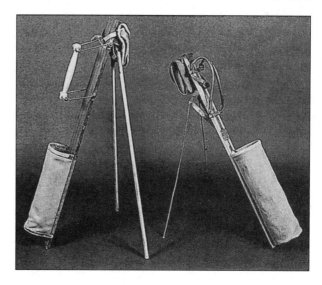

SIMPLE CARRIERS

Another variety of carrier was a simple hand grip with brackets for a half dozen clubs. It usually consisted of a handle with clips to hold clubs by their shafts. The hand grip took the form of a leather handle, a strap or wood bar.

CLUB STANDS

Club stands catered to the golfer who never saw the need for a bag and continued to carry clubs under his arm. When making a shot, instead of laying clubs in the fairway grass, a stand kept the grips in the air, avoiding dampness. Several types of spiked stands were sold. The golfer would stick the pointed end in the ground and rest the club handles in a retaining bar or ring. Another such-device was a three-legged tripod, which supported clubs much like soldiers stacked muskets.

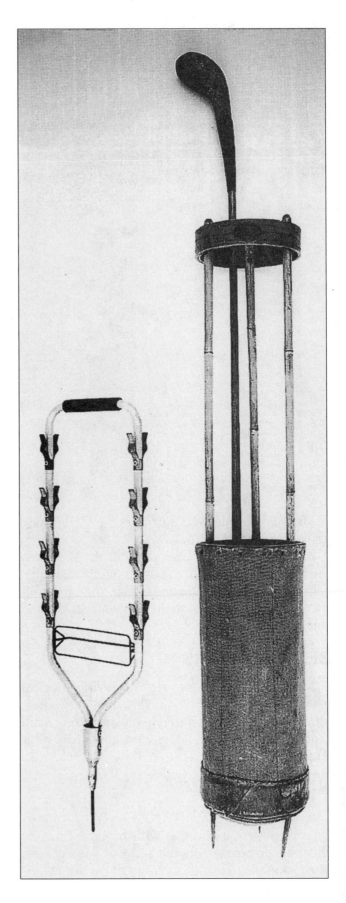

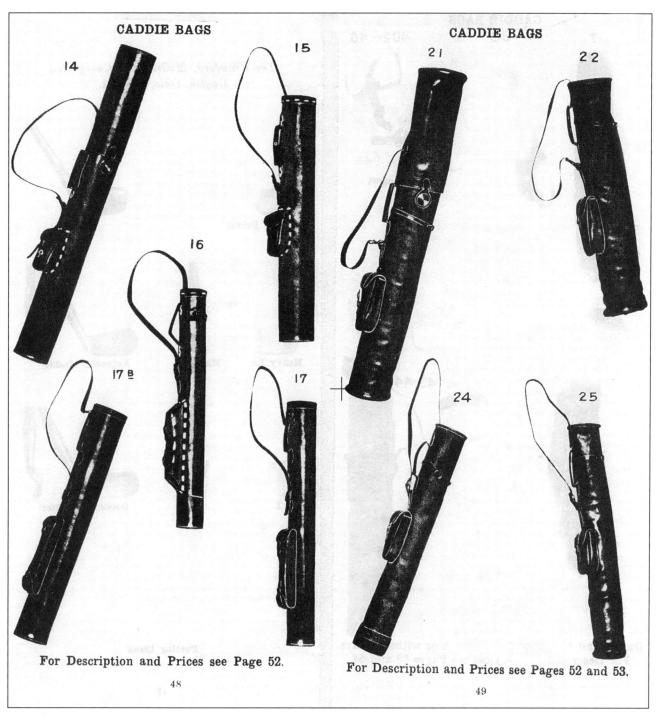

CADDIE BAGS

14 15 16 17 B 17

For Description and Prices see Page 52.

48

CADDIE BAGS

21 22 24 25

For Description and Prices see Pages 52 and 53.

49

Bags from the Mc Gregor Catalogue 1913

D&M "LUCKY DOG" GOLF BAGS

No. 16. An attractive six inch stayless bag of pearl gray whipcord with black trimmings. Rubber top and bottom. Zipper fastenings on ball pocket. Cushioned sling strap, "Easy Grip" handle. Price. $7.50

No. 3L. An extra smart looking 5 inch bag especially designed for ladies. Made of water proofed striped fabric, with red, blue or green trim. Has three metal stays. Zipper ball pocket. Cushioned sling strap. "Easy Grip" handle. Price $7.00

No. 3. Made of khaki colored water proofed whipcord. Has wide laced cuff of tan leather. Rubber top and bottom. Zipper fastening on ball pocket. A splendid 5 inch, three stay bag Price 6.00

No. 2. A 6 inch three stay bag of rubberized water proofed fabric. Hood with eyelets, zipper fastening on ball pocket Rubber top, metal bottom. Choice of light grey or tan. Price 6.00

No. 11. A light and neat looking 5 inch three stay bag made of water proofed grey fabric with black trimmings. Wide cuff Rubber top, metal bottom. Zipper fastening on ball pocket. Price 5.00

No. 1. Made of water proofed fabric with brown leatherette trim. A three stay 5 inch bag, with zipper fastening on ball pocket. Cushioned sling strap. Price . 4.00

No. 0. An excellent bag for the price. Made of covert cloth, leatherette trim. Has three metal stays. Padded sling strap. Buckle fastening on ball pocket. 5 inch bag. Price 3.00

No. 6. A stayless 5 inch Sunday bag made of khaki canvas. Strap and buckle fastening on ball pocket. Wide web sling strap, and "Easy Grip" handle. Price 1.50

[41]

No. 10. A seven inch stayless bag, beautifully made of genuine dark tan elk. Hood tucks inside when not in use. Ball and utility pockets and hood have zipper fasteners. Equipped with cushioned sling strap and "Easy Grip" handle. A bag that will give lasting service and satisfaction. $35.00

No. 27. Identical in style to the No. 10 bag but without the utility pocket. Made of genuine black or tan cowhide. Zipper fasteners on hood and ball pocket. A high grade, seven inch stayless, all-leather bag .30.00

No. 26. An all-leather, stayless bag in six inch size. Made of black cowhide. Ball pocket and hood equipped with zipper fasteners. Cushioned sling strap and "Easy Grip" handle. Price 27.50

No. 7K. Made of heavy pearl gray whipcord, black leather trimmings. Reinforced hard rubber rings around top and at bottom which prevent scarring of clubs and marring anything with which bag comes in contact. Has large utility pocket, ball pocket and hood. Zipper fasteners. Cushioned sling strap, and "Easy Grip" handles. A "De Luxe", seven inch, stayless bag. Price . $20.00

No. 8. An unusual bag for service and appearance. Made of strong tan basket-weave fabric, trimmed with dark tan cowhide. Zipper fasteners on ball pocket and hood. Rubber top and bottom. Reinforced with three metal stays. Six inch size 15.00

No. 7. Similar in construction and material to the No. 7K, except for strap and buckle fastenings in place of zippers on hood, ball and utility pockets. Made of heavy pearl gray whipcord. Rubber top and bottom. A high grade 7 inch stayless bag. $15.00

No. 5. A very attractive four stay, 6 inch bag. Made of heavy water proofed fabric with wide black and orange stripes. Rubber top and bottom. Wide laced cuffs. Zipper fastenings on pocket and hood. Cushioned sling strap. "Easy Grip" handle 10.00

[40]

CHAPTER 17

HOW AND WHERE TO PURCHASE GOLF COLLECTIBLES

Buying and selling at a GCS annual meeting.

KNOW MORE THAN THE ANTIQUE DEALER

One of the most frequently asked questions from beginning collectors who purchased the first edition of my book was: "Where can these items be purchased?" Most collectors and curious golfers begin with garage sales, flea markets and antique stores. Unless you are very knowledgeable, you will be disappointed with your purchases. People selling items at garage sales, flea markets and antique stores usually have very limited knowledge or just enough to be dangerous to you, the beginner.

I get e-mail and phone inquiries by the hundreds telling me of items touted as very rare, owned by "Walter Hagen" or "Gene Sarazen" and, especially, "Robert T. Jones, Jr." clubs with coated steel shafts being offered as hickory shafted clubs.

Make sure the seller has indisputable documentation (provenience or pedigree) to accompany collectibles allegedly having been the property of a famous golfer. There are many misrepresented Arnold Palmer, Jack Nicklaus, Bobby Jones, Gene Sarazen, etc., items being offered at lofty prices. One of the most common is the "Calamity Jane Putter" that Bobby Jones made so famous. I am offered one of the "Original Six" 10-15 times a year! And to my knowledge, Arnold Palmer has never sold or given any of his putters to anyone, yet, I get calls and inquiries on a regular basis regarding his putters being offered for sale.

Unless you like being taken advantage of, you should first: join a golf collector's association or society (listed in Chapter 2), buy a good reference book (you're on the right track by purchasing this one), see the bibliography and contact the contributors. Then, when you are armed with more knowledge than the garage sale, flea market and antique store merchants, you can start having some fun.

ORDERING FROM MAIL ORDER CATALOGUES

The most logical sources from which to buy would be dealers, like myself, who publish catalogues on a regular basis. Jeff Ellis and I are the only club and ball dealers publishing catalogues on a regular basis. Jeff publishes 3 or 4 yearly, while the author publishes monthly. Leo Kelly, Old Chicago Golf Shop, is on the World Wide Web. George Lewis, Golfiana, publishes 2 or 3 extensive book catalogues a year, and there are several dealer/collectors who send lists periodically.

Furjanic, Ellis, Kelly and Lewis are among the most respected authorities in the hobby, and treat customers with respect, answer their inquiries and offer return priviledges on all items. You can order confidently from these dealers as they are committed to the hobby and to the clients they serve.

WHERE TO REACH OUT AND TOUCH THE COLLECTIBLES

There are several antique golf stores, one at the Lodge, Pebble Beach, CA; Scottsdale, AZ; Cincinnati, OH, as well as others scattered about the USA. You can make an appointment to visit the author's offices where you can brouse through thousands of wood shaft clubs and other collectibles. Jeff Ellis, Leo Kelly and George Lewis would also welcome you on an appointment basis.

Gatherings of golf associations and societies (Chapter 2) give collectors the opportunity to meet to buy, sell and exhibit their collectibles. The Golf Collector's Society and British Golf Collectors Society have numerous meetings, swap and trade shows, as well as tournaments where golf with hickory shafted clubs is played.

The BGCS' best attended gathering is during the British Open. "Boot" sales, hickory tournaments, and breaking bread together are the highlights.

The GCS has their national annual meeting in the fall, and approximately 500 members gather to play golf with hickories, buy, sell and trade collectibles, attend the annual dinner and generally have a great time meeting and making friends.

The GCS is divided into 10 regions, and usually, each region has at least one meeting each year. For example, Region 4, (TX, OK, NM, AR & LA) has its annual hickory tournament, show/sale and dinner in the spring of every year in Irving, TX. For the convenience of the collectors, Chuck Furjanic, Inc. also holds a major live auction sale that same weekend. About 100 collectors and dealers attend the two events.

ACQUIRING THROUGH AUCTIONS

Auctions are another source to acquire collectibles, but the "Buyer Beware" adage is in force here. You either must be very knowledgeable or have someone knowledgeable represent you at these sales. Keep in mind, a 10-15% buyers fee is added to the purchase price of each lot.

Chuck Furjanic, Inc., Sotheby's, Christie's, Phillips, Bonham's and Pacific Books conduct live auctions on a regular basis. There are several dealers and collectors who conduct mail sales. Roger Gilchrist conducts three to four absentee auctions each year offering paper and autographed items. Golf's Golden Years, (David Berkowitz) conducts three to four absentee auctions each year offering memorabilia, balls, tees and other golf collectibles.

Chuck Furjanic, Inc. is the only auction house in the USA to conduct two live sales and two absentee sales each year. The catalogues are very helpful to the bidder, whether a beginner or expert. Estimates, indicating the range between wholesale and retail, are listed for each lot. Good descriptions, items rated using the 10-point grading standards (Chapter 3), and numerous photos of the collectibles offered, aid the collector to submit bids confidently.

Chuck Furjanic, Inc. offers absentee bidders, in both live and absentee sales, the courtesy of a "no reasons asked" return priviledge if the collectibles purchased in the auction are not satisfactory. Check with other auction houses on their return policies.

The biggest advantages in buying at auction is attending the live sales of Chuck Furjanic, Inc., Sotheby's, Phillips, etc. and actually being able to view and handle a vast assortment of collectibles, from all areas of the sport, in one place. Rare and seldom offered collectibles are more likely to be offered through major auctions than through dealer listings, the internet or shows. You will also be able to meet and consult with experts and other collectors in attendance. The value of hands-on viewing and inspecting the collectibles, meeting and making new friends with your same interests, and acquiring items at your desired price, can be one of the most rewarding experiences of your life.

Buying over the internet can be costly and dangerous to your collecting health. If you must use the internet, buy from established dealers you know and trust or are recommended to you by dealers or collectors you trust. I put the internet, and internet auctions, in the same category as garage sales, flea markets and antique stores.

SELLING THROUGH AUCTIONS

Auctions are a convenient vehicle for dealers and collectors to sell their collectibles. Established auction houses have extensive mailing lists of clients to whom your collectibles will be exposed, hopefully generating top dollar and fair market value. Most auction houses follow similar guidelines:

Seller's fees ranging from 5% to 20% depending upon the value of the consignment and the value of individual lots.

Consigned items should be in the auctioneer's hands at least 60 days prior to the sale. Proper cataloguing, photographs, printing and mailing the catalogues takes time.

There may be charges to the consignor for unsold lots (listing fees), photography, insurance and storage.

Settlement for payment of sold lots is usually between 30 and 45 days after the sale closes. Items must be paid for and shipped, and items returned may be sent to under bidders.

Depending upon the arrangements made with the auction company, sales may be credited towards purchase of items in that auction. This is a convenient way for the collector to sell duplicates and acquire items for their collection without the exchange of funds.

BIDDING BY REPRESENTATION AT AUCTIONS

In the event you cannot attend the sale yourself, but would like to place bids in a Sotheby's or other British auction houses, there are several dealers who can "represent" you at the sale. Normal procedure is to phone you after the lots of interest have been inspected and discuss the condition and probable value. The dealer will charge a fee for his time and phone expenses.

CHUCK FURJANIC, INC.
Golf Collectibles
P O BOX 165892   IRVING, TX 75016
1-800-882-4825 * 1-972-594-7802 * FAX 972-257-1785
eMail Address: furjanic@onramp.net
Web site: http://www.golfforallages.com
Specializing in Wood Shaft Golf Clubs
Buy . Sell . Trade . Auctions . Appraisals

BIDDING CONTRACT

Chuck Furjanic is hereby contracted to represent

Joe Public, 123 Main St, Anytown, USA 12345

as a bidding agent at

BONHAM'S & DOYLE AUCTION, NYC, OCT. 5, 1999

Fees will include the following services:

1. Inspection of lots
2. Evaluation of lots
3. Communication of the above information before the auction.

Fees are as follows:

1. Lots purchased below the auctioneer's low estimate 15%
2. Lots purchased at or above the auctioneer's low estimate 12%
3. Lots purchased at one bidding increment above agreed amount 10%

All lots purchased at this sale must be picked up and paid for within 10 days of the sale.

By my signature, I agree with the above terms:

X_____Date_____

X_____Date_____

ABSENTEE BIDDING

Auction houses will accept absentee bids. be sure to check with each individual company in regards to their return policy before placing your bids. there is no fee for this service, and the auctioneer will execute your bids as if you were at the sale in person. For example: You submit a bid of $500. on lot #123. when the auctioneer opens lot #123 on the floor, it will be at one increment over the next highest bid (usually 10%) and commences onward until the highest bidder is acknowledged. If the highest bid, other than yours, is $300, the auctioneer opens lot #123 at $350. on your behalf. If no one overbids, the lot is yours at $350., not $500. On the other hand, if a bidder in attendance (live bidder) bids $400., the auctioneer witll the bid $450. on your behalf, as though you were actually in the room. If the live bidder then bids $500. the auctineer will honor his bid, and your $500. bid is "out" as all ties between live and absentee bidders are awarded to the live bidder.

Be very careful when bidding on auction lots based on catalogue descreptions. Many cataloguers assume you will inspect the lots in person, or have someone represent you, and lot descriptions can be very vague such as: "Seven wood shaft putter, a niblick and four others, (12)" or "thirteen steel shaft putters along with 22 wood shaft irons, putters and woods in two bags. (35)".

Today, most aution companies have their sales on the internet. Chuck Furjanic, Inc. provides color phottos to accompany the lists of lots on his internet site: http://www.golfforallages.com

---

Absentee Bid Form

Please read the terms of the sale before you submit bids.
Please remember to sign the Absentee Bid Form.
Please bid by lot numbers only and in WHOLE dollar amounts

MAIL BIDS TO: CHUCK FURJANIC, P O BOX 165892 IRVING, TX 75016

Lot #	BID	Lot #	BID

Name_____
ADDRESS_____
CITY_____ST_____ZIP_____
PHONE O_____H_____
Please charge my purchases and ship immediately!
MC/VISA_____EXP_____
Signature_____
If necessary, please increase my bid(s) by an additional
10%_____ 20%_____ 30%_____

If you choose to charge your purchases using MC or VISA, a processing fee of 3% will be added to your invoice.

---

524 FIVE INTERESTING ITEMS including a PGA "Hole in One" charm, 2 half dollar size buttons with lady golfer and caddy, a black boy "Golden Shred" pin and a 1933 "National Public Links Championship, Portland, Or" blue pin. (5) $90-175

525 AN UNIQUE PAPER WEIGHT of a golf bag, shoes and balls on a red cover book measuring 4 1/2" X 3". A very nice collectible! $225-400

526 WALTER HAGEN WALL PLAQUE circa 1920's from a wall display of Walter Hagen clubs. Oval shaped measuring 6" X 5" and depicting two plus four clad golfers and a caddie. $75-125

527 A BLANKET WITH THE PGA EMBLEM. Approximately 5 X 4 feet in deep navy blue and commemorates the "Northern California PGA Junior Championship". Looks circa 1960's. $90-175

528 "ANTHOLOGY OF THE GOLF BALL". 12 replica balls with the history of Worthington golf balls, 1899-1990. $55-100

529 "ANTHOLOGY OF THE GOLF BALL". 12 replica balls with the history of Worthington golf balls, 1899-1990. $55-100

530 TWO "ANTHOLOGY OF THE GOLF BALL". 12 replica balls in each Anthology with the history of Worthington golf balls, 1899-1990. (2) $110-200

531 THREE MASTERS SERIES BADGES. 1977, Watson, 1992, Couples and 1994, Olazabal. (3) $120-200

532 FIVE MASTERS SERIES BADGES. 1992, Couples and 1994, Olazabal, 1993 Monday practice round and two 1995 Tuesday practice round. (5) $90-150

533 ST. ANDREWS OLD COURSE MAP "Surveyed & Depicted by A. MacKenzie, Golf Course Architect, March 1924". 27" X 13 1/2' and nicely framed. $190-375

534 A PEWTER CIGARETTE BOX circa 1920's with a MESH patern ball and crossed clubs on the lid. 4 X 6 1/2 inches with a hinged lid. $150-275

535 A WILSON PUTTING DISC in the original circa 1920's colorful box. Putting Disc is MINT NEW, box is G-5. $60-100

536 A CYLINDRICAL CIGARETTE HOLDER, silver plated, with a 1 3/4" opening and lid. The Cylinder is 4 1/2" tall with a false bottom 1 3/4". Engraved "Mohawk Golf Club, 1930". A nice item for the desk that can hide small articles underneath! G-8+ $120-200

537 COWBOY BOOT GOLF SHOES. A pair of 8D white cowboy boots with 5 steel spikes in each heel and 6 spikes in the sole. Only in Texas! $50-100

538 THREE PEWTER PLATES. 83rd U S Open, Oakmont, 1982 PGA Southern Hills and 1991 U S Open, Hazeltine, Payne Stewart's first Open victory. (3)$150-300

539 FOUR MINT PACKETS OF TEES from 1937. Five large tees in each match book container stamped "The Canada Wood Specialty Co., Ltd. Orillia, Ont." They come in the original mailing box with return stamp and canceled 4¢ Canadian Stamp. The 1937 stamp dates the box. Tees are G-10. (5) $60-100

540 A STEREOSCOPE VIEWER with one card. "Underwood & Underwood, NY" with patent dates of 1902, 03, & 04 stamped on the bottom. "Mercury Stereoscope, Trade Mark" on the metal part of the viewer. Near Mint. $60-140

541 GOLFER'S PAL WRIST SCORE KEEPER. Looks like a watch and is in the original box. G-10 $75-150

542 TWO GREAT SMOKER'S ITEMS. An ash tray with wood base and golf clubs in bag and a tobacco humidor with golf bag and clubs. (2) $350-550

543 TWO CANVAS GOLF BAGS with leather trim. One from the 1920's in nice condition, however the bottom is broken (can be repaired) and a canvas bag from the 1950's (2) $30-60

544 A GOLF CLUB LAMP. Driver and ball on a two level wood base and a nice beige and nice shade. Much nicer than the lamp offered for $125. by British Links. $75-140

545 A PINEHURST PUTTER BOY SUNDIAL made of copper. 4 1/2 inch round sundial base and putter boy stands 5 1/2 inches tall. $75-150

546 ICE BUCKET WITH GOLF BALL LID. Circa 1950's with red leather trim. Comes with "Ice Cold Without Ice" plastic golf balls "Filled in England with Drinking Water". One dozen "balls" in box. (2) $75-125

547 1971 RYDER CUP BLUE BLAZER belonging to Peter Oosterhuis. An all wool jacket made by Seegan of Hanover Square. Europe Ryder Cup patch on the pocket. $400-600

548 TWO RYDER CUP NECK TIES belonging to Peter Oosterhuis. Both are brown and embroidered with Ryder Cup Trophies. Circa 1970's. (2) $50-100

549 TWO RYDER CUP NECK TIES belonging to Peter Oosterhuis. One red, the other blue and having the Ryder Cup Crossed Flags. Circa 1970's. (2) $50-100

550 TWO RYDER CUP NECK TIES belonging to Peter Oosterhuis. One red with Ryder Cup Trophies, the other blue embroidered with the Ryder Cup patch design that matches the jacket. Circa 1970's. (2) $50-100

551 A VERY SCARCE SHIELD FACE SLOTTED HOSEL MID-IRON. "S C 1 Superior Mid-iron" and "Pat'd May 14, 1918" on back. All original with a marked shaft. See the 1917 Macgregor catalogue reprint. G-8 $190-325

552 A MACGREGOR "T-2" SHIELD FACE "Tomahawk Brand Iron". Original stamped shaft. G-7 $90-160

553 THREE ODD FACE IRONS in above average condition. A Macgregor "XA 1/2 Mashie", a Gibson M-N and a Royal Mashie. (3) $125-200

554 HENDRY & BISHOP DREADNOUGHT NIBLICK with an oversized head. G-7 $75-125

**THANK YOU
FOR BIDDING**

**OUR NEXT AUCTION
IS SCHEDULED FOR**

APRIL 1, 2000

25

Chuck Furjanic, Inc. proudly presents a
GOLF COLLECTIBLES AUCTION

Linda Craft 1939-1993

Featuring the

LINDA CRAFT ESTATE

and Other Consignments

Sunday
May 7, 1995
10:00 AM

To be held at the
DoubleTree Guest Suites
DFW Airport
4650 W Airport Freeway
Irving, Tx. 75062
Just 5 minutes from DFW Airport

Lot viewing: Double Tree Guest Suites

May 6, from Noon to 9:00 pm   **May 7, from 8:00 am to 9:30 am**

Lots for the Mail Bid Auction Sale closing
May 15, 1995 are also included.

SELLING THROUGH INTERNET AUCTIONS

There are numerous internet auctions through which you may list and sell your items, many without a fee. Keep in mind, the internet auction companies only provide the vehicle to offer your collectibles and inform you of the high bidders. You are responsible for collecting the money, being sure the funds are "good" (many bidders want to pay by credit card or with personal checks), physically shipping the items and being prepared for damage to the collectibles while en route. You must also make provisions for returns if your high bidder is not satisfied.

Selling items personally and depositing funds (conducting business) will require you to file IRS Schedule "C" (Profit or Loss from business). If you make sales to buyers within your own state (and your state has a sales tax law), you must have a license to collect sales tax.

Thanks to Bob Gowland, formerly of Phillips, Chester, England, and currently conducting auctions for Bonham's, Southport, England, for contributing information which has been incorporated in this chapter.

BIBLIOGRAPHY

Berdock, Bruce and Baier, Michael
A Century of Golf Cards, 1993
Published in Canada

Biocini, Paul
Signature Golf Ball Collector's Guide, 1995
Paul Biocini, Modesto, CA

British Golf Collectors Society
Through The Green

Christie's, Glasgow, Scotland
Auction Catalogues

Cooper, J. M.
Early U. S. Golf Clubs by Spalding & Bros. 1994
J. M. Cooper, Kannapolis, NC

Donovan, Richard E. and Murdoch, Joseph S. F.
The Game of Golf and The Printed Word 1566-1985, 1988
Castalio Press, Endicott, NY

Furjanic, Chuck
Auction Catalogues
Golf Collectibles, Irving, TX

Furjanic, Chuck
Monthly Catalogues 1989 to Present
Golf Collectibles, Irving, TX

Ellis, Jeffery B.
The Clubmaker's Art, 1997
Zephyr Productions Inc.

Georgiady, Peter
Compendium of British Clubmakers, 1994
Airlie Hall Press, Greensboro, NC

Georgiady, Peter
Wood Shafted Value Guide For 1995
Airlie Hall Press, Greensboro, NC

Georgiady, Peter
Wood Shafted Value Guide For 2000
Airlie Hall Press, Greensboro, NC

Georgiady, Peter
Collecting Antique Golf Clubs, 1996
Airlie Hall Press, Greensboro, NC

Georgiady, Peter and Kelly, Leo M., Jr.
Quick Reference Guide to Antique Golf Club Names, 1993
Old Chicago Golf Shop, Matteson, IL

Gilchrist, Roger E.
Gilchrist's Guide to Golf Collectibles, 1998

Golf Collectors Society
The Bulletin

Hamilton, Charles
Collecting Autographs and Manuscripts, 1993
Modoc Press, Santa Monica, CA

Jackson, Alan F.
The British Professional Golfers, 1887-1930, A Register, 1994
Grant's Books, Worchestershire, England

Kelly, Leo M., Jr.
Antique Golf Ball Reference & Price Guide, 1993
Old Chicago Golf Shop, Richton Park, IL

Kennedy, Patrick
Golf Club Trade Marks, 1984
Thistle Books, S. Burlington, VT

Oliver's
Auction Catalogues
Kennebunk, ME

Olman, John M. and Morton
The Encyclopedia of Golf Collectibles, 1985
Books Americana, Florence, AL

Olman, John and Morton
Olman's Guide to Golf Antiques, 1992
Market Street Press, Cincinnati, OH

Paris, Don
The B.G.I. Company.
self published 1999

Phillips, Chester England
Auction Catalogues

Smedley, Philip and Berdock, Bruce
The Price Guide to Golf Cards, Part I: Tobacco Cards 1994
Published in Canada

Smedley, Philip and Berdock, Bruce
The Price Guide to Golf Cards, Part 2: Non-Tobacco Cards, 1995
Published in Canada

Sotheby's, London, England
Auction Catalogues

Sporting Antiquities Auction Catalogues
Melrose, MA

Sprung, Shirley and Jerry
Decorative Golf Collectibles 1991
Glentiques, LTD., Coral Springs, FL

CONTRIBUTORS

Chuck Furjanic
PO Box 165892
Irving, TX 75062
972-594-7802
972-257-1785 FAX
http://www.golfforallages.com
Furjanic@directlink.net

Wayne Aaron
9950 Huntcliff Trace
Atlanta, GA 30350
770-993-3611

Dr. Hank Alperin
1450 Winter St.
Augusta, GA 30904
706-738-7317

Archie Baird
Greyfriars
Aberlady, East Lothian
Scotland EH32 0RB

Paul Biocini
4505 Bluff Creek Dr.
Modesto, CA 95355
209-527-1162

Bob Burkett
Old Sport Golf
4297 NE Expressway Access Rd.
Doraville, GA 30340
404-493-4344

Jim "Spalding Man" Cooper
1110 Oklahoma St.
Kannapolis, NC 28083
704-782-2493

Lee Crist
109 Woodland Terrace
Duncanville, PA 16635
814-693-9636

Mike Daniels
Gifts For The Golfer
23 Wilshire Dr.
Albany, NY 12205
518-869-7103

Art DiProspero
Highlands Golf
P.O. Box 300
Watertown, CT 06795
860-274-4203

Mark Emerson
4040 Poste Lane Rd.
Columbus, OH 43221
614-771-7272

Jim Espinola
PO Box 54
Dracut, MA 01826
508-459-7165

Keith Foster
5615 Old Poag Rd.
Edwardsville, IL 62035

Pete Georgiady
Airlie Hall Press
PO Box 981
Kernersville, NC 27285
336-996-7836
ahp@greensboro.com

Roger Gilchrist
PO Box 969
Freeport, FL 32439
850-835-1429

Johnny Henry
PO Box 776
Ennis, TX 75020
972-875-7360

Gary Hilgers
14921 White Oak Dr.
Burnsville, MN 55337
612-891-1270

Roger Hill
2875 Cascade Springs. Dr. NE
Grand Rapids, MI 49546
616-285-6130

Tom & Karen Kuhl
No address available

Bob Kuntz
PO Box 300
Dayton, OH 45420
937-228-7767

George Lewis, Golfiana
PO Box 291
Mamaroneck, NY 10543
914-835-5100
www.golfiana.com

Bob Gowland
Bonham's
Southport, England

Gary Hilgers
14921 White Oak Dr.
Burnsville, MN 55337
binkgolf@aol.com

Ralph Livingston
831 Freemont NW. Apt. #4
Grand Rapids, MI 49504
616-451-6020

Forrest Mc Connell
2740 Fernway Dr.
Montgomery, AL 36111
334-263-6146

Dick Moore
640 E. Liberty Ave.
Girard, OH 44420
216-545-2832

Norm Moreau
12A Mary Gapper Cres.
Richmond Hill, Ontario
Canada L4C 7L9
905-737-8629

Joseph Murdoch
Cathedral Village
600 E. Cathedral Rd. #G307
Philadelphia, PA 19128
215-984-8897

Gordon Page
34643 Sunward Loop
Zephyr Hills, FL 33541
1-800-859-9842
gpage@innet.com

Don Paris
98 Sterling Dr.
Kensington, CT 06037
860-828-5170

Will Roberto
381 Hubbard St.
Glastonbery, CT 06063
1-888-653-8666

Jerry Sprung and Glentiques, Ltd.
PO Box 8807
Coral Springs, FL 33075
305-344-9856

INDEX

A

Aaron, Tommy 245
Adams, Douglas 301
Aitken, Alex 59
Allan, John 59
Allaway 185
Allen, Peter 285
All-My-Tee 272
American Golfer 373
American Tobacco Co. 345
Ampco Mfg Co. 60
Anderson 27
Anderson & Blythe 60
Anderson Of Anstruther, Scotland
.... 62, 64
Anderson, Anderson & Anderson 60
Anderson, D. & Sons 60
Anderson, Robert 63
Aoki, Isao 258
Aonian 313
Ariel 193
Armour, Tommy 245, 258, 285
Army & Navy 65
Art Deco 328
Art Deco Co. 324
Arthur Wood & Son 313
Ashford, W & G 65
Ashtray 329
Auchterlonie 187
Auchterlonie, D & W 66
Auchterlonie, Laurie 245
Auchterlonie, Tom 66
Avon Deluxe 199
Avon Double Arm Tee 272
Ayres, F. H. 67
Azinger, Paul 258

B

B. Morris 348
Bakspin Series Irons 113
Ballesteros, Seve 245, 258
Ball Molds 182
Ball Washers 364
Ball-face Irons 106
Baltimore 36
Bamberger, Michael 285
Banner Irons 106
Barber, Miller 258
Barnes, James M. 258, 285
Baugh, Laura 245
Bayer, George 245
Bell, Peggy Kirk 248

Benny Putter 33
Berg, Patty 245, 258
Berlyn, Fexis S. 345
Beveridge, James 69
Biscuit Tin 374
Black Bug Dimple 193
Blackheath Golfers 301
Blacksmith 25
Blacksmith Made 69
Blue Bird 195
Bobby Tees 272
Bolt, Tommy 245
Bookends 375
Boomer, Percy 285
Boros, Julius 245, 258
Braddell 70
Braid, James 259
Brand, Charles 71
Brewer, Gay 259
Brick-face Irons 107
Bridgeport Gun & Implement Co. 71
British Amateur Championship ... 335
British Open Medal 336
Brock, Charles Edmond 301
Bromford 201
Bronze Medals 335
Brown, Kenneth 285
Brown, Michael J. 302
Brown's Rake Iron 35
Browning, R. H. K. 285
Bruce Cored Center 207
Buhrke Co., R. H. 74
Burbank 197
Burke 50-50 199
Burke, Billy 246
Burke, Jack 246
Burke Mfg. Co. 76
Bussey 35
Bussey & Co. 80
Butchart-Nichol's 81

C

Caddie Badges 367
Calamity Jane Putter 135, 139
Cambridge 326
Canadian Open Gold Medal 336
Cann & Taylor 81
Capon Heaton 191
Carltonware 313
Carrick, F. & A. 83
Casper, Billy 246, 259
Cassidy, J. L. 83
Cast-Iron Doorstops 379

Certified 205
Chamberlain, J. 302
Chemico 187
Chemico Triumph 207
Cherokee Putter 108
Chikaramachi 314
Churchman 345
Cigarette Box 329
Cigarette Case 354
Clark, J. & D. 83
Clark, Robert 285
Clincher Cross 212
Cochran, A. & Stobbs, J. 285
Cochrane's Ltd. 84
Cocktail Set 324
Cocktail Shaker 355
Colbert, Jim 259
College Silks 345
Collett, Glenna 259, 285
Condie, Robert 85
Cooper, Harry 246
Cope's Golfers 348
Copeland Spode 314
Cornish, G. & Whitten, R. 286
Cotton, Henry 259, 286
Country Club Cigar Tin 374
Couples, Fred 259
Cousins, Geoffrey 286
Cox, Wiffy 246
Craigie, J. & W. 86
Cran Cleek 34
Cran Irons 144
Cresant 314
Crescent Colonel 212
Crombie, Charles 302
Cruickshank , Bobby 246
Cruickshank Steel Tees 272
Crystal Humidor 327
Cudahy's 197

D

Daly, John 259
Dante, J. & Elliott, L. 286
Darby Flyer 199
Darbyshire, L. Claughton 2 86
Darwin, Bernard 286
Davies, Peter 286
De Hooch, Peter 302
De Passe Mfg. Co. 328
Decanter 323
Deep Grooved 31
Demaret, Jimmy 246, 259, 286
Dent, Jim 259

Desktop Thermometer 379
Diamond Chick 191, 195
Didrikson, (Zaharias), Babe
................................247, 252, 267, 296
Diegel, Leo 259
Dint Patent Golf Co., Ltd. 86
Dobereiner, Peter 286
Dollman, J. 302
Dollman, John Charles 302, 303
Dome Metal Tees 277
Donaldson, J. 86
Donovan & Murdock 287
Donruss 346
Double Waterfall 34
Douglas Sand Tee Gun 273
Doulton 314, 316
Down-it 486 Putter 109
Draper-Maynard 199
Duncan, G. & Darwin, B. 287
Dunlop 199, 220
Dunlop Man 378
Dunn, John D. 87
Dunn, Seymour 87
Dunn, Willie 87
Dunn's Record Ball 187
Duplex 34
Duval, David 259
Dysart, Fife, Scotland 134

E

Earle, L. 303
Elder, Lee 247
Eggcup - Sterling 355
Els, Ernie 259
Eterna Tee 273
Eureka 189
Evans, Chick 259, 287

F

Fairway 205
Faldo, Nick 260
Faroid 193
Farrell, Johnny 247, 260
Feather Balls 183
Finch 185
Flaherty, Tom 287
Flash 205
Fleck, Jack 247
Flower, Clement 303
Floyd, Ray 260
Forbes, Bart 303
Forgan, Andrew 88
Forgan, Robert 88
Fork Spliced 132
Forked Splice Woods 74
Forrester, G. 91

Foster Brothers 92
Foulis, James 92
Frost, A.B. 304

G

G & S Golf Tee 273
Gassiat 35
Gassiat, Jean 93
Geiberger, Al 247,260
Giant Niblick 35, 85, 168
Gibson, Charles 94
Gibson, Nevin 287
Gibson, William 94
Gold Cup 201
Gold Medal Golf Tee 273
Golf Around The Clock Game 369
Golf Bags 381
Golf Ball Paint 365
Golf Ball Slot Machine 370, 372
Golf Course Equipment 372
Golf Illustrated 373
Golf Museums 48
Golf Shoe Spikes 365
Golfer's Magazine 373
Golfing Magazine 373
Goodman, Johnny 260
Goodrich, B. F. 201, 208
Goodyear 209, 210
Gourlay, James 96
Graffis, Herb 287
Graham , David 260
Grant, Sir Francis 304
Gray Goose 199
Gray, John 97
Grimwades 317
Guldahl, Ralph 247, 260
Gustovson, Leland 304
Gutta-Percha Face Iron 123

H

H. Hoffman 328
Hackbarth 35
Hackbarth, Otto 98
Hagen, Walter & L. A. Young Co.
.... 158, 160
Hagen, Walter 247, 260, 288
Halley & Co., James B 98
Hand Hammered Gutta-Percha 184
Hand-Held Golf Games 370
Handkerchief Boxes 374
Handle Ware 317
Harmon, Claude........................... 261
Harrington Special 207
Haskell 208
Hat Pin - Sterling 355
Haultain, A. 288

Hawkes, T. G. & Co. 325
Heavy Colonel 197
Heissey 326
Henderson & Stirk 288
Hendry & Bishop, Ltd 98
Henley 189, 195
Henry's Rifled Ball 195
Hicks, Helen 248
Hiatt & Co. 99
Hill, Dave 288
Hillerich & Bradsby 99
Hilton, Harold 288
Hines, Jimmy 248
Hogan Belt Watch 366
Hogan, Ben 248, 261, 288
Hole-In-One Medals 335
Hollow Back 33
Hope, Bob 261
Houghton, George 288
Humidor With Sterling Lid 339
Hunt Mfg. Co. 104
Hunter, Charles 105
Hunter, Dave 289
Hunter, Robert 289
Hutchinson, Harold 289
Hutchinson, Horace 289
Hutchinson, Jock 248

I

Ice Cream Molds 376
Imperial Golf 105
Inkwell - Silver-Plated 356
International Golf Tee 273
Irwin, Hale 261
Ivora Putter 109

J

Jacklin, Tony 261
Jack Rabbit 201
Jackson 24
Jacobs, John 289
Jacobus Patent Wood 146
Jansen, Lee 261
Jenkins, Dan 289
Jerome, Owen Fox 289
Johnson, Frank A. 105
Jones, Ernest 289
Jones, Robert T., Jr. 262, 289
Jose-Maria Olazabal 264
Just Perfect Tees 274

K

Kargo Card Golf Game 370
K-D Sand Tee Mold 274
Kempshall 211

Kerr, John 290
Keystone Sand Tee Mold 274
Kirkwood, Joe 248
Kroydon 105

L

Lady's Coin Purse 356
Laffoon, Ky 248
Langer, Bernhard 262
Lard Patent 145
Lawn Golf Game 368
Lawson Little 262
Leather-Face Iron 122
Lee, Harry C. 107
Lees, Charles 304
Lehman, Tom 262
Lema, Tony 248, 262, 290
Lenox 318
Leyland & Birmingham Rubber Co.
.... 108
Limoge 318
Line Cut Gutta-Percha 184, 185
Lladro 318
Locke, Bobby 262, 290
Lockwood & Brown 108
Logan, Hugh 108
Longhurst, Henry 290
Lopez, Nancy 249
Love, Davis III 262
Lynx 201

M

MacDonald, C. B. 290
Mackenzie, Alister 290
Makalena, Ted 249
Mangrum, Lloyd 249
Manhattan Tee 277
Mark O'Meara 264
Marr, Dave 249
Martin, H. B. 290
Martin, John Stewart 290
Masters Badges 367
Masters Series Badges 368
Match Book Tees 274
Match Safe 356, 357, 358
Maxim 201
Maxwell Designed Holes 31
McCord, Gary..................... 262
McEwan 24, 114
Media Badges 367
Mehlem , Franz Anton 317
Men's Amateur Contestant Medal ..337
Men's US Open Contestant Medal ..337
Meteor.......................... 209
Meuller Enterprises, Inc. 347
Middlecoff, Cary 249, 262

Midget 197
Millar, Charles 114
Miller, Johnny 249
Miller Press 347
Mills 148, 149, 151
Milosevich, Paul 304
Montgomery, Colin 262
Morris, Tom 115, 189, 263
Morrison, Alex 290
Morristown 137
Murdock, Joseph S. F. 290
Murphy, Bob 263
Musselburgh 37

N

National Exchange Bank 347
Nelson, Byron 249, 263, 290
Nelson, Larry 263
Nicholson, T. 121
Nicklaus, Jack 249, 263, 290
Nobby 205
Noirit 33
No-Looz-Tee 274
Noritake 319
Norman, Greg 264
North British 201, 212
Norwood, Joe 291
Novel Tees 275

O

Ocobo............................ 189
Ogden's Limited 348
Oke, W. G. 123
Oliver, Porky 250
Olman, John & Morton 291
Olympic Putter 140
One-Piece Wood 74, 87, 114
Osmond's Patent 387
Ouimet, Francis 264, 291
Owl Mesh 199

P

P G A 197
Palmer, Arnold 250, 259, 291
Par-It Golf Game 370
Park Royal 190
Park, Willie 123, 125, 292
Park's Pattern Putter 124
Patrick, Alex 126
Pavin, Cory 264
Paxton, Peter 127
Peg Golf Tee 275
Penfold Or Bromford Man 377
Perfec Tee 276
Perfect Golf Tee 276

Perma Tee 276
PGA Championship Medal 336
Philp 24
Philp, Hugh 128, 129
Pin Cushion 359
Pipeshank, George 304
Player, Gary 264, 292
Plimpton, George 292
Pneumatic 209
Pocket Watch 366
Prestwick 37
Price, Charles 292
Price, Nick 265
Primrose Confectionary 348
Pryde's Orange Tee 276

R

"R A" Putter 109
Rake Irons 166, 168
Randall, John 130
Reach Eagle 196
Reach Paramount 201
Reddy Tee......................276
Reid, Sir George 305
Resilient......................191
Revolta, Johnny 250, 265, 292
Rex Mesh 199
Rex Zinc Tees 277
Rice, G. & Briggs, C. 292
Rice, G. & Keeler, O. B. 292
Richard Ginori 319
Rite Pencil Tee 277
Roberts, Clifford 293
Robertson, Allan 178
Rodriguez, Chi-Chi 251
Rodwell, Charles 130
Rola-Bola Golf Game 369
Rollins & Parker 130
Rotella, Robert J. 293
Royal Bayruth 319
Royal Doulton 319, 321
Rustless Golf Club Company 130

S

Sadler, W.D. 305
St. Andrew Golf Co. 147
St. Andrews 37
St. Mungo 197
St. Regis 199
Sampson, Curt 293
Sand Tee Mold 277
Sarazen Fifty 251
Sarazen, Gene 251, 265, 293
Saunders, Fred 131
Sayers, Ben 131
Schaap, Dick 293

Schenectady Putter 107
Schoenhut Golfer 376
Score Keeper 366
Scot-Tee 277
Scott Patent 30
Scott, A. H. 132
Scottie Dog Advertising Figure..... 377
Seely Patent 145
Self-Adjusting Golf Tee 278
Shaw, Joseph T. 293
Sheridan Collectibles 350
Shute, Denny 251, 265
Silver King Advertising Figure 377
Silver Loving Cup 338
Silvertown 190, 212
Simpson, Archie 132
Simpson, R. 132
Simpson, Sir Walter G. 293
Sir Leslie Ward, 'spy' 305
Skoogee Sand Iron 96
Slazenger And Sons 134
Smart, John 305
SMCO 136, 140
Smith, Garden G. 305
Smith, H. & Taylor, D. 293
Smith, Horton 265
Smooth Gutty Mold 178
Snead, Sam 251, 265, 293
Spalding 134,137
Spalding Balls 203, 212
Spalding One-Piece 145
Spalding Special 136
Spalding, A. G. & Brothers 136
Spence & Gourlay 146
Spence, James 147
Spice Tin 374
Spingoff Golf Game 369
Spool Of Pitched Linen 366
Spoons - Sterling Silver 360
Sprague 36
Spring Face 34
Spring Face Irons 144
Springvale 189
Stadium Golf Co. 147
Standard Golf Co. 148
Stanley, Dave 294
Stanley, Louis T. 294
Star Challenger 193
Steel, Donald & Ryde & Wind 294
Steele, C. K. 294
Sterling Loving Cup 340
Sterling Medals 335
Sterling Silver Putter 158
Sterling Tea Pot 339
Stevens, Thomas E. 305
Stewart, Payne 265
Stewart, Tom 152

Streamliner 30
Suggs, Louise 294
Super Harlequin 210

T

Taylor, Alex 251
Taylor, John Henry 265, 294
Tees In Bags 278
Tether Tees 279
Thomas, George G., Jr. 294
Thompson, Peter 265
Tin Box 374
Tomato Can 374
Top Not Tee 278
Travis Putter 140
Travis, Walter J. 294
Trevino, Lee 266
Triple Splice 30
Triple-T Golf Tee 279
Tufts, Richard S. 294
Tulloch, W. W. 295

U

U. S. Tiger 214
U.S. Open Badges 367, 368
U.S. Open Gold Medal 337
U.S. Open Golf Medal 336
U.S. Royal 205
Urquhart 35
Urquhart, Robert 157

V

Vail, Arnold 306
Vaile, P. A. 295
Van De Velde, Adriaen 306
Van Der Linde, Adriaen 306
Van Der Neer, Aert 307
Vardon Flyer 190, 252
Vardon, Harry 266, 295
Venturi , Ken 266
Vicker's Limited 157
Vulcan Golf Co. 157

W

Waffle-Face Iron 107
Walgreen Golf Tees 279
Walgreen's 205
Wannamaker 205
Warwick 208, 321
Water Irons 166, 168
Waterfall 144
Waterford 323

Watson, J.F. 307
Watson, Tom 266
Weaver, Arthur 307
Wedgewood 321
Weller 322
Wethered, Joyce 266
Wethered, Joyce & Roger 295
Whigham, H. G. 295
Whiskey Flask 361
Whit & Barnes 191
White Flat Bramble 214
White Flyer 208
White, Jack 161
White, Robert 161
Whitlatch, Marshall 295
Whiz 201
Why Not 210
Williams, J. H. & Co. 161
Williamsons & Sons 322
Wills 351
Wilson 205
Wilson, R. B. (Buff) 161
Wilson, Robert 162
Wilson, Thomas E. 162
Wilson, Willie 165
Winarick, A. R. Co. 325
Wind, Herbert Warren 296
Wine Decanter 325
Winton, W. & Co., Ltd 165
Wodehouse, P. G. 296
Women's Amateur Contestant Medal
.... 337
Wood, Craig 252
Wood, Harry B. 296
Woods, Tiger 266
World Win Putter 109
Worsham, Lou 252
Worthington 214
Wrapped Balls 215
Wright & Ditson 169, 214
Wright, Mickey 267

X

X L Challenger 199

Y

"Yello" Tee 279

Z

Zome Two 211
Zweifel Card Golf Game 3

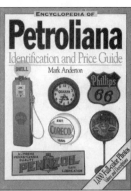

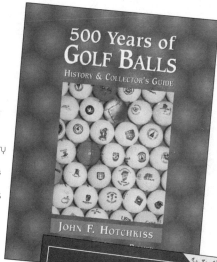